Attack-and-Defense Games for Control Systems

This vital work for researchers and graduate students focuses on resilience estimation and control of cyber-physical networked systems using attacker-defender game theory. It presents attack and defense strategies and describes the design and resilience of control systems to withstand cyberattacks.

Complex control systems, including cyber-physical and cloud control systems, are in open network environments and are often confronted with threats from cyberspace, physical space, and even cloud service. With diversified and intelligent attack patterns and improvements in attack capabilities, non-contact damage can be widespread. In this book, the authors use a formal, mathematical approach to introduce their recent research findings to describe and design attack and defense strategies using a game theoretic method. The book is divided into three sections, focusing on strategies for resilience against deception attacks and DoS attacks, and protecting cloud control systems against threats. In these sections, the authors address topics such as secure and distributed filtering, attack detection and disturbance rejection, resilient state estimation, and resilient control, and techniques such as Stackelberg games, hierarchical games, and active eavesdropping. Through this book readers will be able to design effective defense strategies for a complex control system to achieve resilience for closed-control cyber physical systems, networks, and cloud systems.

This book is a vital resource for graduate students and academic researchers who are familiar with the concepts related to cyberattack and defense and who have a related research background. To maximize their benefit from this book, readers are recommended to have a strong mathematical foundation as the book takes a mathematical approach to the concepts and strategies described within.

Huanhuan Yuan is an Associate Professor with the School of Astronautics, Northwestern Polytechnical University, Xi'an China. She achieved her B.S. and M.S. degrees from Yanshan University in 2013 and 2016, respectively, and her Ph.D. in Control Science and Engineering from Beijing Institute of Technology, Beijing, in 2020.

Yuan Yuan is a Professor with the School of Astronautics, Northwestern Polytechnical University, Xi'an, China. He obtained his B.Sc. from Beihang University in 2009 and Ph.D. in Computer Science and Technology from Tsinghua University in 2015.

Huapeng Dong is currently pursuing a Ph.D. degree at the Unmanned System Research Institute, Northwestern Polytechnical University.

Yuanqing Xia is a Professor with the School of Automation at Beijing Institute of Technology. He received his Ph.D. in Control Theory and Control Engineering from Beijing University of Aeronautics and Astronautics in 2001.

Mengbi Wang received his B.Sc. Degree in Measurement Technology and Instrument from the Department of Precision Instrument, Tsinghua University, Beijing, China, in 2010, and his Ph.D. degree in Instrument Science and Technology from the Department of Precision Instrument, Tsinghua University, Beijing, China, in 2018. He is currently a researcher at the Department of Precision Instrument, Tsinghua University.

Attack-and-Defense Games for Control Systems

Analysis and Synthesis

Huanhuan Yuan, Yuan Yuan, Huapeng Dong,
Yuanqing Xia, and Mengbi Wang

CRC Press
Taylor & Francis Group
Boca Raton London New York

CRC Press is an imprint of the
Taylor & Francis Group, an **informa** business

First edition published 2024
by CRC Press
2385 NW Executive Center Drive, Suite 320, Boca Raton FL 33431

and by CRC Press
4 Park Square, Milton Park, Abingdon, Oxon, OX14 4RN

CRC Press is an imprint of Taylor & Francis Group, LLC

ISBN: 978-1-032-77464-0 (hbk)
ISBN: 978-1-032-77466-4 (pbk)
ISBN: 978-1-003-48325-0 (ebk)

DOI: 10.1201/9781003483250

Typeset in TeXGyreTermesX
by KnowledgeWorks Global Ltd.

Publisher's note: This book has been prepared from camera-ready copy provided by the authors.

Contents

SECTION III Resilient Strategy for CCS Against a Threat

Preface

With the rapid development of computing and communicating technologies, the control system becomes more and more complicated. An control system, including the cyber-physical system and cloud control system, is under an open network environment and is confronted with threats from cyber space, physical space, and even the cloud service. With diversified and intelligent attack patterns and the improvement of attack capability, non-contact damages are achieved through the fact that attacks penetrate into physical space from cyber space, which may wreak havoc. Recently, security incidents involving industrial control systems have taken place frequently, which has attracted a lot of attention from governments and other communities. Meanwhile, some research focusing on attack detection, attack strategy design, and resilient strategy design for security of control systems has been carried out. However, the existing results are conservative and there are many difficulties needing prompt solutions, such as how to build more reasonable models for complex systems under attack and how to design an effective attack-defense mechanism to improve the capability of defense of the control system and then guarantee the system performance; the secure studies on the cloud computing-enabled cloud control system are scarce.

Motivated by these challenges, this book aims at designing effective defense strategies for the complex control system, which include a resilient strategy for filtering the cyber-physical system, an attack-defense strategy for closed-control of a cyber-physical system and security of the network and cloud service for the cloud control system.

Chapter 1 provides a motivation for the research and its history and an overview of the recent development of defense/attack strategy design for complex control systems.

Then, this book consists of three parts:

Part I, including Chapter 2, Chapter 3 and Chapter 4, focuses on the resilient strategy design for a control system under deception attack. First, a filter system with multiple channels under measurement missing and deception attacks is researched. Filtering performance analysis and filter gained design are given for a system with φ-level security. Then, extending the result to a distributed filtering system, the distributed filtering system is subject to the quantization effect. An event-triggered mechanism, and two-stage deception attacks. The H_∞ distributed filter is designed for the system. For a more anti-attack strategy, we research the attack detection and extended state observer to reduced the effect of the deception attack on a multiagent system.

Part II from Chapter 5 to Chapter 8 aims to design resilient strategies to reduce the effect from a Denial-of-Service (DoS) attack by exploiting the signal interference plus noise ratio to note the effect from DoS attack. Both filtering system performance and closed-loop control system performance are investigated in this part. Game theory is introduced to describe the interaction of defender and attacker. When considering a cross-layer performance in the game problems, the closed-from expression of strategies cannot be given easily. Reinforcement learning methods, including value iteration and Q-learning methods, are introduced to solve the game problems in this part.

Part III, including Chapter 9 and Chapter 10, studies the resilient strategies for cloud control systems, in which the features and unsecurity are analyzed for a cloud control system first. Then, a dynamic pricing-based resilient strategy design for a cloud control system under jamming attack is given. For the cloud control system suffering from advanced persistent threats, the Stackelberg-game-based defense analysis is studied, in which both the defense and attack resource strategies are obtained for the large-scale system.

Xi'an, China, *Huanhuan Yuan*
Xi'an, China, *Yuan Yuan*
Xi'an, China, *Huapeng Dong*
Beijing, China, *Yuanqing Xia*
Beijing, China, *Mengbi Wang*
June 8, 2024

1 Introduction

1.1 BACKGROUND

Developments in information science and control science have led to system networking and increased access to system intelligence. Through communication networks, control systems can connect devices in different regions. The control and decision-making capabilities of devices and systems have become very "smart" [26], benefiting from intelligence techniques. The deep combination of the information world and physical entities has spawned many new complex control systems, including the Internet of Things (IoT)[61], the cyber-physical System (CPS)[183], and the cloud control system (CCS)[227].

In recent years, the rapid development of computer technology, network communication technology, and control technology has caused big changes in the human experience. Information systems and physical systems are deeply integrated in modern control systems, such as aerospace systems, power network systems, chemical process systems, intelligent manufacturing, intelligent buildings, intelligent transportation, etc. To represent the interaction of two layer systems, CPS[19, 183] emerges and integrates the main characteristics of complex systems.

During a meeting of the National Science Foundation (NSF) in 2006, CPS was first defined in detail. In 2013, Germany's "Industry 4.0 Implementation Proposal" proposed CPS as the core technology of Industry 4.0. The "Smart Manufacturing 2025" points out that intelligent manufacturing forms such as intelligent equipment and intelligent factories based on CPS are leading a major change in manufacturing methods, and then strengthening the application of CPS.

In the process of deepening the integration and development of manufacturing and the Internet, the Ministry of Industry and Information Technology released the "White Paper on Information-Physical Systems" on March 1, 2017. It was stated that the essence of CPS is to develop closed-loop empowerment systems that use automatic data flow between information and physical spaces for state sensing, real-time analysis, scientific decision-making, and precise execution, meanwhile reducing complexity and uncertainty in manufacturing and application services and making resource allocation more efficient. A key research direction of CPS is industrial control and information security management, including risk assessment and protection capability [37, 60]. The structure of CPS is given in Fig. 1.1. CPS unifies the cyber world and physical world, which depends on the communication technology and becomes more and more open; this leads to the system confronting security threats [101]. In recent years, some security incidents occurred which make the systems operate abnormally. Some security incidents include the following.

(1) In June 2010, an industrial control system vulnerability was used to hack the Bursh nuclear power plant in Iran, resulting in a large number of cases centrifuge failures. Known as the Stuxnet attack, this left nuclear reactors

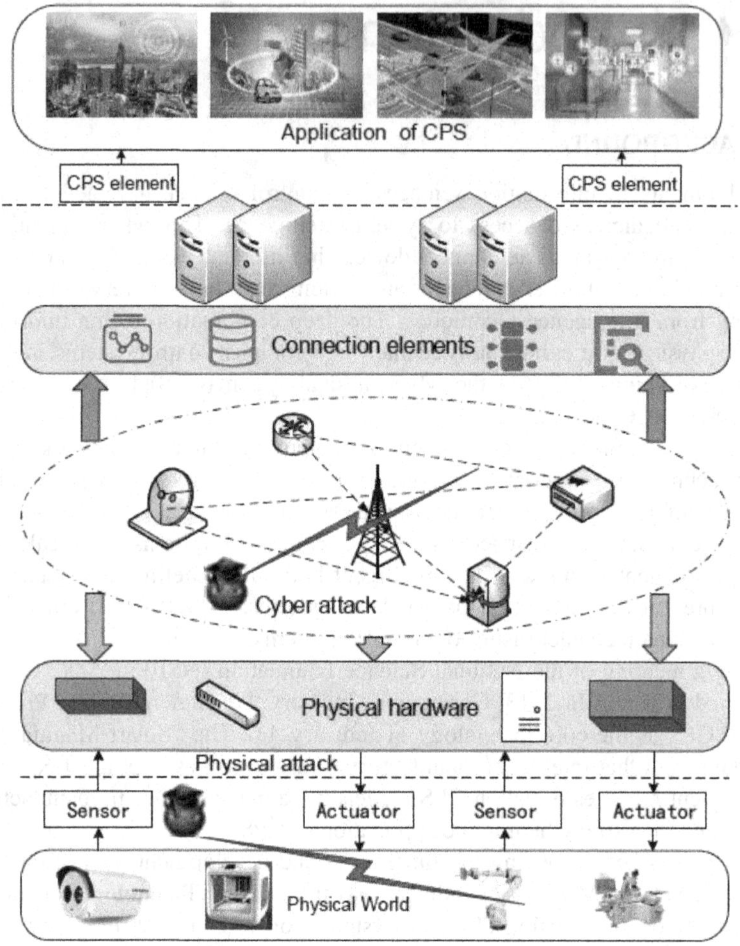

Figure 1.1 Structure of CPS.

out of service for a long time, significantly delaying Iran's nuclear program.

(2) On the afternoon of December 23, 2015, parts of the Ukrainian capital Kiev and other location in Ukraine were attacked by hackers. The homes of 1.4 million people in the West were without power.

(3) In 2016, the cyber security firm Kaspersky Lab detected a way to gain access by sending malicious emails The cyber attack on useful data, called Operation Ghoul, was successful More than 130 industrial and engineering enterprise networks in more than 30 countries around the world were attacked, and the range of its attack is very wide. The effect of the attack was very significant.

(4) In January 2018, the networks of three Dutch banks were hit by a distributed denial of service (DDoS) attack for nearly a week. Denial-of-Service (DDoS) attacks brought down websites and Internet banking services. In addition, the Dutch tax office also came under similar attack.
(5) In 2019, more than 50 large businesses in Russia were ransomed by unknown attackers. Using IoT devices, In particular, routers masqueraded as Slavov, Magnit, and 50 other well-known companies and sent phishing emails to blackmail employees.

Cyber attacks are frequent and the attack methods are increasing; cybersecurity issues have risen to a national strategic level[16, 30]. On May 15, 2018 the U.S. Department of Homeland Security released a cybersecurity strategy that identifies five major directions and seven clear objectives for cybersecurity risk including risk identification, reducing critical infrastructure vulnerabilities, reducing the threat of cybercriminal activity, mitigating the impact of cyber incidents, and achieving cybersecurity outcomes. On June 27, 2019, the EU Cybersecurity Act 2019 came into force. The Act establishes legal regulations for EU institutions, agencies and offices to follow in order to strengthen cybersecurity structures, enhance control of digital technologies, and ensure cybersecurity in dealing with the cybersecurity of individual users, organizations, and businesses, with the aim of promoting the economy and facilitating the functioning of the internal market in key sectors such as health, energy, finance, and transport. The bill is groundbreaking, systematic, scientific, and forward-looking, providing new ideas worthy of reference for the legal design of global networks and information and communication security, international cooperation on cybersecurity protection, and the improvement of the cybersecurity standard system. Our country has implemented a series of policies to support the development of the information security industry since 2012. On December 27, 2016, the Central Network Security and Informatization Leading Group released the "National Network Security Strategy", emphasizing that "there is no national security without network security." On June 1, 2017, the "Network Security Law of the People's Republic of China" was officially implemented. Network security has laws to follow and they are enforced. The network security market space, industrial investment, and construction have entered a stage of sustained and stable development.

The four core elements of CPS include: perception and automation, industrial software, the industrial network, the industrial cloud, and the intelligent service platform, among which the industrial cloud platform has an increasingly critical role in the huge CPS, which can provide reliable assurance for the collection, storage, and analysis of CPS big data and realize the efficient processing of big data for scientific decision-making and precise execution[139]. New concepts, technologies, and models are constantly emerging in the process of deep integration of informationization and industrialization to cope with new applications and development trends. Integrating cloud computing, communication networks, and control technology, Prof. Yuanqing Xia first proposed the concept of CCS[227] in 2012 and conducted a series of explorations and research[228, 229, 231, 232]. Using a Networked Control System (NCS), IoT can achieve interconnection, interoperability, and mutual control, but due to the demands of human production and life, IoT is massive in scale and complex in structure, and in the process of practical application, will generate a tremendous amount of data. Traditional NCS cannot provide reliable data storage and fast calculation of control instructions, and cannot meet the demands of high-quality systems[229]. Combining the advantages of NCS and cloud computing technology, CCS can realize the autonomous intelligent control of the system. As a typical application of CPS, intelligent transportation systems involve many kinds of objects, large amounts of data, and high requirements for transmission and computation scheduling and control ability; in addition, cloud control technology can be used to solve problems related to large data storage and computation, optimization algorithms for scheduling, and real-time control in intelligent transportation systems. Xia Y.[230] that investigated the intelligent traffic information physical fusion CCS, which can be used for predicting traffic flows and congestion on urban roads, while also obtaining the traffic flow control strategy in order to improve the dynamic performance of the traffic system.

CCS is a new framework and concept that will provide powerful tools for complex system control. CCS includes four levels: cloud, network, edge, and end, as shown in Fig. 1.2. The cloud, i.e., the cloud data center, uses data-driven intelligent recognition-based methods to identify system models and form twin systems by interacting with the actual controlled objects. Further, the control tasks are virtualized into workflows, and the intelligent control tasks are efficiently executed in the container environment by designing workflow scheduling algorithms. The network layer will form a hierarchical network interconnection structure centered on the cloud data

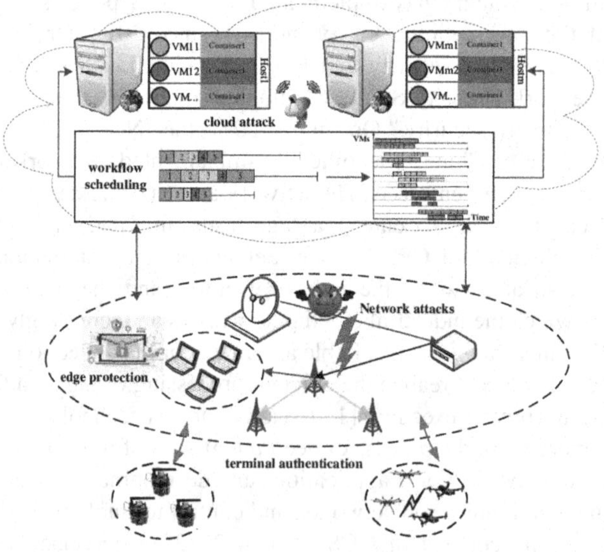

Figure 1.2 The schematic diagram of CCS.

center. This will have features such as large capacity, high carrying capacity, high scalability, and communication security. The edge layer can synthesize task assignment indexes; complete tasks with small data storage, high real-time demand, and low computational processing capability requirements; and assign tasks with large data volume, high computational volume, and a certain latency tolerance to the cloud. The terminal refers to the controlled objects of the system, including the data acquisition system composed of sensors, a monitoring and display system, actuators, and human-computer interaction, etc. Collaborative control between the cloud and the edge is the key in CCS. After the cloud completes the upper-level planning and scheduling, specific tasks are distributed to the edge, and the edge completes local control. To save energy and reduce costs, cloud data centers are usually built in remote areas, which causes data transmission in the network to have a large time delay. At the same time, the shared and dynamic nature of CCS cloud resources makes the computation time of system tasks have a large uncertainty [171]. Therefore, it is very necessary for CCS to consider the impact of time delay in the system design process. CCS externalizes the control tasks to the cloud, which has higher openness and is more vulnerable to attacks from the network and cloud services. How to ensure system security is a prerequisite to guarantee the stable operation of the system.

The security of CCS includes four levels: cloud, network, edge, and end: Cloud security includes both cloud storage[134, 142] and cloud service security[97, 109]. The controlled systems that access the cloud have to transmit their sensory data to the cloud. The cloud data center will serve multiple controlled systems at the same time. As a result, it is vital to ensure that data privacy is maintained. At the same time, CCS has large scale and distributed characteristics, and the effective allocation of security resources is an effective means to improve the overall system performance. The data in CCS is transmitted through a complex network, and the network transmission process may be subject to various forms of network attacks, such as data eavesdropping, denial of service (DoS) attacks[204], replay attacks, and false data injection (FDI) attacks, etc. The use of effective encryption techniques and the design of proactive defense strategies can reduce the impact of attacks on the system. We can combine hardware and software edge security protection systems by designing intrusion detection systems (IDS), protection software, and isolation mechanisms at the edge. The CCS terminals have a large number of heterogeneous devices accessing them, and a differentiated identity identification authentication mechanism can guarantee the security of the devices accessing these terminals[159].

The study of safety issues has become a crucial research element in the field of control systems, including CPS and CCS. System security research is of great importance and urgency in the productive life of society. If the research on malicious attacks is not timely and in-depth, we will be at our wits' end when they really happen, causing serious economic and property losses and even threatening human lives.

1.2 ANALYSIS OF THE CHARACTERISTICS OF CYBER ATTACKS

Industrial control systems have evolved from traditional local area networks to the industrial internet. The open network environment has led to the exposure of

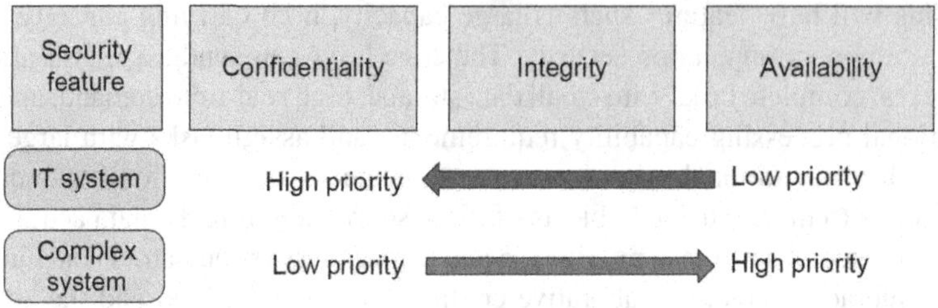

Figure 1.3 System security features.

system nodes and data transmission, which is very likely to cause system security problems. Research institutions and related companies around the world have carried out theoretical and practical research on cyber security of complex control systems [43, 67, 197, 254]. An organic interaction exists between the information world and the physical world through the integration of big data computing, network communication, and traditional control. The computing and network communication link is crucial to ensuring the performance of control systems[77]. In order to gain a deeper understanding of the characteristics of attacks on control systems, we list and compare three characteristics of control system security with those of traditional Information Technology (IT) security concerns.

(1) Confidentiality: Information is collected, transmitted, stored, and processed without leakage to unauthorized users, that is, the requirement to protect the privacy of data [145].
(2) Integrity (Integrity): Information is not tampered with by illegal users during collection, transmission, storage, and processing, and is not unreasonably changed by authorized users, maintaining the consistency of information, i.e., ensuring the integrity of the content of the data [98, 99].
(3) Availability: Information can arrive accurately and on time at the designated receiving location to ensure that the use of information by authorized users is not abnormally denied; i.e., authorized users have reliable and timely access to information and resources [3, 93].

For IT systems, ensuring information security is key, so the greatest concern is confidentiality, followed by integrity, and finally the availability of the three characteristics mentioned above. Unlike traditional IT security, with the development of technology to enhance performance more easily, complex control systems place physical objects in an open network environment. The information can be deleted, tampered with and blocked in the open environment [210]. The control system is more concerned about whether the control performance of the system is satisfied. Therefore, the characteristics of the above three aspects are most concerned about availability, followed by integrity, and finally confidentiality, as shown in Fig. 1.3.

The above three characteristics are the three basic principles of system security. Attackers also compromise information and systems from these three aspects, which

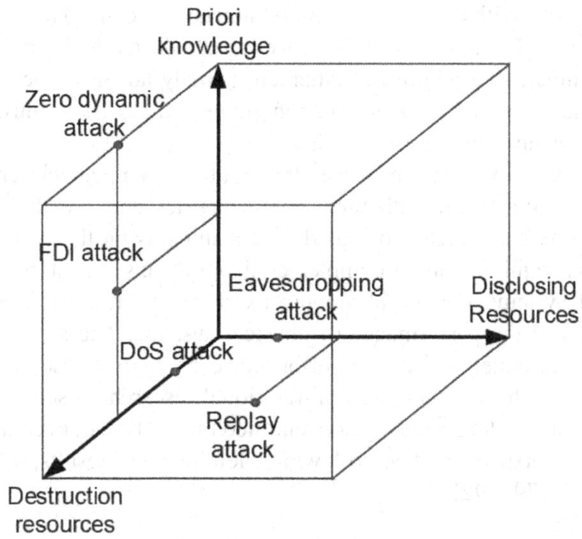

Figure 1.4 Attack behavior space description.

are classified as availability attacks, integrity attacks, and confidentiality attacks:

(1) Availability attacks: As a result of the lack of connectivity that prevents signals from reaching the destination node, DoS attacks are the main method of attack [92, 216]. The high real-time information requirements of modern control systems make them face new challenges in dealing with availability attacks such as DoS.
(2) Integrity attacks: Providing wrong data to spoof the system, the system performs wrong operations with access to wrong external information, which in turn affects the physical system, also known as spoofing attacks, including FDI attacks [44, 161, 205], replay attacks [8, 45], and zero-dynamic attacks [12, 117, 154, 198, 211], etc.
(3) Confidentiality attacks: External attackers can obtain system status information by listening to the communication channel between physical components, and then infer the user's private information, including eavesdropping attacks [117, 198] and wormhole attacks[154].

It can be seen that there are various ways to attack the performance of the damage control system; the demand characteristics of the attacker for the typical attacks on Priori Knowledge, Disclosure Resource and Disruption Resource are represented in Fig. 1.4 [12]. From the figure, it can be seen that a DoS attack only requires the injection of a disruption resource to the system, which is easy to implement and is the most frequent attack method in practice. The shortcomings of the current DoS attack research are summarized in the following section, which is the main research content of this book. With the improvement of attackers' technical means, in addition to the single form of attack described above, an attack method with a long-term, advanced and threatening nature has emerged, namely advanced persistent threats (APTs). This attack method refers to an anonymous and persistent intrusion process that is carefully planned by a person against a specific target [95, 97, 155].

From the above analysis, it can be seen that control system attacks and traditional IT system attacks both start with three characteristics and use the same means. However, the same attack behavior has different impacts on the two systems. The intrinsic security requirements of complex control systems are different from those of traditional IT systems. For complex control systems, their information processing is closely related to the performance of physical systems. The attacks of complex control systems ultimately affect the performance of control systems by affecting the security of the information space. In traditional research on security issues, the relevant theoretical results are mainly concentrated in the IT field. In contrast, security research from the perspective of control, while yielding some results, still faces many challenges [4, 70, 179, 192].

1.3 ATTACK BEHAVIOR MODELING

The essence of the study of system security issues is to master the attacker's attack mode, design a defense strategy, and therefore reduce the impact of the attack on the system. The design of a reasonable defense strategy is based on an in-depth understanding of attack behavior, an in-depth analysis of the nature, so as to establish a reasonable mathematical model of attack behavior. In recent years, researchers have summarized the characteristics of typical attacks, and the models of typical attacks [107, 141, 169, 216] such as DoS attacks, FDI attacks, and replay attacks are given below.

DoS attacks are threats that make system resources unavailable, and from a technical point of view, the attacker achieves this by filling the cache of the user domain or core domain, blocking the network medium or changing the routing protocol. The symbols $\bar{y}_k$ and y_k denote the received data and the transmitted data. After an attack by DoS, if y_k fails to transmit successfully, then $\bar{y}_k \in \emptyset$. Amin et al. model the DoS attack as a binary Bernoulli packet loss process in Ref.[169]. And the impact on sensor and actuator data is represented by the sequence $\{\gamma_1, \gamma_2, \cdots, \gamma_k, \cdots\}$ and $\{\nu_1, \nu_2, \cdots, \nu_k, \cdots\}$ where γ_k and ν_k are independent identically distributed Bernoulli random variables. It is further given that the probability of information loss when the link is subjected to DoS attack and the security policy selection satisfy $\tilde{\gamma}(\nu) = \Pr[\gamma_k = 0 \mid \nu]$ and $\tilde{\nu}(\nu) = \Pr[\nu_k = 0 \mid \nu]$ where $\mathcal{V}$ is the input of the chosen security defense policy. The literature [112] models the DoS attack as a hidden Markov model $\gamma(Z_{k+1})$, where Z_k satisfies the conditional Markov chain $Z_k = A(F_k(Y_{k-1}))Z_{k-1} + V_k$. Yuan et al. model the DoS attack as a one-step time-delay model $y_k = (1-\varsigma)y_{k-1} + y_k$, and solve the controller using a switching control method [235]. In the literature [141], Long et al. model the packet delay variation and loss due to DoS attacks as a queueing model shown in Fig.1.5. During wireless

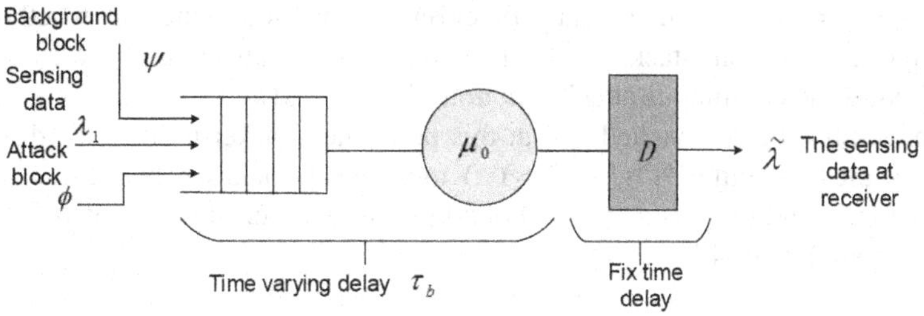

Figure 1.5 DoS attack queue model.

network transmission, DoS attackers block the transmission of system signals by transmitting interfering signals, using Signal-Interference-Plus-Noise Ratio (SINR) to describe the strength of the signal received by the receiver, i.e.,

$$\mathrm{SINR} = \frac{aT}{bJ + N_0}. \tag{1.1}$$

where T is the power of the transmitted signal, J is the power of the attack signal, N_0 is the power spectral density of the background noise, and a and b are the transmission gain and interference gain, respectively[107, 216]. The literature [107] gives the Packet Error Rate (PER) versus SINR in Binary Phase Shift Keying (BPSK).

$$P_{BPSK} = Q(\sqrt{\kappa \mathrm{SINR}}) \tag{1.2}$$

where $Q(\cdot)$ is the Q function of the standard normal distribution and κ is a known constant. In the literature [168], the system performance is studied based on the attack frequency and duration. And the time series of DoS attacks is $\{H_n\}_{n\in\mathrm{N}}$, where $H_n := \{h_n\} \cup [h_n, h_n + \tau_n)$ denotes the nth DoS attack interval and $\{H_n\}_{n\in\mathrm{N}} \in \mathcal{I}_{\mathrm{DaS}}$.

As a type of cyber attack, deception attacks degrade system performance by maliciously modifying packets transmitted in the network. In the literature [34–36], deception attacks are modeled as bounded signals satisfying $||\xi_k|| \leq \delta$. The attacker is energy-constrained, and in order to increase the difficulty of designing defense strategies for the system, the attack signal is often set to be random, satisfying the Bernoulli distribution i.e. $\beta_k \xi_k$, where $\Pr\{\beta_k = 0\} = \bar{\beta}$, $\Pr\{\beta_k = 1\} = 1 - \bar{\beta}$. Pang et al. studied the tracking performance of the system under the influence of FDI attack in the literature [73]. The signal after the attack $\bar{y}_k = y_k + \xi_k$, where y_k is the transmitted signal and ξ_k is the spuriously injected signal. Another typical deceptive attack is the replay attack. The principle is to record a segment of data transmitted by the system in the past. This segment is sent to the system receiver to affect the arrival of the normal signal. This method can increase the stealth of the attack signal and is not easily detected by the system. Zhu et al. give the replay attack model; the attacker records the state data $M^a(k)$ and performs the following steps when launching the attack: (i) erases the data sent by the sender ; (ii) sends the recorded system previous data $M^a(k)$ to the system receiver; (iii) keeps the stored state such that $M^a(k+1) = M^a(k)$.The indicator function $\vartheta(k)$ is used to indicate whether the attacker has launched an attack. $\vartheta(k) = 1$ indicates that an attack has been launched, at which point the continuous attack function $s(k+1) = s(k) + 1$; $\vartheta(k) = 0$ indicates that no attack has been launched, but at this point the attacker is still recording the data sent by the transmitter $M^a(k+1) = \Upsilon$, Υ indicates the data sent by the transmitter at that moment, and there is an upper bound on the number of consecutive attacks, i.e., satisfies $\mathrm{s(k)} \leq \mathrm{S}$[147].

1.4 RESEARCH STATUS AND TRENDS IN CYBER ATTACK OF CONTROL SYSTEMS

Based on the analysis of attack characteristics, it can be seen that the study of security from the control system perspective is a significant research direction. In recent years, this research direction has attracted the attention of scholars. Specifically, the research includes attack detection, attack strategy design, resilient strategy design, and attack and defense confrontation. The research results in these directions are summarized and analyzed below.

1.4.1 RESEARCH ON ATTACK DETECTION

In an insecure environment, the prerequisite for designing and implementing security behavior policies is the detection of attacks. Attack detection is a prerequisite and guarantee for the subsequent implementation of policy correction to mitigate the damage caused by attacks [31, 52, 65, 100, 116, 149, 194, 206]. Kosut [149] investigates a static attack detection method based on the consistency of the system output at the same moment. The static attack detection method does not consider the dynamic characteristics of the system and therefore cannot detect arbitrary attacks suffered by the control system actuators. Hablinger [52] designed detectors based on system dynamics, sensing topology, actuator inputs, and sensor outputs to determine whether there is a spoofing attack. Fawzi [65] proposes dynamic attack detection and reconfiguration algorithms. In addition, the method to discern the presence of deception attacks by randomly interfering with the input and detection output of the system is called active attack detection [202]. Chen [206] gives sufficient conditions for a deception attack signal not to be detected if the initial state information is known, and also gives the forms of attacks that cannot be detected for an arbitrary time horizon.

Ding [31] proposes two options for defending against attacks, pre-protecting critical parts of the system and detecting attacks. In addition, several typical attack detection methods in the existing literature are summarized in that literature: binary-based Bayesian detection for hypothesis making [17] , weighted least squares [165], Kalman filter based χ^2 detector [218] and similar fault detection and isolation techniques [225]. Lee C. [25] studies the problem of detectability of attacks in terms of system observability. For the replay attacks present in CPS, Fang C. [24] uses optimal periodic watermark scheduling methods to reduce the detection cost for non-continuous replay attacks. Most of the detection methods for DoS attacks use computer techniques, and [245] gives a DDoS detection and transfer method based on Software-defined Networking (SDN) technology. Zhu [138] designed a privacy-preserving cross-domain attack detection method for SDNs, which enables the effectiveness and detection accuracy of attack detection with sensitive information secured in their respective domains. The attacker simultaneously emits spoofed attack signals to the system and sensor links to falsify the system state and sensor measurement output, builds a distributed estimator, and transforms the design problem of the finite-time domain distributed estimator into a quadratic minimization problem using the state space model of Krein space, neuralgic analysis, and projection techniques, and further designs a recursive algorithm to solve [201].

With the development of artificial intelligence technology, data-driven attack detection techniques are also a significant research direction in addition to the above-mentioned attack detection methods [2, 5, 71, 150]. A review [150] summarizes the research on IoT intrusion detection mechanisms using machine learning methods. A traffic anomaly detection and estimation scheme based on a neural network (NN) observer was proposed by Niu et al. [71] based on Linear Matrix Inequality (LMI) proposed in the literature [72]. This scheme models the network traffic of important nodes in the NCS as a very linear function and uses an optimal event-triggered NN controller based on an adaptive dynamic programming approach to obtain an efficient scheme that can detect and estimate attacks. Diro et al. designed a distributed detection method for small mutations or novel attacks in the network space using the efficient feature extraction properties of deep learning methods [5].

1.4.2 RESEARCH ON ATTACK STRATEGY DESIGN

To design more effective defense strategies, researchers design the most destructive attack strategy from the perspective of the attacker [248]. Guo et al. give the worst linear attack strategy that is not detected by the χ^2 detector based on the Kalman filtering algorithm [248]. Based on the above study, Guo et al. further proposed the Kullback-Leibler (KL) scattering concealment metric in the literature [250]. A linear attack strategy was designed based on the information, and a recursive expression was given for the covariance of the remote state estimation error under the influence of the attack; the worst-case attack strategy was determined by solving the optimization algorithm. Further, assuming that the attacker has the ability to sense the system state information and intercept the sensor transmission information, the destructiveness of the system using different information design optimal attack strategy is analyzed while avoiding detection by the system [249]. Unlike the above studies where the attack policy design requires real-time state new information, Li and Yang [58, 59] calculate the attack policy offline by designing filters based on the historical data of the system, and this method is easier to implement in practical scenarios. Zhang et al. design two state estimation metrics, mean estimation error and end-point moment error, to construct an energy-constrained optimal attack strategy for the DoS attacker and also to design the optimal attack strategy for counter detection when there is an attack detector inside the filter [89].

In addition to the above-mentioned design of attack strategies for state estimation systems, the attack strategies that minimize the performance of closed-loop control systems are investigated in [62, 63, 167, 207, 208]. Wu et al. study the case where the attacker has limited attack resources and can only attack a finite number of channels, and establish a finite-time domain quadratic objective function for the attacker, based on Pontryagin 's maximization principle to find the attacker's optimal switching strategy [63]. Chen et al. consider the system's forward channel and feedback channel under FDI attack e_t at the same time, set the attacker's control objective and the constraint of not being detected by the system with a certain probability, and solve the optimization problem in two cases: when the induced deviation is zero, the optimization problem is transformed into a linear programming problem; when the induced deviation is at normal values, the optimal solution can be obtained by designing computationally intensive algorithms or suboptimal solutions can be obtained by designing algorithms with lower computational complexity [208]. Against stochastic CPS, Bai a ϵ-Concealment Index based on the Chernoff-Stein Lemma was proposed in [244], giving mean square error estimates related to system parameters, statistical properties of noise, and available information under concealment attacks, where the attacker aims to maximize the performance degradation function of the estimated error covariance and quantifies the relationship between system performance degradation and attack concealment. Zhang et al. study FDI attacks on linear quadratic Gaussian (LQG) systems, where the attacker aims to maximize the quadratic cost of the system while ensuring a certain level of stealth. They design the attack signal as a series of Gaussian noise signals. The eigenvalues of the covariance of the signal are proportional to the increment of the quadratic performance cost[89]. In the literature [90], the problem of optimal attack strategy for DoS attackers of LQG systems in the finite time domain is studied. And the optimal attack strategy and the corresponding cost are given by investigating the nature of the attack strategy and the LQG cost function. The stability of the system is studied at this time, and the research problem is extended to the case of multiple systems. Further, Zhang et al. investigate an optimal energy allocation strategy for DoS attacks under conditions of fading channels using a Markov Decision Process (MDP) in the literature [91].

1.4.3 RESEARCH ON RESILIENT STRATEGIES AGAINST CYBER ATTACKS

The previous section described the current state of research on designing attack strategies from the attacker's perspective. This section will describe the current state of research on resilient defense strategies from the system perspective that can still meet certain system performance requirements under the impact of attacks.

The research results on CPS security state estimation under network attacks are first presented. With the idea of H_∞ filtering, Wang et al. designed a filter that guarantees certain security performance for discrete-time systems with random time delay and sensor saturation [40]. Based on the above research, Wang et al. further established the multi-sensor multi-rate sampling measurement output model under the deceptive attack in [255]. Further, they designed a centralized fusion estimator that guarantees the system's secure filtering performance. The estimated gain is obtained by stochastic analysis techniques. The system is modeled as a two-state switching system, and the frequency and duration of the attack are considered. In order to ensure that the system meets the ideal filtering performance, a sufficient condition is provided based on the theory of switching systems [166]. In the literature [173], the authors study the H_∞ filtering problem under non-periodic DoS interference attacks. In order to compensate for the impact of non-periodic DoS interference attacks on the system, they devised an event-triggering mechanism while at the same time improving the utilization of system resources. By using a time-delay approach, they modeled the system as a switching system and filter, and event-triggered parameters are obtained by solving LMI. In addition, Liu et al. investigated the extended Kalman filtering problem for nonlinear systems under random network attacks [178]. Song et al. researched the setter estimation problem for complex network systems under the influence of unknown linear and nonlinear bounded attacks in the literature [75]. Researchers in [220] and [119] studied the sparse sensor attack problem by switching methods. Based on the above studies of single system state estimation, scholars have also carried out research on the distributed security filtering problem for sensor networks [32, 74, 76, 127, 130, 197]. In [74], the authors consider sensors and estimators in sensor networks. There is a random spoofing attack between the estimator and its neighbor estimator. A model for state estimation under two-channel attacks is developed. The filter gain that meets performance requirements is obtained by solving the H_∞ filtering problem. The literature [32] researches the deceptive attack of multiple coupled subsystems in the process of information transmission, which gives recursive expressions related to the upper bound of the estimation error covariance under the χ^2 detection mechanism. This work implements distributed solutions by the gradient descent method and verifies the effectiveness of the algorithm on grid systems. Based on the real-time transmission of new information, [197] designs a detection mechanism for distinguishing whether the information is under attack, and further develops a distributed Kalman filtering strategy for defending against FDI attacks. Song et al. [76] first gave the necessary and sufficient conditions for the multi-sensor system attack signal not to be detected from the perspective of the attacker. Further, based on the error system of state estimation, the estimator is redesigned under the assumption that the network is attacked.

Next, the current status of research on the security of closed-loop control systems under network attacks is presented. In literature [35], Ding et al. proposed a concept of secure control domain under random DoS attacks and random deception attacks and designed output-based feedback controllers to satisfy control requirements. In [22], Persis and Tesi et al. propose a modeling approach based on the frequency and duration of DoS attacks, and give the conditions to make the system satisfy the attack frequency and duration for input to state stability (ISS). In [193], an event-triggered control strategy that avoids the impact of DoS attacks of specific frequency and duration on system stability is designed. Based on the ISS Lyapunov function, the literature [23] gives the maximum loss ratio of feedback information for nonlinear systems to maintain stability under DoS attacks. Based on the above-mentioned methodology designed for modeling the system under DoS attacks, Hu et al. designed the event-triggered communication scheme under the influence of periodic DoS attack, established the switching system model, and gave the exponential stability indexes related to the attack parameters, event-triggered parameters, sampling period, and decay rate[174]. Further, they designed the bandwidth allocation scheme based on a dynamic event-triggered mechanism under DoS attack [176]. And then, they applied the above theory in a DC micro grid system [175]. In [120], An et al. consider a complex system model consisting of multiple interconnected nonlinear subsystems that are subjected to intermittent DoS attacks. And they design an output feedback-based control strategy to obtain LMI conditions related to attack frequency, duration, and controller parameters using a dwell time approach. In [219, 220], necessary and sufficient conditions are investigated in order to ensure that the system state is observable when the system actuators and sensors are subjected to sparse deceptive attacks simultaneously. By estimating the upper bound of the unknown attack, the author designs a closed-loop control scheme that can ensure the asymptotic stability of the system when the actuator and sensor are subject to time-varying attacks, Ding et al.[122] studied the distributed finite-time resilient control problem of a heterogeneous energy storage system. They designed an attack detection and repair mechanism based on ACK information, and then designed a control mechanism to make the distributed energy system achieve frequency regulation, active energy sharing, and energy level balancing while achieving finite-time tracking.

The following summarizes the security research on multi-intelligent body systems. the problem of multi-sensor consistency estimation in sensor networks under FDI attacks was investigated in [124]. Based on a consistent nonconvex optimization protocol, An et al. proposed a distributed security estimation algorithm for CPS in the literature [121]. The linear multi-intelligent system is subjected to a random attack satisfying a Markov process, and the output information is then used to reconstruct the state of the attacked system, and conditions are given to ensure that the multi-intelligent system is secure under distributed control [233]. Multi-intelligent systems under DoS attack with non-uniform sampling and bound duration, Zhang et al. describe the system as a switched stochastic time-delay system and give sufficient conditions to make the system satisfy consistency [48]. Further, Zhang et al. studied the security of leader-follower heterogeneous multi-intelligent systems. The authors model different attack density cases as time-varying delay models, thereby providing a quantitative relationship between attack density parameters and system consistency [46]. According to the literature [187], the leader-follower consistency problem under DoS attacks is studied using second-order multi-intelligent systems with nonlinear dynamics and event-triggered policies. This study provides the attack frequency, upper bound on duration, and conditions for satisfying the controller parameters for a DoS attack that makes the system consistent. Using Markov stochastic processes to model network attacks, Feng et al. explore the consistency tracking problem for multi-intelligent systems [247]. In the literature [246], Feng et al. further investigate the leaderless and leader-follower multi-intelligent security consistency problem under DoS attacks, respectively. They designed an elastic event trigger control scheme, and gave conditions for attack frequency and duration to satisfy system consistency. He et al. Study the pulse-synchronized control problem of multi-intelligence bulk systems under FDI attack [195]. Modares et al. study the network attack on sensors and actuators of multi-intelligent systems [68], and design an output feedback control protocol that can satisfy both homogeneous and heterogeneous multi-intelligent systems. This protocol can block the impact of the attack on other intelligences in the system. It can also mitigate the impact of the attack on the attacked intelligences by designing adaptive attack compensators.

1.4.4 RESEARCH ON ATTACK-AND-DEFENSE GAME STRATEGIES

In the context of security problems of complex control system, attackers and defenders have opposing objectives. Game theory provides tools for modeling both attackers and defenders. According to the literature [7, 168, 217, 236, 238], attackers and defenders are considered to be two players of the game, and the attack and defense strategies are derived by solving optimization problems.

Gupta [7] considers the problem of attack resource allocation and control policy optimization for finite-time length. The cost function is set to be $J = \mathbb{E}\{\sum_{k=0}^{N-1}(x_k^2 + a_k u_k^2) + x_N^2\}$. Considering the attacking and defending players as a zero-sum game, the saddle point solution of the game problem satisfies $J(\gamma^*, \mu) \leq J(\gamma^*, \mu^*) \leq J(\gamma, \mu^*)$, where γ and μ are the control and attack strategies, respectively. Similar to the above idea, Li [217] studies the security estimation problem for the remote state estimation system by modeling the interaction process of when an energy-constrained sensor transmits information and when an energy-constrained attacker interferes with the information transmission as a zero-sum game. In addition, it provides an algorithm for online solving the state estimation error covariance using Markov chain theory. Yuan et al. define the probability of control signal loss as the attacker's attack density. The attacker disrupts the system performance to the maximum extent with the minimum attack density. The control system minimizes the linear quadratic regulation (LQR) performance of the multitasking system by designing the control to model the attacker and controller as a leader-follower Stackelberg game problem, and obtain the optimal attack strategy and optimal controller by dichotomously finding and solving a convex optimization problem [238]. In the literature [143], the problem of resilient policy design for second-order systems is studied based on game theory. Based on the game theoretic approach, Li et al. studied the problems of resource allocation for false data injection attacks [215]. resource allocation for energy-constrained defenders and FDI attackers in multi-sensor NCS [212], transmission channel and attack channel selection under multi-channel transmission mechanism [115], and defense resource allocation and attack node selection in dynamic network systems [213] are investigated. The problem of offensive and defensive games in wireless sensor networks is studied in the literature [196]. According to Zhang [168], machine learning methods are made more resilient by designing game models assuming that the attacker has access to training data in order to corrupt the training effect.

In addition to the above studies, scholars have also investigated the problem of attack and defense confrontation in real system models. Wang, Hasan, and Ma et al. Study the attack-defense game problem of a power grid system [163, 172, 189]. Xiao et al [135]. study the security problem in Mobile Crowdsensing (MCS) networks. Smart users may provide false information to the MCS server in order to save energy and avoid privacy leakage. The MCS server and smart users are modeled as Stackelberg game model, which is solved using Deep Q-network (DQN) techniques. Yu [199] studies the security cooperation problem of mobile self-organizing networks under noisy and incomplete monitoring based on a game theoretic approach. Based on the attack-and-defense stochastic game of Petri nets, Wang [226] studies the problem of modeling and security analysis of enterprise networks. Chen et al. study the security of infrastructure networks through dynamic games [96]. Based on the Bargaining game approach, the trust problem of information transmission in the Internet of Vehicles is studied in the literature [106]. IoT is coupled with military networks to form the Internet of Battlefield Things (IoBT). Ye et al. investigate the security problems of IoBT systems based on dynamic psychological simulations [209].

Section I

Resilient Strategy to Address a Deception Attack

2 Secure filtering under multiple missing measurements and deception attacks

2.1 INTRODUCTION

Recently, filtering techniques have attracted a lot of attentions because the measurements contain not only useful signals but also complicated random noise. Filtering techniques are important in engineering applications such as trajectory tracking of robots, power control of smart grid systems, and formation control of spacecrafts, where wireless sensors play important roles[47, 49]. Stochastic nonlinearities must be considered in such applications, and efficient results have been developed for filtering problems using the unscented Kalman filtering approach[33] and the extended Kalman filtering approach[178]. Both of them are applicable for nonlinear systems with noises of known statistics. In addition, H_∞ filtering can deal with exogenous disturbances and parameter uncertainties for stochastic nonlinear systems[105, 243, 256].

Time-delay and missing measurements are two main problems in networked operation filtering systems which may result in instability and performance degradation. In addition, network security is important due to the vulnerability of wireless communication channels to cyber attacks, which can reduce the reliability of networks by corrupting sensor or actuator data. According to the implementation types, cyber attacks are classified as DoS attacks and deception attacks. The DoS attack, also known as a jamming attack, is implemented by launching a large quantity of useless information or interference power. The deception attack takes effect by modifying the measurement data or control command[35, 40], and it can be further subdivided into a false data injection attack[73] and a replay attack[147]. Most previous studies assume all sensors have the same data missing probability and the same attack acts on all sensor data in mutual network, but in practice, sensors' data are transmitted in multiple channels, which may have different missing probabilities and attack signals.

In this chapter, the secure filtering problem is investigated for a class of uncertain stochastic time-delay and nonlinear systems.

(1) A novel multiple channel attack model is established to account for the missing measurements and random deception attacks, which are assumed to occur in the secure or insecure networks on both sides of wireless sensors.
(2) The concept of φ-level security is proposed to quantify the degree of security.

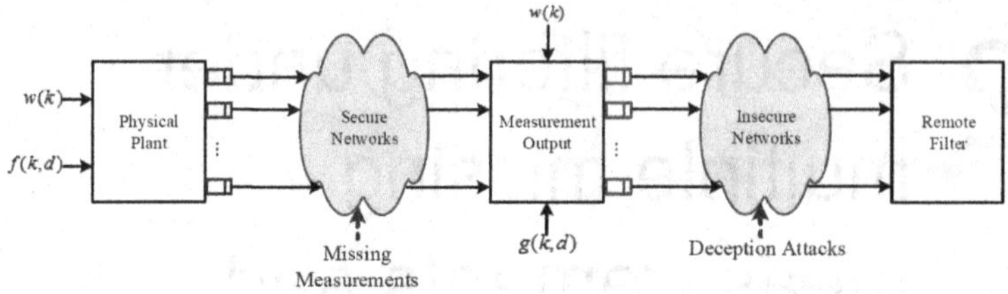

Figure 2.1 Structure for filtering system over secure and insecure networks.

With the techniques of stochastic analysis, sufficient conditions are derived to guarantee the filtering systems to be φ-level security.

(3) A secure filter is designed such that the multiple channel filtering error dynamics achieves the desired secure level, and the filtering gains are obtained by solving a set of inequality constraints.

The rest of this chapter is organized as follows. The problem formulations are given in Section 2.2. In Section 2.3, the main results are given, including the sufficient conditions for φ-level security and design of filter gains. In Section 2.4, numerical simulations are shown to verify the effectiveness of the proposed method. Conclusions are drawn in Section 2.5.

2.2 PROBLEM FORMULATION

In this chapter, the filtering problem is considered for an uncertain discrete-time system with stochastic time-delay and nonlinearities as shown in Fig. 2.1. The physical plant is of the following form

$$\begin{aligned} x(k+1) &= A(k)x(k) + A_d(k)x_d(k) + f(k,d) + E_1 w(k), \\ x(s) &= \varphi(s),\ s \in [-n_M, 0], \end{aligned} \tag{2.1}$$

where $x(k) \in \mathbb{R}^{n_x}$ is the state variable and $\varphi(s)$ is the initial state satisfying $\|\varphi(s)\|^2 < \vartheta^2$, $\forall s \in [-n_M, 0]$. $w(k) \in \mathbb{R}^{n_w}$ is a Gaussian white noise sequence with $\mathbb{E}\{w(k)\} = 0$ and upper bound $\|w(k)\|^2 \le \theta_1^2$. System matrices $A(k) = A + \Delta A(k)$, $A_d(k) = A_d + \Delta A_d(k)$, where the time-varying matrices $\Delta A(k)$ and $\Delta A_d(k)$ are the linear fractional parametric uncertainties defined as

$$\begin{aligned} \begin{bmatrix} \Delta A(k) & \Delta A_d(k) \end{bmatrix} &= M\hat{G}(k) \begin{bmatrix} N_1 & N_2 \end{bmatrix}, \\ \hat{G}(k) &= G(k) \begin{bmatrix} I - HG(k) \end{bmatrix}^{-1}, \end{aligned} \tag{2.2}$$

where M, N_1, and N_2 are known constant real matrices, and $G(k)$ is the unknown time-varying matrix satisfying $G^T(k)G(k) \le I$, $\forall k \ge 0$. Assume that matrix $I - HG(k)$ is invertible for any $G(k)$ and $I - H^T H > 0$. Besides, A, A_d, and E_1 are system matrices with appropriate dimensions.

According to Fig. 2.1, wireless sensors located near the physical plant are to measure the output, where the physical plant and sensors are assumed to be linked by secure networks, whereas, the filter is located remotely, where sensors and filter are built through insecure networks. The multiple channel measurements with sensor data missing in secure networks and randomly occurring deception attacks in insecure networks are described as

$$\begin{aligned} y(k) &= \Xi(k)Cx(k)+g(k,d)+E_2w(k), \\ \tilde{y}(k) &= y(k)+\Sigma(k)v(k), \\ v(k) &= -y(k)+\xi(k), \end{aligned} \tag{2.3}$$

where $y(k) \in \mathbb{R}^{n_y}$ is the measured output vector, $\Xi(k) = \text{diag}\{\alpha_1(k), \cdots, \alpha_{n_y}(k)\}$ represents sensor data missing with $\alpha_i(k)$, $i \in \mathcal{N}_y = \{1,2,\cdots,n_y\}$ being n_y unrelated random variables. The received measurement output $\tilde{y}(k)$ is affected by the randomly occurring deception attacks from the insecure networks between senors and filter. $v(k) \in \mathbb{R}^{n_y}$ is the malicious signal sent by adversaries with $\xi(k) \in \mathbb{R}^{n_y}$ satisfying

$$\|\xi(k)\|^2 \leq \theta_2^2. \tag{2.4}$$

Matrix $\Sigma(k) = \text{diag}\{\beta_1(k), \cdots, \beta_{n_y}(k)\}$ represents the randomness of deception attacks. Stochastic variables $\alpha_i(k)$, $i \in \mathcal{N}_y$ and $\beta_i(k), i \in \mathcal{N}_y$ are mutually independent Bernoulli distributed white sequences taking values 0 or 1 with the probabilities

$$\begin{aligned} &\text{Prob}\{\alpha_i(k)=0\} = 1-\bar{\alpha}_i, \ \text{Prob}\{\alpha_i(k)=1\} = \bar{\alpha}_i, \\ &\text{Prob}\{\beta_i(k)=0\} = 1-\bar{\beta}_i, \ \text{Prob}\{\beta_i(k)=1\} = \bar{\beta}_i. \end{aligned} \tag{2.5}$$

Remark 1 *In this chapter, it is assumed that wireless sensors are exploited to measure the output signals, where networks on both sides of the sensors are considered. The wireless sensors are installed locally, and local area networks with limited bandwidth link the physical plant and sensors. The measurement data missing phenomenon which is the main reason degrading the system performance is taken into consideration. In addition, a filter is installed remotely, where the sensors and remote filter are built through the Internet. The networks between the sensors and remote filter are open to adversaries and vulnerable, and therefore cyber attacks are studied for the filtering system.*

Functions $f(k,d)$ and $g(k,d)$ describing the stochastic nonlinearity of states and delayed states which are bounded in a statistical sense are given as

$$\begin{aligned} &\mathbb{E}\left\{\begin{bmatrix} f(k,d) \\ g(k,d) \end{bmatrix} \Big| x(k)\right\} = 0, \\ &\mathbb{E}\left\{\begin{bmatrix} f(k,d) \\ g(k,d) \end{bmatrix} \begin{bmatrix} f^T(l,d) & g^T(l,d) \end{bmatrix} \Big| x(l)\right\} = 0, \\ &\qquad\qquad\qquad\qquad\qquad\qquad k \neq l, \\ &\mathbb{E}\left\{\begin{bmatrix} f(k,d) \\ g(k,d) \end{bmatrix} \begin{bmatrix} f^T(k,d) & g^T(k,d) \end{bmatrix} \Big| x(k)\right\} \\ &\leq \sum_{j=1}^{q} \begin{bmatrix} \pi_{1j} \\ \pi_{2j} \end{bmatrix} \begin{bmatrix} \pi_{1j} \\ \pi_{2j} \end{bmatrix}^T \times [x^T(k)\phi_j x(k) + x_d^T(k)\psi_j x_d(k)], \end{aligned} \tag{2.6}$$

where nonnegative integer q is a given constant. $\pi_{1j} \in \mathbb{R}^{n_x}$ and $\pi_{2j} \in \mathbb{R}^{n_y}$, $j \in \mathcal{N}_q = \{1, \cdots, q\}$. Matrices ϕ_i and ψ_i are positive-definite with appropriate dimensions. And also, it is assumed that $f(k,d)$ and $g(k,d)$ are unrelated with $\alpha_i(k)$, $\beta_i(k)$, $i \in \mathcal{N}_y$ and $w(k)$.

Considering the multiple channel missing measurements and deception attacks, the following linear filter structure is designed as

$$\begin{aligned} \hat{x}(k+1) &= F\hat{x}(k) + N\tilde{y}(k), \\ \hat{x}(s) &= 0, \ s \in [-n_M, 0], \end{aligned} \tag{2.7}$$

where $\hat{x}(k)$ is state estimation, and F and N are filter parameters to be determined. $\hat{x}(s), s \in [-n_M, 0]$ are the estimations of initial states.

Denoting the filtering error $e(k) = x(k) - \hat{x}(k)$, from equations (2.1), (2.3) and (2.7), the filtering error system yields

$$\begin{aligned} & e(k+1) \\ =& Fe(k) + (A(k) - F - N(I - \Sigma(k))\Xi(k)C)x(k) \\ & + A_d(k)x_d(k) + f(k,d) + E_1 w(k) - N\Sigma(k)\xi(k) \\ & - N(I - \Sigma(k))g(k,d) - N(I - \Sigma(k))E_2 w(k). \end{aligned} \tag{2.8}$$

Augmenting the state variables

$$\tilde{x}(k) = \begin{bmatrix} x(k) \\ e(k) \end{bmatrix}, \ \tilde{x}_d(k) = \begin{bmatrix} x_d(k) \\ e_d(k) \end{bmatrix}, \ h_d(k) = \begin{bmatrix} f(k,d) \\ g(k,d) \end{bmatrix},$$

the filtering error dynamics is given as

$$\begin{aligned} \tilde{x}(k+1) =& (\mathcal{A}(k) + \mathcal{A}_0(k))\tilde{x}(k) + \mathcal{A}_d(k)Z\tilde{x}_d(k) \\ & + \mathcal{C}h_d(k) + \mathcal{E}w(k) + \mathcal{F}\xi(k), \end{aligned} \tag{2.9}$$

where

$$\begin{aligned} \mathcal{A}(k) &= \begin{bmatrix} A(k) & 0 \\ A(k) - F - N(I - \bar{\Sigma})\bar{\Xi}C & F \end{bmatrix}, \\ \mathcal{A}_0(k) &= \begin{bmatrix} 0 & 0 \\ N((I - \bar{\Sigma})\bar{\Xi} - (I - \Sigma(k))\Xi(k))C & 0 \end{bmatrix}, \\ \mathcal{A}_d(k) &= \begin{bmatrix} A_d(k) \\ A_d(k) \end{bmatrix}, \ \mathcal{C}(k) = \begin{bmatrix} I & 0 \\ I & -N(I - \Sigma(k)) \end{bmatrix}, \\ \mathcal{E}(k) &= \begin{bmatrix} E_1 \\ E_1 - N(I - \Sigma(k))E_2 \end{bmatrix}, \ \mathcal{F}(k) = \begin{bmatrix} 0 \\ -N\Sigma(k) \end{bmatrix}, \\ Z &= \begin{bmatrix} I & 0 \end{bmatrix}, \ \bar{\Xi} = \mathbb{E}\{\Xi(k)\}, \ \bar{\Sigma} = \mathbb{E}\{\Sigma(k)\}. \end{aligned}$$

In this chapter, we aim at designing a linear filter such that the filtering error system (2.9) is φ-level security under measurement data missing and randomly occurring deception attacks. Before ending this section, the definition of φ-level security is introduced to quantify the degree of security in the following.

Definition 2.1 *The filtering error dynamics* (2.9) *are said to be φ-level security if one has $\mathbb{E}\{\|e(k)\|^2\} < \varphi$ for all $k \geq n_M + 1$.*

2.3 MAIN RESULTS

In this section, we first give sufficient conditions to guarantee that the nominal system of filtering error dynamics (2.9), i.e., without parameter uncertainties, is φ-level security. Then, the design of the desired filter in equation (2.7) is given. And eventually, the main results are extended to include the robustness.

Theorem 2.1 *Consider filter error dynamics* (2.9) *with given filter gains F and N. If there exist positive-definite matrices P, Q, and positive scalars ε_j, $j \in \mathcal{N}_q$ such that the following inequalities hold, then the filter error dynamics* (2.9) *are φ-level security.*

$$\Omega = \begin{bmatrix} \Omega_{11} & * & * & * \\ \Omega_{21} & \Omega_{22} & * & * \\ \Omega_{31} & 0 & \Omega_{33} & * \\ \Omega_{41} & 0 & 0 & \Omega_{44} \end{bmatrix} < 0, \tag{2.10}$$

$$\Upsilon_{1j} = \begin{bmatrix} -\varepsilon_j & * & * \\ P\bar{C}\bar{\Pi}_j & -P & * \\ \Upsilon_{1j}(3,1) & 0 & -\mathcal{P} \end{bmatrix} < 0,\ j \in \mathcal{N}_q, \tag{2.11}$$

$$-\gamma_0\pi + (\gamma_0 - 1)\lambda_{\max}\{P\} + 2\gamma_0(\gamma_0^{n_M} - 1)\lambda_{\max}\{Z^TQZ\} \le 0, \tag{2.12}$$

and

$$\begin{aligned} &\frac{1}{\lambda_{\min}\{P\}\gamma_0^k}\left(\frac{\gamma_0^{k+1} - \gamma_0}{\gamma_0 - 1}\theta_3^2 + 2n_M\gamma_0^{n_M}\lambda_{\max}\{Z^TQZ\}\right. \\ &\left.\times\vartheta^2 + 2\lambda_{\max}\{P\}\vartheta^2\right) \le \varphi,\ \forall k \in \{1, 2, \cdots, K\}, \end{aligned} \tag{2.13}$$

where

$$\Omega_{11} = diag\{-P + Z^TQZ + \pi I,\ -Q,\ -I\epsilon_2,\ -I\epsilon_1\},$$

$$\Omega_{21} = \begin{bmatrix} 0 & 0 & 0 & P\bar{\mathcal{E}} \\ P\mathcal{A} & P\mathcal{A}_d & P\bar{\mathcal{F}} & 0 \end{bmatrix}, \Omega_{22} = diag\{-P,\ -P\},$$

$$\Omega_{31} = \begin{bmatrix} 0 & 0 & 0 & \Omega_{31}(1,4) \\ \Omega_{31}(2,1) & 0 & \Omega_{31}(2,3) & 0 \\ \Omega_{31}(3,1) & 0 & 0 & 0 \\ 0 & 0 & 0 & \Omega_{31}(4,4) \end{bmatrix},$$

$$\Omega_{33} = diag\{-\mathcal{P},\ -\mathcal{P},\ -\mathcal{P},\ -\mathcal{P}\},$$

$$\Omega_{41} = \begin{bmatrix} \hat{\phi} & 0 & 0 & 0 \\ 0 & \hat{\psi} & 0 & 0 \end{bmatrix}, \Omega_{44} = diag\{-\Theta_1,\ -\Theta_2\},$$

with

$$\Omega_{31}(1,4)=\begin{bmatrix}\sqrt{(1-\bar{\beta}_1)\bar{\beta}_1}P\bar{E}_{21}\\ \sqrt{(1-\bar{\beta}_2)\bar{\beta}_2}P\bar{E}_{22}\\ \vdots\\ \sqrt{(1-\bar{\beta}_{n_y})\bar{\beta}_{n_y}}P\bar{E}_{2n_y}\end{bmatrix},$$

$$\Omega_{31}(2,1)=\begin{bmatrix}(1-\bar{\beta}_1)\bar{\alpha}_1P\bar{C}_1\\ (1-\bar{\beta}_2)\bar{\alpha}_2P\bar{C}_2\\ \vdots\\ (1-\bar{\beta}_{n_y})\bar{\alpha}_{n_y}P\bar{C}_{n_y}\end{bmatrix},\Omega_{31}(2,3)=\begin{bmatrix}\bar{\beta}_1P\bar{N}_1\\ \bar{\beta}_2P\bar{N}_2\\ \vdots\\ \bar{\beta}_{n_y}P\bar{N}_{n_y}\end{bmatrix},$$

$$\Omega_{31}(3,1)=\begin{bmatrix}\sqrt{(1-\bar{\beta}_1)\bar{\alpha}_1-2(1-\bar{\beta}_1)^2\bar{\alpha}_1^2}P\bar{C}_1\\ \sqrt{(1-\bar{\beta}_2)\bar{\alpha}_2-2(1-\bar{\beta}_2)^2\bar{\alpha}_2^2}P\bar{C}_2\\ \vdots\\ \sqrt{(1-\bar{\beta}_{n_y})\bar{\alpha}_{n_y}-2(1-\bar{\beta}_{n_y})^2\bar{\alpha}_{n_y}^2}P\bar{C}_{n_y}\end{bmatrix},$$

$$\Omega_{31}(4,4)=\begin{bmatrix}\sqrt{\bar{\beta}_1-2\bar{\beta}_1^2}P\bar{N}_1\\ \sqrt{\bar{\beta}_2-2\bar{\beta}_2^2}P\bar{N}_2\\ \vdots\\ \sqrt{\bar{\beta}_{n_y}-2\bar{\beta}_{n_y}^2}P\bar{N}_{n_y}\end{bmatrix},$$

$$\Upsilon_{1j}(3,1)=\begin{bmatrix}\sqrt{(1-\bar{\beta}_1)\bar{\beta}_1}P\bar{C}_{01}\bar{\Pi}_j\\ \sqrt{(1-\bar{\beta}_2)\bar{\beta}_2}P\bar{C}_{02}\bar{\Pi}_j\\ \vdots\\ \sqrt{(1-\bar{\beta}_{n_y})\bar{\beta}_{n_y}}P\bar{C}_{0n_y}\bar{\Pi}_j\end{bmatrix},$$

$$\mathcal{A}=\begin{bmatrix}A & 0\\ A-F-N(I-\bar{\Sigma})\bar{\Xi}C & F\end{bmatrix},\ \mathcal{A}_d=\begin{bmatrix}A_d\\ A_d\end{bmatrix},$$

$$\bar{\mathcal{F}}=\begin{bmatrix}0\\ -N\bar{\Sigma}\end{bmatrix},\ \bar{\mathcal{E}}=\begin{bmatrix}E_1\\ E_1-N(I-\bar{\Sigma})E_2\end{bmatrix},$$

$$\bar{C}=\begin{bmatrix}I & 0\\ I & -N(I-\bar{\Sigma})\end{bmatrix},$$

$$\Theta_1=diag\{\varepsilon_1I^{\dagger},\ \cdots,\ \varepsilon_qI^{\dagger}\},$$

$$\Theta_2=diag\{\varepsilon_1I^{\ddagger},\ \cdots,\ \varepsilon_qI^{\ddagger}\},$$

$$\mathcal{P}=diag\{P,\ P,\cdots,\ P\},\ \theta_3=\sqrt{\epsilon_1\theta_1^2+\epsilon_2\theta_2^2},$$

and

$$\hat{\phi}=\begin{bmatrix}\varepsilon_1\sqrt{\bar{\phi}_1}\\ \varepsilon_2\sqrt{\bar{\phi}_2}\\ \vdots\\ \varepsilon_q\sqrt{\bar{\phi}_q}\end{bmatrix},\ \hat{\psi}=\begin{bmatrix}\varepsilon_1\sqrt{\psi_1}\\ \varepsilon_2\sqrt{\psi_2}\\ \vdots\\ \varepsilon_q\sqrt{\psi_q}\end{bmatrix},$$

$$\bar{E}_{2i}=\begin{bmatrix}0\\ NE_{2i}\end{bmatrix},\ \bar{C}_i=\begin{bmatrix}0 & 0\\ NC_i & 0\end{bmatrix},\ \bar{N}_i=\begin{bmatrix}0\\ NI_i\end{bmatrix},$$

$$\bar{C}_{0i}=\begin{bmatrix}0 & 0\\ 0 & -NI_i\end{bmatrix},\ \bar{\phi}_j=\begin{bmatrix}\phi_j & 0\\ 0 & 0\end{bmatrix},\ \bar{\Pi}_j=\begin{bmatrix}\pi_{1j}\\ \pi_{2j}\end{bmatrix},$$

$I^{\dagger}$ *and* $I^{\ddagger}$ *being identity matrices with appropriate dimension,* $\bar{E}_{2i}$ *and* C_i *representing the ith row of matrices E and C, that is,* $E_{2i}=I_iE_2$, $C_i=I_iC$, $I_i=diag\{\underbrace{0,\cdots,0}_{i-1},1,\underbrace{0,\cdots,0}_{n_y-i}\}$.

Proof *A Lyapunov function for system* (2.9) *is chosen as*

$$V(k)=\tilde{x}^T(k)P\tilde{x}(k)+\sum_{s=k-n_M}^{k-1}\tilde{x}^T(s)Z^TQZ\tilde{x}(s). \tag{2.14}$$

The difference of Lyapunov function (2.14) *is calculated as*

$$\begin{aligned}
&\mathbb{E}\{\Delta V(k)\}\\
=&(\mathcal{A}\tilde{x}(k)+\mathcal{A}_dZ\tilde{x}_d(k))^TP(\mathcal{A}\tilde{x}(k)+\mathcal{A}_dZ\tilde{x}_d(k))\\
&+\mathbb{E}\{(\mathcal{A}\tilde{x}(k)+\mathcal{A}_dZ\tilde{x}_d(k))^TP\mathcal{F}(k)\xi(k)\}\\
&+\mathbb{E}\{(\mathcal{F}(k)\xi(k))^TP(\mathcal{A}\tilde{x}(k)+\mathcal{A}_dZ\tilde{x}_d(k))\}\\
&+\mathbb{E}\{(\mathcal{F}(k)\xi(k))^TP\mathcal{A}_0(k)\tilde{x}(k)\}\\
&+\mathbb{E}\{(\mathcal{A}_0(k)\tilde{x})^TP\mathcal{F}(k)\xi(k)\}\\
&+\mathbb{E}\{(\mathcal{A}_0(k)\tilde{x}(k))^TP\mathcal{A}_0(k)\tilde{x}(k)\}\\
&+\mathbb{E}\{(\mathcal{E}(k)w(k))^TP\mathcal{E}(k)w(k)\}\\
&+\mathbb{E}\{(\mathcal{F}(k)\xi(k))^TP\mathcal{F}(k)\xi(k)\}\\
&+\mathbb{E}\{(C(k)h(k,d))^TPC(k)h(k,d)\}-\tilde{x}^T(k)P\tilde{x}(k)\\
&+\tilde{x}^T(k)Z^TQZ\tilde{x}(k)-\tilde{x}_d^T(k)Z^TQZ\tilde{x}_d(k)
\end{aligned}$$

$$
\begin{aligned}
&\le (\mathcal{A}\tilde{x}(k)+\mathcal{A}_d Z\tilde{x}_d(k))^T P(\mathcal{A}\tilde{x}(k)+\mathcal{A}_d Z\tilde{x}_d(k))\\
&+(\mathcal{A}\tilde{x}(k)+\mathcal{A}_d Z\tilde{x}_d(k))^T P\bar{\mathcal{F}}\xi(k)\\
&+(\bar{\mathcal{F}}\xi(k))^T P(\mathcal{A}\tilde{x}(k)+\mathcal{A}_d Z\tilde{x}_d(k))\\
&+\sum_{i=1}^{n_y}((1-\bar{\beta}_i)\bar{\alpha}_i-(1-\bar{\beta}_i)^2\bar{\alpha}_i^2)\tilde{x}^T(k)\bar{C}_i^T P\bar{C}_i\tilde{x}(k)\\
&+\sum_{i=1}^{n_y}(1-\bar{\beta}_i)\bar{\alpha}_i\bar{\beta}_i\tilde{x}^T(k)\bar{C}_i^T P\bar{N}_i\xi(k)\\
&+\sum_{i=1}^{n_y}(1-\bar{\beta}_i)\bar{\alpha}_i\bar{\beta}_i\xi^T(k)\bar{N}_i^T P\bar{C}_i\tilde{x}(k)\\
&+w^T(k)\bar{\mathcal{E}}^T P\bar{\mathcal{E}}w(k)+\sum_{i=1}^{n_y}(1-\bar{\beta}_i)\bar{\beta}_i w^T(k)\bar{E}_{2i}^T P\bar{E}_{2i}w(k)\\
&+\xi^T(k)\bar{\mathcal{F}}^T P\bar{\mathcal{F}}\xi(k)+\sum_{i=1}^{n_y}(\bar{\beta}_i-\bar{\beta}_i^2)\xi^T(k)\bar{N}_i^T P\bar{N}_i\xi(k)\\
&-\tilde{x}^T(k)P\tilde{x}(k)\\
&+\sum_{j=1}^{q}\left([\tilde{x}^T(k)\bar{\phi}_j\tilde{x}(k)+\tilde{x}_d^T(k)Z^T\psi_j Z\tilde{x}_d(k)]\Lambda_j\right)\\
&+\tilde{x}^T(k)Z^T QZ\tilde{x}(k)-\tilde{x}_d^T(k)Z^T QZ\tilde{x}_d(k)\\
&+\epsilon_1(\theta_1^2-w^T(k)w(k))+\epsilon_2(\theta_2^2-\xi^T(k)\xi(k)),
\end{aligned}
$$

where $\Lambda_j = tr\left(\bar{C}\Pi_j\bar{C}^T P+\sum_{i=1}^{n_y}(\bar{\beta}_i-\bar{\beta}_i^2)\bar{C}_{0i}\Pi_j\bar{C}_{0i}^T P\right)$ *and* $\Pi_j=\bar{\Pi}_j\bar{\Pi}_j^T$. *By denoting*

$$
\eta(k)=\begin{bmatrix}\tilde{x}^T(k) & \tilde{x}_d^T(k)Z^T & \xi^T(k) & \omega^T(k)\end{bmatrix}^T,
$$

one has that

$$
\begin{aligned}
\mathbb{E}\{\Delta V(k)\} \le &\mathbb{E}\left\{\eta^T(k)\Omega_0\eta(k)-\eta^T(k)\right.\\
&\left.\times diag\{\pi I,0,0,0\}\eta(k)\right\}+\epsilon_1\theta_1^2+\epsilon_2\theta_2^2,
\end{aligned} \tag{2.15}
$$

where

$$
\Omega_0=\begin{bmatrix}\Omega_0(1,1) & * & * & *\\ \Omega_0(2,1) & \Omega_0(2,2) & * & *\\ \Omega_0(3,1) & \Omega_0(3,2) & \Omega_0(3,3) & *\\ 0 & 0 & 0 & \Omega_0(4,4)\end{bmatrix}
$$

with

$$\begin{aligned}
\Omega_0(1,1) =& \mathcal{A}^T P \mathcal{A} + \sum_{i=1}^{n_y} (\bar{\alpha}_i (1-\bar{\beta}_i) - \bar{\alpha}_i^2 (1-\bar{\beta}_i)^2) \bar{C}_i^T P \bar{C}_i \\
& + \sum_{j=1}^{q} \bar{\phi}_j \varepsilon_j + Z^T Q Z - P + \pi I, \\
\Omega_0(2,1) =& \mathcal{A}_d^T P \mathcal{A}, \\
\Omega_0(2,2) =& \mathcal{A}_d^T P \mathcal{A}_d - Q + \sum_{j=1}^{q} \psi_j \varepsilon_j, \\
\Omega_0(3,1) =& \bar{\mathcal{F}}^T P \mathcal{A} + \sum_{i=1}^{n_y} (1-\bar{\beta}_i) \bar{\alpha}_i \bar{\beta}_i \bar{N}_i^T P \bar{C}_i, \\
\Omega_0(3,2) =& \bar{\mathcal{F}}^T P \mathcal{A}_d, \\
\Omega_0(3,3) =& \bar{\mathcal{F}}^T P \bar{\mathcal{F}} + \sum_{i=1}^{n_y} (1-\bar{\beta}_i) \bar{\beta}_i \bar{N}_i^T P \bar{N}_i - \epsilon_2 I, \\
\Omega_0(4,4) =& \bar{\mathcal{E}}^T P \bar{\mathcal{E}} + \sum_{i=1}^{n_y} (1-\bar{\beta}_i) \bar{\beta}_i \bar{E}_{2i}^T P \bar{E}_{2i} - \epsilon_1 I,
\end{aligned}$$

By Schur complement, inequality $\Omega_0 < 0$ *can be rewritten as* (2.10)*, and the following inequality*

$$\Lambda_j < \varepsilon_j, \ j \in \mathcal{N}_q \tag{2.16}$$

equals to (2.11).

Next, the upper bound of filtering error under measurement data missing and deception attacks is estimated. Obviously, if condition (2.10) *holds, we have*

$$\mathbb{E}\{\Delta V(k)\} \leq -\pi \mathbb{E}\{\|\tilde{x}(k)\|^2\} + \theta_3^2. \tag{2.17}$$

It follows from (2.14) *that*

$$\mathbb{E}\{V(k)\} \leq \lambda_{\max}\{P\} \mathbb{E}\{\|\tilde{x}(k)\|^2\} + \lambda_{\max}\{Z^T Q Z\} \sum_{s=k-n_M}^{k-1} \mathbb{E}\{\|\tilde{x}(s)\|^2\}. \tag{2.18}$$

Together with (2.17)*, the following*

$$\begin{aligned}
& \mathbb{E}\{\gamma^{k+1} V(k+1)\} - \mathbb{E}\{\gamma^k V(k)\} \\
=& \gamma^{k+1} \mathbb{E}\{\Delta V(k)\} + \gamma^k (\gamma - 1) \mathbb{E}\{V(k)\} \\
\leq& \gamma^{k+1} \{-\pi \mathbb{E}\{\|\tilde{x}(k)\|^2\} + \theta_3^2\} + \gamma^k (\gamma - 1) \mathbb{E}\{V(k)\}
\end{aligned} \tag{2.19}$$

holds with scalar $\gamma > 1$. *For integer* $K > n_M + 1$, *summing up both sides of* (2.19) *from* 0 *to* $K-1$, *one has that*

$$
\begin{aligned}
&\mathbb{E}\{\gamma^K V(K)\} - \mathbb{E}\{V(0)\} \\
&\leq \sum_{k=0}^{K-1} \gamma^{k+1}\{-\pi\mathbb{E}\{\|\tilde{x}(k)\|^2\}\} + \sum_{k=0}^{K-1} \gamma^{k+1}\theta_3^2 + \sum_{k=0}^{K-1} \gamma^k(\gamma-1)\lambda_{\max}\{P\}\mathbb{E}\{\|\tilde{x}(k)\|^2\} \\
&\quad + \sum_{k=0}^{K-1} \gamma^k(\gamma-1)\lambda_{\max}\{Z^TQZ\} \sum_{s=k-n_M}^{k-1} \mathbb{E}\{\|\tilde{x}(s)\|^2\} \\
&=(-\gamma\pi + (\gamma-1)\lambda_{\max}\{P\}) \sum_{k=0}^{K-1} \gamma^k \mathbb{E}\{\|\tilde{x}(k)\|^2\} + \frac{\gamma^{K+1}-\gamma}{\gamma-1}\theta_3^2 \\
&\quad + (\gamma-1)\lambda_{\max}\{Z^TQZ\} \sum_{k=0}^{K-1} \sum_{s=k-n_M}^{k-1} \gamma^k \mathbb{E}\{\|\tilde{x}(s)\|^2\},
\end{aligned}
$$

where

$$
\begin{aligned}
&\sum_{k=0}^{K-1} \sum_{s=k-n_M}^{k-1} \gamma^k \mathbb{E}\{\|\tilde{x}(s)\|^2\} \\
&\leq \frac{1-\gamma^{n_M}}{1-\gamma} \sum_{s=-n_M}^{-1} \mathbb{E}\{\|\tilde{x}(s)\|^2\} + \frac{\gamma - r^{n_M+1}}{1-\gamma} \sum_{s=0}^{K-1-n_M} \gamma^s \mathbb{E}\{\|\tilde{x}(s)\|^2\} \\
&\quad + \frac{\gamma - \gamma^{K-s+1}}{1-\gamma} \sum_{s=K-n_M}^{K-1} \gamma^s \mathbb{E}\{\|\tilde{x}(s)\|^2\}.
\end{aligned}
\tag{2.20}
$$

Then, we have

$$
\begin{aligned}
&\mathbb{E}\{\gamma^K V(K)\} - \mathbb{E}\{V(0)\} \\
&\leq(-\gamma\pi + (\gamma-1)\lambda_{\max}\{P\} + 2\gamma(\gamma^{n_M}-1) \times \lambda_{\max}\{Z^TQZ\}) \sum_{k=0}^{K-1} \gamma^k \mathbb{E}\{\|\tilde{x}(k)\|^2\} \\
&\quad + \frac{\gamma^{K+1}-\gamma}{\gamma-1}\theta_3^2 + (\gamma^{n_M}-1)\lambda_{\max}\{Z^TQZ\} \sum_{s=-n_M}^{-1} \mathbb{E}\{\|\tilde{x}(s)\|^2\}.
\end{aligned}
\tag{2.21}
$$

Finding a scalar $\gamma_0 > 1$ *satisfying inequality* (2.12), *it is concluded that*

$$
\begin{aligned}
&\mathbb{E}\{\gamma_0^K V(K)\} - \mathbb{E}\{V(0)\} \\
&\leq \frac{\gamma_0^{K+1}-\gamma_0}{\gamma_0-1}\theta_3^2 + (\gamma_0^{n_M}-1)\lambda_{\max}\{Z^TQZ\} \sum_{s=-n_M}^{-1} \mathbb{E}\{\|\tilde{x}(s)\|^2\}.
\end{aligned}
\tag{2.22}
$$

Since

$$\begin{aligned}\mathbb{E}\{\gamma_0^K V(K)\} \geq& \lambda_{\min}\{P\}\gamma_0^K \mathbb{E}\{\|e(K)\|^2\},\\ \mathbb{E}\{V(0)\} \leq& \lambda_{\max}\{P\}\mathbb{E}\{\|\tilde{x}(0)\|^2\} + 2n_M \lambda_{\max}\{Z^T QZ\}\vartheta^2,\end{aligned} \tag{2.23}$$

we have

$$\begin{aligned}&\mathbb{E}\{\|e(K)\|^2\} \\ &\leq \frac{1}{\lambda_{\min}\{P\}\gamma_0^K}\left(\frac{\gamma_0^{K+1}-\gamma_0}{\gamma_0 - 1}\theta_3^2 + 2n_M\gamma_0^{n_M}\lambda_{\max}\{Z^T QZ\}\vartheta^2 + 2\lambda_{\max}\{P\}\vartheta^2\right).\end{aligned} \tag{2.24}$$

Then, it is known if condition (2.13) *holds, filter error dynamics* (2.8) *are secure.*

In the following, our attention is focused on the calculation of filtering gains F and N for the stochastic time-delay and nonlinear system with multiple missing measurements and deception attacks using the results in Theorem 1. For convenience, the positive-definite matrix P is taken as $P = \text{diag}\{P_1, P_2\}$, where P_1 and P_2 are positive-definite matrices.

Theorem 2.2 *If there exist positive definite matrices $P = diag\{P_1, P_2\}$ and Q, matrices Y_1 and Y_2 such that the following inequalities*

$$\Phi = \begin{bmatrix} \Phi_{11} & * & * & * \\ \Phi_{21} & \Phi_{22} & * & * \\ \Phi_{31} & 0 & \Phi_{33} & * \\ \Phi_{41} & 0 & 0 & \Phi_{44} \end{bmatrix} < 0, \tag{2.25}$$

$$\Upsilon_{2j} = \begin{bmatrix} -\varepsilon_j & * & * \\ \tilde{C}\tilde{\Pi}_j & -P & * \\ \Upsilon_{2j}(3,1) & 0 & -\mathcal{P} \end{bmatrix} < 0,\ j \in \mathcal{N}_q, \tag{2.26}$$

(2.12) *and* (2.13) *hold, the filter error dynamics* (2.9) *are φ-level security. Therefore, the desired filter parameters are given as*

$$F = P_2^{-1}Y_1,\ N = P_2^{-1}Y_2, \tag{2.27}$$

where

$$\Phi_{11} = \Omega_{11},\ \Phi_{22} = \Omega_{22},\ \Phi_{33} = \Omega_{33}, \Phi_{41} = \Omega_{41},\ \Phi_{44} = \Omega_{44},$$

$$\Phi_{21} = \begin{bmatrix} 0 & 0 & 0 & \tilde{\mathcal{E}} \\ \tilde{\mathcal{A}} & \tilde{\mathcal{A}}_d & \tilde{\mathcal{F}} & 0 \end{bmatrix}, \Phi_{31} = \begin{bmatrix} 0 & 0 & 0 & \Phi_{31}(1,4) \\ \Phi_{31}(2,1) & 0 & \Phi_{31}(2,3) & 0 \\ \Phi_{31}(3,1) & 0 & 0 & 0 \\ 0 & 0 & 0 & \Phi_{31}(4,4) \end{bmatrix}, \tag{2.28}$$

with

$$\Phi_{31}(1,4)=\begin{bmatrix}\sqrt{(1-\bar{\beta}_1)\bar{\beta}_1}\tilde{E}_{21}\\ \sqrt{(1-\bar{\beta}_2)\bar{\beta}_2}\tilde{E}_{22}\\ \vdots\\ \sqrt{(1-\bar{\beta}_{n_y})\bar{\beta}_{n_y}}\tilde{E}_{2n_y}\end{bmatrix},\Phi_{31}(2,1)=\begin{bmatrix}(1-\bar{\beta}_1)\bar{\alpha}_1\tilde{C}_1\\ (1-\bar{\beta}_2)\bar{\alpha}_2\tilde{C}_2\\ \vdots\\ (1-\bar{\beta}_{n_y})\bar{\alpha}_{n_y}\tilde{C}_{n_y}\end{bmatrix},$$

$$\Phi_{31}(2,3)=\begin{bmatrix}\bar{\beta}_1\tilde{N}_1\\ \bar{\beta}_2\tilde{N}_2\\ \vdots\\ \bar{\beta}_{n_y}\tilde{N}_{n_y}\end{bmatrix},\Phi_{31}(3,1)=\begin{bmatrix}\sqrt{(1-\bar{\beta}_1)\bar{\alpha}_1-2(1-\bar{\beta}_1)^2\bar{\alpha}_1^2}\tilde{C}_1\\ \sqrt{(1-\bar{\beta}_2)\bar{\alpha}_2-2(1-\bar{\beta}_2)^2\bar{\alpha}_2^2}\tilde{C}_2\\ \vdots\\ \sqrt{(1-\bar{\beta}_{n_y})\bar{\alpha}_{n_y}-2(1-\bar{\beta}_{n_y})^2\bar{\alpha}_{n_y}^2}\tilde{C}_{n_y}\end{bmatrix},$$

$$\Phi_{31}(4,4)=\begin{bmatrix}\sqrt{\bar{\beta}_1-2\bar{\beta}_1^2}\tilde{N}_1\\ \sqrt{\bar{\beta}_2-2\bar{\beta}_2^2}\tilde{N}_2\\ \vdots\\ \sqrt{\bar{\beta}_{n_y}-2\bar{\beta}_{n_y}^2}\tilde{N}_{n_y}\end{bmatrix},\Upsilon_{2j}(3,1)=\begin{bmatrix}\sqrt{(1-\bar{\beta}_1)\bar{\beta}_1}\tilde{C}_{01}\bar{\Pi}_j\\ \sqrt{(1-\bar{\beta}_2)\bar{\beta}_2}\tilde{C}_{02}\bar{\Pi}_j\\ \vdots\\ \sqrt{(1-\bar{\beta}_{n_y})\bar{\beta}_{n_y}}\tilde{C}_{0n_y}\bar{\Pi}_j\end{bmatrix},$$

$$\tilde{\mathscr{A}}=\begin{bmatrix}P_1A & 0\\ P_2A-Y_1-Y_2(I-\bar{\Sigma})\bar{\Xi}C & Y_1\end{bmatrix},\ \tilde{\mathscr{A}}_d=\begin{bmatrix}P_1A_d\\ P_2A_d\end{bmatrix},$$

$$\tilde{\mathscr{F}}=\begin{bmatrix}0\\ -Y_2\bar{\Sigma}\end{bmatrix},\ \tilde{\mathscr{E}}=\begin{bmatrix}P_1E_1\\ P_2E_1-Y_2(I-\bar{\Sigma})E_2\end{bmatrix},$$

$$\tilde{C}=\begin{bmatrix}P_1 & 0\\ P_2 & -Y_2(I-\bar{\Sigma})\end{bmatrix}$$

and

$$\tilde{E}_{2i}=\begin{bmatrix}0\\ Y_2E_{2i}\end{bmatrix},\ \tilde{C}_i=\begin{bmatrix}0 & 0\\ Y_2C_i & 0\end{bmatrix},\tilde{N}_i=\begin{bmatrix}0\\ Y_2I_i\end{bmatrix},\ \tilde{C}_{0i}=\begin{bmatrix}0 & 0\\ 0 & -Y_2I_i\end{bmatrix}.$$

Proof *The proof is omitted here.*

The main result of Theorem 2 is extended to the uncertain parameter cases. The secure filter gains are obtained by solving inequalities similar to the ones in Theorem 2. The following lemma is recalled for the subsequent development.

Lemma 2.1 *[240] Given constant matrices Σ_1, Σ_2 and a symmetric constant matrix Υ, the inequality*

$$\Upsilon+\Sigma_1\hat{G}(t_k)\Sigma_2+\Sigma_2^T\hat{G}^T(t_k)\Sigma_1^T<0$$

holds, where $\hat{G}(t_k)$ is given in (2.2), if and only if there is a scalar $\delta>0$ such that

$$\Upsilon+\begin{bmatrix}\delta^{-1}\Sigma_1^T & \delta\Sigma_2\end{bmatrix}\begin{bmatrix}I & -H\\ -H^T & I\end{bmatrix}^{-1}\begin{bmatrix}\delta^{-1}\Sigma_1\\ \delta\Sigma_2^T\end{bmatrix}<0.$$

Theorem 2.3 *Considering the filtering error dynamics* (2.9) *with parameter uncertainties* (2.2), *if*

$$\Psi = \begin{bmatrix} \Psi_{11} & * \\ \Psi_{21} & \Psi_{22} \end{bmatrix} < 0, \tag{2.29}$$

where

$$\begin{aligned} &\Psi_{11} = \Phi,\ \Psi_{21} = \begin{bmatrix} \varpi_1 & \boldsymbol{0}_{2\times 3} & \varpi_2 & \boldsymbol{0}_{2\times 6} \end{bmatrix}, \\ &\varpi_1 = \begin{bmatrix} \tilde{N}_1 & N_2 \\ 0 & 0 \end{bmatrix},\ \varpi_2 = \begin{bmatrix} 0 \\ \mu \tilde{M}^T P \end{bmatrix}, \\ &\Psi_{22} = \begin{bmatrix} -\mu I & * \\ \mu H^T & -\mu I \end{bmatrix} \end{aligned}$$

with $\tilde{M} = \begin{bmatrix} M \\ M \end{bmatrix}$ *and* $\tilde{N}_1 = \begin{bmatrix} N_1 & 0 \end{bmatrix}$ *and conditions* (2.12), (2.13) *and* (2.26) *hold, then system* (2.9) *with uncertainties is* φ*-level security.*

Proof *Based on Lemma 2.1, there exists a scalar* $\delta > 0$ *such that*

$$\Psi_0 = \Phi + \begin{bmatrix} \delta^{-1}\eta^T & \delta\zeta \end{bmatrix} \mathcal{H}^{-1} \begin{bmatrix} \delta^{-1}\eta \\ \delta\zeta^T \end{bmatrix} < 0, \tag{2.30}$$

where

$$\begin{aligned} &\mathcal{H} = \begin{bmatrix} I & -H \\ -H^T & I \end{bmatrix},\ \eta = \begin{bmatrix} \tilde{N}_1 & N_2 & \boldsymbol{0}_{1\times 10} \end{bmatrix}, \\ &\zeta = \begin{bmatrix} \boldsymbol{0}_{1\times 5} & P\tilde{M} & \boldsymbol{0}_{1\times 6} \end{bmatrix}^T. \end{aligned}$$

By using Schur's complement, $\Psi_0 \leq 0$ *is changed to* $\Psi_1 \leq 0$*, where*

$$\Psi_1 = \begin{bmatrix} \Psi_1(1,1) & * \\ \Psi_1(2,1) & \Psi_1(2,2) \end{bmatrix} \tag{2.31}$$

with

$$\begin{aligned} &\Psi_1(1,1) = \Phi,\ \Psi_1(2,2) = -\mathcal{H}, \\ &\Psi_1(2,1) = \begin{bmatrix} \varphi_1 & \boldsymbol{0}_{2\times 3} & \varphi_2 & \boldsymbol{0}_{2\times 6} \end{bmatrix}, \\ &\varphi_1 = \begin{bmatrix} \delta^{-1}\tilde{N}_1 & \delta^{-1}N_2 \\ 0 & 0 \end{bmatrix},\ \varphi_2 = \begin{bmatrix} 0 \\ \delta \tilde{M}^T P \end{bmatrix}. \end{aligned}$$

Then, pre- and post-multiplying Ψ_1 *by* $diag = \{I, I, I, I, I, I, I, I, I, I, I, I, \delta I, \delta I\}$ *and denoting* $\mu = \delta^2$*, we get inequality* (2.29)*. The proof is at the end.*

A heuristic iterative algorithm is presented for Theorem 2.2 to calculate the secure filter gains.

Algorithm 1 Calculation of secure filter gains F, N

1: Input system parameters A, A_d, C, E_1, E_2, Π_j, ϕ_j, φ_j, $j \in N_q$, n_M, the upper bounds of random parameters ϑ, θ_1, and θ_2, and the values of probabilities $\bar{\Xi}$ and $\bar{\Sigma}$.

2: Initialize $\pi > 0$, $K > n_M + 1$, a small enough searching step size τ.

3: Solve the optimization problem:

$$\begin{aligned} \mathbf{OP}: \quad & \min_{P,Q,Y_1,Y_2} \epsilon_1 + \epsilon_2 \\ & \text{s.t. Inequalities (2.25) and (2.26).} \end{aligned}$$

4: If problem **OP** is solvable, calculate $\lambda_{\min}\{P\}$, $\lambda_{\max}\{P\}$, $\lambda_{\max}\{Q\}$, θ_3^2. Go to *Step* 5. If problem **OP** is not solvable, go to *Step* 7.

5: Calculate γ_0 satisfying (2.12), then go to *Step* 6. If there is no solution γ_0 for (2.12), $\pi \leftarrow \pi + \tau$, go to *Step* 3.

6: Check the condition (2.13). If condition (2.13) holds, calculate the desired secure filtering gains with $F = P_2^{-1} Y_1$ and $N = P_2^{-1} Y_2$. If condition (2.13) does not hold, $\pi \leftarrow \pi + \tau$, go to *Step* 3.

7: The algorithm is infeasible. Stop.

2.4 SIMULATION RESULTS

In this section, a simulation example is presented to illustrate the usefulness of the established secure filtering scheme. Consider a stochastic time-delay and nonlinear system with two sensor transmission channels. The system data of (2.1) and (2.3) are given by

$$A = \begin{bmatrix} 0.1 & 0 \\ 0 & 0.2 \end{bmatrix}, A_d = \begin{bmatrix} 0.1 & 0.05 \\ 0.03 & 0.1 \end{bmatrix}, E_1 = \begin{bmatrix} 0.4 \\ 0.4 \end{bmatrix},$$

$$C = \begin{bmatrix} 0.4 & 0.5 \\ 0.1 & 0.3 \end{bmatrix}, E_2 = \begin{bmatrix} 0.4 \\ 0.1 \end{bmatrix}.$$

The stochastic nonlinear functions satisfy

$$\mathbb{E}\left\{\begin{bmatrix} f(k,d) \\ g(k,d) \end{bmatrix} |x(k)\right\} = 0,$$

$$\mathbb{E}\{f(k,d) f^T(k,d)|x(k)\}$$

$$
\begin{aligned}
&= \begin{bmatrix} 2 \\ 2 \end{bmatrix} \begin{bmatrix} 2 \\ 2 \end{bmatrix}^T \left(x^T(k) \begin{bmatrix} 0.01 & 0 \\ 0 & 0.01 \end{bmatrix} x(k) \right. \\
&\left. + x_d^T(k) \begin{bmatrix} 0.01 & 0 \\ 0 & 0.01 \end{bmatrix} x_d(k) \right), \\
&\mathbb{E}\{g(k,d)g^T(k,d)|x(k)\} \\
&= \begin{bmatrix} 2.2 \\ 2.2 \end{bmatrix} \begin{bmatrix} 2.2 \\ 2.2 \end{bmatrix}^T \left(x^T(k) \begin{bmatrix} 0.01 & 0 \\ 0 & 0.01 \end{bmatrix} x(k) \right. \\
&\left. + x_d^T(k) \begin{bmatrix} 0.01 & 0 \\ 0 & 0.01 \end{bmatrix} x_d(k) \right).
\end{aligned}
$$

The upper bound of disturbance, initial state, and maximum time-delay parameters are set by $\theta_1^2 = 0.09$, $\vartheta^2 = 0.02$ and $n_M = 5$. The packet delivery rates and probabilities of successful deception attacks for two transmission channels are

$$
\bar{\Xi} = \begin{bmatrix} 0.7 & 0 \\ 0 & 0.8 \end{bmatrix}, \quad \bar{\Sigma} = \begin{bmatrix} 0.05 & 0 \\ 0 & 0.1 \end{bmatrix}.
$$

Let the deception attack signals be given as

$$
\xi(k) = \begin{bmatrix} 0.5 * \sin(k) \\ 0.3 * \sin(1.5k) \end{bmatrix}.
$$

Using Matlab Yalmip Toolbox and Algorithm 1 to solve the inequalities (2.12), (2.13), (2.25) and (2.26), we obtain

$$
\begin{aligned}
P_1 &= \begin{bmatrix} 8.0818 & 2.1135 \\ 2.1135 & 8.1492 \end{bmatrix}, \quad P_2 = \begin{bmatrix} 10.7367 & 7.8486 \\ 7.8486 & 13.8080 \end{bmatrix}, \\
Q &= \begin{bmatrix} 2.8755 & -3.2498 \\ -3.2498 & 2.9928 \end{bmatrix}.
\end{aligned}
$$

The secure filtering gains are calculated as

$$
F = \begin{bmatrix} -0.0272 & -0.1280 \\ -0.0743 & -0.0247 \end{bmatrix}, \quad N = \begin{bmatrix} 0.4457 & 0.4989 \\ 0.4219 & 0.5054 \end{bmatrix}.
$$

The initial values of states are chosen as $x(-5) = \cdots = x(-1) = \begin{bmatrix} 0.1 & 0.1 \end{bmatrix}$, $x(0) = 0$. The initial values of estimation states are set by $\hat{x}(-5) = \cdots = \hat{x}(0) = \begin{bmatrix} 0 & 0 \end{bmatrix}$.

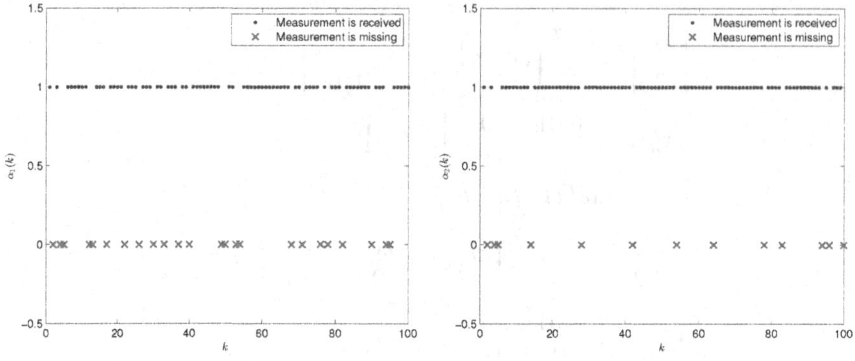

(a) Channel 1. (b) Channel 2.

Figure 2.2 Data transmission in two channels.

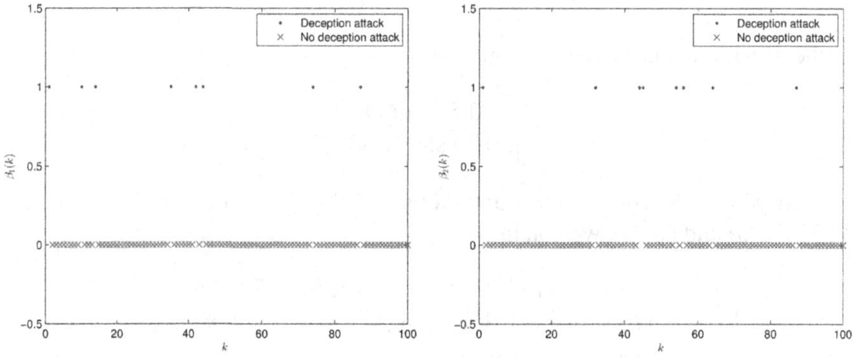

(a) Channel 1. (b) Channel 2.

Figure 2.3 Randomly occurring deception attacks in two channels.

Let us denote the iteration steps as $K = 100$. Fig. 2.2 and Fig. 2.3 show the data transmission and randomly occurring deception attacks in two channels, respectively. Under the influence depicted in Fig. 2.2 and Fig. 2.3, the state trajectories and their estimations are plotted in Fig. 2.4. Fig. 2.5 depicts the evolutions of estimation errors $e_1(k)$ and $e_2(k)$ with and without deception attacks, where we can see that deception attacks significantly degrade the estimation performance.

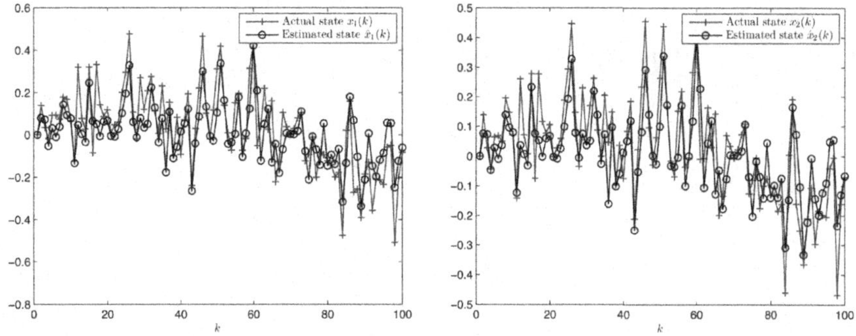

(a) State 1 and its estimation. (b) State 2 and its estimation.

Figure 2.4 Evolution of states and their estimations.

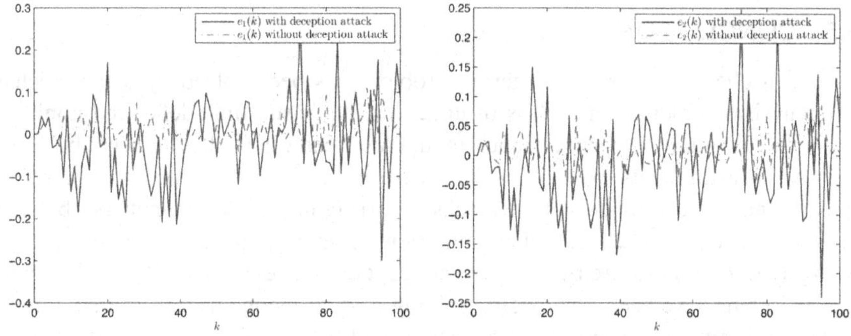

(a) Estimation error of state 1. (b) Estimation error of state 2.

Figure 2.5 Evolution of estimation errors with and without deception attacks.

Fig. 2.6 depicts the relation curves between the upper bound estimation of filter error $\|e(k)\|^2$ and the upper bound of deception attacks θ_2^2, which shows that larger θ_2^2 leads to larger $\|e(k)\|^2$.

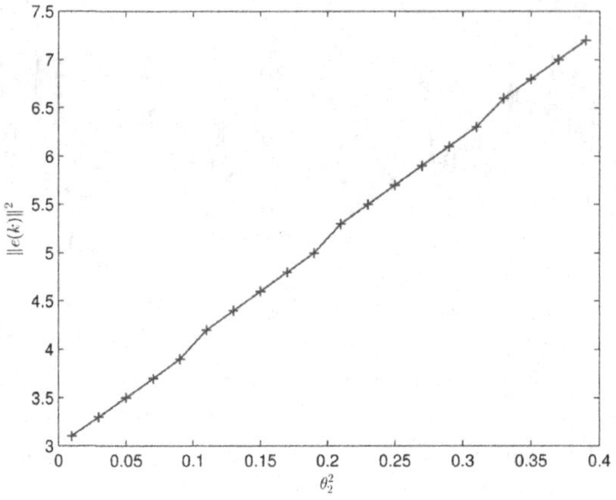

Figure 2.6 Upper bound of filter error $\|e(k)\|^2$ versus θ_2^2.

2.5 CONCLUSION

In this chapter, the secure filtering problem has been solved by using stochastic analysis techniques for a class of uncertain stochastic time-delay and nonlinear systems. The multiple channel attack model has been established to account for the missing measurements existing in the secure network between physical plant and sensors and the random deception attacks occurring in the insecure network between sensors and remote filter. Sufficient conditions have been given to guarantee the filtering system to be secure by using the concept of φ-level security. Then, the secure filtering gains have been obtained by solving a set of inequality constraints. Finally, numerical simulation examples have been provided to verify the effectiveness of the proposed design methodology.

3 Distributed filtering against deception attacks with the quantization effect

3.1 INTRODUCTION

Autonomous sensors with estimation capability are embedded in large-scale systems to enhance sensing, computing, and communication capabilities. Distributed filtering is a major field in sensor networks, but the limited size, energy, and communication capabilities of each installed node bring numerous challenges. Many filtering methods are reported in available researches[20, 29, 34, 126], in which the Kalman filtering and H_∞ filtering are the most effective methods to deal with corresponding Gaussian noise and bounded noise.

In the process of distributed filtering, each sensor observes the output of the physical; meanwhile it can estimate the state of the system by exploiting its own measurements and the information from its neighbors. When large amounts of information are transmitted in limited bandwidth, network issues such as time-delay[190, 191], packet dropout, and packet-disorder emerge. Before the measurements from the physical plant and estimation information from adjacent sensors are transmitted, a quantization strategy can be used to relieve pressure of the limited bandwidth. Besides a quantization strategy, the event-triggered mechanism is another countermeasure to alleviate communication congestion[133].

Large-scale systems linked by networks are vulnerable to cyber attacks; this has attracted many researchers' attention in the studied areas of control and filtering. From the perspective of the defender, a deception attack is randomly implemented, and intermittent deception attack has been studied in[34, 74, 212, 241]. Distributed filtering with deception attacks has not been investigated thoroughly, not to say limited bandwidth resources are provided, which motivates the study of this chapter.

This chapter considers a distributed secure filtering problem for a category of time-varying systems subject to uncertainty and model-reality mismatch, two-stage deception attacks, and bandwidth limitation. Both deception attacks between sensor and corresponding estimator and among estimators appear randomly. To alleviate a communication burden, a quantization strategy is introduced before transmitting measurement and estimation signals. An event-triggered mechanism is employed for each estimator node; thus only necessary data are transmitted to its neighbour sensors when a setting event occurs. The desired target of the problem to be handled is to devise a series of time-varying filters such that the H_∞ secure performance is guaranteed against random deception attacks over a finite time horizon. Sufficient conditions ensuring the existence of time-varying filters under the effect of complex factors are derived, where filter gains are obtained by finding the solution of a sequence of recursive matrix inequalities online. Simulation results in both a numerical example and an industrial continuous-stirred tank reactor system are given to show the validity of the presented methodology.

(1) A novel distributed time-varying filtering system with two-stage deception attacks is established, where deception attacks exist in the channels between sensors and corresponding estimators and among estimators.
(2) To reduce network congestion and save energy for sensors, the quantization strategy and event-triggered communication protocol are exploited, and the effects to the filtering performance are analyzed.
(3) The distributed H_∞ performance for sensor networks is established. The filters are derived by obtaining the solution of a sequence of matrix inequalities for online application.

The structure of this chapter is listed: In Section 3.2, problem formulation for a distributed filtering system is given. The distributed estimator and design purpose are proposed in Section 3.3. Secure performance analysis and filter design are presented in Section 3.4. For verification, Section 3.5 gives the simulation example, and conclusions of this chapter are drawn in Section 3.6.

3.2 PROBLEM FORMULATION

A typical distributed filtering system under communication constraints and two-stage deception attacks as shown in Fig. 3.1 is considered in this chapter. To improve the system performance with limited bandwidth, a quantization strategy and an event-triggered scheme are used. From Fig. 3.1, it is seen that deception attacks exist between sensor and corresponding estimator and among estimators.

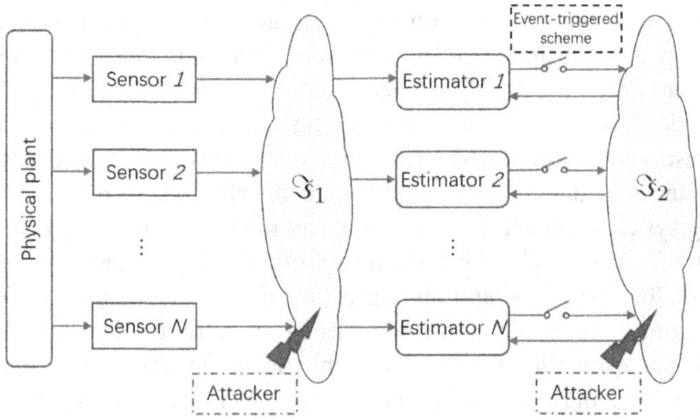

Figure 3.1 Distributed filtering system under deception attacks.

3.2.1 DISTRIBUTED FILTERING SYSTEM

Consider a discrete time-varying system described as follows

$$\begin{aligned} x(k+1) &= (\bar{A}(k)+A_{\Delta}(k))x(k)+B(k)\omega(k), \\ y_i(k) &= C_i(k)x(k)+D_i(k)v_i(k), i \in \mathbf{N} \triangleq \{1,2,\cdots,N\}, \\ z(k) &= M(k)x(k), \end{aligned} \tag{3.1}$$

where $x(k) \in \mathbb{R}^{n_x}$ is the state in time step k, $y_i(k) \in \mathbb{R}^{n_{y_i}}$ is the plant's output measured by the ith sensor, $\omega(k)$ and $v_i(k)$ are the disturbance inputs with $\omega(k) \in l_2([0,\mathrm{T}],\mathbb{R}^{n_\omega})$ and $v_i(k) \in l_2([0,\mathrm{T}],\mathbb{R}^{n_{v_i}})$. $z(k)$ is the output signal to be estimated. $A(k) \triangleq \bar{A}(k)+A_{\Delta}(k), \bar{A}(k) \in \mathbb{R}^{n_x \times n_x}, A_{\Delta}(k) \in \mathbb{R}^{n_x \times n_x}$, $B(k) \in \mathbb{R}^{n_x \times n_\omega}$, $C_i(k) \in \mathbb{R}^{n_{y_i} \times n_x}$, $D_i(k) \in \mathbb{R}^{n_{y_i} \times n_{v_i}}$ and $M(k) \in \mathbb{R}^{n_z \times n_x}$ are known time-varying system matrices, where $A_{\Delta}(k)$ represents the uncertainty and model-reality mismatch satisfying

$$A_{\Delta}(k) = \Gamma_1 F(k) \Gamma_2. \tag{3.2}$$

In formula (3.2), $A_{\Delta}(k) = [\varsigma_{kj}(k)], k,j \in \{1,2,\cdots,n_x\}$, $F(k) = \mathrm{diag}\{\varsigma_{11}(k), \varsigma_{12}(k),\cdots,\varsigma_{kj}(k),\cdots,\varsigma_{n_x n_x}(k)\}$ with $|\varsigma_{kj}(k)| < \bar{\varsigma}$. $\Gamma_1 = [\Gamma_{11},\Gamma_{12},\cdots,\Gamma_{1v},\cdots \Gamma_{1n_x^2}]$, $\Gamma_2 = [\Gamma_{21},\Gamma_{22},\cdots,\Gamma_{2v},\cdots,\Gamma_{2n_x^2}]^T$ with $\Gamma_{1v} = E_k$ and $\Gamma_{2v} = E_j$, $v = (k-1)n_x + j, k,j \in \{1,2,\cdots,n_x\}$. E_k represents the column vector with the kth element being 1 and others being 0. Note that the interval-bounded uncertainty and model-reality mismatch in model (3.2) have been investigated in [55]. The interval-bounded uncertainty is obviously less conservative than the norm-bounded uncertainty considered in [129].

A sensor network encompassing N sensors is deployed to collect the output of the plant as depicted in Fig. 3.1. The connection of sensor nodes is described by a directed graph $\mathbf{G} = \{\mathbf{N},\mathbf{E},\mathbf{A}\}$, where notation $\mathbf{N} \triangleq \{1,2,\cdots,N\}$ is the set of nodes, $\mathbf{E} = \mathbf{N} \times \mathbf{N}$ is the set of edges, and the adjacency matrix is $\mathbf{A} = [a_{ij}]_{N \times N}$ with non-negative adjacency element a_{ij}. $a_{ij} > 0$ represents that node i can receive information from node j, i.e., $(i,j) \in \mathbf{E}$, otherwise $a_{ij} = 0$ and $a_{ii} = 0$ for $i \in \mathbf{N}$. The ith node's neighbours are denoted as set $\mathcal{N}_i = \{j \in \mathbf{N} | (i,j) \in \mathbf{E}\}$.

3.2.2 QUANTIZER

In order to transmit information effectively with limited communication bandwidth, the quantization strategy and event-triggered mechanism are employed before transmission.

In this chapter, logarithmic type quantizers are used for measurement outputs and state estimations. Denote the quantizer for measurement output vector $y_i(k), i \in \mathbf{N}$ as

$$q_{y_i}(y_i(k)) = \left[q_{y_i}^{(1)}(y_i^{(1)}(k)), q_{y_i}^{(2)}(y_i^{(2)}(k)), \cdots, q_{y_i}^{(n_{y_i})}(y_i^{(n_{y_i})}(k))\right]^T, \tag{3.3}$$

where $y_i^{(l)}(k), l \in \{1,2,\cdots,n_{y_i}\}$ represents the lth element of $y_i(k)$. The quantization levels for each $q_{y_i}^{(l)}(\cdot)$ is described by the following set

$$\begin{aligned}\Theta_{y_i,l} =& \{\pm\mu_{y_i,l}^{(m)} | \mu_{y_i,l}^{(m)} = \hbar_{y_i,l}^{m}\mu_{y_i,l}^{(0)}, m = \pm1,\pm2,\cdots\} \cup \{0\},\\ & 0 < \hbar_{y_i,l} < 1,\ \mu_{y_i,l}^{(0)} > 0.\end{aligned} \tag{3.4}$$

The logarithmic quantizer in the sensor corresponding to quantization level (3.4) is presented as follows

$$q_{y_i}^{(l)}(y_i^{(l)}(k)) = \begin{cases} \mu_{y_i,l}^{(m)}, & \frac{1}{1+\ell_{y_i,l}}\mu_{y_i,l}^{(m)} \le y_i^{(l)}(k) \le \frac{1}{1-\ell_{y_i,l}}\mu_{y_i,l}^{(m)},\\ 0, & y_i^{(l)}(k) = 0,\\ -q_{y_i}^{(l)}(-y_i^{(l)}(k)), & y_i^{(l)}(k) < 0, \end{cases} \tag{3.5}$$

where $\ell_{y_i,l} = (1-\hbar_{y_i,l})/(1+\hbar_{y_i,l})$.

To be similar, a quantizer is installed in the estimator node i to quantize the estimation of state as

$$q_{\hat{x}_i}^{(l)}(\hat{x}_i^{(l)}(k)) = \begin{cases} \mu_{\hat{x}_i,l}^{(m)}, & \frac{1}{1+\ell_{\hat{x}_i,l}}\mu_{\hat{x}_i,l}^{(m)} \le \hat{x}_i^{(l)}(k) \le \frac{1}{1-\ell_{\hat{x}_i,l}}\mu_{\hat{x}_i,l}^{(m)},\\ 0, & \hat{x}_i^{(l)}(k) = 0,\\ -q_{\hat{x}_i}^{(l)}(-\hat{x}_i^{(l)}(k)), & \hat{x}_i^{(l)}(k) < 0 \end{cases} \tag{3.6}$$

3.2.3 EVENT DETECTORS

Besides, an event-triggered mechanism is deployed in sensors when transmitting the estimated state as shown in Fig. 3.1. The estimation for system state $x(k)$ in estimator i is denoted as $\hat{x}_i(k) \in \mathbb{R}^{n_x}$. In the framework of distributed filtering, each estimator node in the system is to fuse the information both from its corresponding sensor and its neighbours. For the purpose of reducing unnecessary data transmission between adjacent sensors, a distributed event-triggered communication protocol is designed to decide whether the current estimated state is transmitted to its neighbours or not. For estimator i, the event generator function is chosen as

$$\phi(\hat{x}_i(k), \hat{x}_i(k_i^r), \theta_i(k)) \triangleq \psi_i^T(k)\psi_i(k) - \theta_i(k)\hat{x}_i^T(k)\hat{x}_i(k), \tag{3.7}$$

where k_i^r denotes the last released instant of estimator i, $\psi_i(k) \triangleq q_{\hat{x}_i}(\hat{x}_i(k)) - q_{\hat{x}_i}(\hat{x}_i(k_i^r))$ is the deviation of the ith sensor's estimation between the current instant and the latest released instant, and $\theta_i(k)$ is a positive scalar and is adjustable. If the following condition

$$\phi(\hat{x}_i(k), \hat{x}_i(k_i^r), \theta_i(k)) > 0 \tag{3.8}$$

holds, the event generator is triggered and thus the event-triggered sequences

$$k_i^0 < k_i^1 \cdots < k_i^r < k_i^{r+1} < \cdots$$

can be calculated by

$$k_i^{r+1} = \min\left\{k | \phi(\hat{x}_i(k), \hat{x}_i(k_i^r), \theta_i(k)) > 0, k > k_i^r\right\}. \tag{3.9}$$

Note that with a number of sensors distributed evenly during installation and a limited communication resource, an event-triggered protocol (3.8) is selected. Based on inequality (3.8), it is known that the threshold $\theta_i(k)$ can regulate the update frequency from neighbours, which makes a tradeoff between filtering performance and utilization of resource. That is to say, the tradeoff between the estimation performance and bandwidth load is dependent on the parameter of $\theta_i(k)$. If a precise estimation is needed, a small $\theta_i(k)$ should be chosen. On the other hand, to reduce the communication load, a large $\theta_i(k)$ should be provided. Compared with the centralized event-triggered scheme in previous research [42], the distributed one in this chapter can reduce unnecessary communication and computation resource and meanwhile save energy. Moreover, the state-dependent event-triggered scheme in (3.8) makes the transmission process more efficient.

3.2.4 TWO-STAGE DECEPTION ATTACKS

As depicted in Fig. 3.1, deception attacks exist in two stages of the communication process, that is, in the communication channel from sensor to corresponding estimator denoted by $\Im_1$ and in communication channels among estimators denoted as $\Im_2$. The measurement output $i, i \in \mathbf{N}$ transmitted through networks $\Im_1$ is written by

$$\tilde{y}_i(k) = (1-\gamma_i(k))q_{y_i}(y_i(k)) + \gamma_i(k)\xi_i(k). \tag{3.10}$$

The estimated state $i, i \in \mathbf{N}$ transmitted after channels $\Im_2$ is given by

$$\tilde{\hat{x}}_i(k_i^r) = (1-\beta_i(k_i^r))q_{\hat{x}_i}(\hat{x}_i(k_i^r)) + \beta_i(k_i^r)\rho_i(k_i^r). \tag{3.11}$$

In formulas (3.10) and (3.11), $\gamma_i(k)$ and $\beta_i(k_i^r)$ are two-valued random variables subject to Bernoulli distributions satisfying

$$\begin{aligned} &\Pr\{\gamma_i(k)=1\} = \bar{\gamma}_i,\ \Pr\{\gamma_i(k)=0\} = 1-\bar{\gamma}_i, \\ &\Pr\{\beta_i(k_i^r)=1\} = \bar{\beta}_i,\ \Pr\{\beta_i(k_i^r)=0\} = 1-\bar{\beta}_i, \end{aligned} \tag{3.12}$$

where $\gamma_i(k) = 1$ represents that the ith measurement output is attacked, and otherwise it is not attacked. $\beta_i(k_i^r) = 1$ means that the estimated state from node i is tampered with and otherwise it is transmitted error-free. The bounded signals $\xi_i(k)$ and $\rho_i(k_i^r)$ are the substitutes of corresponding $y_i(k)$ and $\hat{x}_i(k_i^r)$ from attackers when the channels are attacked and satisfy $\|\xi_i(k)\|^2 \le \delta_{\xi_i}^2$ and $\|\rho_i(k)\|^2 \le \delta_{\rho_i}^2$ for all $i \in \mathbf{N}$.

3.3 DISTRIBUTED FILTER AND DESIGN PURPOSE

The following distributed filter for sensor i is designed

$$\begin{aligned} \hat{x}_i(k+1) =& A(k)\hat{x}_i(k) + K_i(k)(\tilde{y}_i(k) - C_i(k)\hat{x}_i(k)) \\ &+ \sum_{j \in N_i} h_{ij}(\tilde{\hat{x}}_j(k_j^r) - q_{\hat{x}_i}(\hat{x}_i(k_i^r))), \\ \hat{z}_i(k) =& M(k)\hat{x}_i(k), \end{aligned} \tag{3.13}$$

where $K_i(k)$ is the filtering parameter to be solved. $H_0 \triangleq [h_{ij}]_{N\times N}$ is the coupling configuration matrix with $h_{ij} = a_{ij}$ for $i \neq j$ and $h_{ii} = -\sum_{j=1,j\neq i}^{N} a_{ij}$. With the quantization rule in (3.5) and (3.6), it is obtained that $q_{y_i}^{(l)}(y_i^{(l)}(k)) = (1+\Delta_{y_i}^{(l)})y_i^{(l)}(k)$ with $|\Delta_{y_i}^{(l)}| < \ell_{y_i,l}$ and $q_{\hat{x}_i}^{(l)}(\hat{x}_i^{(l)}(k)) = (1+\Delta_{\hat{x}_i}^{(l)})\hat{x}_i^{(l)}(k)$ with $|\Delta_{\hat{x}_i}^{(l)}| < \ell_{\hat{x}_i,l}$.

Denoting $e_i(k) \triangleq x(k) - \hat{x}_i(k)$, with the effects of quantizers (3.5) and (3.6), event-triggered mechanism (3.8) and deception attacks in equations (3.10) and (3.11), the filtering error system is obtained as

$$
\begin{aligned}
e_i(k+1) =&(A(k) - K_i(k)C_i(k))e_i(k) + \sum_{j=1}^{N} \tilde{h}_{ij}(1+\Delta_{\hat{x}_j})e_j(k) \\
&- K_i(k)(\Delta_{y_i} - \gamma_i(k)(1+\Delta_{y_i}))C_i(k)x_i(k) \\
&- \sum_{j=1}^{N} \tilde{h}_{ij}(1+\Delta_{\hat{x}_j})x_j(k) + B(k)\omega(k) \\
&- K_i(k)(1-\gamma_i(k))(1+\Delta_{y_i})D_i(k)v_i(k) - K_i(k)\gamma_i(k)\xi_i(k) \\
&+ \sum_{j=1}^{N} \tilde{h}_{ij}\psi_j(k) - \sum_{j=1,j\neq i}^{N} h_{ij}\beta_j(k_j^r)\rho_j(k_j^r) \\
\tilde{z}_i(k) =& M(k)e_i(k),
\end{aligned}
\tag{3.14}
$$

where

$$
\Delta_{y_i} = \text{diag}_{n_{y_i}}\{\Delta_{y_i}^{(l)}\}, \Delta_{\hat{x}_i} = \text{diag}_{n_{\hat{x}_i}}\{\Delta_{\hat{x}_i}^{(l)}\},
$$

$$
\tilde{h}_{ij} = \begin{cases} h_{ij}(1-\beta_j(k)), i \neq j \\ h_{ij}, i = j \end{cases}.
$$

To give a compact form, some notations are presented first.

$$
\begin{aligned}
e(k) &= \text{vec}_N^T\{e_i^T(k)\}, \hat{x}(k) = \text{vec}_N^T\{\hat{x}_i^T(k))\}, \\
\xi(k) &= \text{vec}_N^T\{\xi_i^T(k)\}, \psi(k) = \text{vec}_N^T\{\psi_i^T(k)\}, \\
\rho(k) &= \text{vec}_N^T\{\rho_i^T(k_i^r)\}, v(k) = \text{vec}_N^T\{v_i^T(k)\}, \\
\mathcal{K}(k) &= \text{diag}_N\{K_i(k)\}, \mathcal{B}(k) = \mathbf{1} \otimes B(k), \\
C(k) &= \text{diag}_N\{C_i(k)\}, \mathcal{D}(k) = \text{diag}_N\{D_i(k)\}, \\
z(k) &= \text{vec}_N^T\{z_i^T(k)\}, \bar{M}(k) = I_N \otimes M(k), \\
\gamma(k) &= \text{diag}_N\{\gamma_i(k)I_{n_{y_i}}\}, \\
\bar{\gamma} &= \text{diag}_N\{\bar{\gamma}_i I_{n_{y_i}}\}, \bar{\beta} = \text{diag}_N\{\bar{\beta}_i I_{n_x}\}, \\
\mathcal{N}_i &= \text{diag}\{\underbrace{0,\cdots,0}_{i-1}, I_{n_{y_i}}, \underbrace{0,\cdots,0}_{N-i}\},
\end{aligned}
$$

$$\mathcal{M}_i = \mathrm{diag}\{\underbrace{0,\cdots,0}_{i-1}, I_{n_x}, \underbrace{0,\cdots,0}_{N-i}\},$$
$$\Delta_y = \mathrm{diag}_N\{\Delta_{y_i}\}, \Delta_{\hat{x}} = \mathrm{diag}_N\{\Delta_{\hat{x}_i}\},$$
$$\bar{n} = Nn_x, \bar{m} = \sum_{i=1}^{N} n_{y_i}, \bar{n}_v = \sum_{i=1}^{N} n_{v_i},$$
$$\bar{\tilde{H}}^\dagger = \bar{\tilde{H}} \otimes I_{n_x}, \check{\tilde{H}}^\dagger = \check{\tilde{H}} \otimes I_{n_x},$$
$$H^\dagger = H \otimes I_{n_x}, \tilde{H}^\dagger_{\Delta_{\hat{x}}} = \tilde{H}_{\Delta_{\hat{x}}} \otimes I_{n_x},$$
$$\tilde{H}_1^\dagger = \tilde{H}_1 \otimes I_{n_x}, \tilde{H}^\dagger = \tilde{H} \otimes I_{n_x},$$

where matrices $\bar{\tilde{H}}$, H and $\check{\tilde{H}}^\dagger$ are given as

$$\begin{aligned}
\bar{\tilde{H}} &= \begin{bmatrix} h_{11} & h_{12}(1-\bar{\beta}_2) & \cdots & h_{1N}(1-\bar{\beta}_N) \\ h_{21}(1-\bar{\beta}_1) & h_{22} & \cdots & h_{2N}(1-\bar{\beta}_N) \\ \vdots & \vdots & \ddots & \vdots \\ h_{N1}(1-\bar{\beta}_1) & h_{N2}(1-\bar{\beta}_2) & \cdots & h_{NN} \end{bmatrix}, \\
H &= \begin{bmatrix} 0 & h_{12}\bar{\beta}_2 & \cdots & h_{1N}\bar{\beta}_N \\ h_{21}\bar{\beta}_1 & 0 & \cdots & h_{2N}\bar{\beta}_N \\ \vdots & \vdots & \ddots & \vdots \\ h_{N1}\bar{\beta}_1 & h_{N2}\bar{\beta}_2 & \cdots & 0 \end{bmatrix}, \\
\check{\tilde{H}} &= \begin{bmatrix} 0 & h_{12}(\bar{\beta}_2-\beta_2(k_2^r)) & \cdots & h_{1N}(\bar{\beta}_N-\beta_N(k_N^r)) \\ h_{21}(\bar{\beta}_1-\beta_1(k_1^r)) & 0 & \cdots & h_{2N}(\bar{\beta}_N-\beta_N(k_N^r)) \\ \vdots & \vdots & \ddots & \vdots \\ h_{N1}(\bar{\beta}_1-\beta_1(k_1^r)) & h_{N2}(\bar{\beta}_2-\beta_2(k_2^r)) & \cdots & 0 \end{bmatrix}, \\
\tilde{H} &= \begin{bmatrix} h_{11} & h_{12}(1-\beta_2(k)) & \cdots & h_{1N}(1-\beta_N(k)) \\ h_{21}(1-\beta_1(k)) & h_{22} & \cdots & h_{2N}(1-\beta_N(k)) \\ \vdots & \vdots & \ddots & \vdots \\ h_{N1}(1-\beta_1(k)) & h_{N2}(1-\beta_2(k)) & \cdots & h_{NN} \end{bmatrix}, \\
\tilde{H}_{\Delta_{\hat{x}}} &= \tilde{H} * \begin{bmatrix} 1+\Delta_{\hat{x}_1} \\ 1+\Delta_{\hat{x}_2} \\ \vdots \\ 1+\Delta_{\hat{x}_N} \end{bmatrix}, \\
\tilde{H}_1 &= \begin{bmatrix} 0 & h_{12}\beta_2(k) & \cdots & h_{1N}\beta_N(k) \\ h_{21}\beta_1(k) & 0 & \cdots & h_{2N}\beta_N(k) \\ \vdots & \vdots & \ddots & \vdots \\ h_{N1}\beta_1(k) & h_{N2}\beta_2(k) & \cdots & 0 \end{bmatrix}.
\end{aligned} \tag{3.15}$$

Based on (3.14) and notations above, the distributed filtering error system is rewritten in a compact form as follows

$$\begin{aligned} e(k+1) =&(\Psi_{e0}(k)+\tilde{H}^{\dagger}_{\Delta_{\hat{x}}})e(k)+(\Psi_{x0}(k)-\tilde{H}^{\dagger}_{\Delta_{\hat{x}}})x(k)+\mathcal{B}(k)w(k) \\ &+\Psi_{v0}(k)v(k)+\mathcal{K}(k)\gamma(k)\xi(k)+\tilde{H}^{\dagger}\psi(k)-\tilde{H}^{\dagger}_{1}\rho(k), \\ \tilde{z}(k) =&\bar{M}(k)e(k) \end{aligned} \tag{3.16}$$

with

$$\begin{aligned} \Psi_{e0}(k) =&I_N\otimes A(k)-\mathcal{K}(k)C(k), \\ \Psi_{x0}(k) =&-\mathcal{K}(k)(\Delta_y-\bar{\gamma}(I_{\bar{m}}+\Delta_y))C(k), \\ \Psi_{v0}(k) =&-\mathcal{K}(k)(I_{\bar{m}}-\bar{\gamma})(I_{\bar{m}}+\Delta_y)\mathcal{D}(k). \end{aligned} \tag{3.17}$$

Additionally, with denoting

$$\eta(k)=[x^T(k)\ e^T(k)]^T,$$

the augmented system is obtained in the following

$$\begin{aligned} \eta(k+1) =&(\bar{\mathscr{A}}(k)+\tilde{\mathscr{A}}(k))\eta(k)+\mathscr{B}(k)\omega(k) \\ &+(\bar{\mathscr{C}}(k)+\tilde{\mathscr{C}}(k))v(k)+(\bar{\mathscr{D}}(k)+\tilde{\mathscr{D}}(k))\xi(k) \\ &+(\bar{\mathscr{E}}(k)+\tilde{\mathscr{E}}(k)))\psi(k)+(\bar{\mathscr{F}}(k)+\tilde{\mathscr{F}}(k))\rho(k) \end{aligned} \tag{3.18}$$

where

$$\begin{aligned} \bar{\mathscr{A}}(k) =& \begin{bmatrix} I_N\otimes A(k) & 0 \\ \Psi_{x1}(k) & \Psi_{e1}(k) \end{bmatrix}, \\ \tilde{\mathscr{A}}(k) =& \begin{bmatrix} 0 & 0 \\ \tilde{\mathscr{A}}_{21}(k) & \check{H}^{\dagger}(I_{\bar{n}}+\Delta_{\hat{x}}) \end{bmatrix}, \\ \mathscr{B}(k) =& \begin{bmatrix} \mathcal{B}(k) \\ \mathcal{B}(k) \end{bmatrix}, \bar{\mathscr{C}}(k)=\begin{bmatrix} 0 \\ \Psi_{v1}(k) \end{bmatrix}, \\ \tilde{\mathscr{C}}(k) =& \begin{bmatrix} 0 \\ -\sum_{j=1}^{N}(\bar{\gamma}_j-\gamma_j(k))\mathcal{K}(k)(I_{\bar{m}}+\Delta_y)N_j\mathcal{D} \end{bmatrix}, \\ \bar{\mathscr{D}}(k) =& \begin{bmatrix} 0 \\ -\mathcal{K}(k)\bar{\gamma} \end{bmatrix}, \end{aligned}$$

$$
\begin{aligned}
\tilde{\mathscr{D}}(k) &= \begin{bmatrix} 0 \\ \sum_{j=1}^{N}(\bar{\gamma}_j - \gamma_j(k))\mathcal{K}(k)\mathcal{N}_j \end{bmatrix}, \\
\bar{\mathscr{E}}(k) &= \begin{bmatrix} 0 \\ \bar{\bar{H}}^{\dagger} \end{bmatrix}, \tilde{\mathscr{E}}(k) = \begin{bmatrix} 0 \\ \check{\bar{H}}^{\dagger} \end{bmatrix}, \\
\bar{\mathscr{F}}(k) &= \begin{bmatrix} 0 \\ -H^{\dagger} \end{bmatrix}, \tilde{\mathscr{F}}(k) = \begin{bmatrix} 0 \\ \check{H}^{\dagger} \end{bmatrix}, \\
\tilde{\mathscr{A}}_{21}(k) &= -\sum_{j=1}^{N}(\bar{\gamma}_j - \gamma_j(k))\mathcal{K}(k)(I_{\bar{m}} + \Delta_y)\mathcal{N}_j C - \check{\bar{H}}^{\dagger}(I_{\bar{n}} + \Delta_{\hat{x}}), \\
\Psi_{e1}(k) &= I_N \otimes A(k) - \mathcal{K}(k)C(k) + \bar{\bar{H}}^{\dagger}(I_{\bar{n}} + \Delta_{\hat{x}}), \\
\Psi_{x1}(k) &= -\mathcal{K}(k)(\Delta_y - \bar{\gamma}(I_{\bar{m}} + \Delta_y))C(k) - \bar{\bar{H}}^{\dagger}(I_{\bar{n}} + \Delta_{\hat{x}}), \\
\Psi_{v1}(k) &= -\mathcal{K}(k)(I_{\bar{m}} - \bar{\gamma})(I_{\bar{m}} + \Delta_y)\mathcal{D}(k).
\end{aligned}
$$

The desired target of this chapter is to obtain the filter gains; thus the filtering error system makes the following H_∞ performance hold for given disturbance attenuation performance γ_0 and matrix $W > 0$ over a finite time horizon $[0,\mathrm{T}]$ [133], i.e.,

$$
\begin{aligned}
\frac{1}{N}\sum_{k=0}^{\mathrm{T}}\mathbb{E}\{\|z(k)\|^2\} \leq & \gamma_0^2 \sum_{k=0}^{\mathrm{T}}\mathbb{E}\Big\{\|\omega(k)\|^2 + \frac{1}{N}(\|v(k)\|^2 \\
& + \|\xi(k)\|^2 + \|\rho(k)\|^2)\Big\} + \gamma_0^2\mathbb{E}\{\eta^T(0)W\eta(0)\}.
\end{aligned} \tag{3.19}
$$

Remark 2 *For the time-varying distributed filtering system* (3.1), *we are usually interested in the transient consensus dynamics over a specified time interval. Estimation performance* (3.19) *is proposed to reflect the time-varying manner and characterize the transient estimation performance of the addressed distributed filtering system, which is introduced to evaluate the noise and deception attack attenuation level over the specified horizon* $[0,\mathrm{T}]$. *Thus, the finite time horizon event-triggered filtering scheme is considered in this chapter, which contributes to improving the filtering performance.*

Before ending this part, a useful lemma is introduced to facilitate the further derivation.

Lemma 3.1 *[129] Given real matrices with appropriate dimensions denoted by* Ω_1, Ω_2, *and* Γ, *where* Γ *satisfies inequality* $\Gamma^T\Gamma \leq I$, *for any scalar* $\epsilon > 0$, *it is obtained that* $\Omega_1\Gamma\Omega_2 + (\Omega_1\Gamma\Omega_2)^T \leq \epsilon^{-1}\Omega_1\Omega_1^T + \epsilon\Omega_2\Omega_2^T$.

Lemma 3.2 *[140] Assume* X *and* Y *are the real matrices with compatible dimensions and* $G(k) = diag\{g_1(k), g_2(k), \cdots, g_L(k)\}$ *with* $|g_l(k)| < \delta$ *for* $l = 1, 2, \cdots, L$. *Then, for any real diagonal matrices* $\varpi = diag\{\varpi_1, \varpi_2, \cdots, \varpi_L\} > 0$, *one has the following inequality*

$$
XG(k)Y + Y^TG^T(k)X^T \leq X\varpi X^T + \delta^2 Y^T\varpi^{-1}Y. \tag{3.20}
$$

3.4 MAIN RESULTS

Following design purpose (3.19), the system performance is analyzed in this section and then the distributed filter satisfying H_∞ performance is achieved by getting the solution of a sequence of recursive inequalities.

3.4.1 SECURE PERFORMANCE ANALYSIS

Without taking the effect of quantization into account, in the following theorem sufficient conditions are given to guarantee the augmented system (3.18) satisfying a predetermined H_∞ performance.

Theorem 3.1 *Without considering the effect of quantization, given filtering gains $K_i, i \in \mathcal{N}$, if a positive definite matrix sequence $P(k)$, scalar $\vartheta(k)$, $k \in [0,\mathrm{T}]$ exist which make the following inequalities hold, then the finite time horizon H_∞ performance (3.19) is satisfied.*

$$\begin{aligned}\Pi_0(k) =&\Theta_0(k)+\Theta_1^T(k)P(k+1)\Theta_1(k)\\&+\sum_{j=1}^{N}\Big(\Theta_{2,j}^T(k)P(k+1)\Theta_{2,j}(k)+\Theta_{3,j}^T(k)P(k+1)\Theta_{3,j}(k)\\&+\Theta_{4,j}^T(k)P(k+1)\Theta_{4,j}(k)\Big)<0, k\in[1,\mathrm{T}],\\P(0) <&W,\end{aligned} \tag{3.21}$$

where

$$\begin{aligned}\Theta_0(k) =&diag\{-P(k)+\frac{1}{N}M_1^T(k)M_1(k)+\vartheta(k)\mathcal{I}_1^T\theta(k)\mathcal{I}_1,\\&-\gamma_0^2 I_{n_w},-\frac{1}{N}\gamma_0^2 I_{\bar{n}_v},-\frac{1}{N}\gamma_0^2 I_{\bar{n}},-\vartheta(k)I_{\bar{n}},-\frac{1}{N}\gamma_0^2 I_{\bar{n}}\},\\\mathcal{I}_1 =&[I_{\bar{n}},-I_{\bar{n}}], M_1(k)=[0,\bar{M}(k)],\theta(k)=diag\{\theta_1(k),\cdots,\theta_N(k)\},\\\Theta_1(k) =&[\bar{\mathscr{A}}_0(k),\bar{\mathscr{B}}(k),\bar{\mathscr{C}}_0(k),\bar{\mathscr{D}}(k),\bar{\mathscr{E}}(k),\bar{\mathscr{F}}(k)],\end{aligned}$$

$$\Theta_{2,j}(k)=\begin{bmatrix}\sqrt{\bar{\gamma}_j-\bar{\gamma}_j^2}(\mathcal{K}(k)N_jC)^T\\-\sqrt{\bar{\beta}_j-\bar{\beta}_j^2}(\check{H}^\dagger M_j)^T\\0\\0\\0\\0\\0\end{bmatrix}^T,$$

$$\Theta_{3,j}(k) = \begin{bmatrix} \sqrt{\bar{\gamma}_j - \bar{\gamma}_j^2}(\mathcal{K}(k)\mathcal{N}_j C)^T \\ 0 \\ 0 \\ \sqrt{\bar{\gamma}_j - \bar{\gamma}_j^2}(\mathcal{K}(k)\mathcal{N}_j \mathcal{D})^T \\ \sqrt{\bar{\gamma}_j - \bar{\gamma}_j^2}(\mathcal{K}(k)\mathcal{N}_j)^T \\ 0 \\ 0 \end{bmatrix}^T,$$

$$\Theta_{4,j}(k) = \begin{bmatrix} \sqrt{\bar{\beta}_j - \bar{\beta}_j^2}(\check{H}^\dagger \mathcal{M}_j)^T \\ -\sqrt{\bar{\beta}_j - \bar{\beta}_j^2}(\check{H}^\dagger \mathcal{M}_j)^T \\ 0 \\ 0 \\ 0 \\ \sqrt{\bar{\beta}_j - \bar{\beta}_j^2}(\check{H}^\dagger \mathcal{M}_j)^T \\ \sqrt{\bar{\beta}_j - \bar{\beta}_j^2}(\check{H}^\dagger \mathcal{M}_j)^T \end{bmatrix}^T,$$

The elements in notation $\Theta_1(k)$ are given as

$$\bar{\mathscr{A}}_0(k) = \begin{bmatrix} I_N \otimes A(k) & 0 \\ \Psi_{x10}(k) & \Psi_{e10}(k) \end{bmatrix},$$

$$\bar{\mathscr{C}}_0(k) = \begin{bmatrix} 0 \\ \Psi_{v10}(k) \end{bmatrix},$$

$$\tilde{\mathscr{A}}_0(k) = \begin{bmatrix} 0 & 0 \\ \tilde{\mathscr{A}}_{210}(k) & \check{H}^\dagger \end{bmatrix},$$

$$\tilde{\mathscr{C}}_0(k) = \begin{bmatrix} 0 \\ -\sum_{j=1}^N (\bar{\gamma}_j - \gamma_j(k))\mathcal{K}(k)\mathcal{N}_j \mathcal{D} \end{bmatrix},$$

where

$$\begin{aligned}
\Psi_{e10}(k) =& I_N \otimes A(k) - \mathcal{K}(k)C(k) + \bar{\tilde{H}}^\dagger, \\
\Psi_{x10}(k) =& -\mathcal{K}(k)\bar{\gamma}C(k) - \bar{\tilde{H}}^\dagger, \\
\Psi_{v10}(k) =& -\mathcal{K}(k)(I_{\bar{m}} - \bar{\gamma})\mathcal{D}(k), \\
\tilde{\mathscr{A}}_{210}(k) =& -\sum_{j=1}^N (\bar{\gamma}_j - \gamma_j(k))\mathcal{K}(k)\mathcal{N}_j C - \check{H}^\dagger.
\end{aligned}$$

Proof *For system* (3.18), *the following Lyapunov function candidate is chosen*

$$V(k) = \eta^T(k)P(k)\eta(k). \tag{3.22}$$

Without considering the effect of quantization, that is, $\Delta_y = 0$ *and* $\Delta_{\hat{x}} = 0$*, the difference for two consecutive steps of Lyapunov function* (3.22) *is computed as*

$$\begin{aligned}
&\mathbb{E}\{\Delta V(k)\} = \mathbb{E}\{V(k+1) - V(k)\} \\
&= \mathbb{E}\{\eta^T(k+1)P(k+1)\eta(k+1) - \eta^T(k)P(k)\eta(k)\} \\
&= \psi^T(k)\Theta_0^T(k)P(k+1)\Theta_0(k)\psi(k) + \eta^T(k)\begin{bmatrix} \Upsilon_1(\mathcal{N}_jC(k)) & * \\ -\Upsilon_3(\bar{\tilde{H}}^\dagger \mathcal{M}_j) & \Upsilon_3(\bar{\tilde{H}}^\dagger \mathcal{M}_j) \end{bmatrix}\eta(k) \\
&+ \nu^T(k)\Upsilon_1(\mathcal{N}_j\mathcal{D}(k))\nu(k) + \xi^T(k)\Upsilon_1(\mathcal{N}_j)\xi(k) \\
&+ \varphi^T(k)\Upsilon_3(\bar{\tilde{H}}^\dagger \mathcal{M}_j)\varphi(k) + \rho^T(k)\Upsilon_3(\bar{\tilde{H}}^\dagger \mathcal{M}_j)\rho(k) \\
&+ 2\eta^T(k)\begin{bmatrix} \Upsilon_2(\mathcal{N}_jC(k), \mathcal{N}_j\mathcal{D}(k)) \\ 0 \end{bmatrix}\xi(k) + 2\eta^T(k)\begin{bmatrix} -\Upsilon_3(\bar{\tilde{H}}^\dagger \mathcal{M}_j) \\ \Upsilon_3(\bar{\tilde{H}}^\dagger \mathcal{M}_j) \end{bmatrix}\varphi(k) \qquad (3.23) \\
&+ 2\eta^T(k)\begin{bmatrix} -\Upsilon_3(\bar{\tilde{H}}^\dagger \mathcal{M}_j) \\ \Upsilon_3(\bar{\tilde{H}}^\dagger \mathcal{M}_j) \end{bmatrix}\rho(k) - 2\nu^T(k)\Upsilon_2(\mathcal{N}_j\mathcal{D}(k), \mathcal{N}_j)\xi(k) \\
&+ 2\varphi^T(k)\Upsilon_3(\bar{\tilde{H}}^\dagger \mathcal{M}_j)\rho(k) + \vartheta(k)(\hat{x}^T(k)\theta(k)\hat{x}(k) - \varphi^T(k)\varphi(k)) \\
&+ \frac{1}{N}\{\|z(k)\|^2\} - \gamma_0^2\{\|\omega(k)\|^2 + \frac{1}{N}(\|\nu(k)\|^2 + \|\xi(k)\|^2 + \|\rho(k)\|^2)\} \\
&- \frac{1}{N}\{\|z(k)\|^2\} + \gamma_0^2\{\|\omega(k)\|^2 + \frac{1}{N}(\|\nu(k)\|^2 + \|\xi(k)\|^2 + \|\rho(k)\|^2)\}
\end{aligned}$$

where

$$\begin{aligned}
\psi(k) &= \left[\eta^T(k)\ w^T(k)\ \nu^T(k)\ \xi^T(k)\ \varphi^T(k)\ \rho^T(k)\right]^T, \\
\Upsilon_1(X_1) &= \sum_{j=1}^{N}\sqrt{\hat{\gamma}_j}X_1^T\mathcal{K}^T(k)\mathcal{I}_0^TP(k+1)\mathcal{I}_0\mathcal{K}(k)X_1, \\
\Upsilon_2(X_1, X_2) &= \sum_{j=1}^{N}\sqrt{\hat{\gamma}_j}X_1^T\mathcal{K}^T(k)\mathcal{I}_0^TP(k+1)\mathcal{I}_0\mathcal{K}(k)X_2, \\
\Upsilon_3(X_1) &= \sum_{j=1}^{N}\sqrt{\hat{\beta}_j}X_1^T\mathcal{I}_0^TP(k+1)\mathcal{I}_0X_1, \\
\mathcal{I}_0 &= [0, I_{\bar{n}}]^T, \hat{\gamma}_j = \bar{\gamma}_j - \bar{\gamma}_j^2, \hat{\beta}_j = \bar{\beta}_j - \bar{\beta}_j^2.
\end{aligned}$$

Arranging formula (3.23) *in a compact form, one has*

$$\begin{aligned}
\mathbb{E}\{\Delta V(k)\} =& \psi^T(k)\Pi_0(k)\psi(k) - \frac{1}{N}\{\|z(k)\|^2\} + \gamma_0^2\{\|\omega(k)\|^2 \\
&+ \frac{1}{N}(\|\nu(k)\|^2 + \|\xi(k)\|^2 + \|\rho(k)\|^2)\},
\end{aligned}$$

where $\Pi_0(k)$ *is the matrix given in* (3.21).

With inequality (3.21), *it is concluded that*

$$\begin{aligned}&\mathbb{E}\{\Delta V(k)\}+\frac{1}{N}\{\|z(k)\|^2\}-\gamma_0^2\{\|\omega(k)\|^2\\&+\frac{1}{N}(\|v(k)\|^2+\|\xi(k)\|^2+\|\rho(k)\|^2)\}<0.\end{aligned}\tag{3.24}$$

Calculating the accumulation for inequality (3.24) *from* 0 *to* T *with respect to* k, *it is obtained that*

$$\begin{aligned}\frac{1}{N}\sum_{k=0}^{\mathrm{T}}\mathbb{E}\{\|z(k)\|^2\}\leq&\gamma_0^2\sum_{k=0}^{\mathrm{T}}\mathbb{E}\{\|\omega(k)\|^2+\frac{1}{N}(\|v(k)\|^2\\&+\|\xi(k)\|^2+\|\rho(k)\|^2)\}+\mathbb{E}\{\eta^T(0)P(0)\eta(0)\}.\end{aligned}\tag{3.25}$$

With choosing initial value $P(0)<W$, *the* H_∞ *performance* (3.19) *holds. This completes the proof.*

3.4.2 FILTER DESIGN

On account of the analysis for H_∞ estimation performance and the sufficient conditions presented in Theorem 3.1, it is time to present a method for designing an estimator of the distributed dynamic (3.18).

Theorem 3.2 *Letting the disturbance attenuation level* $\gamma_0>0$, *initial matrix* $W>0$ *be predetermined, the filtering error dynamic* (3.18) *satisfies the* H_∞ *secure performance* (3.19), *if there are positive matrices* $P(k)=diag\{P_1(k),P_1(k)\},k\in[0,\mathrm{T}]$, *a series of matrices* $K_i(k),i\in\mathbf{N},k\in[0,\mathrm{T}]$, *positive scalars* $\varepsilon_j(k),j\in\{1,\cdots,6\},k\in[0,\mathrm{T}]$ *where recursive linear matrix inequalities in the following*

$$\Pi_2(k)=\begin{bmatrix}\Pi_2^{(1,1)}(k)&*&*&*\\\Pi_2^{(2,1)}(k)&\Pi_2^{(2,2)}(k)&*&*\\\Pi_2^{(3,1)}(k)&\Pi_2^{(3,2)}(k)&\Pi_2^{(3,3)}(k)&*\\\Pi_2^{(4,1)}(k)&\Pi_2^{(4,2)}(k)&\Pi_2^{(4,3)}(k)&\Pi_2^{(4,4)}(k)\end{bmatrix}<0,\ k\in[0,\mathrm{T}],\qquad P(0)<W\tag{3.26}$$

hold, where

$$\begin{aligned}P^\dagger(k+1)=&P_1^{-1}(k+1),\\\Pi_2^{(1,1)}(k)=&\Pi_1(k),\end{aligned}$$

$$\Pi_2^{(2,1)}(k)=\begin{bmatrix}S_1^T(k)\\vec_N^T\{S_{2,j}^T(k)\}\\vec_N^T\{S_{3,j}^T\}\\vec_N^T\{S_{4,j}^T\}\\vec_N^T\{S_{5,j}^T(k)\}\\S_6^T\end{bmatrix},$$

$$
\begin{aligned}
\Pi_2^{(2,2)}(k) =& diag\{-\varepsilon_1(k)I_{\bar{m}}, -3\varepsilon_2(k)I_{\bar{m}}, -3\varepsilon_3(k)I_{\bar{n}}, \\
& -3\varepsilon_4(k)I_{\bar{n}}, -3\varepsilon_5(k)I_{\bar{m}}, \varepsilon_6(k)I_{\bar{n}}\}, \\
\Pi_2^{(3,1)}(k) =& \begin{bmatrix} \varepsilon_1(k)\mathcal{T}_1(k) \\ vec_N\{\varepsilon_2(k)\mathcal{T}_{2,j}(k)\} \\ vec_N\{\varepsilon_3(k)\mathcal{T}_{3,j}\} \\ vec_N\{\varepsilon_4(k)\mathcal{T}_{4,j}\} \\ vec_N\{\varepsilon_5(k)\mathcal{T}_{5,j}(k)\} \\ \varepsilon_6(k)\mathcal{T}_6 \end{bmatrix}, \\
\Pi_2^{(3,3)}(k) =& diag\{-\varepsilon_1(k)I_{\bar{m}}, -3\varepsilon_2(k)I_{\bar{m}}, -3\varepsilon_3(k)I_{\bar{n}}, \\
& -3\varepsilon_4(k)I_{\bar{n}}, -3\varepsilon_5(k)I_{\bar{m}}, \varepsilon_6(k)I_{\bar{n}}\}, \\
\Pi_2^{(4,1)}(k) =& [\varpi\check{\tilde{\Gamma}}_1(k) \ \bar{F}\check{\tilde{\Gamma}}_2^T(k)]^T, \\
\Pi_2^{(4,4)}(k) =& diag\{-\varpi I \ -\varpi I\}, \\
\Pi_2^{(3,2)}(k) =& 0, \Pi_2^{(4,2)}(k) = 0, \Pi_2^{(4,3)}(k) = 0
\end{aligned}
$$

with

$$
\begin{aligned}
\Pi_1(k) &= \begin{bmatrix} \Pi_1^{(1,1)}(k) & * \\ \Pi_1^{(2,1)}(k) & \Pi_1^{(2,2)}(k) \end{bmatrix}, \\
\check{\tilde{\Gamma}}_1(k) &= \begin{bmatrix} 0 & \tilde{\Gamma}_1(k) & 0 & 0 & 0 \end{bmatrix}^T, \\
\check{\tilde{\Gamma}}_2(k) &= \begin{bmatrix} \tilde{\Gamma}_2(k) & 0 & 0 & 0 & 0 \end{bmatrix}, \\
\tilde{\Gamma}_1(k) &= \begin{bmatrix} I_N \otimes \Gamma_1(k) & 0 \\ 0 & I_N \otimes \Gamma_1(k) \end{bmatrix}^T, \\
\tilde{\Gamma}_2(k) &= \begin{bmatrix} I_N \otimes \Gamma_2(k) & 0 & 0 & 0 & 0 & 0 & 0 \\ 0 & I_N \otimes \Gamma_2(k) & 0 & 0 & 0 & 0 & 0 \end{bmatrix}.
\end{aligned}
\tag{3.27}
$$

In equation (3.27)*, the elements are*

$$
\Pi_1^{(1,1)}(k) = \Theta_0(k), \Pi_1^{(2,1)}(k) = \begin{bmatrix} \bar{\Theta}_1(k) \\ vec_N\{\Theta_{2,j}(k)\} \\ vec_N\{\Theta_{3,j}(k)\} \\ vec_N\{\Theta_{4,j}(k)\} \end{bmatrix},
$$

$$
\begin{aligned}
\Pi_1^{(2,2)}(k) = diag\Bigg\{ & P^\dagger(k+1), P^\dagger(k+1), \underbrace{\cdots P^\dagger(k+1)\cdots}_{N}, \\
& \underbrace{\cdots P^\dagger(k+1)\cdots}_{N}, \underbrace{\cdots P^\dagger(k+1)\cdots}_{N} \Bigg\}
\end{aligned}
$$

with

$$\begin{aligned}\bar{\Theta}_1(k) =&[\check{\bar{\mathscr{A}}}_0(k)\ \bar{\mathscr{B}}(k)\ \bar{\mathscr{C}}_0(k)\ \bar{\mathscr{D}}(k)\ \bar{\mathscr{E}}(k)\ \bar{\mathscr{F}}(k)],\\ \check{\bar{\mathscr{A}}}_0(k) =&\begin{bmatrix} I_N\otimes\bar{A}(k) & 0\\ \Psi_{x10}(k) & \bar{\Psi}_{e10}(k)\end{bmatrix},\\ \bar{\Psi}_{e10}(k) =&I_N\otimes\bar{A}(k)-\mathcal{K}(k)C(k)+\bar{\bar{H}}^{\dagger}.\end{aligned}$$

In the above matrices, the elements in $\Pi_2^{(2,1)}(k)$ *and* $\Pi_2^{(3,1)}(k)$ *are given by*

$$\begin{aligned}&\mathcal{S}_1(k)=[\,0\,0\,-(\mathcal{K}(k)(I_{\bar{m}}-\bar{\gamma}))^T\,0\,0\,0]^T,\mathcal{T}_1(k)=[\tilde{\mathcal{T}}_1(k)\,0\,0\,0\,0\,0],\\ &\mathcal{S}_{2,j}(k)=[0\,0\,0\,\tilde{S}_{2,j}^T(k)\,0\,0]^T,\mathcal{T}_{2,j}(k)=[\tilde{\mathcal{T}}_{2,j}(k)\,0\,0\,0\,0\,0],\\ &\mathcal{S}_{3,j}=[0\,0\,0\,\tilde{S}_{3,j}^T\,0\,\tilde{S}_{3,j}^T]^T,\mathcal{T}_{3,j}=[\tilde{\mathcal{T}}_{3,j}\,0\,0\,0\,0\,0],\\ &\mathcal{S}_{4,j}=[0\,0\,0\,0\,0\,\tilde{S}_{4,j}^T]^T,\mathcal{T}_{4,j}=[\tilde{\mathcal{T}}_{4,j}\,0\,0\,0\,0\,0],\\ &\mathcal{S}_{5,j}(k)=[0\,0\,0\,0\,\tilde{S}_{5,j}^T(k)\,0]^T,\mathcal{T}_{5,j}(k)=[\tilde{\mathcal{T}}_{5,j}(k)\,0\,0\,0\,0\,0],\\ &\mathcal{S}_6=[0\,0\,\bar{\bar{H}}^{\dagger T}\,0\,0\,0]^T,\mathcal{T}_6=[\tilde{\mathcal{T}}_6\,0\,0\,0\,0\,0],\end{aligned}$$

where

$$\begin{aligned}&\tilde{\mathcal{T}}_1(k)=[\ell_yC(k)\,0\,0\,\ell_y\mathcal{D}(k)\,0\,0\,0], && \tilde{\mathcal{T}}_{2,j}(k)=[\ell_y\mathcal{N}_jC(k)\,0\,0\,0\,0\,0\,0],\\ &\tilde{\mathcal{T}}_{3,j}=[0\,\ell_{\hat{x}}\mathcal{M}_j\,0\,0\,0\,0\,0], && \tilde{\mathcal{T}}_{4,j}=[\ell_{\hat{x}}\mathcal{M}_j\,0\,0\,0\,0\,0\,0],\\ &\tilde{\mathcal{T}}_{5,j}(k)=[0\,0\,0\,\ell_y\mathcal{N}_j\mathcal{D}(k)\,0\,0\,0], && \tilde{\mathcal{T}}_6=[-\ell_{\hat{x}}I_{\bar{n}}\ \ell_{\hat{x}}I_{\bar{n}}\,0\,0\,0\,0\,0],\\ &\tilde{S}_{2,j}(k)=\begin{bmatrix}0\\ \sqrt{\bar{\gamma}_j-\bar{\gamma}_j^2}\mathcal{K}(k)\\ 0\end{bmatrix}, && \tilde{S}_{3,j}=\begin{bmatrix}0\\ -\sqrt{\bar{\beta}_j-\bar{\beta}_j^2}\check{H}^{\dagger}\\ 0\end{bmatrix},\\ &\tilde{S}_{4,j}=-\tilde{S}_{3,j}, && \tilde{S}_{5,j}(k)=\tilde{S}_{2,j}(k).\end{aligned}$$

Proof *Taking the effect of quantization into consideration, with a similar calculation as* (3.23), *the difference of the Lyapunov function is*

$$\begin{aligned}\mathbb{E}\{\Delta V(k)\} =&\mathbb{E}\{V(k+1)-V(k)\}\\ =&\psi^T(k)\tilde{\Pi}_0(k)\psi(k)-\frac{1}{N}\{\|z(k)\|^2\}\\ &+\gamma_0^2\{\|\omega(k)\|^2+\frac{1}{N}(\|v(k)\|^2+\|\xi(k)\|^2+\|\rho(k)\|^2)\},\end{aligned}\tag{3.28}$$

where

$$\begin{aligned}\tilde{\Pi}_0(k) =&\tilde{\Theta}_0(k)+\tilde{\Theta}_1^T(k)P(k+1)\tilde{\Theta}_1(k)+\sum_{j=1}^{N}(\tilde{\Theta}_{2,j}^T(k)P(k+1)\tilde{\Theta}_{2,j}(k)\\ &+\tilde{\Theta}_{3,j}^T(k)P(k+1)\tilde{\Theta}_{3,j}(k)+\tilde{\Theta}_{4,j}^T(k)P(k+1)\tilde{\Theta}_{4,j}(k))\end{aligned}$$

with

$$
\begin{aligned}
\tilde{\Theta}_0(k) =& \Theta_0(k),\\
\tilde{\Theta}_1(k) =& [\bar{\mathscr{A}}(k)\ \bar{\mathscr{B}}(k)\ \bar{\mathscr{C}}(k)\ \bar{\mathscr{D}}(k)\ \bar{\mathscr{E}}(k)\ \bar{\mathscr{F}}(k)],
\end{aligned}
$$

$$
\tilde{\Theta}_2(k) = \begin{bmatrix} \sqrt{\bar{\gamma}_j - \bar{\gamma}_j^2}(\mathcal{K}(k)(I_{\bar{m}}+\Delta_y)\mathcal{N}_j C)^T \\ -\sqrt{\bar{\beta}_j - \bar{\beta}_j^2}(\check{H}^{\dagger}(I_{\bar{n}}+\Delta_{\hat{x}})\mathcal{M}_j)^T \\ 0 \\ 0 \\ 0 \\ 0 \\ 0 \end{bmatrix}^T,
$$

$$
\tilde{\Theta}_3(k) = \begin{bmatrix} \sqrt{\bar{\gamma}_j - \bar{\gamma}_j^2}(\mathcal{K}(k)(I_{\bar{m}}+\Delta_y)\mathcal{N}_j C)^T \\ 0 \\ 0 \\ \sqrt{\bar{\gamma}_j - \bar{\gamma}_j^2}(\mathcal{K}(k)(I_{\bar{m}}+\Delta_y)\mathcal{N}_j \mathcal{D})^T \\ \sqrt{\bar{\gamma}_j - \bar{\gamma}_j^2}(\mathcal{K}(k)\mathcal{N}_j)^T \\ 0 \\ 0 \end{bmatrix}^T,
$$

$$
\tilde{\Theta}_4(k) = \begin{bmatrix} \sqrt{\bar{\beta}_j - \bar{\beta}_j^2}(\check{H}^{\dagger}(I_{\bar{n}}+\Delta_{\hat{x}})\mathcal{M}_j)^T \\ -\sqrt{\bar{\beta}_j - \bar{\beta}_j^2}(\check{H}^{\dagger}(I_{\bar{n}}+\Delta_{\hat{x}})\mathcal{M}_j)^T \\ 0 \\ 0 \\ 0 \\ \sqrt{\bar{\beta}_j - \bar{\beta}_j^2}(\check{H}^{\dagger}\mathcal{M}_j)^T \\ \sqrt{\bar{\beta}_j - \bar{\beta}_j^2}(\check{H}^{\dagger}\mathcal{M}_j)^T \end{bmatrix}^T.
$$

According to Theorem 1, we known that if $\tilde{\Pi}_0(k) < 0$, H_∞ performance (3.19) *sets up. By using Lemmas 3.1 and 3.2, one has that*

$$
\tilde{\Pi}_0(k) \le \tilde{\Pi}_2(k),
$$

where

$$\begin{aligned}\tilde{\Pi}_2(k) =&\Pi_0(k)+\frac{1}{\varepsilon_1(k)}\mathcal{S}_1(k)\mathcal{S}_1^T(k)+\sum_{j=1}^{N}(\frac{1}{\varepsilon_2(k)}\mathcal{S}_{2,j}(k)\mathcal{S}_{2,j}^T(k)\\&+\frac{1}{\varepsilon_3(k)}\mathcal{S}_{3,j}\mathcal{S}_{3,j}^T+\frac{1}{\varepsilon_4(k)}\mathcal{S}_{4,j}\mathcal{S}_{4,j}^T+\frac{1}{\varepsilon_5(k)}\mathcal{S}_{5,j}(k)\mathcal{S}_{5,j}^T(k))\\&+\frac{1}{\varepsilon_6(k)}\mathcal{S}_6\mathcal{S}_6^T+\varepsilon_1(k)\mathcal{T}_1^T(k)\mathcal{T}_1(k)\\&+\sum_{j=1}^{N}(\varepsilon_2(k)\mathcal{T}_{2,j}^T(k)\mathcal{T}_{2,j}(k)+\varepsilon_3(k)\mathcal{T}_{3,j}^T\mathcal{T}_{3,j}+\varepsilon_4(k)\mathcal{T}_{4,j}^T\mathcal{T}_{4,j}\\&+\varepsilon_5(k)\mathcal{T}_{5,j}^T(k)\mathcal{T}_{5,j}(k))+\varepsilon_6(k)\mathcal{T}_6^T\mathcal{T}_6.\end{aligned}$$

With Schur's complement lemma [82], inequality $\Pi_0(k) < 0$ is equivalent to

$$\tilde{\Pi}_1(k)=\begin{bmatrix}\tilde{\Pi}_1^{(1,1)}(k) & *\\ \tilde{\Pi}_1^{(2,1)}(k) & \tilde{\Pi}_1^{(2,1)}(k)\end{bmatrix}<0,$$

where

$$\tilde{\Pi}_1^{(1,1)}(k)=\Pi_1^{(1,1)}(k),\tilde{\Pi}_1^{(2,2)}(k)=\Pi_1^{(2,2)}(k),$$

$$\tilde{\Pi}_1^{(2,2)}(k)=\begin{bmatrix}\Theta_1(k)\\ vec_N\{\Theta_{2,j}(k)\}\\ vec_N\{\Theta_{3,j}(k)\}\\ vec_N\{\Theta_{4,j}(k)\}\end{bmatrix}.$$

Considering the uncertainty and model-reality mismatch in system (3.1), *we have*

$$\begin{aligned}\tilde{\Pi}_1(k)=&\Pi_1(k)+\check{\Gamma}_1(k)diag\{I_N\otimes F(k),I_N\otimes F(k)\}\check{\Gamma}_2(k)\\&+\check{\Gamma}_2^T(k)diag\{I_N\otimes F(k),I_N\otimes F(k)\}\check{\Gamma}_1^T(k)\\ \le&\Pi_1(k)+\check{\Gamma}_1(k)\varpi\check{\Gamma}_1^T(k)+\varsigma^2\check{\Gamma}_2^T(k)\varpi^{-1}\check{\Gamma}_2(k).\end{aligned}\tag{3.29}$$

Combining inequality (3.29) *and $\tilde{\Pi}_2(k)<0$ with applying Schur's complement lemma, it leads to inequality* (3.26). *The proof is completed.*

The distributed H_∞ secure filtering procedure based on Theorem 3.2 is summarized as the following algorithm.

The following optimization problem is presented to obtain the minimized disturbance attenuation performance γ_0.

Corollary 1 *An H_∞ secure estimator* (3.13) *for system* (3.1) *subject to uncertainty* (3.2), *quantization* (3.5), (3.6) *and event-triggered function* (3.7) *is designed by solving the optimization problem*

$$\begin{aligned}&\min_{P(k),K_i(k),\varepsilon_j(k)}\gamma_0\\&s.t.\ Constraint\ (3.26).\end{aligned}\tag{3.30}$$

Algorithm 2 Distributed secure filtering algorithm

1: Give parameters $\gamma_0 > 0$, $W > 0$, $\mathrm{T} > 0$, system matrices $\bar{A}(k)$, $B(k)$, $C_i(k)$, $D_i(k), i \in \mathbf{N}$ and $M(k)$, and topology graph $\mathbf{G}$.
2: Input $P_1(0) < W$, $k = 0$.
3: **While**$\{k \leq \mathrm{T}\}$
4: With given $P_1(k)$ and system parameters, solve inequality (3.26).
5: Output $P_1(k+1) = P^{\dagger^{-1}}(k+1)$, $K_i(k), i \in \mathbf{N}$, $\varepsilon_j(k), j \in \{1, \cdots, 6\}$.
6: Let $k \leftarrow k+1$.
7: **EndWhile**

Remark 3 *Note that the computational complexity of Algorithm 2 relies on solving inequality* (3.26) *in Theorem 2. Denote that the total number of the decision scalars in inequality* (3.26) *is $\hbar$ and the row size of the inequality is ℓ. As a consequence, the computational complexity of the proposed Algorithm 2 is $O(\ell\hbar^3)$. It should be mentioned that parameters $\hbar$ and ℓ are dependent on the system dimension n_x, n_{yi}, n_z and the scale of sensor network N. Thus, with increasing the scale of the sensor network and/or the system dimension, the computational complexity will increase.*

Remark 4 *It is seen from Theorem 2 that the designed problem of the H_∞ secure filter can be solved for the time-varying system* (3.1) *under a deception attack and event-based communication protocol if inequality* (3.26) *holds for all time step $k \in [0, \mathrm{T}]$. It is pointed out that the inequality is dependent on the previous calculation value $P(k)$ and the system parameters. The feasibility of the recursive linear matrix inequality is guaranteed by choosing an appropriate initial value $P(0)$ and is solved with a semidefinition programming approach.*

Remark 5 *For the distributed filtering system* (3.1)*, the factors including uncertainty and model-reality mismatch, two-stage random deception attacks, disturbances, and bandwidth limitation are addressed in the process of filter design which considers a quite comprehensive and practical scene. To save sensor energy consumption and reduce bandwidth burden, a quantization strategy and event-triggered communication protocol are exploited. With taking the uncertainty, model-reality mismatch and disturbance effects into account, the reliability and robustness of the sensor network can be guaranteed in practical application. A finite time horizon H_∞ filter is presented by solving LMIs, which makes the filtering system achieve a satisfactory dynamic and steady filtering performance [200].*

3.5 SIMULATION RESULTS

In this part, two numerical examples are listed to show the validity of the proposed distributed filtering method.

3.5.1 EXAMPLE 1

A sensor network with topology being denoted by a directed graph $\mathbf{G} = \{\mathbf{N}, \mathbf{E}, \mathbf{A}\}$ is considered, in which the set of nodes is $\mathbf{N} = \{1, 2, 3\}$, the set of edges is $\mathbf{E} = \{(1,1), (1,3), (2,1), (2,2), (3,1), (3,3)\}$, and the adjacency matrix is given by $\mathbf{A} =$

$[a_{ij}]_{3\times 3}$ with $a_{ij} = 0.2$ if $(i, j) \in \mathbf{E}$, otherwise $a_{ij} = 0$. The discrete time-varying system in (3.1) considered in this chapter is given over a prescribed finite time horizon $k \in [0, 100]$ in the following form

$$A(k) = \begin{bmatrix} 1.05+0.2\sin(10k) & 0.25 \\ -0.1+\cos(2k) & 0.16 \end{bmatrix},$$

$$B(k) = \begin{bmatrix} 0.13+0.2\sin(10k) \\ 0.15-0.2\cos(2k) \end{bmatrix}.$$

The measurement matrices are given by

$$C_1(k) = \begin{bmatrix} 9+0.3\cos(1-2k) & 0 \\ 0 & 1.8-0.1\cos(3k) \end{bmatrix},$$

$$C_2(k) = \begin{bmatrix} 10+0.23\cos(1-2k) & 0 \\ 0 & 2-0.05\cos(3k) \end{bmatrix},$$

$$C_3(k) = \begin{bmatrix} 8+0.1\cos(1-2k) & 0 \\ 0 & 2.5-0.1\cos(3k) \end{bmatrix},$$

$$D_1(k) = \begin{bmatrix} 0.12 \\ 0.17+0.27\cos(k) \end{bmatrix},$$

$$D_2(k) = \begin{bmatrix} 0.1 \\ 0.12+0.27\cos(k) \end{bmatrix},$$

$$D_3(k) = \begin{bmatrix} 0.1 \\ 0.17+0.27\cos(k) \end{bmatrix}.$$

The disturbances in state equation and measurement equation are selected as $w(k) = 0.1\cos(k)/k$ and $v_i(k) = 0.1\sin(k)/k$, respectively. The attack signals are $\xi_i(k) = \cos(0.5k)$, $\rho_i(k) = \cos(0.5k)$. The following parameters are taken as $\theta_i(k) = 0.1$, $\mu^{(0)}_{y_i,l} = 1$, $\mu^{(0)}_{\hat{x}_i,l} = 1$, $\ell_{y_i,l} = 0.5$, $\ell_{\hat{x}_i,l} = 0.5$, and $\gamma_0 = 0.1$. The probabilities of attacks are $\bar{\gamma}_i = 0.05$ and $\bar{\beta}_i = 0.05$ for all $i \in \mathbf{N}$. Let's implement Algorithm 1 using MATLAB 2014 with YALMIP 3.0. The filter gains calculated based on Theorem 2 are given in Table I.

The filtering results are shown in Figs. 3.2 and 3.3, from which we can see that the states of the plant are tracked well by the distributed filter. To show the effectiveness intuitively, give the definition of mean-square-error (MSE) of the state estimation $\hat{z}_i(k)$ as follows

$$\text{MSE}_i(k) = \frac{1}{L}\sum_{l=1}^{L}\sqrt{\tilde{z}^T_{i,l}(k)\tilde{z}_{i,l}(k)}, \tag{3.31}$$

where $\tilde{z}_{i,l}(k)$ is the estimation error of output signal $z_i(k)$ in the lth simulation and scalar L represents the total number of Monte Carlo simulations. Choosing $L = 100$, from the simulation results in Fig. 3.4, it can be seen that the designed filter is effective under limited bandwidth and deception attacks. And also, the MSEs of $z(k)$ without deception attacks is given in Fig. 3.5. Comparing the curves in Fig. 3.4 and Fig. 3.5, it is seen that deception attacks deteriorate the estimation performance distinctly.

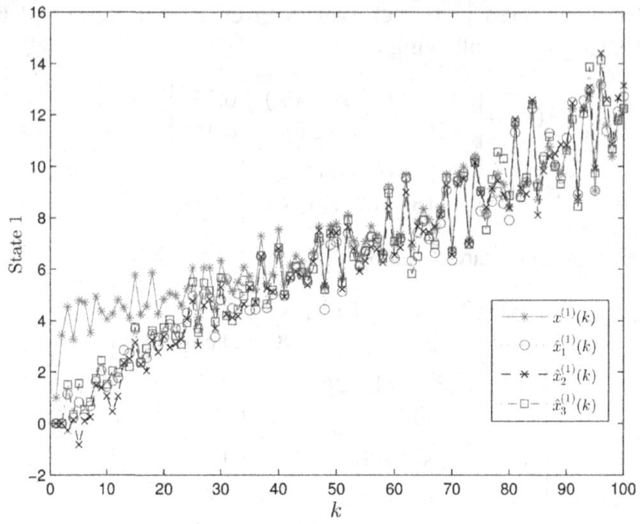

Figure 3.2 State 1 and its estimation.

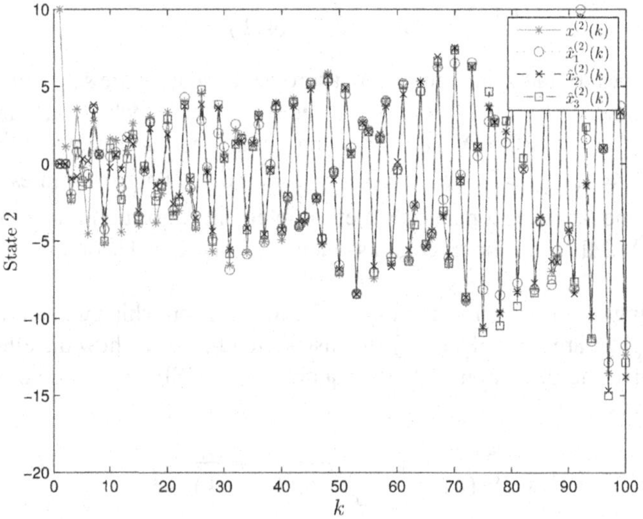

Figure 3.3 State 2 and its estimation.

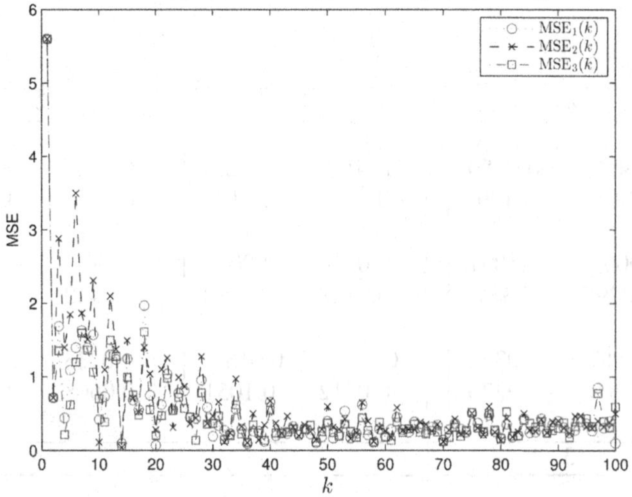

Figure 3.4 MSEs of $z(k)$ with attack.

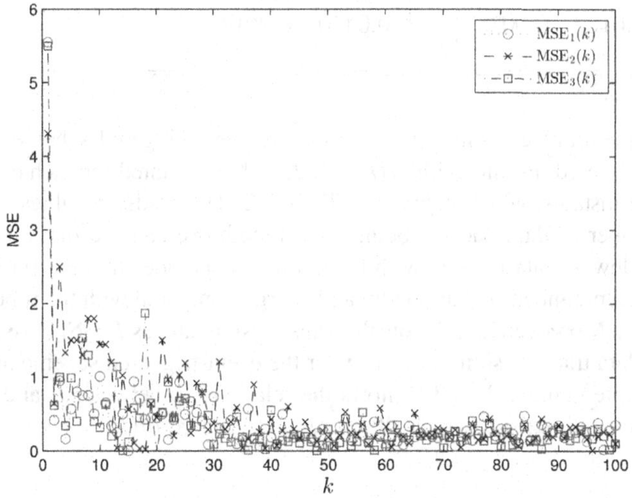

Figure 3.5 MSEs of $z(k)$ without attack.

Table 3.1
Filter gains

k	0	1	2
K_1	$\begin{bmatrix} 0.0409 & -0.0550 \\ -0.0642 & 0.0129 \end{bmatrix}$	$\begin{bmatrix} 0.0103 & 0.0123 \\ -0.0148 & -0.1152 \end{bmatrix}$	$\begin{bmatrix} 0.0087 & -0.0284 \\ 0.0558 & -0.1691 \end{bmatrix}$
K_2	$\begin{bmatrix} 0.0005 & -0.1091 \\ -0.0297 & 0.0314 \end{bmatrix}$	$\begin{bmatrix} -0.0194 & -0.0031 \\ -0.0138 & -0.1180 \end{bmatrix}$	$\begin{bmatrix} -0.0137 & -0.0737 \\ 0.0432 & -0.2421 \end{bmatrix}$
K_3	$\begin{bmatrix} 0.0615 & -0.0326 \\ -0.0846 & -0.0270 \end{bmatrix}$	$\begin{bmatrix} 0.0337 & 0.0181 \\ -0.0212 & -0.1051 \end{bmatrix}$	$\begin{bmatrix} 0.0233 & -0.0008 \\ 0.0608 & -0.1271 \end{bmatrix}$
k	3	4	...
K_1	$\begin{bmatrix} 0.0890 & 0.0093 \\ -0.0159 & 0.0026 \end{bmatrix}$	$\begin{bmatrix} 0.0488 & 0.0065 \\ 0.0401 & 0.0015 \end{bmatrix}$	...
K_2	$\begin{bmatrix} 0.0850 & 0.0035 \\ -0.0144 & 0.0029 \end{bmatrix}$	$\begin{bmatrix} 0.0290 & -0.0058 \\ 0.0273 & 0.0018 \end{bmatrix}$	...
K_3	$\begin{bmatrix} 0.0942 & 0.0102 \\ -0.0169 & 0.0028 \end{bmatrix}$	$\begin{bmatrix} 0.0554 & 0.0062 \\ 0.0420 & 0.0018 \end{bmatrix}$	...

To give quantitative results of the proposed event-triggered scheme (ETS), the number of triggered instants with $\theta_i(k) = 0.2, i \in \mathbf{N}$ is counted for each estimator for 1000 sample instants, which is given in Table 3.2. The boldface values indicate the smallest number of data packets being transmitted. We can see that all estimators transmit the fewest data packets with ETS, which concludes that the ETS will consume lower communication bandwidth and energy compared with the time-triggered scheme (TTS). Moreover, let's denote the transmission ratio as $J_i = \aleph_{\mathrm{ETS}}/\aleph_{\mathrm{TOT}}$, where $\aleph_{\mathrm{ETS}}$ is the data transmission number under the event-triggered scheme and $\aleph_{\mathrm{TOT}}$ is the total sample number. Fig. 3.6 shows the relationship between J_i and parameter $\theta_i(k)$ for each estimator i, which illustrates that a large $\theta_i(k)$ leads to a low data transmission ratio.

3.5.2 EXAMPLE 2

We consider a sensor network for an industrial continuous-stirred tank reactor (CSTR) system [64]. The physical structure of the system is presented in Fig. 3.7 and the CSTR process model developed from energy and material balance equations is

Table 3.2
Number of Transmitted Data Packets

	Estimator 1	Estimator 2	Estimator 3
Total Sample Number	1000	1000	1000
Transmission Number under TTS	1000	1000	1000
Transmission Number under ETS	**314**	**311**	**305**

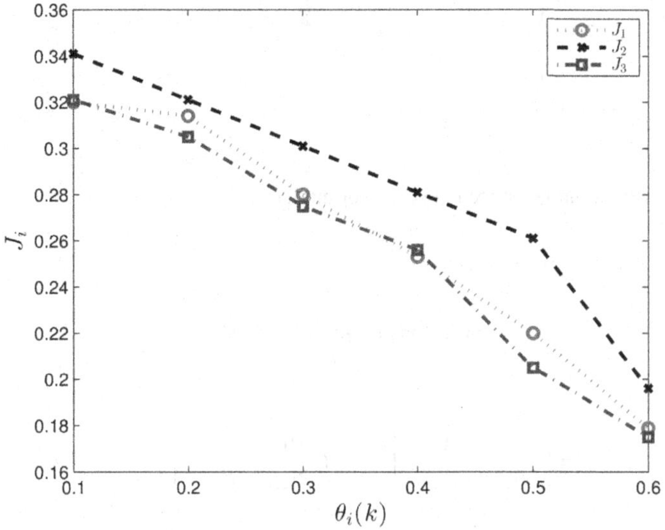

Figure 3.6 Data transmission ratios under event-triggered scheme via different $\theta_i(k)$.

given by [14]

$$\begin{aligned}\frac{dC_O}{dt} &= f_1(C_O,T) = \frac{F}{V}(C_{Of}-C_O) - k_o e^{-(\frac{\Delta E}{RT})} C_O \\ \frac{dT}{dt} &= f_2(C_O,T) = \frac{F}{V}(T_f - T) + \frac{-\Delta H}{\rho c_p} k_o e^{-(\frac{\Delta E}{RT})} C_O - \frac{U_O}{V \rho c_p}(T - T_C).\end{aligned} \tag{3.32}$$

Notations in model (3.32) are listed in the following Table 3.3.

Define the state variable x and the control input variable u as

$$x \triangleq \begin{bmatrix} C_O - C_O^e \\ T - T^e \end{bmatrix}, \ u \triangleq \begin{bmatrix} T_C - T_C^e \\ C_{Of} - C_{Of}^e \end{bmatrix}, \tag{3.33}$$

where $x_e = \begin{bmatrix} C_O^{e\,T} & T^{eT} \end{bmatrix}^T$, $u_e = \begin{bmatrix} T_C^{e\,T} & C_{Of}^{e\ \,T} \end{bmatrix}^T$ are the equilibrium point of the CSTR system. We linearize the system (3.32) with the equilibrium point (x_e, u_e)

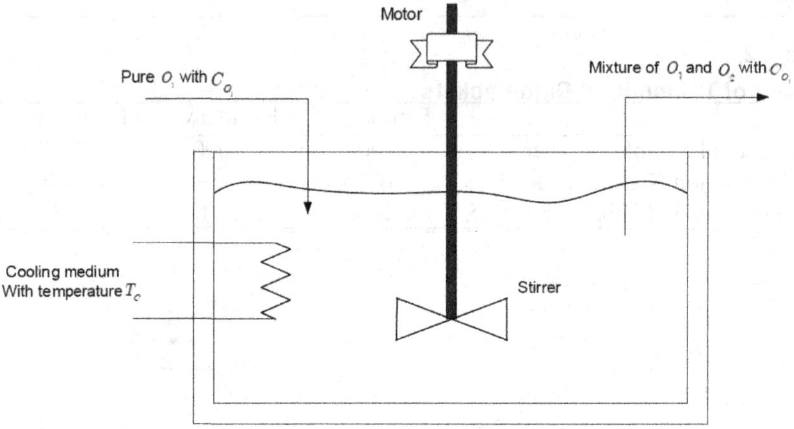

Figure 3.7 The continuous-stirred tank reactor model.

and obtain

$$\dot{x}(t) = Ax(t) + Bu(t), \tag{3.34}$$

where

$$A = \begin{bmatrix} A_{1,1} & A_{1,2} \\ A_{2,1} & A_{2,2} \end{bmatrix}, B = \begin{bmatrix} B_{1,1} & B_{1,2} \\ B_{2,1} & B_{2,2} \end{bmatrix} \tag{3.35}$$

with

$$\begin{aligned}
A_{1,1} &= \frac{\partial f_1(C_O,T)}{C_O}|_{(x_e,u_e)} = -\frac{F}{V} - k_o e^{-\frac{\Delta E}{RT^e}}, \\
A_{1,2} &= \frac{\partial f_1(C_O,T)}{T}|_{(x_e,u_e)} = -C_O^e k_o e^{-\frac{\Delta E}{RT^e}} \frac{\Delta E}{R(T^e)^2}, \\
A_{2,1} &= \frac{\partial f_2(C_O,T)}{C_O}|_{(x_e,u_e)} = -\frac{\Delta H}{\rho c_p} k_o e^{-\frac{\Delta E}{RT^e}}, \\
A_{2,2} &= \frac{\partial f_2(C_O,T)}{T}|_{(x_e,u_e)} = -\frac{F}{V} - \frac{US}{V\rho c_p} - \frac{-\Delta H}{\rho c_p} k_o e^{-\frac{\Delta E}{RT^e}} C_O^e \frac{\Delta E}{R(T^e)^2}
\end{aligned} \tag{3.36}$$

Table 3.3

Parameters in CSTR Process

Parameter	Meaning
S	Area for heat exchange
C_O	Concentration of reactant O in the reactor
C_{Of}	Concentration of O in the feed stream
c_p	Heat capability
k_o	Pre-exponential factor
R	Universal gas constant
T	Reactor temperature
T_f	Feed temperature
T_C	Jacket temperature
U	Overall heat transfer coefficient
V	Reactor volume
ΔE	Active energy
$-\Delta H$	Heat of reaction
ρ	Density of reactor

and

$$
\begin{aligned}
B_{1,1} &= \frac{\partial f_1}{T_C}|_{(x_e,u_e)} = 0 \\
B_{2,1} &= \frac{\partial f_2}{T_C}|_{(x_e,u_e)} = \frac{US}{V\rho c_p} \\
B_{1,2} &= \frac{\partial f_1}{C_{Of}}|_{(x_e,u_e)} = \frac{F}{V} \\
B_{2,2} &= \frac{\partial f_2}{C_{Of}}|_{(x_e,u_e)} = 0.
\end{aligned}
\tag{3.37}
$$

The outputs measured by sensors are a combination of system states, which are interfered with disturbances and deception attacks. There are three sensors in the CSTR system. The set of edges is $\mathbf{E} = \{(1,1),(1,3),(2,1),(2,2),(3,1),(3,3)\}$, and the adjacency matrix is given by $\mathbf{A} = [a_{ij}]_{3\times3}$ with $a_{ij} = 0.2$ if $(i,j) \in \mathbf{E}$, otherwise $a_{ij} = 0$. Substituting values of parameters in Table 3.4 into equation (3.34) which are listed on page 567 of reference [14], the system model of CSTR process is discretized

Table 3.4
Values of Parameters in the CSTR Process

Parameter	Value
F/V	1
k_o	14825*3600
$-\Delta H$	5215
E	11843
ρc_p	500
T_f	25
US/V	250

as system (3.1) with the following matrices [64, 66]

$$\begin{aligned}
A(k) &= \begin{bmatrix} 0.9719+0.05\sin(10k) & 0.0013 \\ -0.034 & 0.8628+0.02\cos(2k) \end{bmatrix}, \\
B(k) &= \begin{bmatrix} 0.0839 & 0.0232 \\ 0.0761 & 0.4144 \end{bmatrix}, \\
C_1(k) &= \begin{bmatrix} -0.1\sin(k) & -0.3 \end{bmatrix}, C_2(k) = \begin{bmatrix} -0.2 & 0.05 \end{bmatrix}, \\
C_3(k) &= \begin{bmatrix} 0.1 & -0.3\sin(k) \end{bmatrix}, \\
D_1(k) &= \begin{bmatrix} 0.1 \end{bmatrix}, D_2(k) = \begin{bmatrix} 0.1 \end{bmatrix}, D_3(k) = \begin{bmatrix} 0.1 \end{bmatrix}.
\end{aligned} \tag{3.38}$$

To give a comparison result, the event generator function (5) in [42] is introduced as follows

$$\phi(\hat{x}_i(k), \hat{x}_i(k_i^r), \theta_i(k)) \triangleq \psi_i^T(k)\psi_i(k) - \theta_i(k)e^{-\alpha k}, \tag{3.39}$$

where $\theta_i(k)$ and α are positive scalars. The transmission ratios J_i under different scenarios are listed in Table 3.5. In Table 3.5, the first scenario means the state-dependent triggered condition (3.7) is applied with parameter $\theta_i(k)$ taking values 0.2. The state-independent triggered scenario means that the event generator function (3.39) is used with $\theta_i(k) = 0.2$, $\alpha = 0.4$. With $\alpha = 0$ and $\theta_i(k)$ taking constant 0.2 for all $k \in [0, \mathrm{T}]$, the event-triggered issue with (3.39) degenerates into a static triggered scenario. When $\theta_i(k) = 0$ and $\alpha = 0$, the periodic sampling scenario is applied in which data are transmitted as long as they are sampled. The boldface values indicate the smallest percentage in the listed four scenarios that data packets are transmitted for different estimators. It is seen that the state-dependent triggered scenario will have the most bandwidth and be the most energy saving. The averaged MSE_1 with $L = 10000$ for each scenario above is shown in Fig. 3.8. We can see that the transmission ratios of both the state-dependent and state-independent scenarios are much less than the static triggered scenario. And also, the state-dependent triggered scenario has better filtering performance than the state-independent one in [42] with the approximate transmission ratios. Setting $\bar{\gamma}_i = \bar{\beta}_i, i \in \{1, 2, \cdots, N\}$, the optimal H_∞ filtering performances in Corollary 1 versus different attack probabilities with and without considering the uncertainty and model-reality mismatch are depicted in Fig. 3.9, which shows a larger attack probability leads to a worse estimation performance

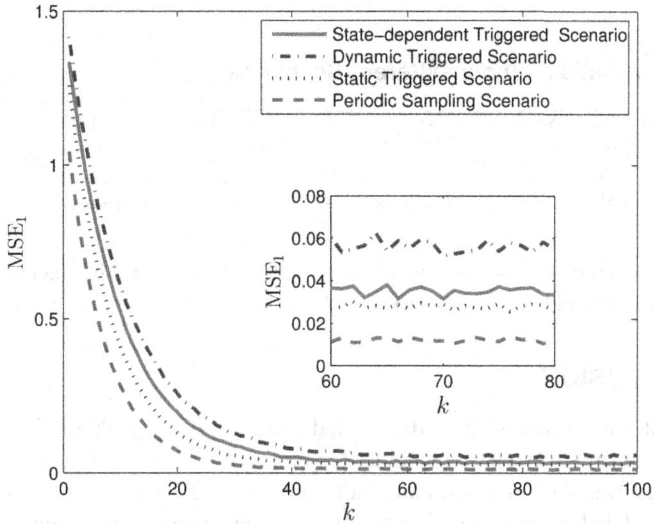

Figure 3.8 MSE$_1$ of $z_1(k)$ under different scenarios.

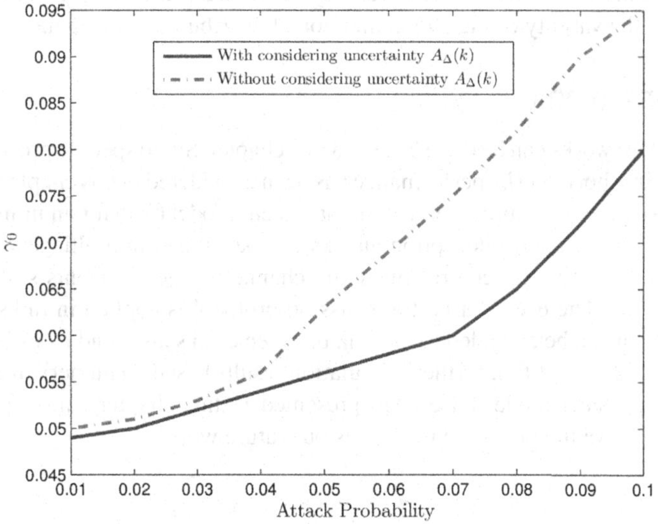

Figure 3.9 The optimal H_∞ filtering performance versus different attack probabilities.

Table 3.5
Transmission Ratio J_i under Different Scenarios

	Estimator 1	Estimator 2	Estimator 3
State-dependent Triggered Scenario $\theta_i(k)=0.2$	**31.4%**	**31.1%**	**30.5%**
State-independent Triggered Scenario in [42] $\theta_i(k)=0.2$, $\alpha=0.4$	33.0%	31.5%	31.7%
Static Triggered Scenario $\theta_i(k)=0.2$, $\alpha=0$	42.7%	40.6%	38.2%
Periodic Sample Scenario $\theta_i(k)=0$, $\alpha=0$	100%	100%	100%

and a better filtering performance is achieved when considering the uncertainty and model-reality mismatch in the system model.

3.6 CONCLUSION

This chapter has investigated a distributed secure filtering problem for a class of time-varying discrete-time systems under the effect of uncertainty and model-reality mismatch, deception attacks, and bandwidth limitation. Two-stage deception attacks have been modeled by random bounded signals. Quantization has been introduced before transmitting measurement and estimation signals to alight communication burden. And also an event-triggered protocol is employed for estimator nodes to reduce the unnecessary data transmission further. H_∞ performance has been designed against random deception attacks over a finite time horizon. Time-varying filters have been obtained online by solving a sequence of recursive matrix inequalities. Simulation examples including a numerical system and a practical system have been given to show the validity of the above-mentioned distributed filtering methodology.

3.7 FUTURE WORK

Several future works can be done based on this chapter. Some specific problems are listed: Finite time horizon H_∞ performance has been considered in this chapter, and we can also investigate the secure filter design for system model (3.1) for an infinite time horizon case. The two-stage deception attacks can be studied in multiagent systems where both the closed-loop control links and channels between agents suffer from deception attacks. The event-based transmission protocol is applied in links among estimators which can be extended to the link between each sensor and its estimator to reduce bandwidth congestion further. Simulation results based on numerical example and a reality physical model have been presented in this chapter, and experiment verification to prove the proposed method is our future work.

4 Attacks detection and disturbance rejection based on ESO/ROESO for a multiagent system

4.1 INTRODUCTION

In the past decades, the multi-agent system has attracted great attention from researchers all over the world because of its broad application prospects. However, in many engineering applications, due to the vulnerability of its own communication link and special mechanism, the system itself will be extremely vulnerable to various interference factors.

False Data Injection Attacks (FDIAs), as a highly common attack, prevent MASs from working normally by affecting the normal transmission of system information, so that it has also been widely researched. The problem of robust control for time-varying systems against false data injection attacks under an event-triggering mechanism has been discussed in [140]. On the basis of the robust controller in [162], reference [140] introduces a novel control protocol composed by an adaptive feedforward compensation mechanism for FDIAs aiming to debase the impact of cyber-attacks.

In addition, some novel methods have been introduced into the research of FDIAs in recent years.The design of an attack signal detection mechanism and an elastic control strategy based on the internal model principle and KL divergence is discussed in[10]. An attack-free approach, as a novel effective method, which is based on adaptive control and the neural network has been studied in[221]. And in [212], game theory method has been introduced to solve the problem of optimal state estimation under FDIAs.

In this chapter, a new circumstance has been discussed, in which attackers launch false data injection attacks against a communication network instead of sensor or actuator. However, False Data Injection Attack is highly concealed and, usually, agents are impotent to distinguish whether they have been attacked or not. For this, similarly to [56], an effective establishment of a detection mechanism for FDIAs is significant in this mission, and unlike a robust and resilient strategy, a novel control strategy has been designed based on Distributed Reduced-Order Extended State Observer (DROESO)[251], [18], for restraining other interference and avoiding using system information with malicious signals from a communication network caused by FDIAs but not mitigating it.

Three main contributions of this work can be summarized as follows:

(1) An effective detection mechanism for FDIAs which is established against a communication network.
(2) For avoiding using system information with malicious signals from a communication network, a novel controller based on DROESO is designed.
(3) Novel application scenarios of multi-spacecrafts has been introduced and the effectiveness of the total algorithm is verified successfully.

The rest of this chapter is organized as follows. Graph theory, the related mathematical symbols used in this chapter, and a system model have been introduced in Section 4.2. The main result including a detection mechanism and novel controller under a contested environment have been presented in Section 4.3. In Section 4.4, an example of a leader-follower multi-spacecraft system has been provided to verify the effectiveness of the proposed algorithm. Finally, the conclusion of this work is drawn in Section 4.5.

4.2 PRELIMINARIES

4.2.1 GRAPH THEORY

In this chapter, we consider a directed graph $\mathcal{G} \subseteq \mathcal{E} \times \mathcal{E}$ for the leader-follower multi-agent system in this work. The Graph $\mathcal{G}$ consists of $N+1$ nodes including $v(\mathcal{G}) = \{v_1, v_2, ..., v_N\}$ followers and one leader 0. The connectivity matrix is defined as $\mathcal{A} = [a_{ij}] \in \mathbb{R}_{n \times n}$ and for any $i, j \in [1, 2, ..., N]$, if $(v_i, v_j) \in \mathcal{G}$, $\mathcal{A}_{ij} > 0$, otherwise, $\mathcal{A}_{ij} = 0$. Therefore, we define the set of the neighbourhood for agent i as $\mathcal{N}_i = \{v_j \in v(\mathcal{G}) : (v_i, v_j) \in \mathcal{E}\}$. Define Laplacian Matrix $\mathcal{L}_1 = [\mathcal{L}_{ij}]_{n \times n}$, while $i = j$, $\mathcal{L}_{ij} = \sum_{j \in \mathcal{N}_i} a_{ij}$; else, $\mathcal{L}_{ij} = -a_{ij}$. Then, we denote the diagonal matrix $G = diag\{g_1, g_2, ..., g_N\}$. There will be connections between the leader and the ith follower while $g_i > 0$. $\mathcal{G}$ has the minimum edges which keep the graph connected as a fixed whole. Define $\mathcal{L} = \mathcal{L}_1 + G$, and $\bar{L} = \begin{bmatrix} 0 & 0_{1 \times N} \\ \mathcal{L}_2 & \mathcal{L} \end{bmatrix}$, $\mathcal{L}_2 = col\{g_1, g_2, ..., g_N\}$.

Lemma 4.1 *[28] There exists a positive definite matrix $\Theta_G = diag\{q_1, q_2, ..., q_{max}\}$, for some positive constant ϱ*

$$\Theta_G \mathcal{L} + \mathcal{L}^T \Theta_G > \varrho I \tag{4.1}$$

where $[q_1, q_2, ..., q_{max}] = (\mathcal{L}^T)^{-1} 1_N$.

4.2.2 MODEL DESCRIPTION

Consider the total multi-agent system that satisfies the leader-follower configuration as depicted in Fig. 4.1. The dynamic of the leader is defined as:

$$\dot{\boldsymbol{x}}_0 = \boldsymbol{A}\boldsymbol{x}_0, \qquad \boldsymbol{y}_0 = \boldsymbol{C}\boldsymbol{x}_0 \tag{4.2}$$

where $\boldsymbol{x}_0 \in \mathbb{R}^{n \times 1}$ and $\boldsymbol{y}_0$ are the state and the output of the leader, respectively. $\boldsymbol{A} \in \mathbb{R}^{n \times n}$, $\boldsymbol{C} = [1 \quad \boldsymbol{0}_{1 \times (n-1)}] \in \mathbb{R}^{1 \times n}$ are system matrix and output matrix, respectively.

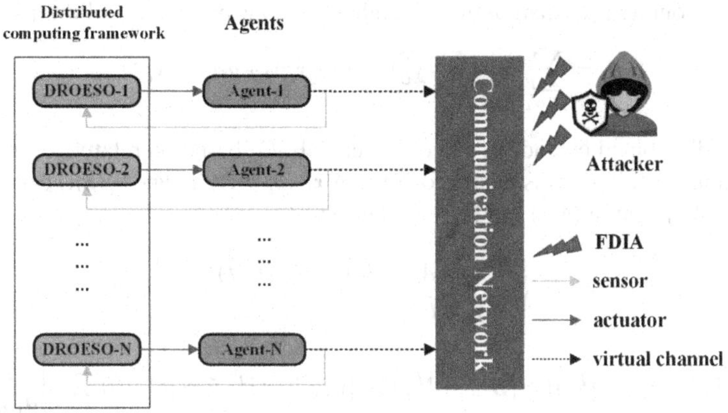

Figure 4.1 Schematic diagram of DROESO.

The dynamic system of each follower is:

$$\begin{cases} \dot{\boldsymbol{x}}_i = \boldsymbol{A}\boldsymbol{x}_i + \boldsymbol{B}(\boldsymbol{u}_i + \varpi_i(t)) \\ \boldsymbol{y}_i = \boldsymbol{C}\boldsymbol{x}_i \end{cases} \tag{4.3}$$

where $\boldsymbol{B} \in \mathbb{R}^{n\times 1}$ is the input matrix and $(\boldsymbol{A}, \boldsymbol{B})$ is controllable, $(\boldsymbol{A}, \boldsymbol{C})$ is observable. $\boldsymbol{x}_i \in \mathbb{R}^{n\times 1} = [\boldsymbol{x}_{i,1}, \boldsymbol{x}_{i,2}, \ldots \boldsymbol{x}_{i,n}]^T$ is the state, and $\varpi_i(t)$ is the bounded nonlinear matched disturbance which satisfies the Lipschitz condition:

$$\|\varpi_i(x) - \varpi_i(y)\| < \gamma\|(x-y)\| \tag{4.4}$$

where γ is Lipschitz constants.

Definition 4.1 *[87]* (Cooperatively Uniformly Ultimately Bounded): For any $m(m = 1, ..., M)$, the tracking error δ^m is said to be Cooperatively Uniformly Ultimately Bounded (CUUB) if there exists a compact set $\Omega^m \subset \mathbb{R}$ with the property that $0 \subset \Omega^m$, so that $\forall \delta^m(t_0) \in \Omega^m$, there exists a bound $\mathcal{B}^m$ and time $T_m(\mathcal{B}^m, \delta^1(t_0), ..., \delta^M(t_0))$, such that $\| \delta^m(t) \| < \mathcal{B}^m, \forall t > t_0 + T_m$.

The control objective in this chapter is to design an effective controller to make the total system stable; that is:

$$lim_{t\to\infty}\|\boldsymbol{x}_i(t) - \boldsymbol{x}_0(t)\| \to \wp \tag{4.5}$$

where $\wp$ is a small domain approaching the equilibrium point. We define the synchronization error of each follower i as:

$$\dot{\boldsymbol{\varepsilon}}_i(t) = \dot{\boldsymbol{x}}_i(t) - \dot{\boldsymbol{x}}_0(t) = \boldsymbol{A}\boldsymbol{\varepsilon}_i + \boldsymbol{B}(\boldsymbol{u}_i + \varpi_i(\boldsymbol{x}_i, t)) \tag{4.6}$$

and relative output information of the neighbouring agent for each follower is:

$$\zeta_i^* = \sum_{j \in N_i} a_{ij}((y_i - y_o) - (y_j - y_o)) + g_i(y_i - y_o). \tag{4.7}$$

Next, the distributed extended state observer (DESO) based on relative observation information for followers is designed. Setting $\boldsymbol{x}_{i,n+1} = \varpi_i(t)$ and $\hbar_i(\boldsymbol{x}_i, t) = \dot{\varpi}_i(\boldsymbol{x}_i, t)$, the original system in (4.3) can be rewritten as:

$$\begin{cases} \dot{\bar{\boldsymbol{x}}}_i = \bar{\boldsymbol{A}}\bar{\boldsymbol{x}}_i + \bar{\boldsymbol{B}}\boldsymbol{u}_i + \boldsymbol{E}\hbar_i(\boldsymbol{x}_i, t) \\ y_i = \bar{\boldsymbol{C}}\bar{\boldsymbol{x}}_i \end{cases} \tag{4.8}$$

and $\bar{\boldsymbol{x}}_i = [\boldsymbol{x}_i^T \quad x_{i,n+1}]^T, \bar{\boldsymbol{B}} = [\boldsymbol{B}^T \quad 0]^T, \boldsymbol{E} = [\boldsymbol{0}_{1\times n} \quad 1]^T, \bar{\boldsymbol{C}} = [\boldsymbol{C} \quad 0], \bar{\boldsymbol{A}} = \begin{bmatrix} \boldsymbol{A} & \boldsymbol{B} \\ \boldsymbol{0}_{1\times n} & 0 \end{bmatrix}$
and the equation in (4.6) can be rewritten as:

$$\dot{\bar{\boldsymbol{\varepsilon}}}_i = \bar{\boldsymbol{A}}\bar{\boldsymbol{\varepsilon}}_i + \bar{\boldsymbol{B}}\boldsymbol{u}_i + \boldsymbol{E}\hbar_i \tag{4.9}$$

The dynamic of DESO is constructed as follows:

$$\begin{cases} \dot{\hat{\bar{\boldsymbol{\varepsilon}}}}_i = \bar{\boldsymbol{A}}\hat{\bar{\boldsymbol{\varepsilon}}}_i + \bar{\boldsymbol{B}}\boldsymbol{u}_i + F\psi_i \\ \psi_i = \sum\limits_{j \in N_i} a_{ij}((y_i - y_j) - \bar{\boldsymbol{C}}(\hat{\bar{\boldsymbol{\varepsilon}}}_i - \hat{\bar{\boldsymbol{\varepsilon}}}_j)) + g_i((y_i - y_o) - \bar{\boldsymbol{C}}\hat{\bar{\boldsymbol{\varepsilon}}}_i) \end{cases} \tag{4.10}$$

Therein, F is the observer gain of DESO which will be designed later. $\hat{\bar{\boldsymbol{\varepsilon}}}_i$ is the estimation for $\bar{\boldsymbol{\varepsilon}}_i$. The estimation error is defined as: $\tilde{\boldsymbol{e}}_i = \bar{\boldsymbol{\varepsilon}}_i - \hat{\bar{\boldsymbol{\varepsilon}}}_i$, and

$$\dot{\tilde{\boldsymbol{e}}}_i = A\tilde{\boldsymbol{e}}_i - F\psi_i + \boldsymbol{E}\hbar_i \tag{4.11}$$

and, we set $T_1 = [I_n \quad \boldsymbol{0}_{n\times 1}], T_2 = [\boldsymbol{0}_{1\times n} \quad 1]$. According to the above, the local control protocol for follower i based on DESO is given as:

$$\boldsymbol{u}_i = KT_1\hat{\bar{\boldsymbol{\varepsilon}}}_i - T_2\hat{\bar{\boldsymbol{\varepsilon}}}_i \tag{4.12}$$

where $K = \boldsymbol{B}^T P_1^{-1}$ is the control gain which will be solved by calculating:

$$\boldsymbol{A}P_1 + P_1\boldsymbol{A}^T - 2\boldsymbol{B}\boldsymbol{B}^T < 0 \tag{4.13}$$

and $T_2\hat{\bar{\boldsymbol{\varepsilon}}}_i$ is the estimation of disturbance which is derived from the DESO for compensating $\boldsymbol{x}_{i,n+1}$ or $\varpi_i(t)$.The global form of the system in (4.9) is:

$$\dot{\boldsymbol{\varepsilon}} = (I_N \otimes (\boldsymbol{A} - \boldsymbol{B}K))\boldsymbol{\varepsilon} + (I_N \otimes \boldsymbol{B}\mathcal{T})\tilde{\boldsymbol{e}} \tag{4.14}$$

In the above, $\mathcal{T} = [K \quad I_1]$, $\boldsymbol{\varepsilon} = [\boldsymbol{\varepsilon}_1, \boldsymbol{\varepsilon}_2, ..., \boldsymbol{\varepsilon}_N]^T$.

Similarly, we can also give the global form of the estimation error in (4.11):

$$\dot{\tilde{\boldsymbol{e}}} = (I_N \otimes \bar{\boldsymbol{A}} - \mathcal{L} \otimes F\bar{\boldsymbol{C}})\tilde{\boldsymbol{e}} + (I_N \otimes \boldsymbol{E})\hbar \tag{4.15}$$

where $\tilde{\boldsymbol{e}} = [\tilde{\boldsymbol{e}}_1, \tilde{\boldsymbol{e}}_2, ..., \tilde{\boldsymbol{e}}_N]^T, \hbar = [\hbar_1, \hbar_2, ..., \hbar_N]^T$.

4.3 MAIN RESULT

4.3.1 ATTACK MODEL AND FDIA DETECTION

It is assumed that the attacker will launch false data injection attacks against the communication network. It means that:

$$\tilde{y}_{j\to i} = y_j + \rho_{ji} f_{ji} \tag{4.16}$$

where $\tilde{y}_{j\to i}$ is the output which is received by node i and transmitted from node j to node i, when the FDIAs have been launched. y_j is the original system output, ρ_{ji} is a Boolean variable.When the attack signal exists, $\rho_{ji} = 1$, conversely, $\rho_{ji} = 0$. f_{ji} is the attack signal acting on the link between node i, j. At the same time, we consider the energy of the attacker is limited so that the upper bound of $\|f_{ji}\|$ is $\bar{f}$.

But, continued use of false information will inevitably lead to the failure of the DESO, and due to strong concealment of FDIAs, it's necessary to design an effective detection mechanism for judging whether the FDIAs exist.

According to (4.16), relative output information of the neighbouring agent for follower i which is under FDIA is:

$$\tilde{\zeta}_i^* = \sum_{j\in N_i} a_{ij}((y_i - y_0) - (\tilde{y}_{j\to i} - y_0)) + g_i(y_i - y_0) \tag{4.17}$$

And the total observation error of the output is:

$$\check{e} = \zeta^* - \bar{C}\hat{\xi}_i^e = (\mathcal{L}\otimes\bar{C})\tilde{e} \tag{4.18}$$

Lemma 4.2 *According to Theorem 4 in [69], there are real matrix $\mathcal{V}$ and diagonal matrix $\mathcal{X}$ containing all the eigenvalues of $\mathcal{L}$, which satisfy:*

$$\mathcal{L} = \mathcal{V}\mathcal{X}\mathcal{V}^{-1} \tag{4.19}$$

Lemma 4.3 *[137] According to the Hölder inequality: for any positive constant a, b which satisfy $\frac{1}{a} + \frac{1}{b} = 1$, and the functions $\mathcal{P}(t)$ and $Q(t)$ are continuous in the interval $[0, T]$, the following equality holds:*

$$\int_0^T |\mathcal{P}(t)Q(t)|dt < (\int_0^T |\mathcal{P}(t)|^a dt)^{\frac{1}{a}} (\int_0^T |Q(t)|^b dt)^{\frac{1}{b}} \tag{4.20}$$

In Theorem 4.1, an effective detection mechanism based on global information is established.

Theorem 4.1 *In order to establish the detection machine for FDIAs against the communication network, according to the above derivation process, a detection function* **DET**(tk) *is given as follows. At arbitrarily moment tk, if:*

$$\begin{cases} \mathbf{J}_{\tilde{\mathbf{e}}}(tk) > \mathbf{DET}(tk), Alarm \\ \mathbf{J}_{\tilde{\mathbf{e}}}(tk) < \mathbf{DET}(tk), Safe \end{cases}$$

Where

$$\begin{cases} \mathbf{J}_{\tilde{\mathbf{e}}}(t) = \check{\mathbf{e}}^T \check{\mathbf{e}} \\ \mathbf{DET}(t) = \alpha_0 \cdot \mathbf{EXP}^{-\alpha_1} \cdot \alpha_2 + \varsigma(t) \end{cases} \tag{4.21}$$

$$\alpha_0 = \kappa \times \lambda_{max}(R \otimes P_2) \times (\lambda_{min}(R \otimes P_2))^{-1}$$
$$\alpha_1 = \lambda_{min}(\Psi) \times \lambda_{max}(P_2)^{-1}, \alpha_2 = V_2(\tilde{\mathbf{e}}(0))$$
$$\varsigma(t) = \kappa \sqrt{\frac{\lambda_{max}(P_2)}{2\lambda_{min}(\Psi)}(1 - \mathbf{EXP}^{-\frac{2\lambda_{min}(\Psi)}{\lambda_{max}(P_2)}t})}$$

At the same time, the observer gain of DESO $F = \frac{1}{\lambda_{min}(\mathcal{L})} P_2^{-1} \bar{\mathbf{C}}^T$ *is obtained by solving LMI as follows:*

$$\begin{bmatrix} \bar{\mathbf{A}}^T P_2 + P_2 \bar{\mathbf{A}} - 2\bar{\mathbf{C}}^T \bar{\mathbf{C}} & P_2 \\ * & -\frac{1}{\lambda_{max}(R)} I_3 \end{bmatrix} < 0$$

Proof *Given the Lyapunov function:*

$$V_2 = \tilde{\mathbf{e}}^T (R \otimes P_2) \tilde{\mathbf{e}} \tag{4.22}$$

$R = (\mathcal{V}^{-1})^T (\mathcal{V}^{-1})$ *and* $P_2 \in \mathbb{R}_{n+1 \times n+1}$ *is the positive-define matrix. Derivation of the Lyapunov function:*

$$\dot{V}_2 = \tilde{\mathbf{e}}^T (R \otimes P_2)((I_N \otimes \bar{\mathbf{A}} - \mathcal{L} \otimes F\bar{\mathbf{C}})\tilde{\mathbf{e}} + (I_N \otimes \mathbf{E})\hbar)$$
$$+(\tilde{\mathbf{e}}^T (I_N \otimes \bar{\mathbf{A}}^T - \mathcal{L}^T \otimes (F\bar{\mathbf{C}})^T))(R \otimes P_2)\tilde{\mathbf{e}}$$
$$+\hbar^T (I_N \otimes \mathbf{E}^T)(R \otimes P_2)\tilde{\mathbf{e}}$$
$$= \tilde{\mathbf{e}}^T (R \otimes (\bar{\mathbf{A}}^T P_2 + P_2 \bar{\mathbf{A}}))\tilde{\mathbf{e}} - 2\tilde{\mathbf{e}}^T (R \otimes P_2 (F\bar{\mathbf{C}}))\tilde{\mathbf{e}}$$
$$+\tilde{\mathbf{e}}^T (R \otimes P_2)(I_N \otimes \mathbf{E})\hbar + \hbar^T (I_N \otimes \mathbf{E}^T)(R \otimes P_2)\tilde{\mathbf{e}}$$

According to Young's inequality:

$$+\tilde{\mathbf{e}}^T (R \otimes P_2)(I_N \otimes \mathbf{E})\hbar + \hbar^T (I_N \otimes \mathbf{E}^T)(R \otimes P_2)\tilde{\mathbf{e}}$$
$$\leq \lambda_{max}(R)\tilde{\mathbf{e}}^T (R \otimes P_2 P_2)\tilde{\mathbf{e}} + \hbar^T (I_N \otimes \mathbf{E}^T \mathbf{E})\hbar$$

Merge the above polynomials:

$$\dot{V}_2 \leq -\frac{\lambda_{min}(\Psi)}{\lambda_{max}(P_3)} V_2 + \hbar^T (I_N \otimes \mathbf{E}^T \mathbf{E})\hbar$$

where $\Psi = \bar{\mathbf{A}}^T P_2 + P_2\bar{\mathbf{A}} - 2\bar{\mathbf{C}}^T\bar{\mathbf{C}} + \lambda_{max}(R)P_2P_2$, P_2 *can be solved by calculating* $\Psi < 0$.

By integration, we obtain:

$$V_2(\tilde{\mathbf{e}}(t)) \leq \mathbf{EXP}^{-\frac{\lambda_{min}(\Psi)}{\lambda_{max}(P_3)}t} V_2(\tilde{\mathbf{e}}(0)) + \int_0^t \mathbf{EXP}^{-\frac{\lambda_{min}(\Psi)}{\lambda_{max}(P_3)}\cdot(t-\tau)} \parallel (\hbar^T(I_N \otimes \mathbf{E}^T\mathbf{E})\hbar) \parallel d\tau$$

Recalling that:

$$\lambda_{min}(R\otimes P_2) \parallel \tilde{\mathbf{e}} \parallel^2 \leq V_2 \leq \lambda_{max}(R\otimes P_2) \parallel \tilde{\mathbf{e}} \parallel^2$$

To sum up, it can be concluded that:

$$\lambda_{min}(R\otimes P_2) \parallel \tilde{\mathbf{e}} \parallel^2 \leq \lambda_{max}(R\otimes P_2)\mathbf{EXP}^{-\frac{\lambda_{min}(\Psi)}{\lambda_{max}(P_2)}t} V_2(\tilde{\mathbf{e}}(0)) \int_0^t \mathbf{EXP}^{-\frac{\lambda_{min}(\Psi)}{\lambda_{max}(P_3)}\cdot(t-\tau)} \parallel (\hbar^T(I_N \otimes \mathbf{E}^T\mathbf{E})\hbar) \parallel d\tau$$

From (4.18), *we can get:*

$$\check{\mathbf{e}}^T\check{\mathbf{e}} = \tilde{\mathbf{e}}^T(\bar{\mathbf{C}}^T \otimes \mathcal{L}^T)(\mathcal{L}\otimes\bar{\mathbf{C}})\tilde{\mathbf{e}} \leq \kappa \parallel \tilde{\mathbf{e}} \parallel^2$$

and $\kappa = \lambda_{max}((\bar{\mathbf{C}}^T \otimes \mathcal{L}^T)(\mathcal{L}\otimes\bar{\mathbf{C}}))$

$$\parallel \check{\mathbf{e}}^T\check{\mathbf{e}} \parallel^2 \leq \frac{\kappa \times \lambda_{max}(R\otimes P_2)}{\lambda_{min}(R\otimes P_2)}\mathbf{EXP}^{-\frac{\lambda_{min}(\Psi)}{\lambda_{max}(P_3)}t} V_2(\tilde{\mathbf{e}}(0)) + \kappa\int_0^t \mathbf{EXP}^{-\frac{\lambda_{min}(\Psi)}{\lambda_{max}(P_3)}\cdot(t-\tau)} \parallel (\hbar^T(I_N \otimes \mathbf{E}^T\mathbf{E})\hbar) \parallel d\tau$$

According to Lemma 3:

$$\begin{aligned}\parallel \check{\mathbf{e}}^T\check{\mathbf{e}} \parallel \leq & \frac{\kappa \times \lambda_{max}(R\otimes P_2)}{\lambda_{min}(R\otimes P_2)}\mathbf{EXP}^{-\frac{\lambda_{min}(\Psi)}{\lambda_{max}(P_3)}t} V_2(\tilde{\mathbf{e}}(0)) \\ & +(\kappa\int_0^t (\mathbf{EXP}^{-\frac{\lambda_{min}(\Psi)}{\lambda_{max}(P_3)}\cdot(t-\tau)})^2 d\tau)^{\frac{1}{2}} \\ & +(\kappa\int_0^t (\parallel (\hbar^T(I_N \otimes \mathbf{E}^T\mathbf{E})\hbar) \parallel)^2 d\tau)^{\frac{1}{2}}\end{aligned}$$

The proof is ended.

Remark 6 *It is worth noting that if the attack signal acts on the communication network, it will lead to the false lead neighbourhood error of output received by the distributed extended state observer and further affect the estimation of the matched disturbance. Therefore, the design of DROESO is very important for its unique structure.*

4.3.2 DESIGN OF DROESO

Setting a new matrix $T_3 = [\mathbf{0}_{(n-1)\times 1} I_{n-1}]$, and defining $\boldsymbol{\eta}_i = T_3\boldsymbol{\varepsilon}_i$, we divide the matrix in equation(4.3):

$$\boldsymbol{A}= \begin{bmatrix} \boldsymbol{A}_1 & \boldsymbol{A}_2 \\ \boldsymbol{A}_3 & \boldsymbol{A}_4 \end{bmatrix} \boldsymbol{B}= \begin{bmatrix} \boldsymbol{B}_1 \\ \boldsymbol{B}_2 \end{bmatrix}$$

$$\boldsymbol{A}_1 = a_{11}, \boldsymbol{A}_2 = \boldsymbol{A}_{1\times(n-1)}, \boldsymbol{A}_3 = \boldsymbol{A}_{(n-1)\times 1}$$
$$\boldsymbol{A}_4 = \boldsymbol{A}_{(n-1)\times(n-1)}\ \boldsymbol{B}_1 = b_1, \boldsymbol{B}_2 = \boldsymbol{B}_{1\times(n-1)}$$

where a_{11} is the element of the first row and the first column of matrix $\boldsymbol{A}$, b_1 is the element of the first row of matrix $\boldsymbol{B}$. Further, we can sort matrix $\bar{\boldsymbol{A}}, \bar{\boldsymbol{B}}, \boldsymbol{E}$ and $\bar{\boldsymbol{\varepsilon}}_i$ into:

$$\bar{\boldsymbol{A}} = \begin{bmatrix} \boldsymbol{A}_1 & \boldsymbol{A}_2 & \boldsymbol{B}_1 \\ \boldsymbol{A}_3 & \boldsymbol{A}_4 & \boldsymbol{B}_2 \\ \mathbf{0}_{1\times 1} & \mathbf{0}_{(n-1)\times(n-1)} & \mathbf{0}_{1\times 1} \end{bmatrix}$$

$$\bar{\boldsymbol{B}}= \begin{bmatrix} \boldsymbol{B}_1 \\ \boldsymbol{B}_2 \\ \mathbf{0}_{1\times 1} \end{bmatrix}, \bar{\boldsymbol{\varepsilon}}_i= \begin{bmatrix} \boldsymbol{\varepsilon}_{i,1} \\ \boldsymbol{\eta}_i \end{bmatrix}, \boldsymbol{E}= \begin{bmatrix} \mathbf{0}_{1\times 1} \\ \mathbf{0}_{(n-1)\times 1} \\ 1_{1\times 1} \end{bmatrix}$$

Based on the above segmentation method, we design a Distributed Reduced-Order Extended State Observer(DROESO) for followers. Setting:

$$\boldsymbol{A}_1^R = \boldsymbol{A}_1, \boldsymbol{A}_2^R = \begin{bmatrix} \boldsymbol{A}_2 & \boldsymbol{B}_1 \end{bmatrix}, \boldsymbol{A}_3^R = \begin{bmatrix} \boldsymbol{A}_3 \\ \mathbf{0}_{1\times 1} \end{bmatrix}, \boldsymbol{B}_2^R= \begin{bmatrix} \boldsymbol{B}_2 \\ \mathbf{0}_{1\times 1} \end{bmatrix},$$

$$\boldsymbol{A}_4^R = \begin{bmatrix} \boldsymbol{A}_4 & \boldsymbol{B}_2 \\ \mathbf{0}_{(n-1)\times(n-1)} & \mathbf{0}_{1\times 1} \end{bmatrix}, \boldsymbol{E}^R = \begin{bmatrix} \mathbf{0}_{(n-1)\times 1} \\ 1_{1\times 1} \end{bmatrix}$$

The dynamic of the reduced-order system is:

$$\dot{\boldsymbol{\eta}}_i = \boldsymbol{A}_3^R T_1 \bar{\boldsymbol{\varepsilon}}_i + \boldsymbol{A}_4^R \boldsymbol{\eta}_i + \boldsymbol{B}_2^R \boldsymbol{u}_i^{\eta} + \boldsymbol{E}^R \hbar \tag{4.23}$$

The DROESO is designed as:

$$\dot{\hat{\boldsymbol{\eta}}}_i = \boldsymbol{A}_3^R T_1 \bar{\boldsymbol{\varepsilon}}_i + \boldsymbol{A}_4^R \hat{\boldsymbol{\eta}}_i + \boldsymbol{B}_2^R \boldsymbol{u}_i^{\eta} + cF^R \boldsymbol{\psi}_i^R \tag{4.24}$$

F^R is the observer gain of DROESO, $\hat{\eta}_i$ is the estimation of η_i, and:

$$\begin{cases} \xi^{\eta} = \sum\limits_{j \in N_i} a_{ij}(\eta_i - \eta_j) + g_i \eta_i \\ \hat{\xi}_i^{\eta} = \sum\limits_{j \in N_i} a_{ij}(\hat{\eta}_i - \hat{\eta}_j) + g_i \hat{\eta}_i \\ \psi_i^R = A_2^R \xi^{\eta} - A_2^R \hat{\xi}^{\eta} \end{cases}$$

but it's noticed that we can't get ξ^{η} directly. Therefore, similar to [18], by integrating the above formula, we can conclude that:

$$\psi_i^R = (\dot{\zeta}^* - A_1^R \zeta^* - B_1(\sum_{j \in N_i} a_{ij}(u_i^{\eta} - u_j^{\eta}) + g_i u_i^{\eta})) - A_2^R \hat{\xi}^{\eta} \tag{4.25}$$

On the premise of constant controller gain K, the local control protocol based on DROESO is:

$$u_i^{\eta} = K\bar{\hat{\xi}}^{\eta} - T_4 \hat{\eta} \tag{4.26}$$

$\bar{\hat{\xi}}^{\eta} = [y_i \quad \eta_i^T]^T, T_4 = [0_{(n-1)\times 1} \quad 1]$. Next, we can define the estimation error $\tilde{\eta}_i = \eta_i - \hat{\eta}_i$,which is between DROESO and the true state. Its form can be written as follows:

$$\dot{\tilde{\eta}}_i = A_4^R \tilde{\eta}_i - cF^R \psi_i^R + E^R \tilde{h}_i \tag{4.27}$$

Further, the expression of global error is:

$$\dot{\tilde{\eta}} = ((I_N \otimes A_4^R - c\mathcal{L} \otimes F^R A_2^R)\tilde{\eta} + (I_N \otimes E^R)\tilde{h} \tag{4.28}$$

where $\tilde{\eta} = [\tilde{\eta}_1, \tilde{\eta}_2, ..., \tilde{\eta}_N]^T, \tilde{h} = [\tilde{h}_1, \tilde{h}_2, ..., \tilde{h}_N]^T$.

Theorem 4.2 *Consider the multi-agent system introduced in* (4.28) *under FDIAs and disturbances. It is assumed that the foregoing assumption is true. If the reduced-order observer gain matrix* $F^R = cQ_R^{-1}\mathbf{A}_2^{R^T}$, *which constant* c *satisfies* $c \geq 2q_{max}/\varrho$. *As time goes, the dynamic tracking error between the DROESO and the state of the agent can be cooperatively uniformly ultimately bounded (CUUB). Positive matrix* Q_R *will be solved by calculating:*

$$\begin{bmatrix} \mathbf{A}_4^{R^T} Q_R + Q_R \mathbf{A}_4^R - 2\mathbf{A}_2^{R^T} \mathbf{A}_2^R & Q_R \\ * & -I_3 \end{bmatrix} < 0 \tag{4.29}$$

Proof *We define the Lyapunov function:*

$$V = \tilde{\eta}^T (\Theta_G \otimes Q_R)\tilde{\eta}$$

And the derivation of the Lyapunov function:

$$\begin{aligned}\dot{V} &= \tilde{\eta}^T (\Theta_G \otimes Q_R)\left(I_N \otimes A_4^R - c\mathcal{L} \otimes F^R A_2^R\right)\tilde{\eta} \\ &+ \tilde{\eta}^T\left(I_N \otimes A_4^{R^T} - \left(c\mathcal{L} \otimes F^R \mathbf{A}_2^R\right)^T\right)(\Theta_G \otimes Q_R)\tilde{\eta} \\ &+ 2\tilde{\eta}^T (\Theta_G \otimes Q_R)\left(I_N \otimes \mathbf{E}^R\right)\hbar\end{aligned}$$

Applying the remaining properties in Lemma 3, we can conclude that:

$$\begin{aligned}\dot{V} = \tilde{\eta}^T &\Big(\Theta_G \otimes \Big(\mathbf{A}_4^{R^T} Q_R + Q_R \mathbf{A}_4^R \\ &-c\left(\Theta_G \mathcal{L} + \mathcal{L}^T \Theta_G\right) \mathbf{A}_2^{R^T} \mathbf{A}_2^R\Big)\Big)\tilde{\eta} + 2\tilde{\eta}^T (\Theta_G \otimes Q_R)\left(I_N \otimes \mathbf{E}^R\right)\hbar\end{aligned}$$

Similar to Theorem 4.1, according to Young's inequality:

$$\begin{aligned}&2\tilde{\eta}^T (\Theta_G \otimes Q_R)\left(I_N \otimes \mathbf{E}^R\right)\hbar \\ &\quad \leq q_{\max}\tilde{\eta}^T (\Theta_G \otimes Q_R Q_R)\tilde{\eta} + \hbar^T\left(I_N \otimes \mathbf{E}^{R^T} \mathbf{E}^R\right)\hbar\end{aligned}$$

Merging polynomials:

$$\begin{aligned}\dot{V}_3 \leq &\tilde{\eta}^T\left(R \otimes \left(\mathbf{A}_4^{R^T} Q_R + Q_R \mathbf{A}_4^R - 2\mathbf{A}_2^{R^T} \mathbf{A}_2^R + q_{\max} Q_R Q_R\right)\right)\tilde{\eta} \\ &+ \hbar^T\left(I_N \otimes \mathbf{E}^{R^T} \mathbf{E}^R\right)\hbar\end{aligned}$$

By solving:

$$\Xi^R = \mathbf{A}_4^{R^T} Q_R + Q_R \mathbf{A}_4^R - 2\mathbf{A}_2^{R^T} \mathbf{A}_2^R + q_{max} Q_R Q_R < 0$$

we can get the positive-definite matrix Q_R, and

$$\|\tilde{\eta}\| \leq \sqrt{\frac{\lambda_{min}(Q_R \otimes \Xi^R)}{N * \|\mathbf{E}\|}}\|\hbar\| \tag{4.30}$$

The multi-agent system can still be realized as Cooperatively Uniformly Ultimately Bounded(CUUB) in the case of using DROESO.

The proof is ended.

4.4 SIMULATION

In this section, an example based on the radial control of multi-spacecrafts in [13] is used to testify the effectiveness of the algorithm. A topology network is shown in Fig. 4.2.

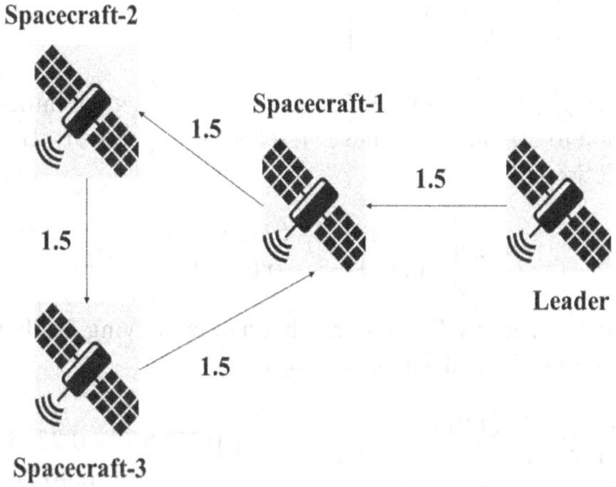

Figure 4.2 Topology graph of multi-spacecraft system.

The system model is constructed as:

$$\begin{cases} \ddot{r} - \dfrac{h^2}{r^3} + \dfrac{\mu}{r^2} = \dfrac{T}{M} sin\beta \\ \dfrac{\dot{h}}{r} = \dfrac{T}{M} cos\beta \\ y_r = \delta r \end{cases}$$

and relative parameters are shown in the following form:

Parameters	Paraphrase
M	The mass of spacecraft
h	Orbital angular momentum
T	Thrust of spacecraft
β	Normal angle
μ	Gravitational constant of the earth
r	Radius of circular orbit

Suppose that we need to control the spacecrafts radially with the expected constant orbital radius r_s and constant angular momentum $h_s = h$; it is noticed that:

$$\frac{3{h_s}^2}{{r_s}^4} - \frac{2\mu}{{r_s}^3} = \frac{\mu}{{r_s}^3} = \omega^2 \tag{4.31}$$

and we set $\beta = \pi/2$. The reference track radius is $r_s = 6578.14$ km; then the control system model can be integrated into:

$$\begin{cases} \begin{bmatrix} \delta\dot{r} \\ \delta\ddot{r} \end{bmatrix} = \begin{bmatrix} 0 & 1 \\ -\omega^2 & 0 \end{bmatrix} \begin{bmatrix} \delta r \\ \delta\dot{r} \end{bmatrix} + \begin{bmatrix} 0 \\ 1 \end{bmatrix} \dfrac{T}{M} \\ y_r = \begin{bmatrix} 1 & 0 \end{bmatrix} \begin{bmatrix} \delta r \\ \delta\dot{r} \end{bmatrix} \end{cases} \tag{4.32}$$

where $\delta r = r - r_s$, $\omega = \sqrt{\mu/r_s{}^3} = 0.00183353$ rad/s. Next, we set the initial state of all agents and observation to 20*rand(2,1) and 5*rand(3,1), respectively. By calculating (4.13), a feasible solution is:

$$P_1 = \begin{bmatrix} 0.4403 & -0.3194 \\ -0.3194 & 0.6526 \end{bmatrix}$$

Setting $\varrho = 2$, the observer gains P_2, Q_R are obtained by solving LMIs which have been introduced in Theorem 1 and Theorem 2 respectively:

$$P_2 = \begin{bmatrix} 5.8454 & 6.0426 & 3.9273 \\ 6.0426 & 13.3621 & 8.2194 \\ 3.9273 & 8.2194 & 9.0685 \end{bmatrix} \quad Q_R = \begin{bmatrix} 0.2775 & -0.2775 \\ -0.2775 & 0.4625 \end{bmatrix}$$

Meanwhile, we can get:

$$F = \begin{bmatrix} -15.8978 & -16.4343 & -10.6812 \end{bmatrix}$$
$$F^R = \begin{bmatrix} -18.0166 & -10.8100 \end{bmatrix}$$

Suppose that the attacker will launch FDIAs on link $3 \rightarrow 1$ and link $2 \rightarrow 3$ within $10 \sim 15$s and $30 \sim 50$s respectively. And $f_{3\rightarrow 1} = 10 * sin(0.25 * t)$ and $f_{2\rightarrow 3} = 10 * cos(0.5 * t)$. The simulation effect of the detection mechanism which has been designed in Theorem 1 is shown in Fig. 4.3. Obviously, according to simulation results, the detection mechanism detected the FDIAs around the 10s and 30s and didn't raise the alarm at other times. The effectiveness of the detection mechanism is verified.

Assume that $\varpi_i = 0.1 * \boldsymbol{EXP}^{sin(0.1*t)}$. From the results shown in Fig. 4.4, it can be seen clearly that all three spacecrafts reach synchronization with the leader. At the same time, as the results show in Fig. 4.5 and Fig. 4.6, the effectiveness of DESO/DROESO has been confirmed regardless of whether the three spacecrafts are under the contested environment. It means that both DESO and DROESO can estimate the state of the spacecraft well and the disturbance can be effectively estimated and further applied to the design of the controller.

4.5 CONCLUSION

We have studied leader-follower synchronization of multi-agent systems using a local controller with matched disturbance. While the multi-agent system is under the

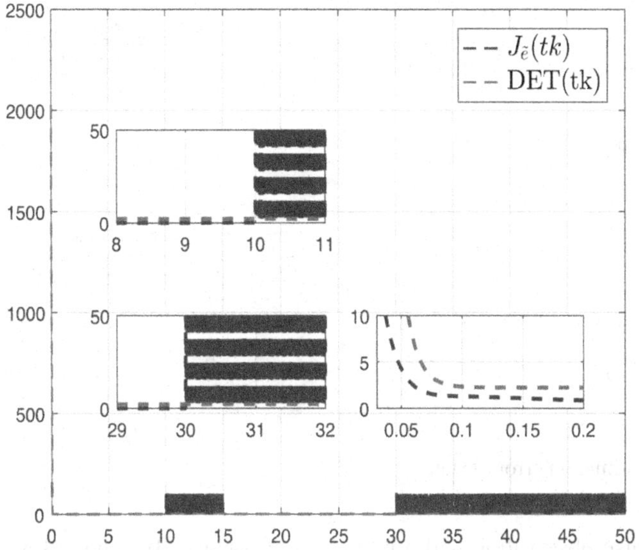

Figure 4.3 Simulation of detection mechanism.

contested environment, we have proposed an effective detection mechanism which is based on DESO. With this mechanism, the MAS can detect FDIAs in a timely manner which are against the communication network. Then, we have designed DROESO to

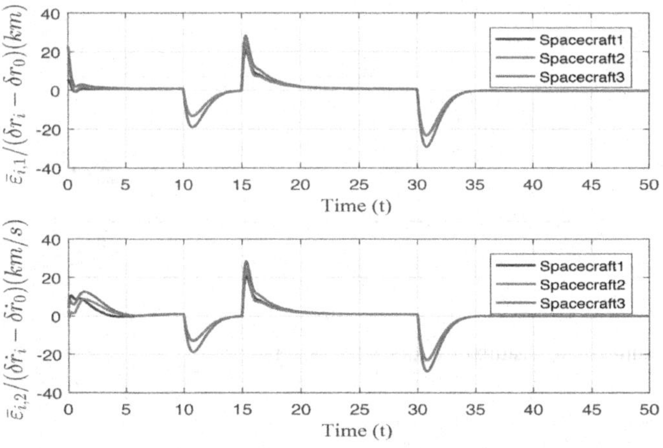

Figure 4.4 States trajectories of spacecrafts.

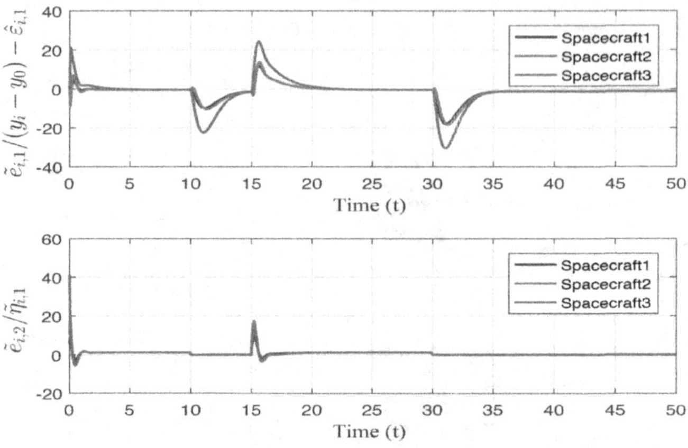

Figure 4.5 Estimation error of states.

ensure that false observation will not be used by agents. By solving LMI, we have obtained the observer gain of DROESO and ensured that the dynamic error system achieves Cooperative CUUB. Finally, an example of multi-spacecrafts has shown the effectiveness of the algorithm.

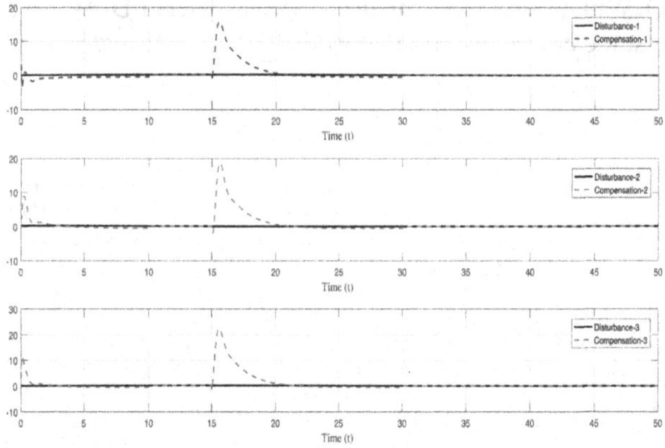

Figure 4.6 Estimation of disturbance for each spacecraft.

Section II

Resilient Strategy to Combat a DoS Attack

5 Resilient state estimation with multi-channel transmission under a DoS attack

5.1 INTRODUCTION

CPSs have enriched human-machine interactions by connecting the cyber world and physical world, especially when wireless sensors and remote state estimators are adopted in CPSs, which operate as a significant portion of the entire monitoring and control system of the industrial process. CPSs always integrate a large number of critical infrastructures, where multiple sensors are installed distributedly [94, 235]. Information transmission of multiple sensors may lead to communication congestion when the communication bandwidth is limited, which can be exploited by a DoS attacker [90]. The energy management of the DoS attack has been explored to maximize the attack effect [93]. In wireless communication networks, simultaneous data transmission will result in signal interference which will further lead to packet dropout and hence degrade the estimation performance. In [216], signal-to-interference-plus-noise ratio (SINR) based power control of a sensor and a DoS attacker has been studied for a remote state estimation system. Compared with [216], where one remote state estimation system is considered, this chapter focuses on multiple sensors transmitting information simultaneously. Multiple channel networks can increase resilience of a system under sudden events, such as communication interruption and cyber attacks [115]. Deploying cochannel operation is of significant interest in CPS and therefore interference management including channel allocation and power control for multiple remote estimation systems is investigated in this chapter.

The wireless network environment is time-varying because of many factors. Energy-constrained wireless sensors installed wide spread with batteries will become more aware of how to choose their actions under time-varying networks, which inspires our work. Works [83, 115, 216] on security of remote estimation systems have been presented where the objective functions are obtained iteratively by using a Q-learning method such that the closed-form of objective functions is not needed. Different from previous works [83, 115, 216], a long-term policy is researched by using a Q-learning method, taking time-varying networks into consideration in this chapter.

This chapter considers a cyber-physical system with multiple remote state estimation subsystems under denial-of-service (DoS) attack. Suppose that there are multiple distributed estimation systems, in each of which a sensor monitors the system and sends its local estimation to a remote estimator over one of multiple wireless channels. A DoS attacker emits noise power to jam the wireless channels. A scheduler is installed to dispatch each sensor to transmit information through a specific channel to minimize the total estimation error covariance on account of energy-saving, whereas, the DoS attacker attempts to jam a channel to realize an opposite objective. With considering interference from other individuals, a multi-sensor multi-channel remote state estimation model is constructed. A myopic policy and a long-term online interaction strategy under a varying network environment are investigated and compared by solving a two-player zero-sum game and a Markov game, respectively. Simulations are provided to demonstrate our results.

(1) A novel multiple channel access issue of multiple remote state estimation systems is analyzed for spectrum efficiency in the presence of a DoS attacker.
(2) For the multiple sensors accessing multiple channels model, feasible strategies are provided for scheduler and attacker. Myopic policies for two players are designed, modeling them using a zero-sum game.
(3) Considering a more practical case that communication networks are time-varying, the long-term interaction of players is modeled with a Markov game. Online minimax-Q learning is applied to solve the game, which has prominent advantages compared with the myopic policy.

The rest of the chapter is organized as follows: In Section 5.2, the system model of multiple remote state estimation systems through wireless networks is set up. A myopic strategy is investigated in Section 5.3. In Section 5.4, a Markov game framework is constructed for long-term running. Minimax-Q learning is applied to obtain the optimal strategies in Section 5.5. Finally, simulation results and conclusions are given in Sections 5.6 and 5.7.

5.2 PROBLEM FORMULATION

In this section, we describe a system model of sensing, communication, and estimation for a CPS with multiple remote state estimation systems and multiple channels as shown in Fig. 5.1.

5.2.1 SYSTEM MODEL WITH LOCAL KALMAN FILTERING

Consider a CPS containing ι sensors and remote estimators as depicted in Fig. 5.1, in which the sensors monitor different linear processes given by

$$\begin{aligned} x_i(k+1) =& A_i x_i(k) + \omega_i(k), \\ y_i(k) =& C_i x_i(k) + v_i(k),\ i \in \iota \triangleq \{1,2,\cdots,\iota\}, \end{aligned} \tag{5.1}$$

where $x_i(k) \in \mathbb{R}^{n_{x_i}}$ is the state vector of system i, $y_i(k) \in \mathbb{R}^{n_{y_i}}$ is the measurement taken by sensor i. The process noise $\omega_i(k) \in \mathbb{R}^{n_{x_i}}$ and measurement noise $v_i(k) \in \mathbb{R}^{n_{y_i}}$ are zero-mean independent and identically distributed Gaussian random variables for all $i \in \iota$, which satisfy $\mathbb{E}[\omega_i(k)\omega_j^T(t)] = \delta_i^j \delta_k^t Q_i, Q_i \geq 0$,

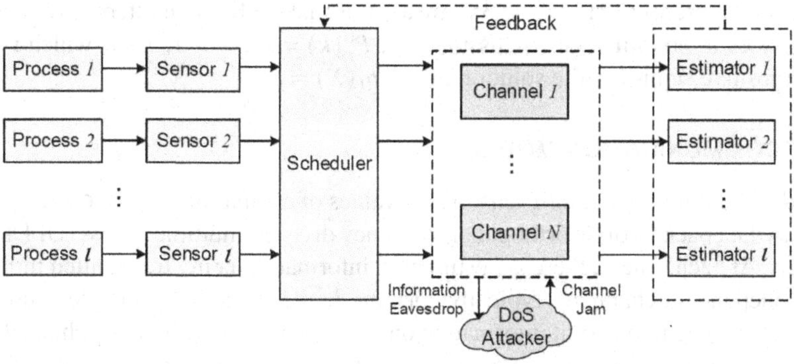

Figure 5.1 Remote state estimation of CPS under a DoS attack.

$\mathbb{E}[v_i(k)v_j^T(t)] = \delta_i^j \delta_k^t R_i, R_i > 0$ and $\mathbb{E}[\omega_i(k)v_j^T(t)] = 0, \forall i, j, k, t$. For each process, the initial state is a zero-mean Gaussian random vector with covariance $\Sigma_i(0) \geq 0$, which is unrelated with $\omega_i(k)$ and $v_i(k)$. Assume that the pair (A_i, C_i) is detectable and $(A_i, Q_i^{1/2})$ is stabilizable.

The smart sensors are assumed to be installed in the plants, where the sensors have the capacity of computing and storage. Hence, Kalman filters run locally to process raw measurement data, which can improve system performance significantly [151]. At each time k, each sensor estimates the state $\hat{x}_i(k)$ based on the measurement information and then sends it to the remote estimator. The estimation error covariance is denoted as

$$P_i^0(k) \triangleq \mathbb{E}\{(x_i(k) - \hat{x}_i(k))(x_i(k) - \hat{x}_i(k))^T | y_i(1), \cdots, y_i(k)\}, \tag{5.2}$$

which are calculated recursively following Kalman filter equations [78]

$$\begin{aligned} \hat{x}_i(k|k-1) &= A_i \hat{x}_i(k-1), \\ P_i^0(k|k-1) &= A_i P_i^0(k-1) A_i^T + Q_i, \\ K_i(k) &= P_i^0(k|k-1) C_i^T (C_i P_i^0(k|k-1) C_i^T + R_i)^{-1}, \\ \hat{x}_i(k) &= \hat{x}_i(k|k-1) + K_i(k)(y_i(k) - C_i \hat{x}_i(k|k-1)), \\ P_i^0(k) &= (I - K_i(k) C_i) P_i^0(k|k-1), \end{aligned} \tag{5.3}$$

where $\hat{x}_i(k|k-1)$ is the priori state estimation and $\hat{x}_i(k)$ is the estimation of states for system i. $P_i^0(k|k-1)$ and $P_i^0(k|k)$ are the priori and posteriori estimate covariance for system i, respectively. $K_i(k)$ is the filtering gain for system i.

To simplify the notation, we define the Lyapunov operator $h_i(\cdot)$ and Riccati operator $g_i(\cdot)$ as

$$\begin{aligned} h_i(X) &\triangleq A_i X A_i^T + Q_i, \\ g_i(X) &\triangleq X - X C_i^T (C_i X C_i^T + R_i)^{-1} C_i X. \end{aligned} \tag{5.4}$$

Similarly to references [216, 217, 235], we assume that the Kalman filters have entered steady states to simplify our discussion, i.e., $P_i^0(k) = \bar{P}_i,\ k > 1,\ i \in \iota$, which is the unique positive semi-definite solution of $g_i \circ h_i(X) = X$.

5.2.2 COMMUNICATION MODEL

As depicted in Fig. 5.1, for ι sensors, the values of estimation $\hat{x}_i(k), i \in \iota$ are transmitted as data packets on N orthogonal frequency division multiple access (OFDMA) channels. At each time k, there is ι estimation information being transmitted through the N independent channels. Typically, for time k, the following principle is used: a sensor is assumed to transmit information on only one channel whereas a channel can be shared by multiple sensors. The sensor will at most select a channel to transmit information and the attacker chooses no more than one to interfere to degrade the signal transmission of estimation information. Denote the following α as the index matrix of channel choice

$$\alpha = \left[\alpha_i^{(n)}\right]_{(\iota+1)\times(N+1)} = \begin{bmatrix} \alpha_0^{(0)} & \alpha_0^{(1)} & \cdots & \alpha_0^{(N)} \\ \alpha_1^{(0)} & \alpha_1^{(1)} & \cdots & \alpha_1^{(N)} \\ \vdots & \vdots & \ddots & \vdots \\ \alpha_\iota^{(0)} & \alpha_\iota^{(1)} & \cdots & \alpha_\iota^{(N)} \end{bmatrix},$$

where $\alpha_i^{(n)},\ i \in \iota, n \in \mathbf{N} \triangleq \{0, 1, \cdots, N\}$ is the binary channel choice index of sensor i and channel n. Typically, $n = 0$ means the sensor adopts a conservative policy to save energy and does not transmit information. $\alpha_i^{(n)} = 1$ if sensor i transmits information by channel n, $\alpha_i^{(n)} = 0$, otherwise. Subscript $i = 0$ represents the player who is the attacker. Index $\alpha_0^{(n)} = 1,\ n \in \mathbf{N}$ means the attacker chooses the nth channel to interfere and especially if $n = 0$ means that the attacker does not jam any channel. Since the sensors and the attacker can each occupy no more than one channel, one has

$$\sum_{n=0}^{N} \alpha_i^{(n)} = 1,\ \forall i \in \{0\} \cup \iota.$$

Let $T_i^{(n)}$ be the transmission power of sensor i on channel n and $J^{(n)}$ be the transmission power of the attacker on channel n. Then, the SINR of sensor i yields

$$\text{SINR}_i = \sum_{n=0}^{N} \frac{\alpha_i^{(n)} g_{i,i}^{(n)} T_i^{(n)}}{\mathcal{I}(n) + \alpha_0^{(n)} g_{i,0}^{(n)} J^{(n)} + (\sigma^{(n)})^2}, \tag{5.5}$$

where $\mathcal{I}(n) = \sum_{j=1, j\neq i}^{\iota} \alpha_j^{(n)} g_{i,j}^{(n)} T_j^{(n)}$, $g_{i,i}^{(n)}$ is the transmission gain from sensor i to the estimator i, $g_{i,j}^{(n)},\ j \neq i$ is the interference gain from the other sensor $j,\ j \neq i$, $g_{i,0}^{(n)}$ denotes the interference gain from the attacker and $(\sigma^{(n)})^2$ is the received background noise at the estimator on channel n, which is assumed to be different on each channel.

Note that the channel gain is determined by transmission distance, shadowing, link fading, carrier frequency, and so on. Hence, the link gains of channels are different and assume that the channel state information (CSI) is available for sensors by using pilot-aided channel estimation technology.

Based on the digital communication theory [110], the inherent relationship between packet error rate (PER) and SINR is depicted as

$$\mathrm{PER}_i = f(\mathrm{SINR}_i), \tag{5.6}$$

where $f(\cdot)$ is a monotonically decreasing function, which depends on the characteristic and modulation schemes. Introduce ι Bernoulli processes $\lambda_i(k), i \in \iota$ to characterize the transmission of sensors. Let $\lambda_i(k) = 0$ denote the estimation $\hat{x}_i(k)$ is lost, otherwise, $\lambda_i(k) = 1$. The overall packet delivery rate depicts that all the bits in a packet arrive at the destination error-free, i.e.,

$$\bar{\beta}_i = \Pr\{\lambda_i(k) = 1\} = (1 - f(\mathrm{SINR}_i))^L, \tag{5.7}$$

where L is the number of bits for a packet. Note that SINR (5.5) is determined by the aggregated channel choices, power strategies of the transmitter and DoS attacker as well as the channel gains. Different levels of SINR lead to different packet dropout rates which further impact the estimation performance as we shall see subsequently.

Remark 7 *The case that different sensors may share the same channel is investigated in this chapter. If the case that different sensors access different channels is realized, enough orthogonal channels must be available for sensors and the channels may not be efficiently used. Compared with the different sensors accessing the different channels case, deploying cochannel sensor operation is able to reuse the spectral resources and, hence, improves the spectral efficiency. Particularly when not enough channels are provided for all sensors, the sensors can also utilize the limited spectrum to transmit information efficiently. We explore the problem of channel allocation and interference management for multiple remote state estimation systems under DoS attack.*

5.2.3 REMOTE STATE ESTIMATION

ι state estimators installed remotely receives signals from N orthogonal channels. $\hat{x}_i(k)$ is the minimum mean-squared error (MMSE) estimation of $x_i(k)$ from the smart sensor according to formula (5.2) and the estimation error covariance is $\bar{P}_i$. The estimation process at the remote estimator is as follows: if $\hat{x}_i(k)$ arrives successfully, the estimator will synchronize the corresponding estimation. Otherwise, the estimator predicts the estimation based on the previous information $\tilde{x}_i(k-1)$ and the system model. In a word, the MMSE estimation at the remote estimator is denoted by

$$\tilde{x}_i(k) = \begin{cases} \hat{x}_i(k), & \lambda_i(k) = 1, \\ A_i\tilde{x}_i(k-1), & \lambda_i(k) = 0. \end{cases}$$

Based on equation (5.2), the associated error covariance at remote estimator $P_i(k)$ for all $k > 1$ is

$$P_i(k) = \begin{cases} \bar{P}_i, & \lambda_i(k) = 1, \\ h_i(P_i(k-1)), & \lambda_i(k) = 0, \end{cases}$$

where $h_i(\cdot)$ is the Lyapunov operator given in (5.4).

It is assumed that the remote estimator transmits acknowledgement (ACK) messages whether the data packet is received successfully or not by the scheduler by reliable transmission link. Meanwhile, the attacker can eavesdrop upon the ACKs to infer the process purposefully.

For sensor i, define $\tau_i(k)$ as the holding time between the present moment and the most recent time when the data packet arrived successfully, i.e., $\tau_i(k) \triangleq k - \max_{0 \le l \le k}\{l : \lambda_i(l) = 1\}$. The relationship between the holding time and estimation error covariance at the remote estimator is $P_i(k) = h_i^{\tau_i(k)}(\bar{P}_i)$.

5.3 ONE-STEP OPTIMIZATION CASE

In this section, a myopic policy aiming at minimizing the expected payoff at the next time is proposed. For sensor i, the expected error covariance is

$$\begin{aligned} \mathrm{Tr}\{\mathbb{E}[P_i(k)]\} =& \beta_i \mathrm{Tr}\{\bar{P}_i\} + (1-\beta_i)\mathrm{Tr}\{h_i^{\tau_i(k-1)+1}(\bar{P}_i)\} \\ =& \beta_i \mathrm{Tr}(\bar{P}_i - h_i^{\tau_i(k-1)+1}(\bar{P}_i)) + \mathrm{Tr}(h_i^{\tau_i(k-1)+1}(\bar{P}_i)). \end{aligned}$$

Radio jamming is a kind of DoS attack in wireless communication that targets disrupting communication by keeping the wireless spectrum busy. It is assumed that a malicious user works to cause most damage to the sensors. On the other side, the transmission of all sensors is coordinated by a scheduler. We take the energy consumption into consideration in the objective function. The objective function is given as follows

$$\begin{aligned} & V(\{\alpha_i^{(n)}, i \in \iota, n \in \mathbf{N}\}, \{\alpha_0^{(n)}, n \in \mathbf{N}\}) \\ =& \sum_{i=1}^{\iota} \left(\mathrm{Tr}\{\mathbb{E}[P_i(k)]\} + \phi_T \sum_{n=1}^{N} \alpha_i^{(n)} T_i^{(n)} \right) - \phi_J \sum_{n=1}^{N} \alpha_0^{(n)} J^{(n)}, \end{aligned}$$

where $\phi_T, \phi_J \ge 0$ are the cost of per power consumption. The scheduler wants to minimize the state estimation error covariance, the power cost of all sensors, and prefers more resource to be consumed by the attacker. In practice, if the performance degradation of the estimation system can bring much cost to the attacker, the attacker tends to invest less to destroy the system. When the resource cost of the attacker is included in the objective function of the scheduler, it reflects that the reward of the scheduler is in terms of how much cost attacker. On the contrary, the jamming attacker wants to interfere with the transmission and in the same analysis procedure, the attacker aims to maximize the payoff. Thus, the scheduler and attacker have opposite objectives and their interactions are well modeled as a noncooperative game. To be more specific, the elements of the game are presented as follows:

1) *Player:* The scheduler and DoS attacker.
2) *Action:* The channel allocation for all sensors, i.e., $\mathcal{A}_T = \{\alpha_i^{(n)}, \forall i \in \iota | \alpha_i^{(n)} \in \{0,1\}, \sum_{n=0}^{N} \alpha_i^{(n)} = 1\}$. The channel choice of the attacker, which is given by $\mathcal{A}_J = \{\alpha_0^{(n)} | \alpha_0^{(n)} \in \{0,1\}, \sum_{n=0}^{N} \alpha_0^{(n)} = 1\}$.
3) *Payoff:* The payoff function of the scheduler is $V(\alpha_i^{(n)}, \alpha_0{}^{(n)*})$, which is a minimizer. The attacker has the opposite objective.

Based on the usage principle, it is known that there are $N+1$ choices for each sensor. The channel choices of all sensors are

$$\vec{\gamma}_T = [n_1, n_2, \cdots, n_\iota], \tag{5.8}$$

where n_i is the index of channel choice for sensor i. Thus, there are $(N+1)^\iota$ strategies for the scheduler. To demarcate each strategy of the scheduler and then give the expression of SINR corresponding to each strategy, the following proposition is introduced.

Proposition 1 *The superscript of strategy $\vec{\gamma}_T^{(r)}$ for the scheduler can be mapped to the sequence $r \in \boldsymbol{R} \triangleq \{1, 2, \cdots, (N+1)^\iota\}$ by using mapping $\mathcal{R}(\cdot)$*

$$r = \mathcal{R}(\vec{\gamma}_T) = \sum_{i=1}^{\iota} (N+1)^{i-1} n_i + 1. \tag{5.9}$$

Moreover, with a known r, the value of n_i is derived by mapping $\Upsilon_i(\cdot), i \in \iota$ as

$$n_i = \Upsilon_i(r) = mod\left(\left\lfloor \frac{r-1}{(N+1)^{i-1}} \right\rfloor, N+1\right), \tag{5.10}$$

where $\lfloor a \rfloor$ denotes the maximum integer not greater than a and $mod(a,b)$ represents the unique nonnegative remainder on division of the integer a by positive integer b.

Proof *Obviously, it is seen that the values of r obtained by* (5.9) *satisfy $r \in \boldsymbol{R}$. We prove that n_i can be derived by* (5.10). *For a given $r \in \boldsymbol{R}$, it yields*

$$\Upsilon_i(r) = mod\left(\left\lfloor \frac{r-1}{(N+1)^{i-1}} \right\rfloor, N+1\right) = mod\left(\sum_{j=i}^{\iota} (N+1)^{j-i} n_i, N+1\right) = n_i. \tag{5.11}$$

This ends the proof.

It is assumed that the sensors and attacker use a fixed power level in a certain channel, where sensors and attacker's power levels are given as

$$\vec{T}_i = [0, T_i^{(1)}, T_i^{(2)}, \cdots, T_i^{(N)}], i \in \iota,$$
$$\vec{J} = [0, J^{(1)}, J^{(2)}, \cdots, J^{(N)}].$$

Notation $\vec{\gamma}_T^{(r)}$ is used to represent the strategy of the scheduler, which can take value from set $\boldsymbol{\gamma}_T = \{\vec{\gamma}_T^{(1)}, \vec{\gamma}_T^{(2)}, \cdots, \vec{\gamma}_T^{((N+1)^\iota)}\}$ and typically, the superscript r is the index of the strategy to correlate with the channel allocation of all sensors. Meanwhile, notation $\vec{\gamma}_J^{(m)} \in \gamma_J = \{\vec{\gamma}_J^{(1)}, \vec{\gamma}_J^{(2)}, \cdots, \vec{\gamma}_J^{(N+1)}\}$ is the strategy of the attacker, where m represents the index of the selected channel to congest.

When the scheduler uses strategy $\vec{\gamma}_T^{(r)}$ and strategy $\vec{\gamma}_J^{(m)}$ is applied by the attacker, based on formula (5.6), the PER of sensor i is

$$\mathrm{PER}_i^{(rm)} = f(\mathrm{SINR}_i^{(rm)}), \tag{5.12}$$

where $\mathrm{SINR}_i^{(rm)}$ is a deformation of equation (5.5) with abusing the symbols of n_i, n_j and n_0, which are defined in the following. According to mapping (5.10), we obtain

$$\Upsilon_i(r) = n_i,\ \Upsilon_j(r) = n_j,\ j \neq i, \tag{5.13}$$

which represents when the scheduler chooses the rth strategy, sensor i selects channel n_i to transmit the data packet, and sensor j uses channel $n_j, j \neq i$. If the attacker uses strategy $\vec{\gamma}_J^{(m)}$, let us denote that he chooses channel n_0. The SINR in equation (5.12) is given by

$$\mathrm{SINR}_i^{(rm)} = \frac{\alpha_i^{(n_i)} g_{i,i}^{(n_i)} T_i^{(n_i)}}{\mathcal{I}(n_i) + \alpha_0^{(n_i)} g_{i,0}^{(n_i)} J^{(n_i)} + (\sigma^{(n_i)})^2} \tag{5.14}$$

with $\mathcal{I}(n_i) = \sum_{j=1, j\neq i}^{\iota} \alpha_j^{(n_i)} g_{i,j}^{(n_i)} T_j^{(n_i)}$, where the binary indexes of channel choices for sensors and attacker are as follows

$$\alpha_i^{(n_i)} = 1,\ \alpha_j^{(n_i)} = \delta_{n_i}^{n_j},\ \alpha_0^{(n_i)} = \delta_{n_i}^{n_0}. \tag{5.15}$$

The scheduler and attacker have opposite objectives, and it forms a zero-sum game. The payoff matrix is given by

$$\mathbf{V} = [V(\vec{\gamma}_T^{(r)}, \vec{\gamma}_J^{(m)})]_{\forall r \in \mathbf{R}, \forall m \in \mathbf{N}}. \tag{5.16}$$

Definition 5.1 *In the two-player zero-sum game between the scheduler and attacker, the Nash equilibrium is a strategy profile* $(\vec{\gamma}_T^{(r^*)}, \vec{\gamma}_J^{(m^*)})$ *that no one can benefit from changing strategies while the other one keeps his strategy unchanged, i.e.,* $V(\vec{\gamma}_T^{(r^*)}, \vec{\gamma}_J^{(m^*)}) \leq V(\vec{\gamma}_T^{(r)}, \vec{\gamma}_J^{(m^*)})$ *and* $V(\vec{\gamma}_T^{(r^*)}, \vec{\gamma}_J^{(m^*)}) \geq V(\vec{\gamma}_T^{(r^*)}, \vec{\gamma}_J^{(m)})$.

Lemma 5.1 *Let* $A = [a_{ij}]_{\forall i,j}$ *be an* $m \times n$ *matrix game with* $\min_i \max_j a_{ij} = \max_j \min_i a_{ij} = V^*(A)$. *Then, matrix A has a saddle point in pure strategies and the optimal value* $V^*(A)$ *is unique.*

For the matrix game of scheduler and attacker with payoff matrix (5.16), if the following equation

$$\min_{r \in \mathbf{R}} \max_{m \in \mathbf{N}} V(\vec{\gamma}_T^{(r)}, \vec{\gamma}_J^{(m)}) = \max_{m \in \mathbf{N}} \min_{r \in \mathbf{R}} V(\vec{\gamma}_T^{(r)}, \vec{\gamma}_J^{(m)}) \tag{5.17}$$

holds, it is concluded that the zero-sum matrix game has a pure strategy Nash equilibrium, where the optimal strategies are denoted as $\vec{\gamma}_T^{(r^*)}$ and $\vec{\gamma}_J^{(m^*)}$. Then, the zero-sum game of scheduler and attacker with payoff function (5.16) is solved, where the channel allocation for sensors is given by $n_i^* = \Upsilon_i(r^*), i \in \iota$. The binary index for sensor $i, i \in \iota$, is $\alpha_i^{(n_i^*)*} = \delta_\vartheta^{n_i^*}$ and the channel choice of attacker is $\alpha_0^{(m^*)*} = \delta_\vartheta^{m^*}$, where ϑ takes value from 0 to N.

For the zero-sum game, the scheduler and attacker's objective functions lead to the well known inequality [185]

$$\min_{r\in\mathbf{R}}\max_{m\in\mathbf{N}} V(\vec{\gamma}_T^{(r)}, \vec{\gamma}_J^{(m)}) \geq \max_{m\in\mathbf{N}}\min_{r\in\mathbf{R}} V(\vec{\gamma}_T^{(r)}, \vec{\gamma}_J^{(m)}). \tag{5.18}$$

According to the previous analysis, it is known that the pure strategy does not exist for most cases. Yet, to obtain an equilibrium solution in matrix game that do not possess a saddle point, a feasible scheme is to enlarge the strategy spaces. That is, allow the players to base their decisions on the outcome of random events which leads to the mixed strategy. A mixed strategy for a player is a probability distribution on the space of his pure strategies. Equivalently, it is a random variable whose values are the players' pure strategy. The following lemma is given to summarize the above results.

Lemma 5.2 *Considering the game between the scheduler and attacker with finite discrete strategy set, it is concluded that the game has a mixed strategy Nash equilibrium in the form of the probability of the finite dimensional action set.*

In Lemma 5.2, the mixed strategy Nash equilibrium for scheduler and attacker is discussed. The strategy of the scheduler is

$$\vec{\pi}_T = \left[\pi_T^{(1)}, \pi_T^{(2)}, \cdots, \pi_T^{(r)}, \cdots, \pi_T^{((N+1)^\iota)}\right]^T,$$

where $\pi_T^{(r)}$, $r \in \mathbf{R}$ represents the probability of choosing the combination of channel assignment r for the scheduler. The strategy of the attacker is

$$\vec{\pi}_J = \left[\pi_J^{(1)}, \pi_J^{(2)} \cdots, \pi_J^{(m)}, \cdots, \pi_J^{(N+1)}\right]^T,$$

where $\pi_J^{(m)}$, $m \in \mathbf{N}$ is the probability of mth choosing a strategy for the attacker.

The strategy of the scheduler and attacker is denoted as $(\vec{\pi}_T, \vec{\pi}_J) \in \hbar$, where $\hbar = (\hbar_T, \hbar_J)$ is the strategy sets for two players with

$$\hbar_T = \left\{\vec{\pi}_T \in \mathbb{R}^{(N+1)^\iota}, \vec{\pi}_T \geq 0, \sum_{r=1}^{(N+1)^\iota} \pi_T^{(r)} = 1\right\}$$

and

$$\hbar_J = \left\{\vec{\pi}_J \in \mathbb{R}^{(N+1)}, \vec{\pi}_J \geq 0, \sum_{r=1}^{(N+1)} \pi_J^{(r)} = 1\right\}.$$

The optimization problem of the scheduler for the zero-sum game is transformed to solve the linear programming

$$\begin{aligned} 1/V^* &= \max_{\xi} \xi^T \mathbf{1}_{(N+1)^\iota} \\ s.t.\ \mathbf{V}^T \xi &\leq \mathbf{1}_{N+1}, \\ \xi &\geq 0, \end{aligned} \tag{5.19}$$

where the optimal mixed strategy of the scheduler is calculated as $\vec{\pi}_T^* = \xi V^*$. The optimal mixed strategy of attacker $\vec{\pi}_J^*$ can be obtained by solving the dual problem of (5.19).

Remark 8 *In the above formulations, it is assumed that only one power level is utilized by each sensor in a certain channel. The situation that multiple power levels are available for sensors can be easily extended. Assume that there are $L_i^{(n)}$ power levels for sensor i in channel n given by $\boldsymbol{T}_i^{(n)} = \{T_i^{(n)}(1), T_i^{(n)}(2), \cdots, T_i^{(n)}(L_i^{(n)})\}$, and sensor i can choose one power level from set $\boldsymbol{T}_i^{(n)}$ to transmit the estimation information if he chooses channel n. Then the channel choice and power control strategy of all sensors are*

$$\begin{aligned} \vec{\gamma}_T =& [T_1^{(n_1)}(l_1^{(n_1)}), T_2^{(n_2)}(l_2^{(n_2)}), \cdots, T_i^{(n_i)}(l_i^{(n_i)}), \cdots, T_\iota^{(n_I)}(l_\iota^{(n_\iota)})], \\ l_i^{(n_i)} \in& \{1, 2, \cdots, L_i^{(n_i)}\}. \end{aligned} \tag{5.20}$$

There are $\prod_{i=1}^{\iota}(1+\sum_{n=1}^{N} L_i^{(n)})$ strategies for the scheduler and $1+\sum_{n=1}^{N} L_0^{(n)}$ strategies for the attacker. What's more, the proposed method in this chapter can also be extended to the case of multiple attackers.

5.4 INFINITE TIME-HORIZON OPTIMIZATION CASE

The monitoring of sensor data continues for a long period, and the jammer will be able to afford to jam the network for a long time. A long-term consideration can present preferable performance compared with the myopic policy especially with time-varying networks. Thus, assume that the secure game is played for an infinite number of stages. A Markov game $\mathcal{G} = \langle \imath, \mathfrak{s}, \hbar, \mathfrak{p}, \mathfrak{U} \rangle$ is set up to depict the interactive process for the scheduler and attacker and the elements in $\mathcal{G}$ represent player, state, action, state transition, and payoff function, respectively. We go into the details of the stochastic game formulation in the following.

5.4.1 PLAYER

The channel allocation for all sensors is coordinated by a scheduler to achieve the optimal benefit. The malicious DoS attacker aims to cause the most damage to the estimation systems. The scheduler $\imath_s$ and DoS attacker $\imath_a$ are viewed as two players of game $\mathcal{G}$, and the two players are assumed to be selfish and rational.

5.4.2 STATE

We consider that there are N channels available for the ι remote state estimation systems. The usability of each channel depends on many factors; for example the main one is that the band is occupied or released by a user with higher priority than the sensors. According to empirical studies on the primary users' access pattern [170], the states of channel $n \in \mathbf{N} \setminus \{0\}$ denoted by $\phi^{(n)}$ can be modeled by a two-state Markov chain, where if the primary user vacates channel n, $\phi^{(n)} = 1$, otherwise, $\phi^{(n)} = 0$. The transition probabilities are denoted by $p_{0,1}^{(n)} = \Pr\{\phi^{(n)}(k+1) = 1 | \phi^{(n)}(k) = 0\}$ and $p_{1,1}^{(n)} = \Pr\{\phi^{(n)}(k+1) = 1 | \phi^{(n)}(k) = 1\}$. For all channels, the access of channels is denoted by $\boldsymbol{\phi} = (\phi^{(1)}, \phi^{(2)}, \cdots, \phi^{(N)})$.

The sensors achieve certain gains by utilizing the spectrum opportunity. The gains are affected by many aspects, including environment change, multi-path propagation, channel fading, and so on. The channel gains can reflect data throughput, delay, environment, or other quality of service measures, which are often increasing functions with respect to channel quality. The fluctuation of channel quality leads to channel gains being time-varying. We assume that the gain of channel n is denoted as $\boldsymbol{g}^{(n)} \triangleq \{g_{ij}^{(n)}, \forall i \in \iota, \forall j \in \{0\} \cup \iota\}$. The channel quality $\boldsymbol{g}^{(n)}$ is often modeled as a finite state Markov chain, which takes value from a set of discrete values, i.e., $\boldsymbol{g}^{(n)} \in \{\mathbf{0}, \boldsymbol{q}_1^{(n)}, \cdots, \boldsymbol{q}_L^{(n)}\}$. The transition probability for channel n is depicted as $p_{l,l'}^{g^{(n)}} = \Pr\{\boldsymbol{g}^{(n)}(k+1) = \boldsymbol{q}_{l'}^{(n)} | \boldsymbol{g}^{(n)}(k) = \boldsymbol{q}_l^{(n)}\}$. For all channels, the channel variation is given by $\boldsymbol{G} = (\boldsymbol{g}^{(1)}, \boldsymbol{g}^{(2)}, \cdots, \boldsymbol{g}^{(N)})$. Note that when the channel $n, n \in \mathbf{N} \setminus \{0\}$ is not available for sensors, the channel gain yields $g_{ij}^{(n)} = 0, \forall i \in \iota, \forall j \in \{0\} \cup \iota$. The finite state Markov chain $(\boldsymbol{\phi}, \boldsymbol{G})$ is used to capture the joint dynamics of both the channel access and quality.

In the above, we have discussed the dynamics of channels' availability and channel gains' fluctuation. Clearly, these dynamics will affect the scheduler and attacker's decisions about how to allocate the channels to transmit estimation data and which channel to choose to interfere with. The decisions of scheduler and attacker lead to a packet dropout rate and affect the estimation error covariance of each sensor at time k, i.e., $P_i(k)$. Denote the estimation error covariance $P_i(k-1)$ of sensor i as the state of the process at step k, which is denoted as $s_i(k) \triangleq P_i(k-1)$. We have $s_i(k) \in \mathbf{S}_i \triangleq \{\bar{P}_i,\ h_i(\bar{P}_i),\ h_i^2(\bar{P}_i),\ \cdots\}$, $i \in \iota$. For the player who is the scheduler, the state $\boldsymbol{s}$ is defined as the combination of all sensors' error covariance, where $\boldsymbol{s}(k) \triangleq (s_1(k), s_2(k), \cdots, s_\iota(k))$. If the scheduler uses channel allocation strategy r and the attacker chooses channel m, the transition probability for sensor i is derived as follows

$$\Pr\{s_i(k+1) | s_i(k)\} = \begin{cases} \bar{\beta}_i^{(rm)}, & \text{if } P_i(k) = \bar{P}_i, \\ 1 - \bar{\beta}_i^{(rm)}, & \text{if } P_i(k) = h_i(P_i(k-1)), \\ 0, & \text{otherwise}, \end{cases} \tag{5.21}$$

where $\bar{\beta}_i^{(rm)}$ is obtained by substituting (5.14) into (5.7).

In summary, the state of the Markov game $\mathcal{G}$ is defined as $\mathfrak{s} = (\boldsymbol{\phi}, \boldsymbol{G}, \boldsymbol{s})$, which denotes the state associated with channel access, channel quality, and estimation error covariance containing all channels and all sensors.

5.4.3 ACTION

The game moves forward over time. The scheduler needs to choose which combination of channel assignments for sensors to send the estimation packets. The attacker will choose a channel to block and then degrade the transmission performance. In this part, the principle that only one channel is available for each sensor and each channel can be chosen by multiple sensors simultaneously is still observed by the scheduler. Thus, there are $(N+1)^{\iota}$ strategies for the scheduler, and the strategy is $\vec{\gamma}_T \in \gamma_T$ and the attacker's action is $\vec{\gamma}_J \in \gamma_J$, which are the same as the ones in Section III. Note that if a certain channel n is not available for the sensors, we also assume that the scheduler can assign a sensor to transmit information on it, where it has been assumed that the channel gain $g_{ij}^{(n)} = 0, \forall i \in \iota, \forall j \in \{0\} \cup \iota$ in Subsection IV.B, which results in zero SINR in channel n.

5.4.4 STATE TRANSITION

With the defined state and action space, the state transition rule is discussed in this part. It is assumed that the scheduler and attacker choose their actions at each time independently. We first discuss the transition process of channels' status and channel condition.

The transition probability of the finite Markov chain for channel n with state $(\phi^{(n)}, \boldsymbol{g}^{(n)})$ is derived. When the nth channel is not available for sensors in two consecutive time slots, one has that

$$\Pr\{\phi^{(n)}(k+1) = 0, \boldsymbol{g}^{(n)}(k+1) = \boldsymbol{0} | \phi^{(n)}(k) = 0, \boldsymbol{g}^{(n)}(k) = \boldsymbol{0}\} = 1 - p_{0,1}^{(n)}. \quad (5.22)$$

When the nth channel is not available in time slot k, while it is available in time slot $k+1$ with gain $\boldsymbol{q}_l^{(n)}$, we have

$$\Pr\{\phi^{(n)}(k+1) = 1, \boldsymbol{g}^{(n)}(k+1) = \boldsymbol{q}_l^{(n)} | \phi^{(n)}(k) = 0, \boldsymbol{g}^{(n)}(k) = \boldsymbol{0}\} = p_{0,1}^{(n)} p_{0,l}^{\boldsymbol{g}^{(n)}}. \quad (5.23)$$

If the nth channel is available for sensors in two consecutive time slots, the state transition probability is given by

$$\Pr\{\phi^{(n)}(k+1) = 1, \boldsymbol{g}^{(n)}(k+1) = \boldsymbol{q}_{l'}^{(n)} | \phi^{(n)}(k) = 1, \boldsymbol{g}^{(n)}(k) = \boldsymbol{q}_l^{(n)}\} = p_{1,1}^{(n)} p_{l,l'}^{\boldsymbol{g}^{(n)}}. \quad (5.24)$$

Finally, when the nth channel turns unavailable from time slot k to time slot $k+1$, the transition probability is

$$\Pr\{\phi^{(n)}(k+1) = 0, \boldsymbol{g}^{(n)}(k+1) = \boldsymbol{0} | \phi^{(n)}(k) = 1, \boldsymbol{g}^{(n)}(k) = \boldsymbol{q}_l^{(n)}\} = 1 - p_{1,1}^{(n)}. \quad (5.25)$$

We assume that the status and condition of each channel are independent, and consequently the transition probability for all of the N channels yields

$$\Pr\{\boldsymbol{\phi}(k+1),\boldsymbol{G}(k+1)|\boldsymbol{\phi}(k),\boldsymbol{G}(k)\} = \prod_{n=1}^{N}\Pr\{\phi^{(n)}(k+1),\boldsymbol{g}^{(n)}(k+1)|\phi^{(n)}(k),\boldsymbol{g}^{(n)}(k)\}.$$

Effected by the channel variations and players' strategies and based on equation (5.21), the transition probability cannot be written in the form of each sensor's transition. Thus the process of state transition given in

$$\Pr\{\mathfrak{s}(k+1)|\mathfrak{s}(k),\vec{\gamma}_T^{(r)}(k),\vec{\gamma}_J^{(m)}(k)\} \tag{5.26}$$

is related to all sensors' strategies and channel variations.

5.4.5 PAYOFF FUNCTION

The average estimation error covariance is used to quantify the the system performance, which is denoted as $\mathbb{E}[P_i(k)]$ for sensor $i, i \in \iota$. To be energy saving, the power consumption is taken into account. For simplification, the fixed transmission power levels are assumed for each sensor and attacker in different channels. Then, the payoff for the scheduler at time step k is written as

$$\begin{aligned} &C_k(\mathfrak{s}(k),\vec{\gamma}_T^{(r)}(k),\vec{\gamma}_J^{(m)}(k)) \\ &= \sum_{i=1}^{\iota}\left\{\mathrm{Tr}\{\mathbb{E}[P_i(k)]\} + \phi_T\sum_{n=0}^{N}\alpha_i^{(n)}(k)T_i^{(n)}\right\} - \phi_J\sum_{n=0}^{N}\alpha_0^{(n)}(k)J^{(n)}. \end{aligned} \tag{5.27}$$

In general, sensors have a long sequence of data to transmit. Thus, it is assumed that the Markov game is played for an infinite number of stages. Moreover, the players treat the payoff in different stages differently; e.g., in delay-sensitive applications, delayed messages will be worth less. A recent payoff should weight more than a payoff that will be received in the faraway future. So players' optimal strategies should be derived based on the expected sum of discount payoff function

$$F(\mathfrak{s},\vec{\pi}_T,\vec{\pi}_J) = \sum_{k=0}^{+\infty}\rho^k\mathbb{E}\{C_k|\vec{\pi}_T,\vec{\pi}_J,\mathfrak{s}_0=\mathfrak{s}\}, \tag{5.28}$$

where $\mathfrak{s}_0$ is the initial state, C_k is the reward at time step k, scalar ρ is the discount factor, which can take values from interval $(0,1)$. The discount functions $\mathfrak{U} = (F_T, F_J)$ for scheduler and attacker are the following, respectively.

$$F_T = F(\mathfrak{s},\vec{\pi}_T,\vec{\pi}_J),\ F_J = -F(\mathfrak{s},\vec{\pi}_T,\vec{\pi}_J).$$

Remark 9 *Typical methods dealing with the Markov game, such as value iteration, policy iteration, and dynamic programming, etc, require the knowledge of information* *including system parameters, state transition probability, and the closed-form of reward function. Based on the analysis in subsection IV.D, the state transition* (5.26) *is related to and coupled with all sensors' strategies and channel variations. Thus, the state transition probability cannot be calculated and the closed-form expression of reward function cannot be obtained. The Q-learning method just needs the knowledge of system parameters to obtain the value of the reward and provides a practical way to solve a Markov game with limited information which motivates us to use the Q-learning method to solve the Markov game problem in the next section.*

5.5 SOLUTION FOR MARKOV GAME $\mathcal{G}$

It is known that the game between the scheduler and attacker is a zero-sum Markov game. In order to attain the optimal strategy with a long-term interest as formula (5.28), the minimax-Q learning method is introduced, which can allow the players to find their optimal game payoffs and their optimal strategies when not knowing the transition probabilities. The following lemma is provided for further analysis.

Lemma 5.3 *[128] Considering the discounted cost problem* (5.28) *which can be regarded as a Markov decision process, the optimal value of objective function* $F^*(\mathfrak{s})$ *satisfies the optimal Bellman equation as follows*

$$F^*(\mathfrak{s}) = \min_{\vec{\pi}_T} \max_{\vec{\pi}_J} \left\{ C(\mathfrak{s}, \vec{\gamma}_T^{(r)}, \vec{\gamma}_J^{(m)}) + \rho \sum_{\mathfrak{s} \in \mathfrak{S}} Pr\{\mathfrak{s}' | \mathfrak{s}, \vec{\gamma}_T^{(r)}, \vec{\gamma}_J^{(m)})\} F^*(\mathfrak{s}') \right\}, \quad (5.29)$$

where $\mathfrak{S}$ *is the set of all possible state* $\mathfrak{s}$.

Since the expression of transition probability of the Markov game is complex or even unknown for us, the Q-function updating method [128] is applied instead of the value iteration method [181] in this chapter. We define a function Q such that

$$\mathrm{Q}^*\left(\mathfrak{s}, \gamma_T^{(r)}, \gamma_J^{(m)}\right) = C\left(\mathfrak{s}, \gamma_T^{(r)}, \gamma_J^{(m)}\right) + \rho \sum_{\mathfrak{s} \in \mathfrak{S}} \Pr\left\{\mathfrak{s}' \mid \mathfrak{s}, \gamma_T^{(r)}, \gamma_J^{(m)}\right\} F^*(\mathfrak{s}'), \quad (5.30)$$

where $\mathrm{Q}^*(\mathfrak{s}, \vec{\gamma}_T^{(r)}, \vec{\gamma}_J^{(m)})$ is the total discounted payoff when taking action $\vec{\gamma}_T^{(r)}$ and $\vec{\gamma}_J^{(m)}$ in state $\mathfrak{s}$. $\mathfrak{S}$ is the set of all possible state $\mathfrak{s}$. Comparing equation (5.30) with equation (5.29), it is known that

$$F^*(\mathfrak{s}) = \min_{\vec{\pi}_T} \max_{\vec{\pi}_J} \mathrm{Q}^*(\mathfrak{s}, \vec{\gamma}_T^{(r)}, \vec{\gamma}_J^{(m)}). \quad (5.31)$$

Then, the problem is turned to find the function $\mathrm{Q}^*(\mathfrak{s}, \vec{\gamma}_T^{(r)}, \vec{\gamma}_J^{(m)})$ and $F^*(\mathfrak{s})$ will be obtained by a minimax operation. Q-learning is an updating procedure, in which players choose an initial value $\mathrm{Q}_0(\mathfrak{s}, \vec{\gamma}_T^{(r)}, \vec{\gamma}_J^{(m)}), \forall \mathfrak{s} \in \mathfrak{S}, \forall \vec{\gamma}_T^{(r)} \in \boldsymbol{\gamma}_T, \forall \vec{\gamma}_J^{(m)} \in \boldsymbol{\gamma}_J$ and then iterate as

$$\begin{aligned}\mathrm{Q}_{k+1}(\mathfrak{s},\vec{\gamma}_T^{(r)},\vec{\gamma}_J^{(m)}) =&(1-\varrho_k(\mathfrak{s},\vec{\gamma}_T^{(r)},\vec{\gamma}_J^{(m)}))\mathrm{Q}_k(\mathfrak{s},\vec{\gamma}_T^{(r)},\vec{\gamma}_J^{(m)})\\ &+\varrho_k(\mathfrak{s},\vec{\gamma}_T^{(r)},\vec{\gamma}_J^{(m)})[C(\mathfrak{s},\vec{\gamma}_T^{(r)},\vec{\gamma}_J^{(m)})\\ &+\rho\min_{\vec{\pi}_T}\max_{\vec{\pi}_J}\mathbf{Q}_k(\mathfrak{s}')],\end{aligned} \tag{5.32}$$

where $\mathbf{Q}_{k+1}(\mathfrak{s}) = [\mathrm{Q}_{k+1}(\mathfrak{s},\vec{\gamma}_T^{(r)},\vec{\gamma}_J^{(m)})]_{r\in\mathbf{R},m\in\mathbf{N}}$ and $\varrho_k(\mathfrak{s},\vec{\gamma}_T^{(r)},\vec{\gamma}_J^{(m)})$ is the learning rate sequence.

Assumption 1 *For the proof of convergence of Q-learning, the infinite sampling and decaying of learning rate $\varrho_k(\mathfrak{s},\vec{\gamma}_T^{(r)},\vec{\gamma}_J^{(m)})$ are assumed as follows [78]:*

1) *The state $\mathfrak{s}\in\mathfrak{S}$ and actions $\vec{\gamma}_T^{(r)}\in\boldsymbol{\gamma}_T$ and $\vec{\gamma}_J^{(m)}\in\boldsymbol{\gamma}_J$ of the scheduler and attacker are visited infinitely often.*
2) *The learning rate should satisfy $\varrho_k(\mathfrak{s},\vec{\gamma}_T^{(r)},\vec{\gamma}_J^{(m)})\in[0,1)$, $\sum_{k=0}^{+\infty}\varrho_k(\mathfrak{s},\vec{\gamma}_T^{(r)},\vec{\gamma}_J^{(m)}) = +\infty$ and $\sum_{k=0}^{+\infty}\varrho_k^2(\mathfrak{s},\vec{\gamma}_T^{(r)},\vec{\gamma}_J^{(m)}) < +\infty$. $\varrho_k(\mathfrak{s},\vec{\gamma}_T^{(r)},\vec{\gamma}_J^{(m)}) = 0$, if the state and the strategies are not the same as the current ones. That is, the players only update the Q-value corresponding to the current state and actions.*

Lemma 5.4 *[103] Denoting $\mathbb{Q}$ as the space of function $\boldsymbol{Q}$, define an operator $\mathcal{P}:\mathbb{Q}\to\mathbb{Q}$. Under the two items in Assumption 1, the minimax-Q learning*

$$\boldsymbol{Q}_{k+1}(\mathfrak{s}) = (1-\varrho_k(\mathfrak{s}))\boldsymbol{Q}_k(\mathfrak{s}) + \varrho_k(\mathfrak{s})[\mathcal{P}\boldsymbol{Q}(\mathfrak{s})] \tag{5.33}$$

will converge to the optimal value $\boldsymbol{Q}^*(\mathfrak{s})$ if the following conditions hold:

1) *Q function defined in space $\mathbb{Q}$ satisfies $\boldsymbol{Q}^*(\mathfrak{s}) = \mathbb{E}\{\mathcal{P}\boldsymbol{Q}^*(\mathfrak{s})\}$.*
2) *For all $\mathfrak{s}\in\mathfrak{S}$, $\boldsymbol{Q}(\mathfrak{s})$, $\boldsymbol{Q}^*(\mathfrak{s})\in\mathbb{Q}$, if there exist $0<\varpi<1$ and ς_k converging to zero with probability 1 such that*

$$\|\mathcal{P}\boldsymbol{Q}(\mathfrak{s}) - \mathcal{P}\boldsymbol{Q}^*(\mathfrak{s})\| \le \varpi\|\boldsymbol{Q}(\mathfrak{s}) - \boldsymbol{Q}^*(\mathfrak{s})\| + \varsigma_k,$$

then iteration $\boldsymbol{Q}_k(\mathfrak{s})$ given in (5.33) converges to $\boldsymbol{Q}^*(\mathfrak{s})$ with probability 1.

Theorem 5.1 *Without knowing the transition probability, $\boldsymbol{Q}(\mathfrak{s})$ is updated as iteration (5.32), where learning rate $\varrho_k(\mathfrak{s})$ takes the form of the reciprocal of the times of the occurrence for the state and action pair, i.e.,*

$$\varrho_k(\mathfrak{s},\vec{\gamma}_T^{(r)},\vec{\gamma}_J^{(m)}) = \begin{cases} a/(b+count(\mathfrak{s},\vec{\gamma}_T^{(r)},\vec{\gamma}_J^{(m)})),\\ \text{if } (\mathfrak{s},\vec{\gamma}_T^{(r)},\vec{\gamma}_J^{(m)}) = (\mathfrak{s}(k),\vec{\gamma}_T^{(r)}(k),\vec{\gamma}_J^{(m)}(k))\\ 0, \qquad\qquad \text{otherwise,}\end{cases} \tag{5.34}$$

where $a>0, b>0$, $a<b$ and $count(\mathfrak{s},\vec{\gamma}_T^{(r)},\vec{\gamma}_J^{(m)})$ is the times of the occurrence for pair $(\mathfrak{s},\vec{\gamma}_T^{(r)},\vec{\gamma}_J^{(m)})$. With large enough iteration steps, iteration (5.32) will converge to $\boldsymbol{Q}^*(\mathfrak{s})$, where the game value is calculated as (5.31) and the Nash strategies are π_T^*, π_J^*.

Proof *The learning rate $\varrho_k(\mathfrak{s})$ in the form of (5.34) satisfies Assumption 1 [103]. Based on Lemma 5.3, the discount payoff function (5.28) is turned to solve equation (5.29). For all $\mathfrak{s} \in \mathfrak{S}, r \in \boldsymbol{R}, m \in \boldsymbol{N}$, define the operator $\mathcal{P}$ as*

$$\mathcal{P}Q(\mathfrak{s}, \vec{\gamma}_T^{(r)}, \vec{\gamma}_J^{(m)}) = C(\mathfrak{s}, \vec{\gamma}_T^{(r)}, \vec{\gamma}_J^{(m)}) + \rho F^*(\mathfrak{s}'),$$

which is rewritten in a compact form

$$\mathcal{P}\boldsymbol{Q}^*(\mathfrak{s}) = \boldsymbol{C}(\mathfrak{s}) + \rho F^*(\mathfrak{s}')\boldsymbol{I}$$

where $\boldsymbol{Q}^* \in \mathbb{Q}$ with $\boldsymbol{C}_k(\mathfrak{s}(k)) = [C_k(\mathfrak{s}(k), \vec{\gamma}_T^{(r)}(k), \vec{\gamma}_J^{(m)}(k)]_{r \in \boldsymbol{R}, m \in \boldsymbol{N}}$. By deduction

$$\begin{aligned} \mathbb{E}\{\mathcal{P}\boldsymbol{Q}^*(\mathfrak{s})\} &= \sum_{\mathfrak{s}' \in \mathfrak{S}} Pr\{\mathfrak{s}'|\mathfrak{s}\}\{\boldsymbol{C}(\mathfrak{s}) + \rho F^*(\mathfrak{s}')\boldsymbol{I}\} \\ &= \boldsymbol{C}(\mathfrak{s}) + \rho \sum_{\mathfrak{s}' \in \mathfrak{S}} Pr\{\mathfrak{s}'|\mathfrak{s}\} F^*(\mathfrak{s}')\boldsymbol{I}\} \\ &= \boldsymbol{Q}^*(\mathfrak{s}), \end{aligned}$$

where it is known Item 1) in Lemma 5.4 satisfies. Let $\boldsymbol{Q}_1(\mathfrak{s})$ and $\boldsymbol{Q}_2(\mathfrak{s})$ be elements in space $\mathbb{Q}$. The distance of the two functions is defined as

$$\|\boldsymbol{Q}_1(\mathfrak{s}) - \boldsymbol{Q}_2(\mathfrak{s})\| = \max_{\vec{\gamma}_T^{(r)} \in \gamma_T, \vec{\gamma}_J^{(m)} \in \gamma_J} \|Q_1(\mathfrak{s}, \vec{\gamma}_T^{(r)}, \vec{\gamma}_J^{(m)}) - Q_2(\mathfrak{s}, \vec{\gamma}_T^{(r)}, \vec{\gamma}_J^{(m)})\|. \tag{5.35}$$

By defining $|\boldsymbol{Q}(\mathfrak{s})| = [|\boldsymbol{Q}(\mathfrak{s}, i, j)|]_{i \in \boldsymbol{R}, j \in \boldsymbol{N}}$, it is obviously known that

$$|\boldsymbol{Q}_1(\mathfrak{s}) - \boldsymbol{Q}_2(\mathfrak{s})| \leq \|\boldsymbol{Q}_1(\mathfrak{s}) - \boldsymbol{Q}_2(\mathfrak{s})\|\boldsymbol{I}. \tag{5.36}$$

With (5.35) and (5.36), it is obtained that

$$\begin{aligned} \boldsymbol{Q}_1(\mathfrak{s}) &\leq \boldsymbol{Q}_2(\mathfrak{s}) + \|\boldsymbol{Q}_1(\mathfrak{s}) - \boldsymbol{Q}_2(\mathfrak{s})\|\boldsymbol{I}, \\ \boldsymbol{Q}_1(\mathfrak{s}) &\geq \boldsymbol{Q}_2(\mathfrak{s}) - \|\boldsymbol{Q}_1(\mathfrak{s}) - \boldsymbol{Q}_2(\mathfrak{s})\|\boldsymbol{I}. \end{aligned} \tag{5.37}$$

Obviously, for matrices A, B, if $A \geq B$, then $\min\max A \geq \min\max B$. Taking the minimax operation for (5.37), we have

$$|\min_{\vec{\pi}_T} \max_{\vec{\pi}_J} \boldsymbol{Q}_1(\mathfrak{s}) - \min_{\vec{\pi}_T} \max_{\vec{\pi}_J} \boldsymbol{Q}_2(\mathfrak{s})| \leq \|\boldsymbol{Q}_1(\mathfrak{s}) - \boldsymbol{Q}_2(\mathfrak{s})\|. \tag{5.38}$$

With inequality (5.38), one has that

$$\begin{aligned} \|\mathcal{P}\boldsymbol{Q}(\mathfrak{s}) - \mathcal{P}\boldsymbol{Q}^*(\mathfrak{s})\| &= \rho |\min_{\vec{\pi}_T} \max_{\vec{\pi}_J} \boldsymbol{Q}(\mathfrak{s}) - \min_{\vec{\pi}_T} \max_{\vec{\pi}_J} \boldsymbol{Q}^*(\mathfrak{s})| \\ &\leq \rho \|\boldsymbol{Q}(\mathfrak{s}) - \boldsymbol{Q}^*(\mathfrak{s})\|, \forall \mathfrak{s} \in \mathfrak{S}. \end{aligned}$$

It is concluded that $\mathcal{P}$ is a contraction operator and by Lemma 5.4 with $\varsigma_k = 0$, $\boldsymbol{Q}(\mathfrak{s}) \to \boldsymbol{Q}^*(\mathfrak{s})$ with probability 1, for all $\mathfrak{s} \in \mathfrak{S}$.

Algorithm 3 Minimax-Q learning algorithm

1: Initialize $Q_0(\mathfrak{s},\vec{\gamma}_T^{(r)},\vec{\gamma}_J^{(m)})$, $F^*(\mathfrak{s})$, for all $\mathfrak{s}\in\mathfrak{S}$, $\vec{\gamma}_T^{(r)}\in\gamma_T$, $\vec{\gamma}_J^{(m)}\in\gamma_J$. Initialize $\pi_T^{(r)}\leftarrow 1/(N+1)^\iota,\forall r\in\mathbf{R}$ and $\pi_J^{(m)}\leftarrow 1/(N+1),\forall m\in\mathbf{N}$. Set $k\leftarrow 0$, $\text{flag}_0(\mathfrak{s},\vec{\gamma}_T^{(r)},\vec{\gamma}_J^{(m)})\leftarrow 0,\forall\mathfrak{s}\in\mathfrak{S},\forall\vec{\gamma}_T^{(r)}\in\gamma_T,\forall\vec{\gamma}_J^{(m)}\in\gamma_J$. Give parameters ρ,ϕ_T,ϕ_J and a small enough parameter ε.
2: **while** $\|\mathbf{Q}_{k+1}(\mathfrak{s})-\mathbf{Q}_k(\mathfrak{s})\|>\varepsilon$ **do**
3: With probability p_{exp}, return actions uniformly at random. Otherwise, select actions $\vec{\gamma}_T^{(r')}(k)$ and $\vec{\gamma}_J^{(m')}(k)$ for the scheduler and attacker based on the mixed strategies $\vec{\pi}_T^*$ and $\vec{\pi}_J^*$ randomly.
4: Observing the next state $\mathfrak{s}(k+1)$, update the Q-value in formula (5.32).
5: Calculate the Nash equilibrium based on equation (5.31) by using linear programming (5.19).
6: Compute the corresponding mixed strategy $\vec{\pi}_T^*$ and $\vec{\pi}_J^*$.
7: $k\leftarrow k+1$.
8: **end while**

Remark 10 *If we do not consider the attacker and only sensors exist in the CPS, the Markov game $\mathcal{G}$ can be transformed into a Markov decision process. The Q-learning process* (5.32) *is replaced by*

$$\begin{aligned}Q_{k+1}(\mathfrak{s},\vec{\gamma}_T^{(r)}) =&(1-\varrho_k(\mathfrak{s},\vec{\gamma}_T^{(r)}))Q_k(\mathfrak{s},\vec{\gamma}_T^{(r)})\\&+\varrho_k(\mathfrak{s},\vec{\gamma}_T^{(r)})[C(\mathfrak{s},\vec{\gamma}_T^{(r)})+\rho\min_{\vec{\gamma}_T^{(r)}}Q_{k+1}(\mathfrak{s}')],\end{aligned}\tag{5.39}$$

where

$$C_k(\mathfrak{s}(k),\vec{\gamma}_T^{(r)}(k))=\sum_{i=1}^{\iota}\left\{Tr\{\mathbb{E}[P_i(k)]\}+\phi_T\sum_{n=0}^{N}\alpha_i^{(n)}(k)T_i^{(n)}\right\}.$$

Remark 11 *There are some other algorithmic techniques for solving the stochastic game, including value iteration and Newton's method. However, these methods require the reward for all states, which are not always available for the scheduler and attacker. The disadvantages can be overcome by using the minimax-Q learning method employed in this chapter, where the transition probability is hard to calculated as in* (5.26)*. The executing of minimax-Q learning as Algorithm 1 just requires the system parameters, such as $\bar{P}_i$, A_i, Q_i, C_i, R_i, ϕ_T, and ϕ_J, and the ACK messages for players. The space complexity of the learning Algorithm 1 is $(N+1)^{(I+1)}|\mathfrak{s}|$. The computational complexity is dominated by the calculation of the Nash equilibrium in the matrix game.*

Corollary 2 *When the process noise and measurement noise are related, if (A_i,C_i) is detectable and $(A_i-\Theta_iR_i^{-1}C_i,Q_i-\Theta_iR_i^{-1}\Theta_i^T)$ is stabilizable, the operators in* *equation* (5.4) *are redefined as [188]*

$$\begin{aligned} h_i(X) &\triangleq (A_i - \Theta_i R_i^{-1} C_i) X (A_i - \Theta_i R_i^{-1} C_i)^T + Q_i - \Theta_i R_i^{-1} \Theta_i^T, \\ g_i(X) &\triangleq X - X C_i^T (C_i X C_i^T + R_i)^{-1} C_i X, \end{aligned} \tag{5.40}$$

where Θ_i *is the covariance matrix of* $\omega_i(k)$ *and* $v_i(k)$, *i.e.,* $\mathbb{E}[\omega_i(k) v_j^T(t)] = \delta_i^j \delta_k^t \Theta_i, \forall i, j, k, t$. *Denoting* $\bar{P}_i^c$ *as the steady state by iterations in* (5.40), *when there are* $\tau_i(k)$ *consecutive packet dropouts, the estimation error covariance at the remote estimator is*

$$P_i(k) = h_i^{\tau_i(k)}(\bar{P}_i^c),$$

and the proposed Markov game method of this chapter still holds for the noise correlation case.

5.6 SIMULATION RESULTS

In this section, some examples are presented to illustrate the validity of the proposed method in this chapter. Here, we consider a CPS with two state estimation processes and remote state estimators. The system parameters of the monitored dynamic processes are given by

$$\begin{aligned} &A_1 = \begin{bmatrix} 1 & 0.5 \\ 0 & 1.05 \end{bmatrix}, \ C_1 = \begin{bmatrix} 1 \\ 0 \end{bmatrix}^T, \ Q_1 = \begin{bmatrix} 0.8 & 0 \\ 0 & 0.8 \end{bmatrix}, \\ &A_2 = \begin{bmatrix} 1 & 0 \\ 0 & 1.05 \end{bmatrix}, \ C_2 = \begin{bmatrix} 1 \\ 0 \end{bmatrix}^T, \ Q_2 = \begin{bmatrix} 0.5 & 0 \\ 0 & 0.5 \end{bmatrix}, \\ &R_1 = \begin{bmatrix} 0.8 \end{bmatrix}, \ R_2 = \begin{bmatrix} 0.5 \end{bmatrix}. \end{aligned}$$

It is assumed that two channels are available for the two estimation processes. The channel gains and interference gains $g_{i,j}^{(n)}, i \in \iota, j \in \{0\} \bigcup \iota, n \in \mathbf{N} \setminus \{0\}$ are listed in Table 5.1. The additive white noise powers of channels are $(\sigma^{(1)})^2 = 1$, $(\sigma^{(2)})^2 = 3$. The transmission powers of sensors on different channels are shown in Table 5.2. We adopt a specific form of $f(\cdot)$ in (5.6), i.e., $f(\text{SINR}) = e^{-\text{SINR}}$ when it is assumed that the wireless channels are fast-fading.

Table 5.1
Channel gains $g_{i,j}^{(1)}, g_{i,j}^{(2)}$

	$j=0$	$j=1$	$j=2$
$i=0$	-	-	-
$i=1$	0.4, 0.1	0.7, 0.8	0.2, 0.3
$i=2$	0.3, 0.2	0.4, 0.2	0.5, 0.9

Table 5.2
Transmission power

	$J^{(n)}$	$T_1^{(n)}$	$T_2^{(n)}$
$n=0$	0	0	0
$n=1$	1.5	4	2
$n=2$	2	2	3

5.6.1 LONG-TERM CASE STUDY WITHOUT ATTACKER

We assume that only one estimation process exists in the CPS and a long-term running under a dynamic network environment are taken into account in this part. There are two states of the channel gains, which are $\boldsymbol{G}_1 = (0.25, 0.8)$ and $\boldsymbol{G}_2 = (0.1, 0.3)$. The transition probabilities are $\Pr\{\boldsymbol{G}_1|\boldsymbol{G}_1\} = 0.6$ and $\Pr\{\boldsymbol{G}_1|\boldsymbol{G}_2\} = 0.6$. We restrict that the state set $\mathbf{S}_1$ is finite and equals $\mathbf{S}_1 = \{\bar{P}_1, h_1(\bar{P}_1), h_1^2(\bar{P}_1)\}$. For learning rate (5.34), the values $a = 10$ and $b = 15$ are taken.

The learning process is shown in Fig. 5.2, where different states are represented by solid lines in different colours. The converged Q-values are shown in Table 5.3. The boldface value is the optimal Q-value in each state, which shows that the sensor will choose channel 2, 1, 1, 0, 0, 0, respectively. It is known that the sensor tends to not transmit the estimation information when the channel gains are low.

The accumulated average payoff at each iteration k is calculated as

$$C_{av}(k) = \frac{1}{k}\sum_{l=0}^{k} C_l(\mathfrak{s}(l), \vec{\gamma}_T^{(r)*}(l)). \tag{5.41}$$

Two different scenarios are presented:

1. Time-varying network scenario: The learning process and optimal strategies are obtained based on time-varying networks;
2. Invariant network scenario: The learning process and optimal strategies are obtained based on an invariant network, i.e., state (G_1, S_1).

In practice, the network is time-varying, which is jumping between states G_1 and G_2. The accumulated average payoff $C_{av}(k)$ under the time-varying network scenario and invariant network scenario is shown in Fig. 5.3, which illustrates that the strategies obtained with the time-varying scenario achieve better performance. In Fig. 5.4, we present the optimal payoff $\min_{\vec{\gamma}_T^{(r)}} \mathbf{Q}$ of all states versus per power cost ϕ_T, which shows that the worse performance can be obtained with higher cost of per power.

5.6.2 LONG-TERM CASE STUDY OF SENSORS AND ATTACKER

For simplification, we consider the two estimation processes as (5.41) that transmit information in two channels. To reduce the computational burden, it is assumed that

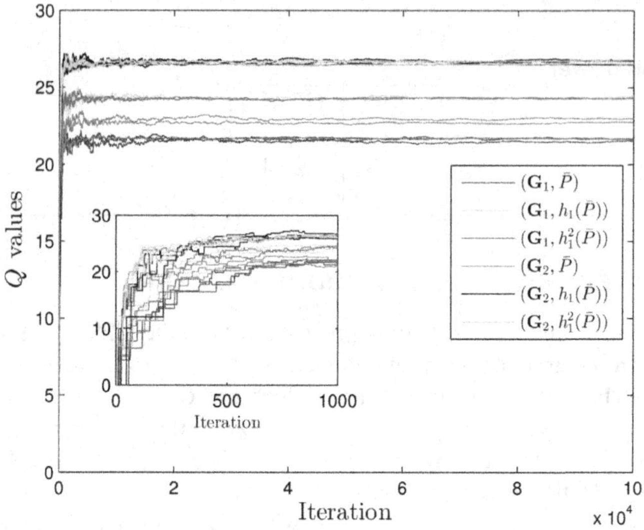

Figure 5.2 Learning process of Q-values with time-varying networks.

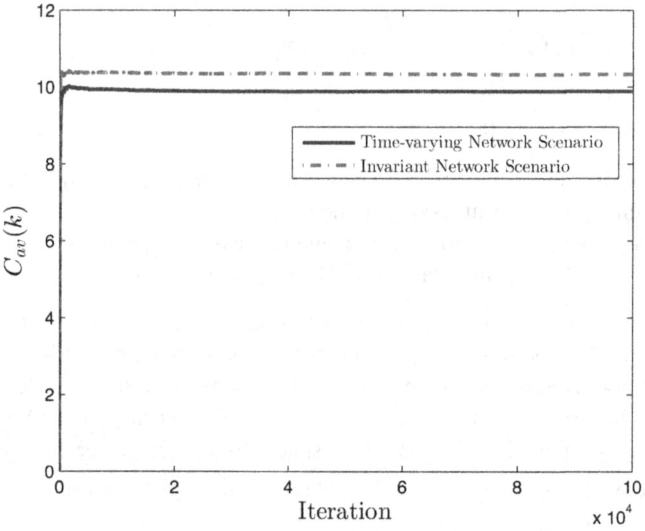

Figure 5.3 Performance comparison with time-varying networks.

Table 5.3
Converged Q values for the sensor

	$n = 0$	$n = 1$	$n = 2$
$(G_1, \bar{P}_1)$	21.6697	21.5911	**21.4982**
$(G_1, h_1(\bar{P}_1))$	26.4741	**24.2407**	24.4108
$(G_1, h_1^2(\bar{P}_1))$	26.5169	**24.2638**	24.3038
$(G_2, \bar{P}_1)$	**21.6625**	22.9828	22.7399
$(G_2, h_1(\bar{P}_1))$	**26.4789**	26.7958	26.7213
$(G_2, h_1^2(\bar{P}_1))$	**26.5350**	26.7969	26.6697

Table 5.4
Optimal mixed strategies of scheduler and attacker in different states

State	$\vec{\pi}_T^*$	$\vec{\pi}_J^*$
$\bar{P}_1, \bar{P}_2$	[0,0,1,0,0,0,0,0,0]	[1,0,0]
$h_1^1(\bar{P}_1), \bar{P}_2$	[0,0,1,0,0,0,0,0,0]	[1,0,0]
$h_1^2(\bar{P}_1), \bar{P}_2$	[0,0,1,0,0,0,0,0,0]	[1,0,0]
$\bar{P}_1, h_2^1(\bar{P}_2)$	[0,0,0,0,0,0.9438, 0,0,0.0562]	[0.0986,0.9014,0]
$h_1^1(\bar{P}_1), h_2^1(\bar{P}_2)$	[0,0,0,0,0,1,0,0,0]	[0,1,0]
$h_1^2(\bar{P}_1), h_2^1(\bar{P}_2)$	[0,0,0,0,0,1,0,0,0]	[1,0,0]
$\bar{P}_1, h_2^2(\bar{P}_2)$	[0,0,0,0,0,0.9165, 0,0,0.0835]	[0.1002,0.8998,0]
$h_1^1(\bar{P}_1), h_2^2(\bar{P}_2)$	[0,0,0,0,0,1,0,0,0]	[0,1,0]
$h_1^2(\bar{P}_1), h_2^2(\bar{P}_2)$	[0,0,0,0,0,1,0,0,0]	[0,1,0]

the two channels are always available and channel gains are invariable. The state set of process $i, \forall i \in \iota$ is restricted to be $\mathbf{S}_i = \{\bar{P}_i, h_i(\bar{P}_i), h_i^2(\bar{P}_i)\}$. In this scene, there are 9 strategies for the scheduler, 3 strategies for the attacker, and 9 states of the Markov game process. For example, by applying Algorithm 1, the learning process of Q-values for the 9×3 channel selection combinations when the state is $(\bar{P}_1, \bar{P}_2)$ is shown in Fig. 5.5. The evolution of the optimal Nash-Q values in different states is depicted in Fig. 5.6, and we can see that the Q-values all converge in different states. The optimal mixed strategies of scheduler and attacker in different states are listed in Table 5.4.

We compare the performance of the scheduler when he adopts the stationary strategy obtained by using the minimax-Q learning with other scenarios to evaluate the proposed game and the learning algorithm. It is assumed that the attacker uses the optimal stationary policy trained against the scheduler who exploits the minimax-Q learning. The following three scenarios of the scheduler are listed for comparison.

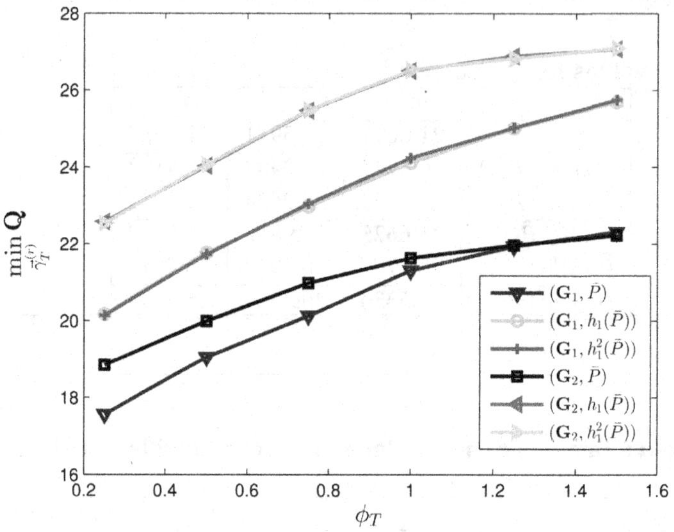

Figure 5.4 Optimal performance under power constraint without attacker.

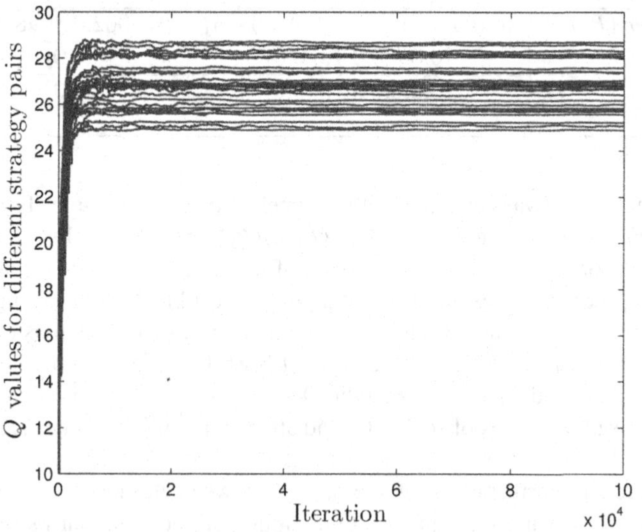

Figure 5.5 Learning process of Q-values in state $(\bar{P}_1, \bar{P}_2)$ for 9×3 strategy pairs.

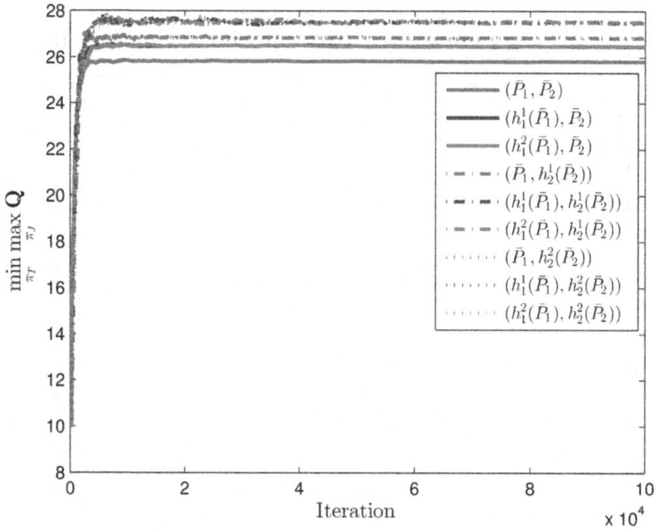

Figure 5.6 Evolution of Nash-Q values in different states.

1. Proposed: The optimal stationary strategy obtained by minimax-Q learning proposed in this chapter is adopted by the scheduler;
2. Myopic: One-step optimization policy attained in Section III is used by the scheduler;
3. Fixed: The scheduler adopts a fixed strategy, that is, he chooses action uniformly from the action space γ_T for each time step k.

The comparison results are shown in Fig. 5.7, where average accumulated payoff is used to assess the system performance, which is calculated similarly to equation (5.41). We can see that the case of 'Proposed' has lower payoff than scenarios 'Myopic' and 'Fixed', which illustrates the effectiveness of the proposed Markov game method in this chapter. Especially, the proposed strategy and myopic strategy are superior to the fixed scenario evidently, because both the 'Proposed' and 'Myopic' scenarios minimize the worst-case performance, whereas the fixed strategy only uniformly picks action regardless of the attacker's strategy.

5.7 CONCLUSION

In this chapter, the problem of channel allocation for the scheduler and channel selection for the attacker has been investigated. A myopic policy has been studied by using an associated two-player zero-sum game. Furthermore, with the time-varying network environment, a long-term interaction between the scheduler and attacker has been analyzed. A Markov game framework has been proposed to attain the optimal strategies for two players. To solve the Markov game without knowing the closed-

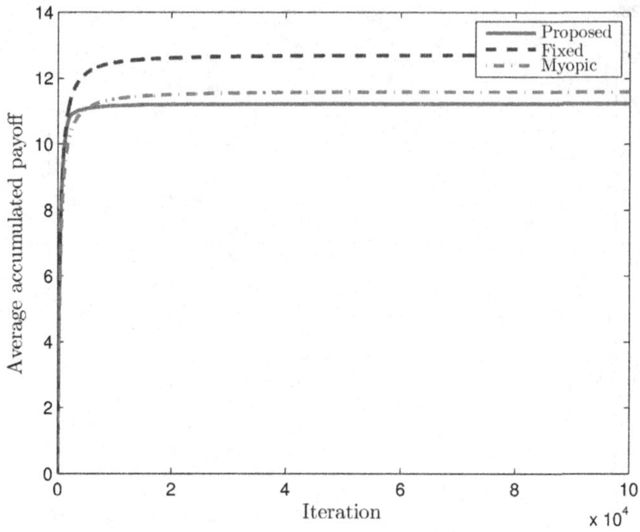

Figure 5.7 Average payoff with different scenarios.

form of reward function and transition probabilities, the minimax-Q learning method has been applied to obtain the optimal payoff and players' optimal strategies. Finally, the validity and advantage of the proposed method have been verified by numerical simulations.

6 Resilient strategy under DoS attack over a multi-channel transmission framework

6.1 INTRODUCTION

There are two main approaches to secure cyber-physical systems (CPSs) from cyber attacks: attack-tolerant and attack-compensation methods. In the attack-tolerant method, one can verify if the system remains in the safety zone with applied secure control strategy[147]. However, in serious attacks, the attack-compensation method is necessary to counteract the degradation of system performance caused by attack-induced phenomena. Various studies have investigated the optimal scheduling strategy for linear quadratic Gaussian (LQG) single and multiple subsystem cases[93], as well as channel and power level selection of the transmitter and attacker in remote state estimation through wireless networks[90, 115, 216]. The development of compensation strategies for CPSs under cyber attacks is of great significance.

Practically, for the control system of CPSs, state variables are not available to the controller, but always a disturbance corrupted output is. Generally, without knowing the statistical processes of the disturbance and noise, which are treated as being controlled by adversaries, we can deal with the estimation and control problem by using the minimax control approach [108]. Additionally, the sampling frequency of CPSs becomes higher and higher owing to the development of sensing and computing techniques.The delta operator approach has been recognized in addressing the sampling issue. Numerical-stiffness caused by fast sampling can be overcome by using the delta operator approach [81]. In a delta operator system, the sampling period can be tuned according to the network environment [237]. Furthermore, related results for both continuous and discrete-time systems have been unified in the delta domain [239]. These series of advantages inspire us to study the security of CPSs by minimax control schemes in the delta domain.

In this chapter, we aim at addressing the resilient strategy for a class of CPS under DoS attack. A minimax control approach in the delta domain is studied for the worst-case state estimation and controller design under imperfect state measurement (IPSM). Then, a multi-channel transmission framework is established for the transmitter and attacker, based on which zero-sum Markov stochastic game is presented for the two players. Especially, the main contributions of this chapter are highlighted as follows

(1) On account of a CPS having the effect of an attack-induced packet dropout, a minimax controller in the delta domain is derived under IPSM with the worst-case disturbance and noise scenario.
(2) Under DoS attack, a novel multi-channel transmission framework is constructed to reduce the probability of being attacked.
(3) The optimal mixed strategies of transmission power for transmitter and attacker are obtained to solve a zero-sum Markov stochastic game using a value iteration method.

The rest of this chapter is organized as follows: In Section 6.2, the problem formulation including a system model and communication model is presented. In Section 6.3, the design objectives are derived. The resilient strategies are solved in Section 6.4. In Section 6.5, numerical simulations are given to demonstrate the validity of the proposed approach. Conclusions are drawn in Section 6.6.

6.2 PROBLEM FORMULATION

Our interest lies in the security of a CPS under DoS attack as depicted in Fig. 6.1. A system model is constructed under IPSM in the delta domain. Then, a novel multi-channel transmission framework is proposed for the transmitter and DoS attacker.

6.2.1 SYSTEM MODEL

A linear time-varying delta operator system is considered in the following form

$$\begin{aligned}\delta x(t_k) =& A(t_k)x(t_k) + B(t_k)u(t_k) + D(t_k)\omega(t_k),\\ \bar{y}(t_k) =& C(t_k)x(t_k) + E(t_k)v(t_k),\\ y(t_k) =& \beta(t_k)\bar{y}(t_k),\end{aligned} \tag{6.1}$$

where $x(t_k) \in \mathbb{R}^{n_x}$, $u(t_k) \in \mathbb{R}^{n_u}$ and $\bar{y}(t_k) \in \mathbb{R}^{n_y}$ are the system state, control input, and measurement output taken by the sensor, respectively. $\omega(t_k) \in \mathbb{R}^{n_\omega}$, and $v(t_k) \in \mathbb{R}^{n_v}$ are the disturbance input and measurement noise. $t_k = \sum_{l=0}^{k-1} \mathrm{T}_l$ is the time instant with T_l being the sampling period. $A(t_k) \in \mathbb{R}^{n_x \times n_x}$, $B(t_k) \in \mathbb{R}^{n_x \times n_u}$, and $D(t_k) \in \mathbb{R}^{n_x \times n_\omega}$ are known time-varying system matrices as well as $C(t_k) \in \mathbb{R}^{n_y \times n_x}$ and $E(t_k) \in \mathbb{R}^{n_y \times n_v}$ are the measurement matrices. As shown in Fig. 6.1, it is assumed that the sensor and remote estimation are linked by wireless network and the controller and physical plant are built by a reliable network. Between the sensor and remote estimator, a DoS attacker tends to interfere with the transmission of measurement signals. A binary random process $\beta(t_k)$ is used to characterize the impact of the DoS attack, where $\beta(t_k) = 1$ represents that the packet is received error-free and otherwise $\beta(t_k) = 0$. Thus, $y(t_k)$ represents the output signal corrupted by the DoS attack.

Remark 12 *[81] The definition of delta operator is given as*

$$\delta x(t_k) = \begin{cases} \frac{dx(t)}{dt}, & \mathrm{T}_k = 0 \\ \frac{x(t_{k+1}) - x(t_k)}{\mathrm{T}_k}, & \mathrm{T}_k \neq 0, \end{cases} \tag{6.2}$$

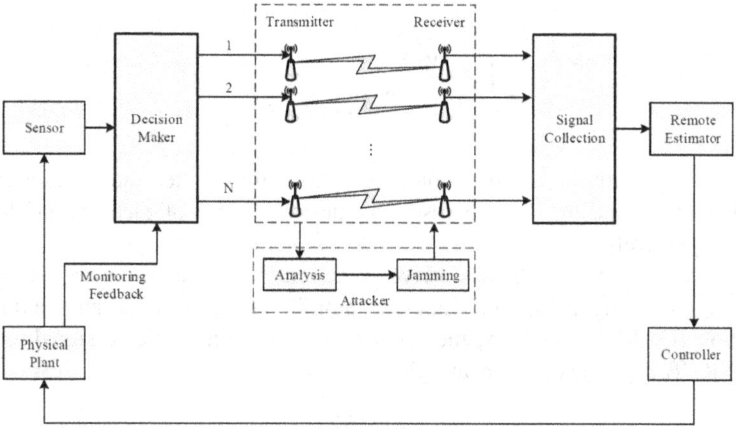

Figure 6.1 Multi-channel transmission framework under DoS attack.

where T_k is the sampling period, t is the continuous time index, and k is the time step with $t_k = \sum_{l=0}^{k-1} T_l$. According to the definition of delta operator, system (6.1) *can be obtained from its continuous-time system equation directly.*

6.2.2 COMMUNICATION MODEL

A wireless communication network is adopted to link the sensor and remote estimator, where the typical attacker can jam the communication link and then degrade the overall system performance. To reduce the damage from a DoS attacker, a multi-channel transmission framework is constructed. It is assumed that there exist N channels between the sensor and remote estimator, where the N channels have an independent communication environment. That is, there are different channel gains η_i, ξ_i for the transmitter and attacker as well as different additive white Gaussian noise ϱ_i^2 in each channel i, $i \in \mathbf{N} \triangleq \{1, 2, \cdots, N\}$.

A Markovian jump mechanism is exploited for the decision maker in Fig. 6.1 to choose to which channel to transmit the measurement signal. The transition probability from channel i at time n to channel j at time $n+1$ yields

$$\Pr\{\theta(n+1) = j|\theta(n) = i\} = p_T^{ij},\ i, j \in \mathbf{N}. \tag{6.3}$$

For the DoS attacker, the same mechanism is applied and the transition probability is

$$\Pr\{\sigma(n+1) = j|\sigma(n) = i\} = p_A^{ij},\ i, j \in \mathbf{N}. \tag{6.4}$$

To be energy saving, the values of transition probabilities for the transmitter and attacker are set by

$$p_T^{ij} = \begin{cases} e^{-T_n/a_i}, & j = i \\ \frac{a_j(1-e^{-T_n/a_i})}{\sum_{l \neq i}^{N} a_l}, & j \neq i \end{cases} \tag{6.5}$$

and

$$p_A^{ij} = \begin{cases} e^{-W_n/b_i}, & j = i \\ \frac{b_j(1-e^{-W_n/b_i})}{\sum_{l\neq i}^{N} b_l}, & j \neq i, \end{cases} \tag{6.6}$$

where T_n and W_n are the transmission power of the transmitter and attacker at time n. Coefficients a_i and b_i, $i \in \mathbf{N}$ represent the desire to serve of each channel for two players, respectively.

In reality, the data packets may arrive at the remote estimator unsuccessfully because of signal fading, noise, and malicious jamming. By using quadrature amplitude modulation (QAM) technology, the relationship between SINR or signal-to-noise ratio (SNR) $\Re$ and packet-error-rate (PER) is given by [6]

$$\text{PER} = 2\mathbf{Q}\left(\sqrt{\kappa \Re}\right), \tag{6.7}$$

where

$$\mathbf{Q}(x) \triangleq \frac{1}{\sqrt{2\pi}} \int_x^{\infty} \exp(-\tau^2/2)d\tau$$

and scalar κ is a constant, $\Re = \frac{\eta T}{\xi W + \varrho^2}$ if an adversary congests the communication network, and otherwise $\Re = \frac{\eta T}{\varrho^2}$.

Thus, the packet transmission in the forward channel can be denoted as a Bernoulli distribution, which yields

$$\Pr\{\beta(t_k) = 1\} = \bar{\beta}, \ \Pr\{\beta(t_k) = 0\} = 1 - \bar{\beta}, \tag{6.8}$$

where

$$\bar{\beta} = 1 - \text{PER}.$$

Under the multi-channel transmission framework between sensor and remote estimator, the possible SINR or SNR in all channels at time n is given as the following matrix

$$\begin{aligned} \Upsilon &= [\Upsilon_{ij}]_{N\times N} \\ &= \begin{bmatrix} \frac{\eta_1 T_n}{\xi_1 W_n + \varrho_1^2} & \frac{\eta_1 T_n}{\varrho_1^2} & \cdots & \frac{\eta_1 T_n}{\varrho_1^2} \\ \frac{\eta_2 T_n}{\varrho_2^2} & \frac{\eta_2 T_n}{\xi_2 W_n + \varrho_2^2} & \cdots & \frac{\eta_2 T_n}{\varrho_2^2} \\ \vdots & \vdots & \ddots & \vdots \\ \frac{\eta_N T_n}{\varrho_N^2} & \frac{\eta_N T_n}{\varrho_N^2} & \cdots & \frac{\eta_N T_n}{\xi_N W_n + \varrho_N^2} \end{bmatrix}, \end{aligned} \tag{6.9}$$

where $\Upsilon_{ij}, i, j \in \mathbf{N}$ represents the SINR or SNR when the transmitter chooses channel i and the attacker chooses channel j.

For analysis convenience, the two stochastic processes $\theta(n)$ and $\sigma(n)$ in (6.3) and (6.4) are reformulated to one unified Markov chain. We set an one-to-one correspondence to pair $(\theta(n), \sigma(n))$ as the stochastic variable $r(n)$. Therefore, the Markovian jump processes of the transmitter and attacker can be mapped to the sequence $r(n) \in \mathbf{R} \triangleq \{1, 2, \cdots, N \times N\}$, which is defined as

$$r(n) = \Theta(\theta(n), \sigma(n)) = \sigma(n) + (\theta(n) - 1)N. \tag{6.10}$$

With a given $r(n)$, the values of $\theta(n)$ and $\sigma(n)$ are derived as

$$\begin{aligned} \theta(n) &= \Phi_1(r(n)) \triangleq 1 + \left\lfloor \frac{r(n) - 1}{N} \right\rfloor, \\ \sigma(n) &= \Phi_2(r(n)) \triangleq 1 + \text{mod}(r(n) - 1, N), \end{aligned} \tag{6.11}$$

where '$\lfloor \cdot \rfloor$' represents the largest integer not greater than '$\cdot$' and 'mod(a,b)' denotes the unique nonnegative remainder on the division of a by b. According to mappings described by (6.10) and (6.11), the transition probability matrix $\mathcal{P} = [p^{hl}]_{(N \times N) \times (N \times N)}$ of Markov chain $r(n)$ is

$$\begin{aligned} p^{hl}(n) =& \Pr\{r(n+1) = l | r(n) = h\} \\ =& \Pr\{\theta(n+1) = \Phi_1(l) | \theta(n) = \Phi_1(h)\} \\ & \Pr\{\sigma(n+1) = \Phi_2(l) | \sigma(n) = \Phi_2(h)\} \\ =& p_T^{\Phi_1(h)\Phi_1(l)} p_A^{\Phi_2(h)\Phi_2(l)}. \end{aligned} \tag{6.12}$$

Based on mappings (6.10) and (6.11), matrix (6.9) is mapped as

$$\mathfrak{R}(r(n)) = \Upsilon_{ij}, \; r(n) \in \mathbf{R}, \; i, j \in \mathbf{N}, \tag{6.13}$$

where $i = \Phi_1(r(n)), \; j = \Phi_2(r(n))$.

Remark 13 *For analysis simplification, we consider that the DoS attack occurs in the forward channel and the feedback link is built by a reliable network. Actually, the model setup and addressed methods can be extended to deal with attacks in networks on both sides of the physical plant, which will be involved in our future work.*

6.3 OBJECTIVE SETUP

To enhance the resilience of CPS under an adversarial environment, the design objectives are set up for the control system and communication network, respectively.

6.3.1 MINIMAX CONTROL

Assume that system (6.1) is under the transmission control protocol (TCP) structure, and the TCP-like information available to the controller is given by

$$\mathcal{I}(t_k) = \{y(t_0), y(t_1), \cdots, y(t_k), \beta(t_0), \beta(t_1), \cdots, \beta(t_k)\}.$$

For convenience, the zero-input strategy is adopted when the data packet does not arrive at the remote estimator. Denote $\mathcal{U}$ and $\mathcal{V}$ as sets of control and disturbance strategies. The control and disturbance strategies are $u(t_k) = \mu(\mathcal{I}(t_k)) \in \mathcal{U}$ and $\omega(t_k) = \nu(\mathcal{I}(t_k)) \in \mathcal{V}, k \in \mathbf{K} \triangleq \{0, 1, \cdots, K\}$. In the spirit of the worst-case approach, it is assumed that the disturbance knows everything the controller does. The objective of the control system is to obtain the optimal feedback controller when considering the DoS attack, which minimizes the following cost function

$$\Gamma_\mu^K = \sup_{x(t_0),\omega(t_k),k\in\mathbf{K}} \frac{J^K(\mu,\nu)^{\frac{1}{2}}}{\mathbb{E}\left\{\|x(t_0)\|_{Q_0}^2 + \mathrm{T}_k \sum_{k=0}^{K-1} \mathcal{M}(t_k)\right\}^{\frac{1}{2}}}, \tag{6.14}$$

where

$$J^K(\mu,\nu) = \mathbb{E}\left\{\|x(t_K)\|_{Q_K}^2 + \mathrm{T}_k \sum_{k=0}^{K-1} (\|x(t_k)\|_Q^2 + \|u(t_k)\|_R^2)\right\},$$

$$\mathcal{M}(t_k) = \|\omega(t_k)\|^2 + \beta(t_k)\|v(t_k)\|^2$$

with $Q \geq 0$, $Q_K \geq 0$, $R > 0$ and $Q_0 > 0$. For parameterized disturbance attention level $\gamma > 0$, the following zero-sum dynamic game is introduced for system (6.1).

$$\begin{aligned} J_\gamma^K(\mu,\nu) = \mathbb{E}\Big\{&\|x(t_K)\|_{Q_K}^2 - \gamma^2\|x(t_0)\|_{Q_0}^2 + \\ &\mathrm{T}_k \sum_{k=0}^{K-1} (\|x(t_k)\|_Q^2 + \|u(t_k)\|_R^2 - \gamma^2 \mathcal{M}(t_k))\Big\} \end{aligned} \tag{6.15}$$

The main objective of the physical system is to obtain the controller such that the cost function (6.15) is minimized under the worst-case disturbance and adversarial environment. In other words, a pair (μ^*, ν^*) is characterized as the saddle-point for the zero-sum dynamic game system (6.15) in terms of γ, if the following inequality

$$\mathbf{P}_1: \; J_\gamma^K(\mu^*,\nu) \leq J_\gamma^K(\mu^*,\nu^*) \leq J_\gamma^K(\mu,\nu^*) \tag{6.16}$$

holds. It is pointed out that a critical issue is to guarantee the existence of a saddle-point solution for the minimax control problem, which is dependent on the value of γ. That is, a finite value of J_γ^K will be obtained under the minimax controller above the smallest value of γ denoted as $\hat{\gamma}$. Therefore, the smallest disturbance attention level $\hat{\gamma}$ can depict the scope of operation of the system (6.1) under disturbance and an adversarial environment, which will be considered in the resilient strategy design of the next section.

Before ending this part, an instrument lemma is introduced to develop our main results.

Lemma 6.1 *[81] For time functions $x(t_k)$ and $y(t_k)$, the following property of the delta operator holds*

$$\delta(x(t_k)y(t_k)) = \delta x(t_k)y(t_k) + x(t_k)\delta y(t_k) + T_k \delta x(t_k)\delta y(t_k),$$

where T_k is the sampling period.

6.3.2 STOCHASTIC ZERO-SUM GAME

If the decision maker installed in the sensor can monitor the performance of the physical plant as well as the opponent's strategy, meanwhile, the attacker can also eavesdrop upon the information, such that the sensor and attacker can make decisions based on the current and previous information. Therefore, a dynamic jamming game is set up to deal with the interactive process. The cost of the sensor in state r at time n is written as

$$R_n(r,T_n,W_n) = c_0\hat{\gamma}(n) + c_1T_n - c_2W_n + C_0, \tag{6.17}$$

where positive scalars c_0, c_1, and c_2 are weight coefficients, parameter C_0 denotes the inherent cost, and $\hat{\gamma}(n)$ represents the system performance of the physical plant. However, the cost function of the attacker is the opposite. The discounted costs for the sensor and attacker are

$$\mathscr{F}_T(r) = \mathscr{F}(r),\ \mathscr{F}_A(r) = -\mathscr{F}(r), \tag{6.18}$$

respectively, where

$$\mathscr{F}(r) = \sum_{n=1}^{+\infty} \rho^n R_n(r,T_n,W_n) \tag{6.19}$$

with r being the initial state taken in set $\mathbf{R}$. Parameter $\rho \in [0,1)$ is the discount factor.

It is addressed to look for the Nash equilibrium (T^*,W^*) for the zero-sum game of the discounted cost function (6.19) such that

$$\mathbf{P}_2:\ \mathbf{F}(T^*,\ W) \leq \mathbf{F}(T^*,\ W^*) \leq \mathbf{F}(T,\ W^*) \tag{6.20}$$

holds, where $\mathbf{F} = \begin{bmatrix} \mathscr{F}^*(1) & \mathscr{F}^*(2) & \cdots & \mathscr{F}^*(N\times N) \end{bmatrix}$.

6.4 RESILIENT STRATEGY DESIGN

Now that the researched problem and design objectives have been identified, we will proceed to develop the control and power transmission strategies to enhance the resilience of the entire CPS.

6.4.1 RESILIENT CONTROL STRATEGY

For the control system, there is no separation between control and estimation due to the worst-case being considered. The solution procedure is based on a certain equivalence principle of minimax control as follows [186]: a) At time t_k, calculate the state feedback minimax controller when assuming that the controller has the actual state; b) Find the minimax state estimation with TCP-like information; c) Using a) and b) together, characterize the worst-case state estimation $\hat{x}_k$. Then, the actual minimax controller can be obtained by replacing $x(t_k)$ with $\hat{x}(t_k)$.

First, we address a state feedback minimax controller in the delta domain based on TCP-like information assuming that we know the perfect state information.

Theorem 6.1 *Considering the zero-sum dynamic game (6.15), for given disturbance attention level $\gamma > 0$, then*

1) There exists the unique saddle-point solution if and only if for all $k \in \mathbf{K} \setminus K$

$$\begin{aligned} R + T_k B^T(t_k) Z(t_{k+1}) B(t_k) > 0, \\ T_k D^T(t_k) Z(t_{k+1}) D(t_k) < \gamma^2 I, \end{aligned} \tag{6.21}$$

where $Z(t_k) \geq 0$ satisfies the Riccati equation

$$\begin{aligned} -\delta Z(t_k) =& Q + P_u^T(t_k) R P_u(t_k) - \gamma^2 P_\omega^T(t_k) P_\omega(t_k) + \\ & T_k \mathcal{A}^T(t_k) Z(t_{k+1}) \mathcal{A}(t_k) \\ & + \mathcal{A}^T(t_k) Z(t_{k+1}) + Z(t_{k+1}) \mathcal{A}(t_k), \\ Z(t_k) =& Z(t_{k+1}) - T_k \delta Z(t_k), \end{aligned} \tag{6.22}$$

where

$$\begin{aligned} P_u(t_k) =& (R + T_k B^T(t_k) \Lambda_u(t_k) Z(t_{k+1}) B(t_k))^{-1} \\ & B^T(t_k) \Lambda_u(t_k) Z(t_{k+1})(T_k A(t_k) + I), \\ P_\omega(t_k) =& (\gamma^2 I - T_k D^T(t_k) \Lambda_\omega(t_k) Z(t_{k+1}) D(t_k))^{-1} \\ & D^T(t_k) \Lambda_\omega(t_k) Z(t_{k+1})(T_k A(t_k) + I), \\ \mathcal{A}(t_k) =& A(t_k) - B(t_k) P_u(t_k) + D(t_k) P_\omega(t_k) \end{aligned} \tag{6.23}$$

with

$$\begin{aligned} \Xi_1(t_k) =& R + T_k B^T(t_k) Z(t_{k+1}) B(t_k), \\ \Xi_2(t_k) =& \gamma^2 I - T_k D^T(t_k) Z(t_{k+1}) D(t_k), \\ \Lambda_u(t_k) =& I + T_k Z(t_{k+1}) D(t_k) \Xi_2^{-1}(t_k) D^T(t_k), \\ \Lambda_\omega(t_k) =& I - T_k Z(t_{k+1}) B(t_k) \Xi_1^{-1}(t_k) B^T(t_k). \end{aligned}$$

2) The feedback saddle-point policies (μ^*, ν^*) are obtained as

$$u^*(t_k) = -P_u(t_k) x(t_k), \; \omega^*(t_k) = P_\omega(t_k) x(t_k), \; \forall k \in \mathbf{K} \setminus K. \tag{6.24}$$

Proof *An induction method is employed here. Supposing that when the controller has the actual state, the claim is true for step $k+1$; the cost function at $k+1$ is constructed as a quadratic form*

$$Y_{k+1}(x(t_{k+1})) = x^T(t_{k+1}) Z(t_{k+1}) x(t_{k+1}), \tag{6.25}$$

where $Z(t_{k+1}) \geq 0$. According to Lemma 6.1, one has that

$$\begin{aligned} & Y_{k+1}(x(t_{k+1})) \\ =& T_k \delta(x^T(t_k) Z(t_k) x(t_k)) + x^T(t_k) Z(t_k) x(t_k) \\ =& T_k \delta x^T(t_k) Z(t_{k+1}) x(t_k) + T_k x^T(t_k) Z(t_{k+1}) \delta x(t_k) \\ & + T_k^2 \delta x^T(t_k) Z(t_{k+1}) \delta x(t_k) + x^T(t_k) Z(t_{k+1}) x(t_k). \end{aligned}$$

By using the dynamic programming method, the cost at step k is given by

$$\begin{aligned} &Y_k(x(t_k)) \\ &= \min_{u(t_k)} \max_{\omega(t_k)} \{\|x(t_k)\|^2_{T_kQ} + \|u(t_k)\|^2_{T_kR} - T_k\gamma^2\|\omega(t_k)\|^2 + Y_{k+1}(x(t_{k+1}))\} \\ &= \min_{u(t_k)} \max_{\omega(t_k)} \Big\{\|x(t_k)\|^2_{T_kQ} + \|u(t_k)\|^2_{T_kR} - T_k\gamma^2\|\omega(t_k)\|^2 \\ &+T_k\delta x^T(t_k)Z(t_{k+1})x(t_k) + T_kx^T(t_k)Z(t_{k+1})\delta x(t_k) \\ &+T_k^2\delta x^T(t_k)Z(t_{k+1})\delta x(t_k) + x^T(t_k)Z(t_{k+1})x(t_k)\Big\} \end{aligned} \tag{6.26}$$

Under Condition (6.21), $Y_k(x(t_k))$ *given in* (6.26) *is strictly convex with respect to* $u(t_k)$ *and concave in* $\omega(t_k)$. *The optimal control and disturbance strategies can be obtained by solving* $\partial Y_k(x(t_k))/\partial u(t_k) = 0$ *and* $\partial Y_k(x(t_k))/\partial\omega(t_k) = 0$. *Thus, the optimal control and disturbance satisfy*

$$\begin{aligned} &(R + T_kB^T(t_k)Z(t_{k+1})B(t_k))u(t_k) \\ &+B^T(t_k)Z(t_{k+1})((T_kA(t_k)+I)x(t_k) + T_kD(t_k)\omega(t_k)) = 0, \end{aligned} \tag{6.27}$$

$$\begin{aligned} &(-\gamma^2 + T_kD^T(t_k)Z(t_{k+1})D(t_k))\omega(t_k) \\ &+D^T(t_k)Z(t_{k+1})((T_kA(t_k)+I)x(t_k) + T_kB(t_k)u(t_k)) = 0. \end{aligned} \tag{6.28}$$

Combining (6.27) *and* (6.28), *the saddle-point is given by equation* (6.24), *and the Riccati equation* (6.22) *is arrived at substituting* (6.24) *into* (6.26). *This completes the proof.*

Next, we consider the minimax estimation problem over the TCP-like information structure.

Theorem 6.2 *For the zero-sum dynamic game* (6.15) *with* $\bar{\beta} \in [0,1]$ *and a fixed* $\gamma > 0$, *if and only if*

$$T_k\Sigma(t_k)Q < \gamma^2 I, \forall k \in \boldsymbol{K}\setminus K, \tag{6.29}$$

where $\Sigma(t_k)$ *satisfies the following generalized stochastic Riccati equation (GSRE)*

$$\begin{aligned} \delta\Sigma(t_k) =& T_kA(t_k)\Pi^{-1}(t_k)A^T(t_k) + A(t_k)\Pi^{-1}(t_k) \\ &+\Pi^{-1}(t_k)A^T(t_k) + (\Pi^{-1}(t_k) - \Sigma(t_k))/T_k + T_kD(t_k)D^T(t_k), \\ \Sigma(t_{k+1}) =& \Sigma(t_k) + T_k\delta\Sigma(t_k),\ \Sigma(t_0) = Q_0^{-1}, \end{aligned} \tag{6.30}$$

with $\Pi(t_k) = \Sigma^{-1}(t_k) + T_k\beta(t_k)C^T(t_k)V(t_k)C(t_k) - T_k\gamma^{-2}Q$, *there exists a stochastic minimax estimator (SME)*

$$\begin{aligned} \delta\bar{x}(t_k) =& A(t_k)\bar{x}(t_k) + B(t_k)u(t_k) + \beta(t_k)(T_kA(t_k)+I)\Pi^{-1}(t_k)C^T(t_k)V(t_k) \\ &(y(t_k) - C(t_k)\bar{x}(t_k)) + \gamma^{-2}(T_kA(t_k)+I)\Pi^{-1}(t_k)Q\bar{x}(t_k). \end{aligned} \tag{6.31}$$

Proof *A forward dynamic programming approach is applied by introducing a quadratic cost-to-come function* $H_k(x(t_k)) = \mathbb{E}\{-\|x(t_k) - \bar{x}(t_k)\|^2_{M(t_k)} + l(t_k)|\ell(t_{k-1})\}$, *where* $M(t_k) > 0$, $M(t_0) = \gamma^2 Q_0$ *and* $\ell(t_k) = \{\mathcal{I}(t_k), u(t_k)\}$. *Then, the cost from initial state to stage* $k+1$ *can be written as*

$$\begin{aligned}
&\mathbb{E}\{\|x(t_{k+1}) - \bar{x}(t_{k+1})\|^2_{M(t_{k+1})} - l(t_{k+1})|\ell(t_k)\} \\
= &\min_{\omega(t_k), x(t_k)} \mathbb{E}\Big\{-\|x(t_k)\|^2_{T_k Q} - \|u(t_k)\|^2_{T_k R} \\
&+ T_k\gamma^2\|\omega(t_k)\|^2 + \gamma^2\|y(t_k) - \beta(t_k)C(t_k)x(t_k)\|^2_{V(t_k)} \\
&+ \|x(t_k) - \bar{x}(t_k)\|^2_{M(t_k)} - l(t_k)\Big|\ell(t_k)\} \\
= &\min_{\omega(t_k), x(t_k)} \mathbb{E}\Big\{\|x(t_k)\|^2_{U(t_k)} + T_k\gamma^2\|\omega(t_k)\|^2 + 2b(t_k)x(t_k) + m(t_k)\Big\},
\end{aligned} \tag{6.32}$$

where

$$\begin{aligned}
V^{-1}(t_k) &= E(t_k)E^T(t_k), \\
U(t_k) &= -T_k Q + M(t_k) + T_k\gamma^2\beta(t_k)C^T(t_k)V(t_k)C(t_k), \\
b(t_k) &= -\gamma^2\beta(t_k)y^T(t_k)V(t_k)C(t_k) - \bar{x}^T(t_k)M(t_k)
\end{aligned}$$

and $m(t_k)$ *represents the part independent of* $x(t_k)$ *and* $\omega(t_k)$. *To calculate the optimal solution, the optimization problem* (6.32) *with constraint* (6.1) *is augmented as*

$$\begin{aligned}
&\min_{\zeta(t_k)} \|\zeta(t_k)\|^2_{\mathcal{T}(t_k)} + 2\mathcal{C}(t_k)\zeta(t_k) \\
&s.t.\ \mathcal{F}\zeta(t_k) = c(t_k),
\end{aligned} \tag{6.33}$$

where

$$\begin{aligned}
&\zeta(t_k) = \begin{bmatrix} x(t_k) \\ \omega(t_k) \end{bmatrix}, \mathcal{F} = \begin{bmatrix} A & D \end{bmatrix}, \\
&c(t_k) = x(t_{k+1}) - T_k B u(t_k), \\
&\mathcal{T}(t_k) = \begin{bmatrix} U(t_k) & 0 \\ 0 & T_k\gamma^2 I \end{bmatrix}, \mathcal{C}(t_k) = \begin{bmatrix} b(t_k) \\ 0 \end{bmatrix}.
\end{aligned} \tag{6.34}$$

Based on Lemma 6.2 in [186], we have

$$\begin{aligned}
&\mathbb{E}\{\|x(t_{k+1}) - \bar{x}(t_{k+1})\|^2_{M(t_{k+1})} - l(t_{k+1})|\ell(t_k)\} = \\
&\mathbb{E}\Big\{\|c(t_k) + (T_k A(t_k) + I)U^{-1}(t_k)b^T(t_k)\|^2_{\bar{M}^{-1}(t_k)} - \|b^T(t_k)\|^2_{U^{-1}(t_k)} + m(t_k)\Big\},
\end{aligned} \tag{6.35}$$

where $\bar{M}(t_k) = (T_k A(t_k) + I)U^{-1}(t_k)(T_k A(t_k) + I)^T + T_k^2\gamma^{-2}D(t_k)D^T(t_k)$. *Comparing both sides of* (6.35), *we know* $M(t_{k+1}) = \bar{M}^{-1}(t_k)$, *and the GSRE* (6.30) *and SME* (6.31) *are obtained by denoting* $\Sigma(t_k) = \gamma^2 M^{-1}(t_k)$. *The proof is complete.*

Finally, the existence condition for the worst-case state estimator and the mininmax state feedback controller is derived under IPSM.

Theorem 6.3 *For any fixed γ and $\bar{\beta}$, if there exist the state feedback controller and the SME, i.e., conditions* (6.21) *and* (6.29) *hold for all $k \in \boldsymbol{K} \setminus K$, then*

1) If

$$\Sigma(t_k)Z(t_k) < \gamma^2 I, \ \forall k \in \boldsymbol{K} \setminus K, \tag{6.36}$$

the worst-case state estimator exists.

2) Under Condition 1), the worst-case state estimator is given by

$$\hat{x}(t_k) = (I - \gamma^{-2}\Sigma(t_k)Z(t_k))^{-1}\bar{x}(t_k), \tag{6.37}$$

where $\bar{x}(t_k)$ is generated by SME (6.31).

3) The feedback saddle-point (6.24) *in Theorem 1 is rewritten as*

$$u^*(t_k) = -P_u(t_k)\hat{x}(t_k), \ \omega^*(t_k) = P_\omega(t_k)\hat{x}(t_k), \ \forall k \in \boldsymbol{K} \setminus K. \tag{6.38}$$

4) The controller achieves the disturbance attention level γ, and we have $\Gamma_{\mu^*}^{K*} \leq \gamma$.

Proof *The worst-case state estimation is obtained by solving the following optimization problem*

$$\hat{x}(t_k) = arg \max_{x(t_k)} \mathbb{E}\{Y_k(x(t_k)) - \gamma^2 \|x(t_k) - \bar{x}(t_k)\|^2_{\Sigma^{-1}(t_k)} + l(t_k) | \ell(t_k)\}. \tag{6.39}$$

It is concluded that the worst-case state estimation is given as equation (6.37). *Therefore, the state feedback minimax controller under IPSM can be obtained by replacing $x(t_k)$ in* (6.24) *by $\hat{x}(t_k)$, which yields equation* (6.38). *If condition* (6.36) *holds, the system performance $J_\gamma^*(\mu^*, \nu^*)$ is finite. That is, the controller can achieve the disturbance attention level γ and $\Gamma_{\mu^*}^{K*} < \gamma$. The proof is complete.*

Remark 14 *In many practical situations, it is not realistic that statistical information of the disturbance and sensor noise is available. Even if it is available, there is a mismatch between the statistical and true information. Thus, the minimax controller dealing with a control problem under IPSM with unknown arbitrary disturbance and sensor noise controlled by adversaries is considered in this chapter. When $\gamma \to \infty$, the minimax control problem* (6.15) *converges to the corresponding LQG control problem as in [223].*

Remark 15 *The advantages of results in the delta domain in theorems of this section are summarized as follows:*

1) The numerical-stiffness can be circumvented when the involved results are applied into industrial control systems with high frequency.

2) The sampling interval in Theorems 1 and 2 becomes an explicit parameter and can be tuned according to the network environment.

3) The results in Theorems 1 and 2 can be seen as a unified form of the results for both discrete- and continuous-time systems. To be specific, let us take Theorem 1 as an example. The delta domain results in Theorem 1 can be easily converted to its discrete-domain analog by using $A_z(k) = T_k A(t_k) + I$, $B_z(k) = T_k B(t_k)$ *and* $D_z(k) = T_k D(t_k)$. *The results to equivalence of the continuous-time form are verified as follows: When* $T_k \to 0$, *denote that* $A(t_k) \to A_s(t)$, $B(t_k) \to B_s(t)$, $D(t_k) \to D_s(t)$ *and* $Z(t_k) \to Z(t)$. *Then, the feedback gains in* (6.24) *become*

$$P_u(t) = R^{-1} B_s^T(t) Z(t), \; P_\omega(t) = \gamma^{-2} D_s^T(t) Z(t). \tag{6.40}$$

With equation (6.40) *and* $\lim_{T_k \to 0} \delta Z(t_k) = \dot{Z}(t)$, *the Riccati backward iteration* (6.22) *becomes*

$$\begin{aligned} -\dot{Z}(t) =& Q + Z(t) B_s(t) R^{-1} B_s^T Z(t) - \gamma^{-2} Z^T(t) D_s(t) D_s^T(t) Z(t) \\ &+ \mathcal{A}_s^T(t) Z(t) + Z(t) \mathcal{A}_s(t) \end{aligned} \tag{6.41}$$

with

$$\mathcal{A}_s(t) = A_s(t) - B_s(t) R^{-1} B_s^T(t) Z(t) + \gamma^{-2} D_s(t) D_s^T(t) Z(t).$$

Note that (6.40) *and* (6.41) *are consistent with the feedback strategies and Riccati recursion in the continuous-time systems [186]. Therefore, it is concluded that Theorem 1 unifies the results in discrete- and continuous-time systems.*

6.4.2 RESILIENT POWER TRANSMISSION STRATEGY

To achieve the Nash equilibrium of $\mathbf{P}_2$, the following lemma is provided.

Lemma 6.2 *[6] Considering the discounted cost problem* (6.19) *which can be regarded as a Markov decision process, the optimal value of objective function* $\mathcal{F}^*(r)$ *satisfies the optimal Bellman equation as follows*

$$\mathcal{F}^*(r) = \min_{T_n} \max_{W_n} \left\{ R(r, T_n, W_n) + \rho \sum_{r' \in R} Pr\{r' | r\} \mathcal{F}^*(r') \right\}. \tag{6.42}$$

In practice, the transmission power of the transmitter and attacker is limited, i.e., $T_n \in [0, T^{\max}]$ and $W_n \in [0, W^{\max}]$. The transmission power of a physical element can not be an analog signal, which is always quantized coarsely to be sent. Therefore, we assume that there are finite power levels L when applying the value iteration algorithm. The power levels of the transmitter and attacker are denoted as $\mathbf{T} = \{T^1, T^2, \cdots, T^{L_T}\}$ and $\mathbf{W} = \{W^1, W^2, \cdots, W^{L_W}\}$, respectively.

Define an auxiliary matrix $\mathbf{Q}(r) = [Q^{ij}(r)]_{L_T \times L_W}, r \in \mathbf{R}$, where

$$Q^{ij}(r, T^i, W^j) = R(r, T^i, W^j) + \rho \sum_{r' \in \mathbf{R}} \Pr\{r' | r\} \mathscr{F}^*(r')$$

with $i \in \mathbf{L}_T \triangleq \{1, 2, \cdots, L_T\}$, $j \in \mathbf{L}_W \triangleq \{1, 2, \cdots, L_W\}$.

In the sequence, the Nash equilibrium strategies are derived in the form of mixed strategies, which is involved in the probability space over finite-dimensional set. The following theorem is presented to give the optimal mixed strategies.

Theorem 6.4 *The discounted, zero-sum, stochastic game* (6.20) *has the optimal value* $\mathscr{F}^*(r)$, $\forall r \in \boldsymbol{R}$, *which is the unique solution of equation*

$$\mathscr{F}^*(r) = \min_{\pi_T} \max_{\pi_W} \{\boldsymbol{Q}(r)\}, \tag{6.43}$$

where $\pi_T \in \mathbb{P}(\boldsymbol{T})$ *and* $\pi_W \in \mathbb{P}(\mathbf{W})$ *with* $\mathbb{P}(\boldsymbol{T})$, $\mathbb{P}(\mathbf{W})$ *are sets of probability distribution over power level sets* $\boldsymbol{T}$ *and* $\mathbf{W}$.

Proof *The results can be obtained by using the Shapley Theorem [181], and we omit the proof here.*

A value iteration method is employed for solving the zero-sum stochastic game (6.43). With an initial approximate game value, we iterate according to

$$\mathscr{F}^*_{n+1}(r) = \min_{\pi_T} \max_{\pi_W} \{\mathbf{Q}_n(r, \mathscr{F}^*_n(r))\}, \ \forall r \in \mathbf{R}. \tag{6.44}$$

Algorithms 1 and 2 are proposed for the joint resilient strategy design of the entire CPS.

Algorithm 4 Optimal disturbance attention level $\hat{\gamma}$

1: For specific packet delivery rate $\bar{\beta}$, take a sufficient large value $\gamma > 0$ and a small enough scalar $\Delta\gamma$.
2: Solve the Riccati equation (6.22) and GSRE (6.30).
3: **if** Conditions (6.21), (6.29), and (6.36) hold **then**
4: $\quad \gamma \leftarrow \gamma - \Delta\gamma$, go to *Step* 2.
5: **else**
6: $\quad \hat{\gamma} = \gamma$.
7: **end if**

6.5 SIMULATION RESULTS

To demonstrate the effectiveness and applicability, we apply the proposed scheme to a load frequency control problem of a three-area power system. The three-area interconnected power system is given as

$$\begin{aligned} \dot{x}(t) &= Ax(t) + Bu(t) + D\omega(t), \\ \bar{y}(t) &= Cx(t) + Ev(t), \end{aligned} \tag{6.46}$$

Algorithm 5 Optimal joint defense strategy design

Given ρ, power level sets $\mathbf{T}$, $\mathbf{W}$, weight coefficients c_0, c_1, c_2, inherent cost C_0.
Initialize $n = 0$, $\mathbf{F}_0$.
while $\|\mathbf{F}_{n+1} - \mathbf{F}_n\| > \varepsilon$ **do**
  for $r = 1 : N \times N$ **do**
    Calculate pricing matrix $\mathbf{Q}_n(r) = [Q_n^{ij}(r)]_{L_T \times L_W}$ based on Algorithm 1, equation (6.17) and

$$Q_n^{ij}(r, T^i, W^j) = R_n(r, T^i, W^j) + \rho \sum_{r' \in \mathbf{R}} \Pr\{r'|r\} \mathscr{F}_n^*(r').$$

    Find the Nash value $\mathscr{F}_{n+1}^*(r)$, $\forall r \in \mathbf{R}$ based on (6.43) according to the linear programming

$$\begin{aligned} \mathbf{P}_3 :\ & 1/\mathscr{F}_{n+1}^*(r) = \max_t t^T \mathbf{1}_{L_T} \\ & s.t.\ \mathbf{Q}_n^T(r) t \leq \mathbf{1}_{L_W}, \\ & \quad t \geq 0. \end{aligned} \tag{6.45}$$

  end for
  $n \leftarrow n + 1$.
end while
The optimal mixed strategy of transmitter is obtained as $\pi_T^* = t\mathscr{F}_n^*(r)$. By solving the dual problem of $\mathbf{P}_3$, we get the optimal mixed strategy of attacker π_W^*.
Output the joint resilient strategies (μ^*, π_T^*) with adversarial environment and worst-case control under imperfect state information.

where

$$\begin{aligned} x(t) &= \begin{bmatrix} x^{1T}(t) & x^{2T}(t) & x^{3T}(t) \end{bmatrix}^T, \\ u(t) &= \begin{bmatrix} u^{1T}(t) & u^{2T}(t) & u^{3T}(t) \end{bmatrix}^T, \\ \omega(t) &= \begin{bmatrix} \Delta P_d^{1T}(t) & \Delta P_d^{2T}(t) & \Delta P_d^{3T}(t) \end{bmatrix}^T, \\ A &= \begin{bmatrix} A^{11} & A^{12} & A^{13} \\ A^{21} & A^{22} & A^{23} \\ A^{31} & A^{32} & A^{33} \end{bmatrix},\ B = \operatorname{diag}\{\ B^1 \quad B^2 \quad B^3\ \}, \\ C &= \operatorname{diag}\{\ C^1 \quad C^2 \quad C^3\ \}^T,\ D = \operatorname{diag}\{\ D^1 \quad D^2 \quad D^3\ \}, \end{aligned}$$

with

$$A^{ii} = \begin{bmatrix} -\frac{1}{T_{P_i}} & \frac{K_{P_i}}{T_{P_i}} & 0 & 0 & -\frac{K_{P_i}}{2\pi T_{P_i}} \sum_{j \in \mathbf{S}, j \neq i} K_{s_{ij}} \\ 0 & -\frac{1}{T_{T_i}} & \frac{1}{T_{T_i}} & 0 & 0 \\ -\frac{1}{R_i T_{G_i}} & 0 & -\frac{1}{T_{G_i}} & \frac{1}{T_{G_i}} & 0 \\ K_{E_i} K_{B_i} & 0 & 0 & 0 & \frac{K_{E_i}}{2\pi} \sum_{j \in \mathbf{S}, j \neq i} K_{s_{ij}} \\ 2\pi & 0 & 0 & 0 & 0 \end{bmatrix},$$

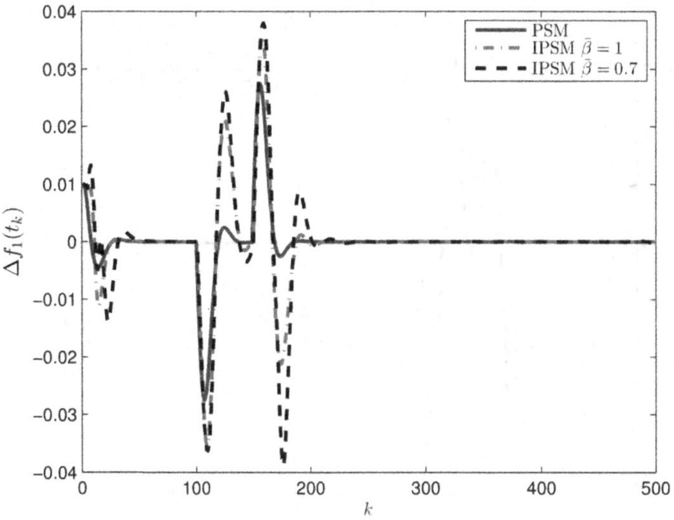

Figure 6.2 State evolution of $\Delta f_1(t_k)$.

$$B^i = \begin{bmatrix} 0 & 0 & \frac{1}{T_{G_i}} & 0 & 0 \end{bmatrix}^T,$$

$$C^i = \begin{bmatrix} 1 & 0 & 0 & 0 & 0 \end{bmatrix}^T,\ D^i = \begin{bmatrix} \frac{K_{P_i}}{T_{P_i}} & 0 & 0 & 0 & 0 \end{bmatrix}^T,$$

$$A^{ij} = \begin{bmatrix} 0 & 0 & 0 & 0 & -\frac{K_{P_i}}{2\pi T_{P_i}} K_{s_{ij}} \\ 0 & 0 & 0 & 0 & 0 \\ 0 & 0 & 0 & 0 & 0 \\ 0 & 0 & 0 & 0 & \frac{K_{E_i}}{2\pi} K_{s_{ij}} \\ 0 & 0 & 0 & 0 & 0 \end{bmatrix},$$

$$x^i(t) = \begin{bmatrix} \Delta f_i(t) & \Delta P_{g_i}(t) & \Delta X_{g_i}(t) & \Delta E_i(t) & \Delta\delta_i(t) \end{bmatrix}^T,$$
$$i, j \in \mathbf{S} \triangleq \{1,2,3\}.$$

Variables $\Delta f_i(t)$, $\Delta P_{g_i}(t)$, $\Delta X_{g_i}(t)$, $\Delta E_i(t)$, and $\Delta\delta_i(t)$ are the changes of frequency, power output, governor valve position, integral control, and rotor angle deviation, respectively. $\Delta P_d^i(t)$ is the vector of load disturbance. Parameters T_{p_i}, T_{T_i}, and T_{G_i} are time constants of the power system, turbine, and governor, respectively. Constants K_{p_i}, K_{E_i}, K_{B_i}, $K_{s_{ij}}$ are power system gain, integral control gain, and frequency bias factor, and the interconnection gain between area i and j ($i \neq j$). Parameter R_i is the speed regulation coefficient. Some specific parameters of the system are shown in Table I of [222].

To illustrate the effectiveness of the controller against adverse disturbance and noise, we give the following setup. The disturbance attention level is $\gamma = 30$. The sampling period is $T_k = 0.05\ s$ and $K = 500$. The weight coefficients are $Q = I_{15\times15}$ and $R = I_{3\times3}$. The initial state is $x^i(t_0) = \begin{bmatrix} 0.01 & 0 & 0 & 0 & 0 \end{bmatrix}^T$, $\bar{x}^i(t_0) = \hat{x}^i(t_0) =$

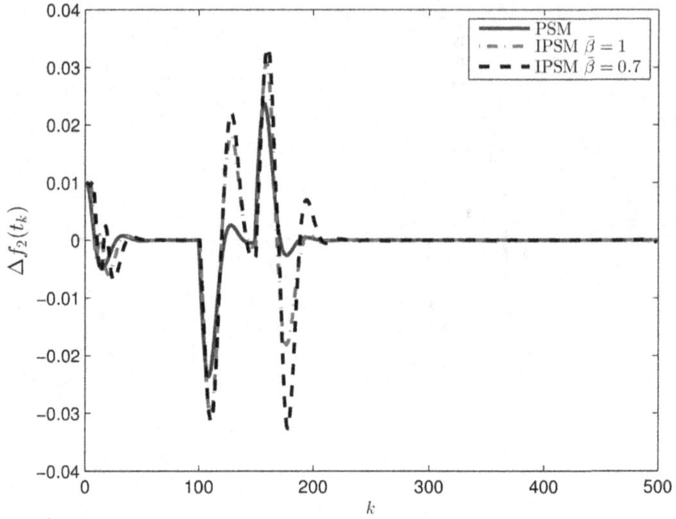

Figure 6.3 State evolution of $\Delta f_2(t_k)$.

$\begin{bmatrix} 0 & 0 & 0 & 0 & 0 \end{bmatrix}^T$, $i \in \mathbf{S}$, and

$$E = 0.01 * \begin{bmatrix} 1 & 0.5 & 0.3 \\ 0.5 & 0.8 & 0.1 \\ 1 & 0.5 & 0.8 \end{bmatrix}, \; v(t_k) = 0.01 * \begin{bmatrix} \sin(t_k)/k \\ \cos(t_k)/k \\ \cos(t_k)/k \end{bmatrix}.$$

A positive load of $\Delta P_d^i(t_k) = 2\ pu, i \in \{1,\ 2\}$ is added in the first two areas of the power system between 5 s and 7.5 s. The resultant curves of $\Delta f_i(t_k)$, $i \in \mathbf{S}$ in the three areas are shown in Fig. 6.2-6.4, which include the cases of perfect state measurements (PSM), IPSM without DoS attack, and IPSM with DoS attack when $\bar{\beta} = 0.7$. It is observed that both the imperfect state information and DoS attack degrade system performance and the overall power system are interconnected.

To demonstrate the validity of the resilient power transmission strategy, we assume that there are two channels with different characteristics. The parameters for two channels are set by $\eta_1 = 0.5$, $\eta_2 = 0.3$, $\xi_1 = 0.3$, $\xi_2 = 0.1$, $a_1 = 0.4$, $a_2 = 0.5$, $b_1 = 1$, $b_2 = 0.3$, and $\varrho_1^2 = \varrho_2^2 = 0.05$. The transmission power of the transmitter and attacker are divided into two levels, i.e., $\mathbf{T} = \{1, 2\}$, $\mathbf{W} = \{0.5, 1\}$. Weight coefficients in equation (6.17) are $c_0 = 0.5$, $c_1 = 0.1$, $c_2 = 0.2$, and $C_0 = \begin{bmatrix} 0.5 & 0.3 \\ 0.3 & 0.5 \end{bmatrix}$. Let the iteration initial value be $\mathbf{F}_0 = \begin{bmatrix} 5 & 4 & 7 & 4 \end{bmatrix}$. By using Algorithm 2, the evolutions of the optimal value $\mathscr{F}_n^*(r)$, $r \in \mathbf{R}$ are depicted as Fig. 6.5. The optimal mixed strategies of each player under four combinations of channel choice are illustrated in Table 6.1, where i is the channel chosen by the transmitter, and j is the channel chosen by attacker.

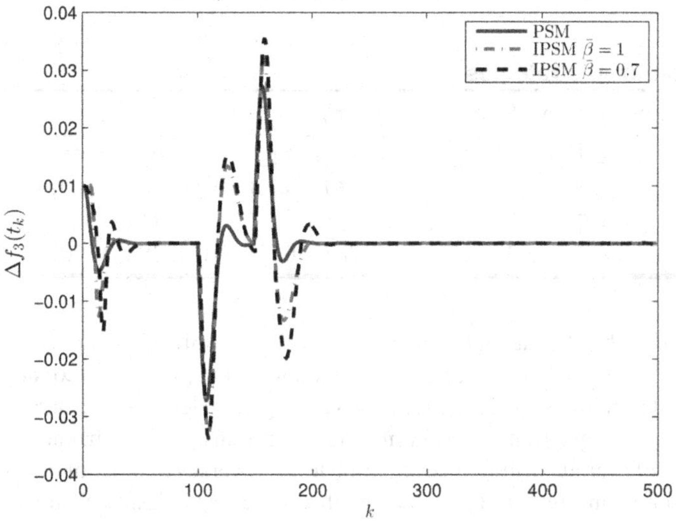

Figure 6.4 State evolution of $\Delta f_3(t_k)$.

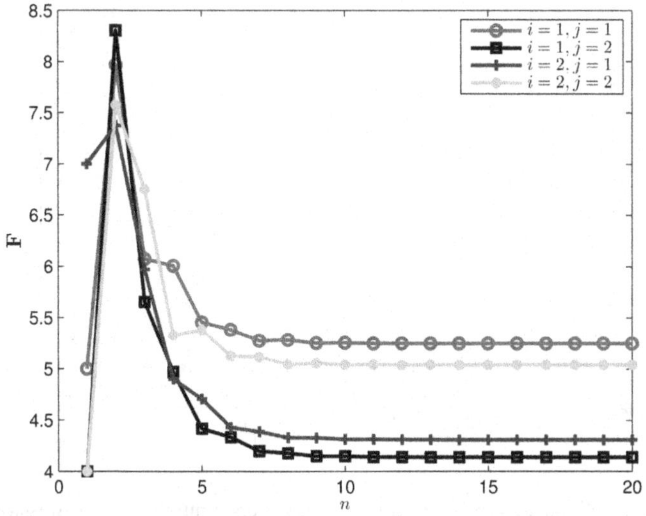

Figure 6.5 Evolutions of cost values $\mathbf{F}_n$.

Table 6.1
The optimal mixed strategies

Transmission Channel	π_T^*	π_W^*
$i=1,\ j=1$	[0.4458 0.5542]	[0.7405 0.2595]
$i=1,\ j=2$	[0.1156 0.8844]	[0.6860 0.3140]
$i=2,\ j=1$	[0 1]	[1 0]
$i=2,\ j=2$	[0.4378 0.5622]	[0.8430 0.1570]

Let us choose the channel gains in each channel randomly for two players, that is, $\eta_i \in [0.3,\ 0.5]$, $\xi_j \in [0.1,\ 0.3]$, $i, j \in \mathbf{N}$. The parameters in (6.5) and (6.6) are chosen as $a_i \in [0.1,\ 1]$ and $b_j \in [0.1,\ 1]$, $i, j \in \mathbf{N}$. Other parameters are the same setup as above. We apply Algorithm 2 1000 times for $1-5$ transmission channels, and the relation curve of average disturbance attention level γ^* versus number of transmission channels is shown in Fig. 6.6. It is observed that more transmission channels lead to better system performance, which demonstrates the effectiveness of the multi-channel defense framework.

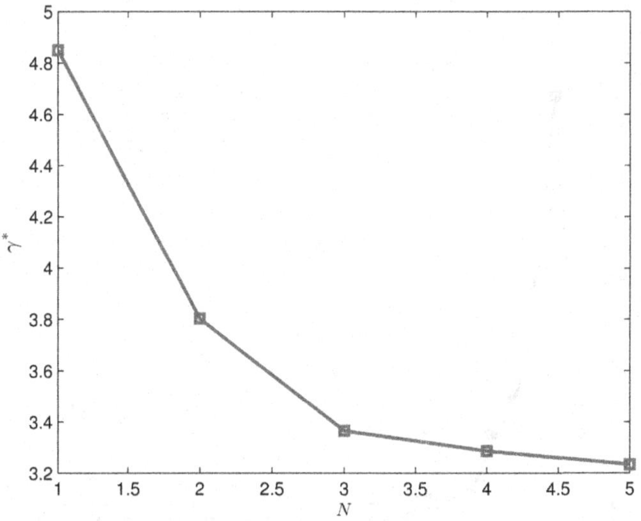

Figure 6.6 The optimal disturbance attention level γ^* versus number of transmission channels N.

6.6 CONCLUSION

In this chapter, the resilient strategy design problem has been investigated for a class of CPS under DoS attack. The system model in the delta domain under DoS attack occurring in a wireless network between sensor and remote estimation has been set up. The minimax control strategy has been obtained in the delta domain under IPSM. Then, the multi-channel transmission framework has been constructed, which can reduce the damage to the control system from a DoS attack. A two-player Markov stochastic game has been built to model the interactive decision-making of both sides under energy budget constraints. We have applied the dynamic programming and value iteration methods to derive the resilient strategies for the control system and communication network. Finally, numerical simulations have been presented to illustrate the validity of the design scheme.

7 Resilient control under DoS attack via a hierarchical game

7.1 INTRODUCTION

Cyber attacks on control systems are commonly classified as two types: integrity attacks [224] and availability attacks [90]. The integrity attacks take effect by modifying the control or measurement signal and require comprehensive resources. In contrast, availability attacks do not need prior knowledge and make the control or measurement signal unavailable to its destination. The availability attacks are also known as denial of-service (DoS) attacks or jamming attacks, and they are realized by corrupting the communication network. Researchers [90, 216, 217, 224, 238] studied the security issues of control systems and obtained many useful results. From this literature, it is known that the transmitter and attacker have a finite power budget and the attacker prefers to remain undetected in practice. Therefore, one essential issue of transmitter and attack is competition with a limited energy budget. It makes practical sense to investigate SINR-based attack scheme-based game theoretic approaches to enhance resilience of the closed-loop WNCSs.

In practice, all the control systems operate in the presence of disturbances. To achieve optimal performance under disturbances, the H_∞ minimax control theory is used[238] . However, nowadays the sampling intervals in industrial control systems become smaller and smaller with the rapid development of sensing technology. Designing a control algorithm by using a traditional shift operator may cause serious numerical problems especially under a finite-word length constraint, as in references [158, 238, 241, 242]. In the last decades, some inspiring control results which are a unified form of discrete- and continuous-time results have been reported for the control problems in the delta domain of NCSs [80, 237]. To the best of the authors' knowledge, the H_∞ minimax control problem has not been studied adequately by using a delta operator approach for WNCSs, not to mention that the WNCSs are under DoS attacks. Here, this chapter will shorten such a gap.

In this chapter, a SINR-based DoS attack model under a dynamic network environment is investigated for a WNCS, which is stratified as the cyber and physical layer. In the presence of DoS attack, a two player zero-sum game framework is introduced to model the interaction between transmitter and attacker who subject to energy constraints in the cyber layer. Then, for the physical layer, an H_∞ minimax control problem in delta domain is studied to guarantee the optimal system performance for WNCS with time-varying network conditions under disturbance. Iterative algorithms are given to solve the cross layer optimization problem. The main contributions of this chapter are mainly threefold:

(1) A two player zero-sum Markov game scheme is established to model the SINR-based power transmission strategies for transmitter and attacker in cyber-layer of the WNCS.
(2) Under the impact of DoS attack-induced two-state Markov packet dropout, an H_∞ optimal controller is obtained by solving a minimax problem for the WNCS in delta domain.
(3) A hierarchical game structure is exploited for the cross layer resilient control design. The value iteration and Q-learning methods are used to attain the optimal transmission and control strategies.

The rest of this chapter is organized as follows. The problem formulation and design objectives are given in Section 7.2. In Section 7.3, the zero-sum Markov game in the cyber layer is analyzed when the transition probability of the dynamic network is known and unknown. The H_∞ minimax controller is given in the form of a saddle-point solution with dynamic programming. The value iteration and Q-learning algorithms are used for the couple design of WNCS. In Section 7.4, numerical simulations on a two-area load frequency control system is shown to verify the effectiveness of the proposed method. Conclusions are drawn in Section 7.5.

7.2 PROBLEM SETUP

As shown in Fig. 7.1, a WNCS under DoS attack is stratified as the cyber and physical layer. In the WNCS, the controller and actuator are linked by wireless network, as well as the sensor and controller communicate by reliable network.

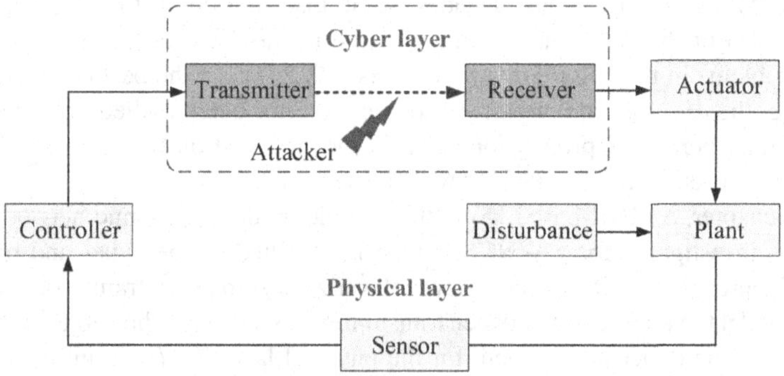

Figure 7.1 WNCS under DoS attack.

There exists a DoS attacker which aims at interfering the transmission of the control signal between the transmitting and receiving modules. Under the DoS attacker and disturbance, system models are set up for cyber and physical layer, respectively.

7.2.1 TRANSMISSION MODEL WITH SINR

In the cyber layer, the transmission power of transmitter p_m is chosen in M levels denoted as $\mathbf{p} = \{p_1, p_2, \cdots, p_M\}$, $\mathcal{M} = \{1, 2, \cdots, M\}$. The transmission strategy of the attacker is denoted as w_l which is chosen from $\mathbf{w} = \{w_1, w_2, \cdots, w_L\}$, $\mathcal{L} = \{1, 2, \cdots, L\}$. Actually, the environment of the wireless communication network fluctuates over time. Assume that the wireless network is random which subjects it to a discrete-time Markov jump process in a finite set $\Pi = \{1, 2, \cdots, S\}$ [50]. The channel fading gain of the transmitter in network mode $s, s \in \Pi$ is given as ζ_s, denoting that $\zeta_s \in \Xi = \{\zeta_1, \zeta_2, \cdots, \zeta_S\}$ and the channel gain of the attacker is η_s, where $\eta_s \in \Gamma = \{\eta_1, \eta_2, \cdots, \eta_S\}$. The stationary transition probability from mode s at time n to s' at time $n+1$ is

$$\lambda_{s,s'} = \mathbb{P}\{s'(n+1) | s(n)\}, \ s'(n+1), s(n) \in \Pi \tag{7.1}$$

and one has that $\sum_{s' \in \Pi} \lambda_{s,s'} = 1, \forall s \in \Pi$. In the presence of the transmitter and DoS attacker, the SINR at the receiver yields

$$\gamma_{T,s} = \frac{\zeta_s p_m}{\eta_s w_l + \sigma^2}, \ s \in \Pi, \ m \in \mathcal{M} \text{ and } l \in \mathcal{L}, \tag{7.2}$$

where σ^2 is the additive white Gaussian noise. Assume that the communication between controller and actuator is modulated by the quadrature amplitude technique. Based on digital communication theory [110], the relationship between symbol error rate (SER) and SINR is shown as

$$\text{SER}(s) = 2\mathbf{Q}\left(\sqrt{\kappa \gamma_{T,s}}\right), \tag{7.3}$$

where

$$\mathbf{Q}(x) \triangleq \frac{1}{\sqrt{2\pi}} \int_x^{\infty} \exp(-\tau^2/2) \mathrm{d}\tau$$

and $\kappa > 0$ is a constant.

Function $r : \Pi \times \mathbf{p} \times \mathbf{w} \to \mathbb{R}$ is defined as the cost of a possible action pair (p_m, w_l) in a certain network mode s. The cost function is given as

$$r(s, p_m, w_l) = \mathcal{F}(J_p(s), p_m, w_l, C_{ml}), \tag{7.4}$$

where $J_p(s)$ is the physical-layer system performance. Scalar C_{ml} denotes the inherent cost when taking the action pair (p_m, w_l). Note that the transmitter as a part of the WNCS wants to help the plant obtain good system performance with little equipment loss. The transmitter that is working as an isolated node which is battery charged should consider the cost of energy consumption. Additionally, more cost of energy consumption is preferred for the opponent participant. Instead of explicit energy constraints, we take the energy consumption of players into consideration in the objective function [216]. Thus, function $\mathcal{F}(\cdot)$, chosen based on the actual scene, is always increasing with respect to parameters $J_p(s), p_m, C_{ml}$ and decreasing in w_l. The transmitter is a minimizer, which minimizes the cost function $r(s, p_m, w_l)$. In contrast, the attacker has an opposite objective; it wants to maximize the cost function. The transmitter and attacker are involved in a two player zero-sum game, and the relation is presented as

$$r(s, p_m, w_l) = r_T(s, p_m, w_l) = -r_J(s, p_m, w_l).$$

To give a formal model of the Markov dynamic jamming game, the distribution vectors are given subsequently. Denote that $f_m(s) \in [0,1]$ and $g_l(s) \in [0,1]$ are the probabilities that the transmitter and attacker choose action $p_m \in \mathbf{p}$ and $w_l \in \mathbf{w}$ in mode s. For specific mode s, we have $\sum_{m=1}^{M} f_m(s) = 1$ and $\sum_{l=1}^{L} g_l(s) = 1$. Then, denote that $\mathbf{f}(s) = [f_1(s), f_2(s), \cdots, f_M(s)]$, $\mathbf{g}(s) = [g_1(s), g_2(s), \cdots, g_L(s)]$, $\forall s \in \Pi$, and for all states $\mathbf{F} = [\mathbf{f}(1), \mathbf{f}(2), \cdots, \mathbf{f}(S)]$, $\mathbf{G} = [\mathbf{g}(1), \mathbf{g}(2), \cdots, \mathbf{g}(S)]$.

The following cost function J_c is introduced to quantify the discounted sum of the expected cost in cyber layer

$$J_c(s) = \mathbb{E}_s^{\mathbf{f}(s), \mathbf{g}(s)} \left(\sum_{n=1}^{+\infty} \rho^n r(s, p_m, w_l) \right), \tag{7.5}$$

where s is the initial state choosing in Π. n is the time step, which is on the time scale of the varying of the network environment. Parameter $\rho \in (0,1)$ is the discount factor for discounting the future rewards.

7.2.2 CONTROL MODEL UNDER DISTURBANCE

The control problem in the physical layer of the WNCS is described in this subsection. Consider a general continuous linear time-invariant plant with disturbance as follows

$$\dot{x}(t) = A_0 x(t) + B_0 u(t) + D_0 \omega(t), \tag{7.6}$$

where $x(t) \in \mathbb{R}^n$ is the state vector, $u(t) \in \mathbb{R}^m$ is the control signal, and $\omega(t) \in \mathbb{R}^p$ is the disturbance. $A_0 \in \mathbb{R}^{n \times n}$, $B_0 \in \mathbb{R}^{n \times m}$, and $D_0 \in \mathbb{R}^{n \times p}$ are system matrices. When taking different network load conditions into consideration, system (7.6) is discretized with time-varying sampling period T_k by a delta operator approach as

$$\delta x(t_k) = A(t_k) x(t_k) + \nu(t_k) B(t_k) u(t_k) + D(t_k) \omega(t_k), \tag{7.7}$$

where $A(t_k) = \frac{e^{A_0 \mathrm{T}_k} - I}{\mathrm{T}_k}$ $B(t_k) = \frac{1}{\mathrm{T}_k} \int_0^{\mathrm{T}_k} e^{A_0(\mathrm{T}_k - \tau)} B_0 d\tau$,and
$D(t_k) = \frac{1}{\mathrm{T}_k} \int_0^{\mathrm{T}_k} e^{A_0(\mathrm{T}_k - \tau)} D_0 d\tau$. In equation (7.7), the delta operator is given as follows

$$\delta x(t_k) = \frac{x(t_k + \mathrm{T}_k) - x(t_k)}{\mathrm{T}_k},$$

where T_k is the sampling period, t is the continuous time, and k is the time step with $t_k = \sum_{l=0}^{k-1} \mathrm{T}_l$. The initial state $x(t_0)$ is assumed to be a Gaussian random vector with mean 0 and covariance Σ. In equation (7.7), notation $\{v(t_k)\}$ represents the attack-induced packet dropout which is modeled as a Markov stochastic process. The process $\{v(t_k)\}$ obeys the following probability distribution

$$\begin{bmatrix} \mathbb{P}(v(t_{k+1})=0\,|\,v(t_k)=0) & \mathbb{P}(v(t_{k+1})=1\,|\,v(t_k)=0) \\ \mathbb{P}(v(t_{k+1})=0\,|\,v(t_k)=1) & \mathbb{P}(v(t_{k+1})=1\,|\,v(t_k)=1) \end{bmatrix} = \begin{bmatrix} 1-\alpha & \alpha \\ \beta & 1-\beta \end{bmatrix}. \tag{7.8}$$

In the sequence, probabilities that a packet is received or not are depending on the previous packet. The variables satisfy $0 < \alpha \leq 1$ and $0 < \beta \leq 1$. It is known that the Markov packet dropout model is a generalization of the Bernoulli packet dropout. The average sojourn time in the mode of packet loss is $(1-\alpha)/\alpha$ [57]. Scalar α which is a critical condition for the convergence of the cost is in sense "more critical" than β. A DoS attacker tends to destroy the system by making the system packet lost consecutively [223]. Therefore, parameter α strictly connected with the probability to have a long "bursts" of packet losses is seen as the consequence of the game between the transmitter and DoS attacker. Then, based on equation (7.3) and the preceding discussion, we have

$$\alpha = 1 - \mathrm{SER}. \tag{7.9}$$

Remark 16

1) For the physical layer, the communication channel with memory occurs in practice; that is, the channel generally does not vary separately in time [148]; thus independent trials fail to simulate such a packet loss process adequately. To capture the possible temporal correlation of channel conditions, a two-state Markov packet loss process is adopted based on the particular Gilbert-Elliott channel model [57, 82].

2) Note that the two-state Markov packet dropout model in the physical layer always evolves on the time scale of seconds, whereas, the Markov jump process of the cyber layer may be on the order of hours [164]. The time scale of varying of the network environment is usually much larger than the evolution of physical systems. Therefore, when studying the transmission and attack strategies in the cyber layer, we assume that the control system has entered the steady state [216, 217].

For the stationary situation, in the absence of any past information, the probability is always the same for all steps, that is, $\mathbb{P}(v(t_0)=0) = \cdots = \mathbb{P}(v(t_k)=0) = \beta/(\alpha+\beta)$ and $\mathbb{P}(v(t_0)=1) = \cdots = \mathbb{P}(v(t_k)=1) = \alpha/(\alpha+\beta), \forall k > 0$.

Transmission control protocol (TCP) is applied in the WNCS and the information set $\mathcal{I}(t_k)$ given as

$$\mathcal{I}(t_0) = \{x(t_0)\},\ \mathcal{I}(t_k) = \{x(t_0), \cdots, x(t_k), v(t_0), \cdots, v(t_{k-1})\} \tag{7.10}$$

is acknowledged at each step k. Denote the control sequence $\{u(t_k)\}$ and disturbance sequence $\{\omega(t_k)\}$ as $\mu(\mathcal{I}(t_k))$ and $\nu(\mathcal{I}(t_k))$, respectively. The goal of this chapter is to determine the optimal action $\mu^*(\mathcal{I}(t_k))$ such that the following system performance

$$\begin{aligned} J_p(\mu,\nu,\mathbf{F}^*,\mathbf{G}^*) = \mathbb{E}_{\nu(t_k)}\Big\{ & x^T(t_K)Q^K x(t_K) + \\ & \mathrm{T}_k \sum_{k=0}^{K-1}\{x^T(t_k)Qx(t_k)+\nu(t_k)u^T(t_k)Ru(t_k)-\gamma^2\omega^2(t_k)\}\Big\} \end{aligned} \tag{7.11}$$

is minimized with the worst-case disturbance for a prescribed fixed value γ, where γ is an upper bound on the desired $\mathcal{L}_2$ gain disturbance attenuation.

7.2.3 DESIGN OBJECTIVES

According to the previous subsections, both the cyber- and physical-layer have two participants which possess opposite design goals. Then, we present them as two player zero-sum games given in the following.

Problem 1 *Let the strategy pair (μ,ν) be fixed. A pair $(\mathbf{F}^*,\mathbf{G}^*)$ is a saddle-point of the ρ-discount game if the following inequality*

$$\mathcal{G}_1 : \boldsymbol{J}_c(\boldsymbol{F}^*,\boldsymbol{G}) \leq \boldsymbol{J}_c(\boldsymbol{F}^*,\boldsymbol{G}^*) \leq \boldsymbol{J}_c(\boldsymbol{F},\boldsymbol{G}^*) \tag{7.12}$$

holds, where $\boldsymbol{J}_c = [J_c(1),J_c(2),\cdots,J_c(S)]$.

Problem 2 *With given cyber layer periodical optimal strategy $(\boldsymbol{F}^*,\boldsymbol{G}^*)$, if for all feasible strategy (μ,ν), there exists*

$$\mathcal{G}_2 : J_p(\mu^*,\nu,\boldsymbol{F}^*,\boldsymbol{G}^*) \leq J_p(\mu^*,\nu^*,\boldsymbol{F}^*,\boldsymbol{G}^*) \leq J_p(\mu,\nu^*,\boldsymbol{F}^*,\boldsymbol{G}^*), \tag{7.13}$$

then (μ^*,ν^*) is the saddle-point equilibrium, and the optimal system performance is $J_p(\mu^*,\nu^*,\boldsymbol{F}^*,\boldsymbol{G}^*)$.

A hierarchical game structure is introduced to characterize the cross layer relation of the whole WNCS. In the hierarchical game, the cyber-layer game and physical-layer game are updated nestedly. The optimal cyber-layer strategy $(\mathbf{F}^*,\mathbf{G}^*)$ leads to a specific Markov packet dropout transition probability α. On the other hand, the control system performance effected by Markov packet dropout is also considered as a part of the cost in the cyber layer. Based on game theory, the optimal transmission strategy under attack and optimal H_∞ controller are given in the form of saddle-point equilibriums, where the joint defense strategies in two layers can enhance the resilience of WNCS.

Remark 17

> *1) The disturbance caused by the environment is assumed to be variable and controlled by an adversary, which aims to provide a worst case for the design of the controller. Thus, the controller and disturbance are regarded as two players with opposite goals in Problem 2, where the designed controller based on the worst case will be robust to actual stochastic disturbance [186].*

2) For analysis simplification, we consider that the DoS attack occurs in the feedback channel and the forward link is built by a reliable network. Actually, the model setup and addressed methods can be extended to deal with attacks in networks on both sides of the physical plant. For example, it can be realized by augmenting a strategy set of transmitter and attacker and considering a linear quadratic gaussian (LQG) problem in the cyber and physical layer, respectively.

7.3 MAIN RESULTS

In this section, solutions of the design objectives for WNCS are presented with saddle-point equilibriums for the cyber and physical layer. The couple relationship between cyber and physical layers is captured as a hierarchical game. The value iteration and Q-learning methods are employed with known and unknown transition probability cases, respectively.

7.3.1 STRATEGY DESIGN FOR $\mathcal{G}_1$

To obtain the mixed Nash equilibrium strategy of $\mathcal{G}_1$, the value iteration and Q-learning methods are exploited for the known and unknown transition probability matrix cases of the network environment, respectively. The following lemma is provided for further analysis.

Lemma 7.1 *[128] The standard solution to problem* (7.5) *above is through an iterative search method that searches for a fixed point of the following Bellman equation*

$$Q(s,p_m,w_l) = r(s,p_m,w_l) + \rho \sum_{s' \in \Pi} \mathbb{P}(s'|s) J_c(s',n). \tag{7.14}$$

Theorem 7.1 *The discounted, zero-sum, stochastic game has a value vector $\boldsymbol{J}_c^*$ which is the unique solution of equation*

$$\boldsymbol{J}_c^* = val([\boldsymbol{Q}(s)]_{s\in\Pi}), \tag{7.15}$$

where $val(\cdot)$ is a function yielding the game value of a zero-sum matrix game. $\boldsymbol{Q}(s)$ is an auxiliary matrix which is given as

$$\boldsymbol{Q}(s) = [Q(s,p_m,w_l)]_{m\in\mathcal{M}, l\in\mathcal{L}}, \tag{7.16}$$

where $Q(s,p_m,w_l)$ is shown as equation (7.14) *of Lemma 7.1.*

Proof *The results are obtained by using Shapley's Theorem [181] and the proof is omitted.*

As in [181], the value iteration method is used for solving the zero-sum stochastic game (7.15). With an initial approximate game value, iterate according to

$$\mathbf{J}_c(n+1) = \mathrm{val}([\mathbf{Q}(s,\mathbf{J}_c(n))]_{s\in\Pi}). \tag{7.17}$$

Obviously, the transition probability matrix of the dynamic network environment must be known by the transmitter and attacker when using the value iteration method in Theorem 7.1. However, the transmitter and attacker may not have access to such information. Therefore, the Q-learning method is introduced to obtain the optimal value with limited information. The instrumental lemma is provided for the subsequent theorem in the following.

Lemma 7.2 *[103] Let $\mathbb{Q}$ be the space of all $\boldsymbol{Q}$ functions. Define an operator $\mathcal{P}_n$: $\mathbb{Q} \to \mathbb{Q}$ that satisfies the following equation*

1$\boldsymbol{Q}^*(s) = \mathbb{E}\{\mathcal{P}_n \boldsymbol{Q}^*(s)\}$.
2For all $s \in \Pi$, $\boldsymbol{Q}(s), \boldsymbol{Q}^*(s) \in \mathbb{Q}$, there exists

$$\|\mathcal{P}_n \boldsymbol{Q}(s) - \mathcal{P}_n \boldsymbol{Q}^*(s)\| \leq \varpi \|\boldsymbol{Q}(s) - \boldsymbol{Q}^*(s)\| + \lambda_n,$$

where $0 < \varpi < 1$ and the sequence $\lambda_n > 0$ converges to 0 with probability 1.

Then, the iteration

$$\boldsymbol{Q}_{n+1}(s) = (1 - \varsigma_n)\boldsymbol{Q}_n(s) + \varsigma_n[\mathcal{P}_n \boldsymbol{Q}_n(s)]$$

converges to $\boldsymbol{Q}^*$ with probability 1, if the learning rate satisfies

$$\varsigma_n \in [0,1), \sum_{n=0}^{+\infty} \varsigma_n = +\infty, \sum_{n=0}^{+\infty} \varsigma_n^2 < +\infty. \tag{7.18}$$

Remark 18

1) Note that typical methods, like value iteration, for solving the Markov game require the knowledge of system parameters, including system performance of physical layer $J_p(s)$, inherent cost C_{ml}, closed-form expression for the reward function $\mathcal{F}(\cdot)$, and transition probability $\lambda_{s,s'}, \forall s, s' \in \Pi$; whereas, the Q-learning method is a form of model-free reinforcing learning, which only needs the system parameters and provides a more practical way to solve the Markov game [78]. In the Q-learning method, the players endow the capability of learning to act optimally in an online patten. The idea of Q-leaning is to try different actions to update the knowledge when little information is available in the early time, and when the players have sufficient information, less emphasis is put on the learning process [103, 128, 180]. With the advantages of the Q-learning method, it has been applied to many fields, such as the security issue on remote state estimation [216], mode-free H_∞ control [1], spectrum management in cognitive wireless networks [21] and so on.

2) It is worth mentioning that iteration methods, i.e., value iteration and Q-learning methods, are investigated in this chapter, which allows that the cost function $\mathcal{F}(\cdot)$ has an extensive form according to the practice scene but is not confined to a convex or linear form as many optimization problems [160, 238].

Theorem 7.2 *If the transition probability $\lambda_{s,s'}, \forall s, s' \in \Pi$ is not known, $Q_{n+1}(s, p_m, w_l)$ is updated as follows*

$$\begin{aligned} Q_{n+1}(s,p_m,w_l) =& (1-\theta_n(s,p_m,w_l))Q_n(s,p_m,w_l)+ \\ & \theta_n(s,p_m,w_l)\left(r(s,p_m,w_l)+\rho J_c^*(s')\right), \end{aligned} \tag{7.19}$$

where $Q_{n+1}(s,p_m,w_l)$ is the $(n+1)$th iteration of (7.19). *Scalar $\theta_n(s,p_m,w_l)$ is the learning rate, which is chosen as*

$$\theta_n(s,p_m,w_l) = \begin{cases} 1/(flag_n(s,p_m,w_l)+1), \ \text{if } (s,p_m,w_l) = (s(n),p_m(n),w_l(n)), \\ 0, \ \text{otherwise}, \end{cases} \tag{7.20}$$

where $flag_n(s,p_m,w_l)$ is the number of times visiting state s, performing action p_m and w_l until step n. The saddle value $J_c^*(s')$ is obtained as

$$J_c^*(s') = \min_{f(s')}\max_{g(s')} \sum_{p_m,w_l} Q(s',p_m,w_l) f_m(s') g_l(s'). \tag{7.21}$$

Proof *Obviously, the learning rate* (7.20) *satisfies conditions* (7.18) *in Lemma 7.2. Then, it is known that $Q_{n+1}(s,p_m,w_l)$ converges if Conditions 1) and 2) hold in Lemma 7.2. Let the operator $\mathcal{P}_n$ be defined as*

$$\mathcal{P}_n \boldsymbol{Q}(s) = [r(s,p_m,w_l)]_{m\in\mathcal{M},l\in\mathcal{L}} + \rho val(\boldsymbol{Q}_n(s'))\boldsymbol{I} \tag{7.22}$$

for all $\boldsymbol{Q} \in \mathbb{Q}$. Denote that $\boldsymbol{Q}^*(s)$ in the following is the steady state of equation (7.14) *if it converges.*

$$\boldsymbol{Q}^*(s) = [r(s,p_m,w_l)]_{m\in\mathcal{M},l\in\mathcal{L}} + \rho \sum_{s'\in\Pi} \mathbb{P}(s'|s)\boldsymbol{J}_c^*(s')\boldsymbol{I} \tag{7.23}$$

Based on (7.23), *we have*

$$\begin{aligned} \boldsymbol{Q}^*(s) =& [r(s,p_m,w_l)]_{m\in\mathcal{M},l\in\mathcal{L}} + \rho \sum_{s'\in\Pi} \mathbb{P}(s'|s)\boldsymbol{J}_c^*(s')\boldsymbol{I} \\ =& \sum_{s'\in\Pi} \mathbb{P}(s'|s)([r(s,p_m,w_l)]_{m\in\mathcal{M},l\in\mathcal{L}} + \rho val(\boldsymbol{Q}_n(s'))\boldsymbol{I}) \\ =& \mathbb{E}\{\mathcal{P}_n \boldsymbol{Q}^*(s)\}. \end{aligned}$$

It is concluded that Condition 1) holds. Next we will show the contraction property. By matrix game theory, if $A \geq B$, we have $val(A) \geq val(B)$. It is obtained that

$$\begin{aligned} & val(\boldsymbol{Q}_2(s)) \geq val(\boldsymbol{Q}_1(s)) - \|\boldsymbol{Q}_1(s) - \boldsymbol{Q}_2(s)\|, \\ & val(\boldsymbol{Q}_2(s)) \leq val(\boldsymbol{Q}_1(s)) + \|\boldsymbol{Q}_1(s) - \boldsymbol{Q}_2(s)\| \end{aligned}$$

and then

$$|val(\boldsymbol{Q}_1(s)) - val(\boldsymbol{Q}_2(s))| \leq \|\boldsymbol{Q}_1(s) - \boldsymbol{Q}_2(s)\|. \tag{7.24}$$

According to inequality (7.24), for all $s \in \Pi$, one has that

$$\begin{aligned}\|\mathcal{P}_n\boldsymbol{Q}-\mathcal{P}_n\boldsymbol{Q}^*\|_\infty =&\rho \max_{s\in\Pi}|val(\boldsymbol{Q}(s))-val(\boldsymbol{Q}^*(s))|\\ \le&\rho \max_{s\in\Pi}\|\boldsymbol{Q}(s)-\boldsymbol{Q}^*(s)\|\\ =&\rho\|\boldsymbol{Q}-\boldsymbol{Q}^*\|_\infty.\end{aligned}$$

By Lemma 7.2, it is concluded that $\boldsymbol{Q}_n \to \boldsymbol{Q}^*$. This completes the proof.

From Theorem 7.2, it is known that the discount factor ρ is related to the convergence rate of the Q-learning method. With the optimal auxiliary matrix $\mathbf{Q}^*$, the mixed saddle-point equilibrium strategies $\mathbf{f}^*(s)$, $\mathbf{g}^*(s)$ and optimal value $J_c^*(s)$, $s \in \Pi$ are obtained by equation (7.21).

7.3.2 STRATEGY DESIGN FOR $\mathcal{G}_2$

With the periodical optimal transmission and attack strategies $(\mathbf{F}^*, \mathbf{G}^*)$, the following theorem is given to provide solutions for Problem 2. The instrumental lemma is introduced first, which will be used in the theorems.

Lemma 7.3 *[81] For any time function $x(t_k)$ and $y(t_k)$, there exists the following property of the delta operator*

$$\delta(x(t_k)y(t_k)) = y(t_k)\delta x(t_k) + x(t_k)\delta y(t_k) + T_k\delta x(t_k)\delta y(t_k),$$

where T_k is the sampling period.

The preliminary notations of Riccati equations are given as

$$\begin{aligned}-\delta\mathcal{S}(t_k) =&Q+\alpha P_{u0}^T(t_k)RP_{u0}(t_k)-\gamma^2P_{\omega0}^T(t_k)P_{\omega0}(t_k)\\ &+(1-\alpha)(\mathrm{T}_k\mathcal{X}_{\mathcal{S}_0}^T(t_k)\mathcal{S}(t_{k+1})\mathcal{X}_{\mathcal{S}_0}(t_k)\\ &+\mathcal{S}(t_{k+1})\mathcal{X}_{\mathcal{S}_0}(t_k)+\mathcal{X}_{\mathcal{S}_0}^T(t_k)\mathcal{S}(t_{k+1}))+\alpha(\mathrm{T}_k\mathcal{X}_{\mathcal{R}_0}^T(t_k)\mathcal{R}(t_{k+1})\mathcal{X}_{\mathcal{R}_0}(t_k)\\ &+\mathcal{R}(t_{k+1})\mathcal{X}_{\mathcal{R}_0}(t_k)+\mathcal{X}_{\mathcal{R}_0}^T(t_k)\mathcal{R}(t_{k+1}))+\frac{\alpha}{\mathrm{T}_k}(\mathcal{R}(t_{k+1})-\mathcal{S}(t_{k+1})),\\ \mathcal{S}(t_k) =&\mathcal{S}(t_{k+1})-\mathrm{T}_k\delta\mathcal{S}(t_k),\end{aligned} \tag{7.25}$$

$$\begin{aligned}-\delta\mathcal{R}(t_k) =&Q+(1-\beta)P_{u1}^T(t_k)RP_{u1}(t_k)-\gamma^2P_{\omega1}^T(t_k)P_{\omega1}(t_k)\\ &+\beta(\mathrm{T}_k\mathcal{X}_{\mathcal{S}_1}^T(t_k)\mathcal{S}(t_{k+1})\mathcal{X}_{\mathcal{S}_1}(t_k)\\ &+\mathcal{S}(t_{k+1})\mathcal{X}_{\mathcal{S}_1}(t_k)+\mathcal{X}_{\mathcal{S}_1}^T(t_k)\mathcal{S}(t_{k+1}))+(1-\beta)(\mathrm{T}_k\mathcal{X}_{\mathcal{R}_1}^T(t_k)\mathcal{R}(t_{k+1})\mathcal{X}_{\mathcal{R}_1}(t_k)\\ &+\mathcal{R}(t_{k+1})\mathcal{X}_{\mathcal{R}_1}(t_k)+\mathcal{X}_{\mathcal{R}_1}^T(t_k)\mathcal{R}(t_{k+1}))+\frac{\beta}{\mathrm{T}_k}(\mathcal{S}(t_{k+1})-\mathcal{R}(t_{k+1})),\\ \mathcal{R}(t_k) =&\mathcal{R}(t_{k+1})-\mathrm{T}_k\delta\mathcal{R}(t_k),\end{aligned}$$

where

$$\Theta(t_k) = R + \mathrm{T}_k B^T(t_k)\mathcal{R}(t_{k+1})B(t_k),$$
$$\Lambda_0(t_k) = -\gamma^2 + (1-\alpha)\mathrm{T}_k D^T(t_k)\mathcal{S}(t_{k+1})D(t_k) + \alpha\mathrm{T}_k D^T(t_k)\mathcal{R}(t_{k+1})D(t_k),$$
$$\Lambda_1(t_k) = -\gamma^2 + \beta\mathrm{T}_k D^T(t_k)\mathcal{S}(t_{k+1})D(t_k) + (1-\beta)\mathrm{T}_k D^T(t_k)\mathcal{R}(t_{k+1})D(t_k),$$
$$\Pi_{u0}(t_k) = \Theta(t_k) - \alpha\mathrm{T}_k^2 B^T(t_k)\mathcal{R}(t_{k+1})D(t_k)\Lambda_0^{-1}(t_k)D^T(t_k)\mathcal{R}(t_{k+1})B(t_k),$$
$$\Pi_{\omega0}(t_k) = \Lambda_0(t_k) - \alpha\mathrm{T}_k^2 D^T(t_k)\mathcal{R}(t_{k+1})B(t_k)\Theta^{-1}(t_k)B^T(t_k)\mathcal{R}(t_{k+1})D(t_k),$$
$$\Pi_{u1}(t_k) = \Theta(t_k) - (1-\beta)\mathrm{T}_k^2 B^T(t_k)\mathcal{R}(t_{k+1})D(t_k)\Lambda_1^{-1}(t_k)D^T(t_k)\mathcal{R}(t_{k+1})B(t_k),$$
$$\Pi_{\omega1}(t_k) = \Lambda_1(t_k) - (1-\beta)\mathrm{T}_k^2 D^T(t_k)\mathcal{R}(k+1)B(t_k)\Theta^{-1}(t_k)B^T(t_k)\mathcal{R}(t_{k+1})D(t_k),$$
$$\Xi_{u0}(t_k) = I - \mathrm{T}_k D(t_k)\Lambda_0^{-1}(t_k)((1-\alpha)D^T\mathcal{S}(t_{k+1}) + \alpha D^T\mathcal{R}(t_{k+1})),$$
$$\Xi_{\omega0}(t_k) = (1-\alpha)\mathcal{S}(t_{k+1}) + \alpha\mathcal{R}(t_{k+1}) - \alpha\mathrm{T}_k D^T\mathcal{R}(t_{k+1})B\Theta^{-1}(k)B^T\mathcal{R}(t_{k+1}),$$
$$\Xi_{u1}(t_k) = I - \mathrm{T}_k D\Lambda_1^{-1}D^T(\beta\mathcal{S}(t_{k+1}) + (1-\beta)\mathcal{R}(t_{k+1})),$$
$$\Xi_{\omega1}(t_k) = \beta\mathcal{S}(t_{k+1}) + (1-\beta)\mathcal{R}(t_{k+1})$$
$$-(1-\beta)\mathrm{T}_k D^T(t_k)\mathcal{R}(t_{k+1})B(t_k)\Theta^{-1}(t_k)B^T(t_k)\mathcal{R}(t_{k+1}),$$
$$P_{u0}(t_k) = -\Pi_{u0}^{-1}(t_k)B^T(t_k)\mathcal{R}(t_{k+1})\Xi_{u0}(t_k)(\mathrm{T}_k A(t_k) + I),$$
$$P_{\omega0}(t_k) = -\Pi_{\omega0}^{-1}(t_k)D^T(t_k)\Xi_{\omega0}(t_k)(\mathrm{T}_k A(t_k) + I),$$
$$P_{u1}(t_k) = -\Pi_{u1}^{-1}(t_k)B^T(t_k)\mathcal{R}(t_{k+1})\Xi_{u1}(t_k)(\mathrm{T}_k A(t_k) + I),$$
$$P_{\omega1}(t_k) = -\Pi_{\omega1}^{-1}(t_k)D^T(t_k)\Xi_{\omega1}(t_k)(\mathrm{T}_k A(t_k) + I),$$
$$\mathcal{X}_{\mathcal{S}_0}(t_k) = A(t_k) + D(t_k)P_{\omega0}(t_k),\ \mathcal{X}_{\mathcal{R}_0}(t_k) = A(t_k) + B(t_k)P_{u0}(t_k) + D(t_k)P_{\omega0}(t_k),$$
$$\mathcal{X}_{\mathcal{S}_1}(t_k) = A(t_k) + D(t_k)P_{\omega1}(t_k),\ \mathcal{X}_{\mathcal{R}_1}(t_k) = A(t_k) + B(t_k)P_{u1}(t_k) + D(t_k)P_{\omega1}(t_k).$$

Theorem 7.3 *With specific transmission and DoS attack strategies, information set $\mathcal{I}(t_k)$, a fixed $\gamma > 0$, and finite time-level K, the following constraint and conclusions are presented for the physical-layer game $\mathcal{G}_2$*

1) The game $\mathcal{G}_2$ exists with the unique saddle-point solution if and only if

$$\Theta(t_k) > 0,\ \Lambda_0(t_k) < 0,\ \Lambda_1(t_k) < 0, \forall k \in \{0, 1, \cdots, K-1\}, \tag{7.26}$$

where $\mathcal{R}(t_k)$ and $\mathcal{S}(t_k)$ satisfy the Riccati recursive equations (7.25) and (7.26), respectively. Furthermore, it is assumed that $\mathcal{R}(t_K) = \mathcal{S}(t_K) = Q^K$.

2) If matrices $\Pi_{u0}(t_k)$, $\Pi_{\omega0}(t_k)$, $\Pi_{u1}(t_k)$, and $\Pi_{\omega1}(t_k)$ are invertible, under Condition 1), the feedback saddle-equilibrium $(\mu^*(\mathcal{I}(t_k)), \nu^*(\mathcal{I}(t_k)))$ is given by

- $\nu(t_{k-1}) = 0$

$$\begin{cases} u_0(t_k) = \mu^*(\mathcal{I}(t_k)) = P_{u0}(t_k)x(t_k), \\ \omega_0(t_k) = \nu^*(\mathcal{I}(t_k)) = P_{\omega0}(t_k)x(t_k), \end{cases} \tag{7.27}$$

- $\nu(t_{k-1}) = 1$

$$\begin{cases} u_1(t_k) = \mu^*(\mathcal{I}(t_k)) = P_{u1}(t_k)x(t_k), \\ \omega_1(t_k) = \nu^*(\mathcal{I}(t_k)) = P_{\omega1}(t_k)x(t_k). \end{cases} \tag{7.28}$$

3) The corresponding system performance is

$$J_K^* = \frac{\Sigma}{\alpha+\beta}(\beta\mathcal{S}(t_0)+\alpha\mathcal{R}(t_0)). \tag{7.29}$$

Proof *Under the two-state Markov packet dropout process in physical-layer, we construct the quadratic cost functions $V(x(t_k))$ based on states at t_{k-1} as*

$$V(x(t_k)) = \begin{cases} \mathbb{E}\{x^T(t_k)\mathcal{S}(t_k)x(t_k)\},\ v(t_{k-1})=0, \\ \mathbb{E}\{x^T(t_k)\mathcal{R}(t_k)x(t_k)\},\ v(t_{k-1})=1. \end{cases}$$

For step $k+1$, we have

$$V(x(t_{k+1})) = \begin{cases} \mathbb{E}\{T_k\delta(x^T(t_k)\mathcal{S}(t_k)x(t_k))+x^T(t_k)\mathcal{S}(t_k)x(t_k)\},\ v(t_k)=0, \\ \mathbb{E}\{T_k\delta(x^T(t_k)\mathcal{R}(t_k)x(t_k))+x^T(t_k)\mathcal{R}(t_k)x(t_k)\},\ v(t_k)=1. \end{cases}$$

According to Lemma 7.3, one has that

$$V(x(t_{k+1})) = \begin{cases} T_k^2\delta x_{\mathcal{S}}^T(t_k)\mathcal{S}(t_{k+1})\delta x_{\mathcal{S}}(t_k)+T_k\delta x_{\mathcal{S}}^T(t_k)\mathcal{S}(t_{k+1})x(t_k) \\ +T_kx^T(t_k)\mathcal{S}(t_{k+1})\delta x_{\mathcal{S}}(t_k)+x^T(t_k)\mathcal{S}(t_{k+1})x(t_k),\ v(t_k)=0, \\ T_k^2\delta x_{\mathcal{R}}^T(t_k)\mathcal{R}(t_{k+1})\delta x_{\mathcal{R}}(t_k)+T_k\delta x_{\mathcal{R}}^T(t_k)\mathcal{R}(t_{k+1})x(t_k) \\ +T_kx^T(t_k)\mathcal{R}(t_{k+1})\delta x_{\mathcal{R}}(t_k)+x^T(t_k)\mathcal{R}(t_{k+1})x(t_k),\ v(t_k)=1, \end{cases}$$

where

$$\begin{aligned} \delta x_{\mathcal{S}}(t_k) &= A(t_k)x(t_k)+D(t_k)\omega(t_k), \\ \delta x_{\mathcal{R}}(t_k) &= A(t_k)x(t_k)+B(t_k)u(t_k)+D(t_k)\omega(t_k). \end{aligned}$$

By using dynamic programming, when $v(t_{k-1})=0$ the cost function at t_k is

$$\begin{aligned} & V(x(t_k)) = \mathbb{E}\{x^T(t_k)\mathcal{S}(t_k)x(t_k)\} \qquad (7.30) \\ = & \min_{u_0(t_k)}\max_{\omega_0(t_k)} \mathbb{E}\{T_kx^T(t_k)Qx(t_k)+T_kv(t_k)u_0^T(t_k)Ru_0(t_k)-T_k\gamma^2\omega_0^2(t_k)+V(x(t_{k+1}))\} \\ = & \min_{u_0(t_k)}\max_{\omega_0(t_k)} \mathbb{E}\Big\{T_kx^T(t_k)Qx(t_k)+T_kv(t_k)u_0^T(t_k)Ru_0(t_k)-T_k\gamma^2\omega_0^2(t_k) \\ & +\mathbb{P}(v(t_k)=0|v(t_{k-1})=0)(T_k^2\delta x_{\mathcal{S}}^T(t_k)\mathcal{S}(t_{k+1})\delta x_{\mathcal{S}}(t_k)+T_k\delta x_{\mathcal{S}}^T(t_k)\mathcal{S}(t_{k+1})x(t_k) \\ & +T_kx^T(t_k)\mathcal{S}(t_{k+1})\delta x_{\mathcal{S}}(t_k)+x^T(t_k)\mathcal{S}(t_{k+1})x(t_k)) \\ & +\mathbb{P}(v(t_k)=1|v(t_{k-1})=0)(T_k^2\delta x_{\mathcal{R}}^T(t_k)\mathcal{R}(t_{k+1})\delta x_{\mathcal{R}}(t_k)+T_k\delta x_{\mathcal{R}}^T(t_k)\mathcal{R}(t_{k+1})x(t_k) \\ & +T_kx^T(t_k)\mathcal{R}(t_{k+1})\delta x_{\mathcal{R}}(t_k)+x^T(t_k)\mathcal{R}(t_{k+1})x(t_k))\Big\} \\ = & \min_{u_0(t_k)}\max_{\omega_0(t_k)} \Big\{T_kx^T(t_k)Qx(t_k)+T_k\alpha u_0^T(t_k)Ru_0(t_k)-T_k\gamma^2\omega_0^2(t_k) \\ & +(1-\alpha)((T_kA(t_k)+I)x(t_k)+T_kD(t_k)\omega_0(t_k))^T\mathcal{S}(t_{k+1})((T_kA(t_k)+I)x(t_k) \\ & \quad +T_kD(t_k)\omega_0(t_k)) \\ & +\alpha((T_kA(t_k)+I)x(t_k)+T_kB(t_k)u_0(t_k)+T_kD(t_k)\omega_0(t_k))^T\mathcal{R}(t_{k+1}) \\ & ((T_kA(t_k)+I)x(t_k)+T_kB(t_k)u_0(t_k)+T_kD(t_k)\omega_0(t_k))\}. \end{aligned}$$

Under $\Theta(t_k) > 0$ and $\Lambda_0(t_k) < 0$ in Condition 1) of Theorem 7.3, it is shown that $V(x(t_k))$ is convex with respect to $u_0(t_k)$, yet it is concave in $\omega_0(t_k)$. The first order derivation of $V(x(t_k))$ in $u_0(t_k)$ and $\omega_0(t_k)$ is given as

$$\frac{\partial V(x(t_k))}{\partial u_0(t_k)} = 2\alpha T_k R u_0(t_k) + 2\alpha T_k^2 B^T(t_k)\mathcal{R}(t_{k+1})B(t_k)u_0(t_k)$$
$$+2\alpha T_k B^T(t_k)\mathcal{R}(t_{k+1})(T_k A(t_k)+I)x(t_k) + 2\alpha T_k^2 B^T(t_k)\mathcal{R}(t_{k+1})D(t_k)\omega_0(t_k),$$

$$\frac{\partial V(x(t_k))}{\partial \omega_0(t_k)} = -2\gamma^2 T_k\omega_0(t_k) + 2(1-\alpha)T_k D^T(t_k)\mathcal{S}(t_{k+1})(T_k A(t_k)+I)x(t_k)$$
$$+2(1-\alpha)T_k^2 D^T(t_k)\mathcal{S}(t_{k+1})D(t_k)\omega_0(t_k) + 2\alpha T_k^2 D^T(t_k)\mathcal{R}(t_{k+1})D(t_k)\omega_0(t_k)$$
$$+2\alpha T_k D^T(t_k)\mathcal{R}(t_{k+1})(T_k A(t_k)+I)x(t_k) + 2\alpha T_k^2 D^T(t_k)\mathcal{R}(t_{k+1})B(t_k)u_0(t_k).$$

Thus, the first order sufficient and necessary condition for the convexity and concavity are

$$\begin{aligned}&(R + T_k B^T(t_k)\mathcal{R}(t_{k+1})B(t_k))u_0(t_k)\\ &= -(B^T(t_k)\mathcal{R}(t_{k+1})(T_k A(t_k)+I)x(t_k) + T_k B^T(t_k)\mathcal{R}(t_{k+1})D(t_k)\omega_0(t_k))\end{aligned} \tag{7.31}$$

and

$$\begin{aligned}&(-\gamma^2 + (1-\alpha)T_k D^T(t_k)\mathcal{S}(t_{k+1})D(t_k) + \alpha T_k D^T(t_k)\mathcal{R}(t_{k+1})D(t_k))\omega_0(t_k)\\ &= -((1-\alpha)D^T(t_k)\mathcal{S}(t_{k+1})(T_k A(t_k)+I)x(t_k) + \alpha D^T(t_k)\mathcal{R}(t_{k+1})(T_k A(t_k)+I)x(t_k)\\ &\quad+\alpha D(t_k)^T\mathcal{R}(t_{k+1})B(t_k)u_0(t_k)).\end{aligned} \tag{7.32}$$

Combining (7.31) *and* (7.32)*, the saddle-point equilibrium $\mu^*(\mathcal{I}(t_k))$ and $\nu^*(\mathcal{I}(t_k))$ is obtained as* (7.27)*. Similarly, substituting* (7.31) *and* (7.32) *into* (7.30)*, the Riccati recursive equation is obtained as* (7.25)*.*

With the same technique, when $\nu(t_{k-1}) = 1$ holds, the saddle-point equilibrium (7.28) *and Riccati recursive equation* (7.26) *are concluded.*

The optimal value J_p^* for a finite-time horizon system performance optimization problem is

$$\begin{aligned}J_p^* &= \mathbb{E}\{V(x(t_0))\}\\ &= \mathbb{P}(\nu(t_{-1})=0)(\mathbb{E}\{x^T(t_0)\mathcal{S}(t_0)x(t_0)\}) + \mathbb{P}(\nu(t_{-1})=1)(\mathbb{E}\{x^T(t_0)\mathcal{R}(t_0)x(t_0)\}).\end{aligned}$$

Since the Markov packet dropout process is assumed to be irreducible and stationary, it is concluded that $\mathbb{P}(\nu(t_{-1})=0) = \beta/(\alpha+\beta)$, $\mathbb{P}(\nu(t_{-1})=1) = \alpha/(\alpha+\beta)$ and then

$$J_p^* = \frac{1}{\alpha+\beta} tr(\beta\Sigma\mathcal{S}(t_0) + \alpha\Sigma\mathcal{R}(t_0)). \tag{7.33}$$

This completes the proof.

Remark 19 *Note that in a control system, all signals are sampled by a sampler, and an appropriate sampling period interval should be chosen based on network load conditions. The sampling period in delta operator systems is an explicit parameter; thus it is easy to observe and analyze the control effect with different network load conditions. Therefore, in this chapter time varying sampling periods are applied for a control system in a delta domain which can present many advantages when network load conditions are changing. The physical layer is in a small time scale relative to the cyber layer. Sampling intervals of a modern industrial control system are always quite small, and the sampling problem becomes vital in control system design. Thus, the delta operator approach is used in the physical layer to overcome the numerical defects for high frequency sampling [81].*

Next, it is assumed that a fixed sample period T is applied; then system equation (7.7) is rewritten as

$$\delta x(t_k) = Ax(t_k) + v(t_k)Bu(t_k) + D\omega(t_k). \tag{7.34}$$

We extend the finite-time problem (7.11) to an infinite-time horizon case and define the infinite-time horizon average cost as $J_p^{\infty} = \lim_{K\to\infty} J_p/K$. In the following, the sufficient and necessary condition is provided to guarantee a finite J_p^{∞} when the disturbance attenuation γ tends to ∞.

Corollary 3 *Suppose that A is unstable and B is invertible. It is concluded that $\alpha > 1 - 1/\lambda_{\max}^2(A)$ is the sufficient and necessary condition of the controller for control system with $\gamma \to \infty$ under stochastic noise to ensure the system to be stable; that is, the infinite-time horizon cost J_p^{∞} is finite.*

Proof *For an actual case, assume that the disturbance $\omega(t_k)$ is a zero mean Gaussian white noise with covariance Ξ. The objective function* (7.11) *of the physical layer is rewritten as*

$$J_p(\mu, \boldsymbol{F}^*, \boldsymbol{G}^*) = \\ \mathbb{E}_{v(t_k)}\left\{x^T(t_K)Q^K x(t_K) + T\sum_{k=0}^{K-1}\{x^T(t_k)Qx(t_k) + v(t_k)u^T(t_k)Ru(t_k)\}\right\}, \tag{7.35}$$

which is a special case of Theorem 3 with $\gamma \to \infty$. Letting γ tend to ∞, the corresponding Riccati equations and controller are obtained as follows based on Theorem 3.

$$\begin{aligned} -\delta\mathcal{S}(t_k) &= Q + \alpha(TA^T\mathcal{R}(t_{k+1})A + A^T\mathcal{R}(t_{k+1}) + \mathcal{R}(t_{k+1})A) - \\ &\alpha(TA+I)^T\mathcal{R}(t_{k+1})B(R + TB^T\mathcal{R}(t_{k+1})B)^{-1}B^T\mathcal{R}(t_{k+1})(TA+I) + \\ &(1-\alpha)(TA^T\mathcal{S}(t_{k+1})A + A^T\mathcal{S}(t_{k+1}) + \mathcal{S}(t_{k+1})A) + \frac{\alpha}{T}(\mathcal{R}(t_{k+1}) - \mathcal{S}(t_{k+1})), \end{aligned} \tag{7.36a}$$

$$
\begin{aligned}
&-\delta\mathcal{R}(t_k) = Q + (1-\beta)(TA^T\mathcal{R}(t_{k+1})A + A^T\mathcal{R}(t_{k+1}) + \mathcal{R}(t_{k+1})A) \\
&-(1-\beta)(TA+I)^T\mathcal{R}(t_{k+1})B(R+TB^T\mathcal{R}(t_{k+1})B)^{-1}B^T\mathcal{R}(t_{k+1})(TA+I) \\
&+\beta(TA^T\mathcal{S}(t_{k+1})A + A^T\mathcal{S}(t_{k+1}) + \mathcal{S}(t_{k+1})A) + \frac{\beta}{T}(\mathcal{S}(t_{k+1}) - \mathcal{R}(t_{k+1})),
\end{aligned} \tag{7.36b}
$$

$$
\begin{aligned}
&-\delta c(t_k) = \alpha Ttr\{D^T\mathcal{R}(t_{k+1})D\Xi\} + (1-\alpha)Ttr\{D^T S(t_{k+1})D\Xi\} \\
&+\frac{\alpha}{T}(d(t_{k+1}) - c(t_{k+1})),
\end{aligned} \tag{7.36c}
$$

$$
\begin{aligned}
&-\delta d(t_k) = (1-\beta)Ttr\{D^T\mathcal{R}(t_{k+1})D\Xi\} + \beta Ttr\{D^T\mathcal{S}(t_{k+1})D\Xi\} \\
&+\frac{\beta}{T}(c(t_{k+1}) - d(t_{k+1})),
\end{aligned} \tag{7.36d}
$$

$$
\mathcal{S}(t_K) = \mathcal{R}(t_K) = Q,\ c(t_K) = d(t_K) = 0,
$$

and

$$
u^*(t_k) = -(R+TB^T\mathcal{R}(t_{k+1})B)^{-1}B^T\mathcal{R}(t_{k+1})(TA+I)x(t_k), \tag{7.37}
$$

where $c(t_k)$ and $d(t_k)$ are given to quantify the induced cost of Gaussian noise. The optimal system performance is given as

$$
J_p^* = \frac{1}{\alpha+\beta} tr\left\{\beta\Sigma\mathcal{S}(t_0) + \alpha\Sigma\mathcal{R}(t_0) + T^2\sum_{k=1}^{K-1} D^T(\alpha\mathcal{R}(t_{k+1}) + \beta\mathcal{S}(t_{k+1}))D\Xi\right\}. \tag{7.38}
$$

By denoting $\mathcal{A} = TA+I$ and defining

$$
\begin{aligned}
\mathcal{S} &= TQ + \alpha\mathcal{A}^T\mathcal{R}\mathcal{A} + (1-\alpha)\mathcal{A}^T\mathcal{S}\mathcal{A} - \alpha T\mathcal{A}^T\mathcal{R}B(R+TB^T\mathcal{R}B)^{-1}B^T\mathcal{R}\mathcal{A}, \\
\mathcal{R} &= TQ + \beta\mathcal{A}^T\mathcal{S}\mathcal{A} + (1-\beta)\mathcal{A}^T\mathcal{R}\mathcal{A} - (1-\beta)T\mathcal{A}^T\mathcal{R}B(R+TB^T\mathcal{R}B)^{-1}B^T\mathcal{R}\mathcal{A},
\end{aligned}
$$

according to Theorem 3 in [223], it is known that if and only if $\alpha > 1 - 1/\lambda_{\max}^2(A)$, the control system (7.34) with a Markov packet dropout is stable. Then, the deduction is concluded that condition $\alpha > 1 - 1/\lambda_{\max}^2(A)$ is sufficient and necessary for the controller $u^*(t_k)$ to ensure the optimal cost J_p^∞ to be finite. The proof is complete.

From Corollary 3, the control system with stochastic noise is guaranteed to be stable during the iteration process, if and only if

$$
\min_{\forall s\in\Pi,\ m\in\mathcal{M},\ l\in\mathcal{L}} \alpha = 1 - 2\mathbf{Q}\left(\sqrt{\kappa\frac{\zeta(s)p_m}{\eta(s)w_l + \sigma^2}}\right) > 1 - 1/\lambda_{\max}^2(A) \tag{7.39}
$$

holds. We can see that parameter α is monotonously decreasing with transmission power w_l. When the attacker is powerful and emits a large enough power to interfere with the transmission of the control signal, condition (7.39) will not hold which means that the control system may diverge.

7.3.3 ITERATION ALGORITHMS FOR A HIERARCHICAL GAME

In the hierarchical game of CPS proposed in this chapter, the cyber layer impacts physical system performance through parameter α. On the other hand, the players in the cyber layer can detect the running state of the physical system and take the system performance into consideration, i.e., $J_p(s)$ is a part of the cost function of the transmitter and attacker as in equation (7.4). The mixed-saddle point equilibrium strategies of the cyber layer are obtained as $\mathbf{f}^*(s)$ and $\mathbf{g}^*(s)$ by value iteration and Q-learning methods. Algorithms 1 and 2 are proposed for the two methods. The algorithms involve iteration for computing the stationary mixed saddle-point equilibrium of the hierarchical game. Especially, since the game here is zero-sum and finite, the value iteration method of Algorithm 1 converges to the stationary saddle-point equilibrium [180, 181]. The convergence of the Q-learning method is shown in Theorem 7.2. In what follows, the detailed implementation steps are provided in Algorithm 1 and Algorithm 2.

7.4 SIMULATION EXAMPLE

To demonstrate the validity of the proposed method, the design scheme is applied into a load frequency control problem of a two-area interconnected power system. In the power system model, the control signal is transmitted by wireless network, and we assume that a DoS attacker exists, which is shown as Fig. 7.2. The system equation of the two-area interconnected power system is

$$\dot{x}(t) = Ax(t) + Bu(t) + FP_d(t), \tag{7.40}$$

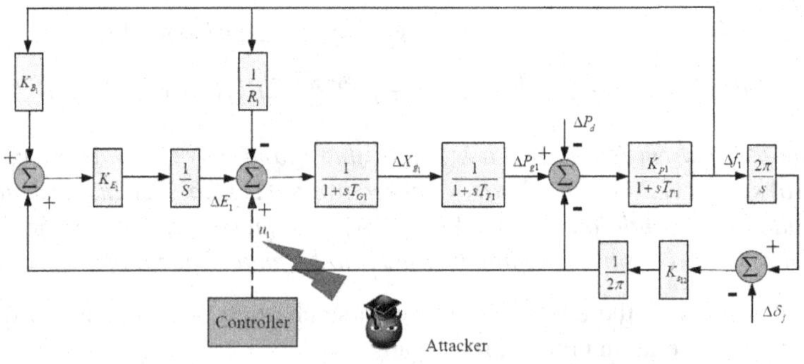

Figure 7.2 Structure of load frequency control system under DoS attack.

Algorithm 6 Value iteration algorithm

Require: $p_m \in \mathbf{p}$, $w_l \in \mathbf{w}$.

1: Initialize ρ, $J_c(s,0)$, $\forall s \in \Pi$ and give a small enough scalar ε.

2: **while** $\|\mathbf{J}_c(n+1) - \mathbf{J}_c(n)\| > \varepsilon$ **do**

3:     **for** $s = 1, 2, \cdots, S$ **do**

4:         Calculate recursive Riccati equations and optimal control strategies according to equations (7.25), (7.26), (7.27) and (7.28). Obtain the optimal system performance $J_p^*(s,n)$, and then compute cost $r(s, p_m, w_l)$ using (7.4).

5:         Calculate the cost matrix $\mathbf{Q}(s)$ using (7.16).

6:         Find $J_c^*(s, n+1)$ by solving the following linear programming problem (LP1).

$$(\text{LP1}) \quad 1/J_c(s, n+1) = \max_{\tilde{y}(s)} \tilde{y}^T(s)\mathbf{1}_M$$

$$\text{s.t.} \ \ \mathbf{Q}^T(s)\tilde{y}(s) \leq \mathbf{1}_L,$$

$$\tilde{y}(s) \geq 0.$$

7:     **end for**

8:     $n \leftarrow n+1$.

9: **end while**

10: The optimal mixed strategy $\mathbf{F}^*$ is obtained using $\mathbf{f}^*(s) = \tilde{y}(s)J_c^*(s, n)$, $s \in \Pi$. For attacker, the optimal mixed strategy $\mathbf{G}^*$ is obtained by solving the dual problem of (LP1).

11: Output the optimal transmission and control strategies under different system modes induced by the dynamic network environment.

---

where

$$x(t) = \begin{bmatrix} x^{1T}(t) & x^{2T}(t) \end{bmatrix}^T, \ u(t) = \begin{bmatrix} u^{1T}(t) & u^{2T}(t) \end{bmatrix}^T,$$

$$A = \begin{bmatrix} A^{11} & A^{12} \\ A^{21} & A^{22} \end{bmatrix}, \ B = \text{diag}\begin{bmatrix} B^1 & B^2 \end{bmatrix}, \ F = \begin{bmatrix} F^1 & F^2 \end{bmatrix}^T,$$

$$A^{ii} = \begin{bmatrix} -\frac{1}{T_{Pi}} & \frac{K_{Pi}}{T_{Pi}} & 0 & 0 & -\frac{K_{Pi}}{2\pi T_{Pi}}\sum_{j\in S, j\neq i} K_{Sij} \\ 0 & -\frac{1}{T_{Ti}} & \frac{1}{T_{Ti}} & 0 & 0 \\ -\frac{1}{R_i T_{Gi}} & 0 & -\frac{1}{T_{Gi}} & \frac{1}{T_{Gi}} & 0 \\ K_{Ei}K_{Bi} & 0 & 0 & 0 & \frac{K_{Ei}}{2\pi}\sum_{j\in S, j\neq i} K_{Sij} \\ 2\pi & 0 & 0 & 0 & 0 \end{bmatrix},$$

$$B^i = \begin{bmatrix} 0 & 0 & \frac{1}{T_{Gi}} & 0 & 0 \end{bmatrix}^T, \ F^i = \begin{bmatrix} \frac{K_{Pi}}{T_{Pi}} & 0 & 0 & 0 & 0 \end{bmatrix}^T,$$

$$A^{ij} = \begin{bmatrix} 0 & 0 & 0 & 0 & -\frac{K_{Pi}}{2\pi T_{Pi}}K_{Sij} \\ 0 & 0 & 0 & 0 & 0 \\ 0 & 0 & 0 & 0 & 0 \\ 0 & 0 & 0 & 0 & \frac{K_{Ei}}{2\pi}K_{Sij} \\ 0 & 0 & 0 & 0 & 0 \end{bmatrix}, \ x^i(t) = \begin{bmatrix} \Delta f_i(t) \\ \Delta P_{gi}(t) \\ \Delta X_{gi}(t) \\ \Delta E_i(t) \\ \Delta \delta_i(t) \end{bmatrix}, \ i, j \in \{1, 2\}.$$

Algorithm 7 Q-learning algorithm

Require: $p_m \in \mathbf{p}$, $w_l \in \mathbf{w}$.

1: Initialize ρ, N, $Q(s, p_m, w_l)$, $\forall s \in \Pi, m \in \mathcal{M}, l \in \mathcal{L}$.

2: **while** $n \leq N$ **do**

3: Choose action p_m. Observe the action of attacker w_l and the next Markov mode s'.

4: Calculate recursive Riccati equations and optimal control strategies with equations (7.25), (7.26), (7.27) and (7.28). Obtain the optimal system performance $J_p^*(s,n)$. Calculate cost $r(s, p_m, w_l)$ by using (7.4).

5: Update $\mathbf{Q}_{n+1}(s)$ with (7.19).

6: Calculate $J_c^*(s)$ and mixed strategy $\mathbf{f}^*(s)$, $\mathbf{g}^*(s)$ by using (7.21).

7: $n \leftarrow n+1$.

8: **end while**

9: Output the optimal transmission and control strategies $\mathbf{f}^*(s)$, $\mathbf{g}^*(s)$, $\forall s \in \Pi$, $\mu^*(\mathcal{I}(t_k))$ and $\nu^*(\mathcal{I}(t_k))$.

Variables $\Delta f_i(t)$, $\Delta P_{g_i}(t)$, $\Delta X_{g_i}(t)$, $\Delta E_i(t)$, and $\Delta\delta_i(t)$ are the changes of frequency, power output, governor valve position, integral control, and rotor angle deviation, respectively. $\Delta P_{d_i}(t) \in \mathbb{R}^k$ is the vector of load disturbance. Parameters T_{P_i}, T_{T_i}, and T_{G_i} are time constants of the power system, turbine, and governor, respectively. Constants K_{P_i}, K_{E_i}, K_{B_i} are power system gain, integral control gain, and frequency bias factor, and $K_{S_{ij}}$ is the interconnection gain between area i and j $(i \neq j)$. Parameter R_i is the speed regulation coefficient. Some basic parameters of the system are shown in Table I of [222].

In the attack model, two network modes are considered, i.e., $\Pi = \{1,2\}$. The sets of channel gains are $\Xi = [0.5, 0.2]$ and $\Gamma = [0.3, 0.1]$. The transition probability from mode 1 to mode 2 is assumed to be 0.4, and from mode 2 to mode 1 is 0.3. The strategy sets of transmitter and attacker are $\mathbf{p} = [8,3]$, $\mathbf{w} = [0.5,2]$. Typically, it is considered that the cost function has the following form

$$r(s, p_m, w_l) = c_0 J_p(s) + c_1 p_m - c_2 w_l + C_{ml},$$

where $c_0 > 0$ is a weighting coefficient. Parameters c_1 and c_2 are cost per unit energy consumption of transmitter and attacker. Specific values are taken as $c_0 = 0.05$, $c_1 = 1$ and $c_2 = 2$. The inherent cost is neglected, i.e., $C_{ml} = 0, \forall m \in \mathcal{M}, l \in \mathcal{L}$. Set network parameters $\kappa(1) = 0.8$, $\kappa(2) = 0.9$ and background noise $\sigma^2 = 0.05$. Background packet dropout rate in two network modes are given as $\beta(1) = 0.4$ and $\beta(2) = 0.6$. For the control system model, the sampling period is uniformly distributed in $[0.04, 0.06]$. The weighting matrices are $Q^K = Q = I_{10\times10}$, $R = I_{2\times2}$, and $\mathcal{S}(t_K) = \mathcal{R}(t_K) = Q^K$. Set the attenuation level as $\gamma = 10$, the variance of initial state as $\Sigma = 1$, and finite time-level $K = 300$.

Set the initial value as $J_c(1,0) = 40$, $J_c(2,0) = 40$ and the optimization accuracy $\varepsilon = 0.001$. By using Algorithm 1, the evolution of optimal values for game $\mathcal{G}_1$

Table 7.1
Comparison of optimal values between Algorithm 6 and Algorithm 7

	$J_c^*(1)$	$J_c^*(2)$
Value Iteration $\rho = 0.5$	47.4786	47.9884
Value Iteration $\rho = 0.05$	24.8460	25.4236
Q-learning $\rho = 0.5$	47.4768	47.9851
Q-learning $\rho = 0.05$	24.8460	25.4236

with $\rho = 0.5$ and $\rho = 0.05$ is shown in Fig. 7.3. Set that $N = 10000$, initial value $Q(s, p_m, w_l) = 40, \forall s \in \Pi, m \in \mathcal{M}, l \in \mathcal{L}$. The evolution of optimal values by using the Q-learning method is shown in Fig. 7.4. The optimal values of Algorithm 1 and Algorithm 2 are compared in Table I and Table II. It is concluded that using the Q-learning method, close results to the value iteration method are obtained, which illustrates the Q-learning method is effective when the transition probability is unknown. What's more, we know that the Q-learning method converges more slowly than the value iteration method, which is because the transition probability must be learned through iterations in Algorithm 2. Figs. 7.5 and 7.6 are presented to illustrate the evolution of the transmitter's and attacker's strategies under different discount factors. Under the optimal mixed strategies, the evolution of control input and disturbance are shown as Fig. 7.7 and Fig. 7.8. Fig. 7.9 depicts the relation curves between physical-layer system performance J_p^* versus per power cost c_1, which shows that when the unit power cost of the transmitter increases, the system performance of physical layer J_p^* increases. This illustrates that when the cost of per power consumption increases, the transmitter is not willing to transmit information with large power, so that system performance is deteriorated in the physical layer. As the verification of Corollary 3, we assume that the disturbance $\omega(t_k)$ is a zero mean Gaussian white noise with covariance $\Xi = 0.1$. Fig. 7.10 is depicted to show that if the attacker is powerful, the control process diverges fast.

Table 7.2
Comparison of mixed strategies between Algorithm 6 and Algorithm 7

	$\mathbf{f}(1)$	$\mathbf{f}(2)$	$\mathbf{g}(1)$	$\mathbf{g}(2)$
Value Iteration $\rho = 0.5$	[0.8967 0.1033]	[0.4470 0.5530]	[0.7793 0.2207]	[0.0786 0.9214]
Value Iteration $\rho = 0.05$	[0.8967 0.1033]	[0.4471 0.5529]	[0.7793 0.2207]	[0.0786 0.9214]
Q-learning $\rho = 0.5$	[0.8966 0.1034]	[0.4434 0.5566]	[0.7760 0.2240]	[0.0863 0.9137]
Q-learning $\rho = 0.05$	[0.8966 0.1034]	[0.4456 0.5544]	[0.7797 0.2203]	[0.0787 0.9213]

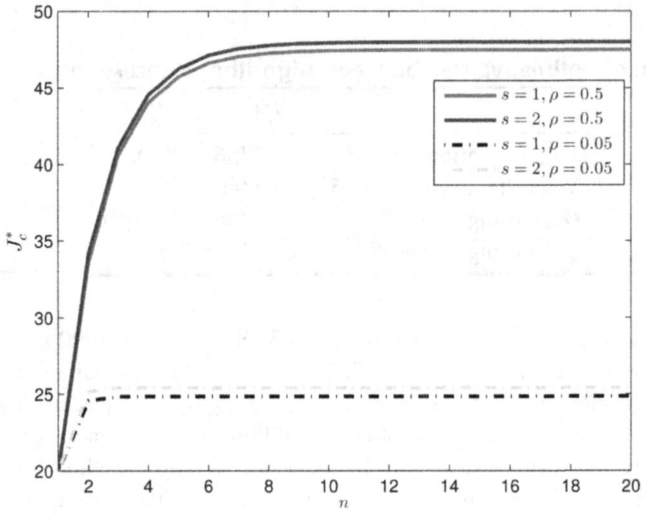

Figure 7.3 Evolution of cost value J_c^* by Algorithm 6.

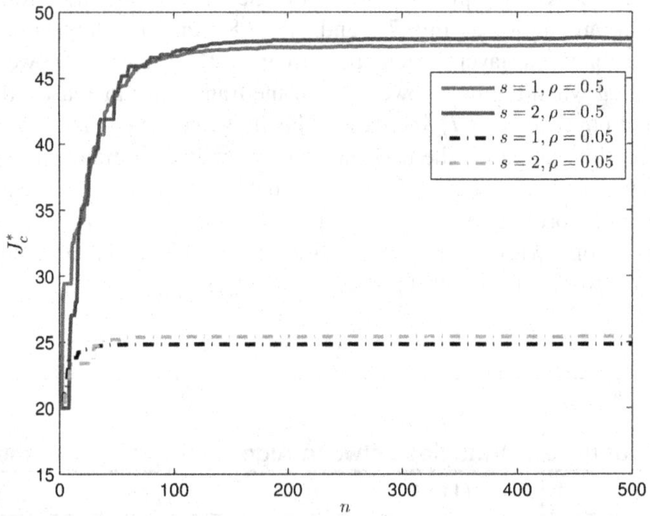

Figure 7.4 Evolution of cost value J_c^* by Algorithm 7.

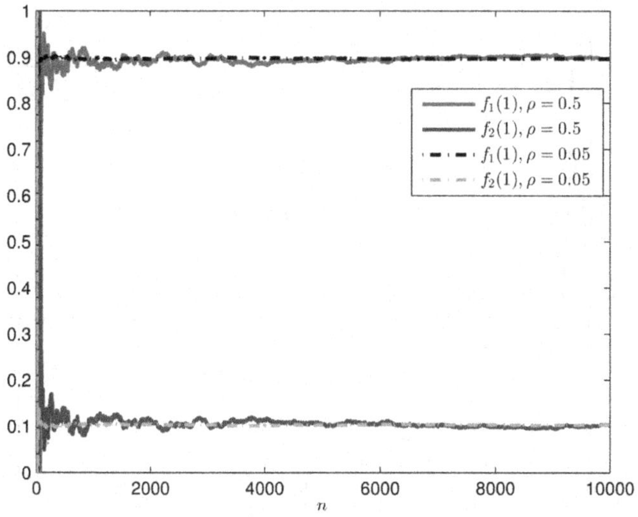

Figure 7.5 Evolution of optimal strategies of transmitter using Algorithm 7.

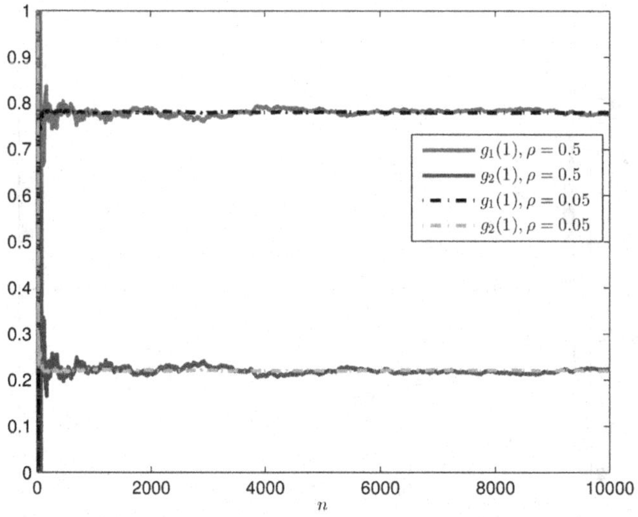

Figure 7.6 Evolution of optimal strategies of attacker using Algorithm 7.

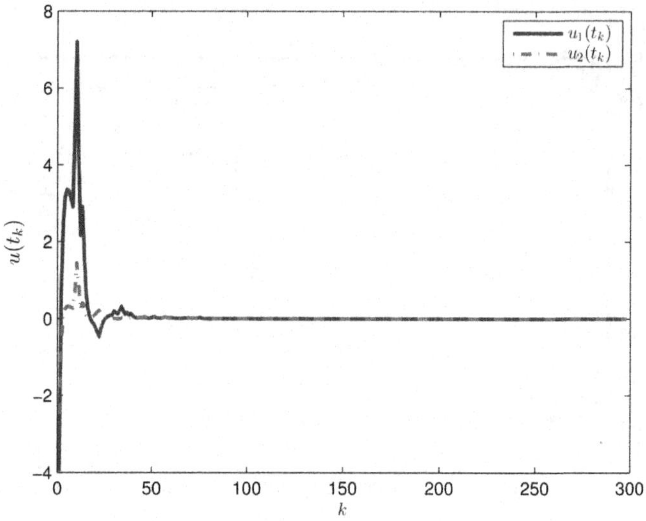

Figure 7.7 The evolution of control input $u(t_k)$.

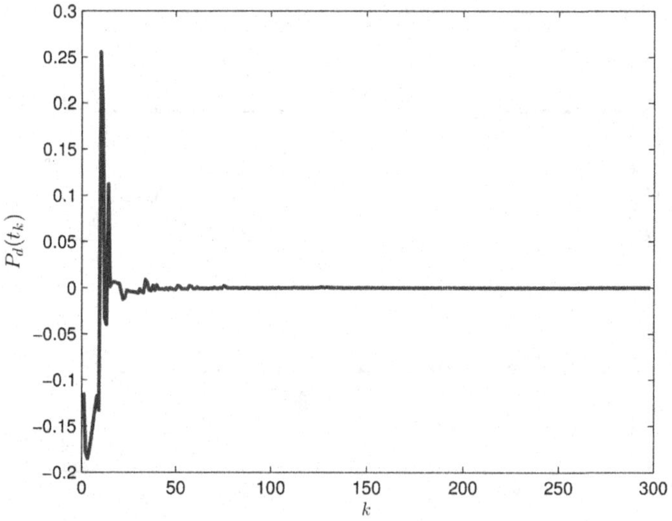

Figure 7.8 The evolution of disturbance $P_d(t_k)$.

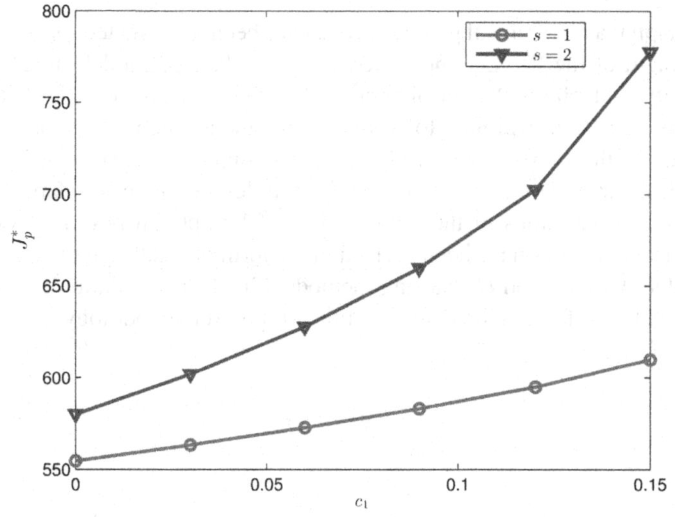

Figure 7.9 System performance J_p^* versus c_1.

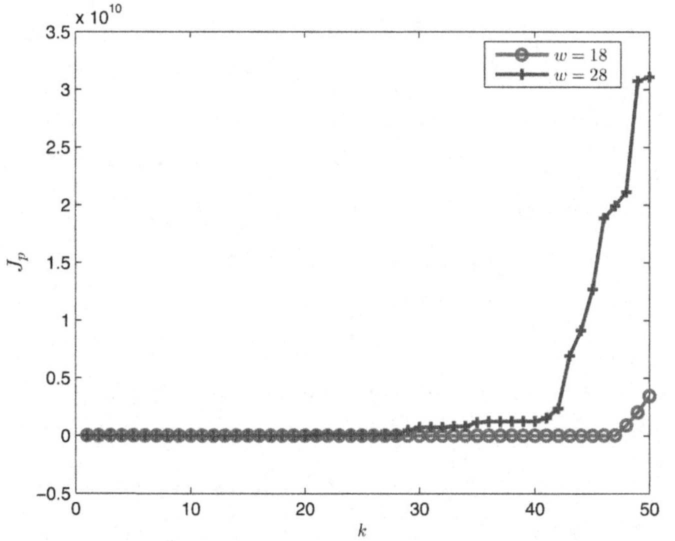

Figure 7.10 The divergence of the control process against a powerful attacker.

7.5 CONCLUSION

In this chapter, a hierarchical game approach has been investigated for the resilient control problem of the WNCS under DoS attack. A layered model integrating the cyber security and physical control process has been established. The zero-sum Markov game has been exploited to model the interaction between transmitter and DoS attacker in the cyber layer. Under the attack-induced packet loss, a control system with disturbance has been modeled in the delta domain to adapt the time-varying network conditions of the physical layer. The optimal power transmission and H_∞ control strategies have been derived in the form of saddle-point equilibriums by using value iteration and Q-learning methods. Finally, a simulation example has been provided to verify the effectiveness of the proposed methodology.

8 Resilient strategy design under an active eavesdropping attack

8.1 INTRODUCTION

The state estimation problem is vital for CPS in which many sensors are always installed distributedly and communicate through wireless networks [182]. With the constraint of deployment in practical applications, sensors are usually battery powered. It is verified remote state estimation provides an effective scenario for high precise estimation with limited energy [151].

There are three main types of cyber attacks on CPS, which are identified as integrity attack, denial of service (DoS) attack, and eavesdropping. The eavesdropping threaten is a kind of passive attack impacting the confidentiality and privacy of CPS, which however has not been discussed sufficiently especially for control and/or estimation issues of CPS.The eavesdropper probes important or sensitive data of the control system. By exploiting the secret information, eavesdropping attacks may result in severe economic losses or even threaten human survival[118, 159, 241].

In this chapter, we focus on the privacy issue of remote state estimation in CPS. Different from a traditional passive eavesdropping attack, an active eavesdropper is assumed to exist in the estimation system. The active eavesdropping jams in order to improve the quality of wiretapped information. This is because that when the link between sensor and estimator is jammed, the sensor will increase its transmission power or frequency to improve the data reception at the estimator [203].

Encryption techniques are used to protect information from interception attacks [131]. But they may not be enough when the transmitter is limited and the eavesdropper is strong [11]. Some works have studied how to schedule transmission and interference to prevent eavesdropping over packet dropout links [132, 177]. This chapter extends [132] and uses game theory to optimize both the defense and attack strategies for a worst-case scenario.

This chapter captures the scene that active eavesdropping attacks exist in the transmission link of the remote state estimation process of CPS. A full-featured eavesdropper with both passive eavesdropping and active jamming is considered which can simultaneously sabotage data transferred to the estimator and improve its own data reception. To defend against the powerful adversary, the sensor is endowed with new function that injects noise to the wiretapping link. In summary, the contributions of this current work are:

1) A synthetic defense and attack mechanism is proposed for corresponding sensor and eavesdropper such that better performance can be obtained from

an opposite perspective.

2) The average estimation error covariances of both estimator and eavesdropper subtracting their own power consumption are used to construct the utility functions for sensor and attacker. A nonzero-sum stochastic game is presented for the two opposing players.
3) The mixed Nash equilibrium is discussed for a degenerated one-stage game of two players with open-loop information. Moreover, the Nash Q-learning method is exploited to solve the stochastic game with feedback information of players' strategies.

The remainder of this chapter is organized as follows: Section 8.2 gives a system description for a remote state estimation of CPS under eavesdropping attack. A Markov nonzero-sum game for two-players is constructed in Section 8.3. In Section 8.4, a degenerated nonzero-sum game for two players is solved. A Nash Q-learning method is introduced to find the solution to a stochastic game in Section 8.5. In Section 8.6, a numerical simulation example is presented to verify the effectiveness of the proposed method. Section 8.7 draws the conclusions.

8.2 SYSTEM DESCRIPTION

As depicted in Fig. 8.1, the state information from a sensor is estimated and sent to the remote estimator where the transmission link is in the presence of an active eavesdropper. The active eavesdropper works in two modes, i.e., passive eavesdropping and active eavesdropping. In passive eavesdropping mode, the attacker eavesdrops the transmitted information from sensor to estimator. In active eavesdropping mode, the attacker jams the communication link between sensor and estimator which makes the attacker achieve a better signal reception. Meanwhile, two antennas are installed in the sensor where one is used to transmit state estimation and the other is used to jam the eavesdropping link. The system structure is introduced in detail with the following problem description.

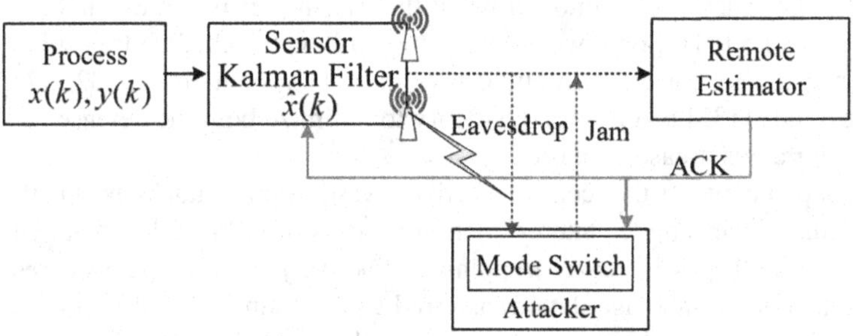

Figure 8.1 Remote state estimation of CPS under an eavesdropping attack.

8.2.1 LOCAL STATE ESTIMATION IN SENSOR

Consider a class of linear time-invariant discrete process as follows

$$\begin{aligned} x(k+1) &= Ax(k)+w(k), \\ y(k) &= Cx(k)+v(k),\ k \geq 0, \end{aligned} \tag{8.1}$$

where $x(k) \in \mathbb{R}^{n_x}$ is the system state, $y(k) \in \mathbb{R}^{n_y}$ is the measurement output at time k obtained by the sensor. $A \in \mathbb{R}^{n_x \times n_x}$ and $C \in \mathbb{R}^{n_x \times n_y}$ are corresponding known system and measurement matrices. $w(k) \in \mathbb{R}^{n_x}$ and $v(k) \in \mathbb{R}^{n_y}$ are the corresponding process noise and observation noise, which obey independent identically distributed (i.i.d) Gaussian processes with zero means and the covariances satisfy $\mathbb{E}[w(k)w^T(t)] = \delta_k^t Q_w, Q_w \geq 0$, $\mathbb{E}[v(k)v^T(t)] = \delta_k^t Q_v, Q_v \geq 0$. Moreover, the pair $(A, \sqrt{Q_w})$ is stabilizable and pair (A, C) is observable, respectively.

The sensor depicted in Fig. 8.1 is smart; it can estimate the current state of process (8.1) by running the following Kalman filtering procedure locally.

$$\begin{aligned} &\hat{x}(k|k-1) = A\hat{x}(k-1), \\ &P_0(k|k-1) = AP_0(k-1)A^T + Q_w, \\ &K(k) = P_0(k|k-1)C^T(CP_0(k|k-1)C^T + Q_v)^{-1}, \\ &\hat{x}(k) = \hat{x}(k|k-1) + K(k)(y(k) - C\hat{x}(k|k-1)), \\ &P_0(k) = (I - K(k)C)P_0(k|k-1). \end{aligned} \tag{8.2}$$

In the above equations, $\hat{x}(k)$ is the estimation of system state $x(k)$ based on measurement information at time k, i.e., $\hat{x}(k) \triangleq \mathbb{E}\{x(k)|y(0)\cdots y(k)\}$. $\hat{x}(k|k-1)$ is the priori estimation. Notation $P_0(k)$ is the error covariance matrix which is defined by $P_0(k) = \mathbb{E}\{(x(k)-\hat{x}(k))(x(k)-\hat{x}(k))^T|y(0)\cdots y(k)\}$. And $P_0(k|k-1)$ is the priori estimation error covariance matrix. $K(k)$ is the filtering gain. For notation simplification, the following Lyapunov and Riccati operators h and g are defined

$$\begin{aligned} h(X) &\triangleq AXA^T + Q_w, \\ g(X) &\triangleq X - XC^T(CXC^T + Q_v)^{-1}CX. \end{aligned} \tag{8.3}$$

It has been verified that the error covariance matrix converges to a unique point $\bar{P}$ of function $h \circ g(x)$ exponentially under the detectability and stabilizability assumption [188]. Furthermore, the steady error covariance $\bar{P}$ is endowed with the following property.

Lemma 8.1 *[84] With $0 \leq \tau_1 \leq \tau_2$, one has inequality*

$$Tr\{\bar{P}\} \leq Tr\{h^{\tau_1}(\bar{P})\} \leq Tr\{h^{\tau_2}(\bar{P})\} \tag{8.4}$$

for operator h.

8.2.2 ACTIVE EAVESDROPPING AND DEFENSE MODEL

After obtaining the local estimation $\hat{x}(k)$, the sensor transmits this value to the remote estimator through a vulnerable channel subject to eavesdropping attack. In most of the previous works, the security research for CPS studies that the eavesdropper is capable of listening; that is, it can only work in the traditional passive eavesdropping mode. In this work, we consider that the eavesdropper is a powerhouse who can not only listen the transmission information in communication link but can also disrupt the link actively with the purpose of improving its listening ability [203].

Traditional encryption techniques focusing on information hiding have been verified to be effective defense means against eavesdropping attacks. Nevertheless, it may be difficult to carry out expensive protection through encryption techniques, since alternative sensors in CPS have merely a limited resource. For instance, the public key in encryption algorithms requires setting up, sharing for public key infrastructure, which brings overheads for CPS including consumption of communication and computing resources. Designing a defense strategy from the physical transmission layer is an urgent task. As shown in Fig. 8.1, to protect the privacy of estimation data from being eavesdropped, there are two antennas installed in the sensor which can work in a full-duplex model. With the smart sensor knowing the existence of the eavesdropper [132, 177], it can send noise to the eavesdropping channel along with estimation data transmission. The communication links between sensor and estimator as well as between sensor and eavesdropper are suffering from channel fading, and the channel gains are given by $g_{s,e}$ and $g_{s,a}$, respectively. Additive white Gaussian noises exist in these channels, and the noise powers are denoted as σ_e^2 and σ_a^2.

First, the eavesdropper working in passive eavesdropping mode is considered. The concept of signal-plus-interference-to-noise ratio (SINR) is introduced to quantify the performance of signal transmission. Typically, the SINR for the estimator at time k is represented as

$$\text{SINR}_e = \frac{g_{s,e}p}{\sigma_e^2}, \tag{8.5}$$

where $p \geq 0$ is the transmission power of the estimation packet. The SINR received by the eavesdropper is written by

$$\text{SINR}_a = \frac{g_{s,a}p}{g'_{s,a}\xi(k) + \sigma_a^2}, \tag{8.6}$$

where $\xi(k)$ is the interference power launched by the sensor which has M levels, i.e., $\xi(k) \in \boldsymbol{\xi} \triangleq \{\xi_1, \xi_2, \cdots, \xi_M\}$. $\xi_1 = 0$ means that the sensor transmits the estimation state only and it does not launch any interference noise. $g'_{s,a}$ is the interference gain from sensor to eavesdropper. With the influence of channel fading, the estimate information from the sensor may arrive at the remote estimator unsuccessfully which leads to packet dropout. Referencing [110], the reception rate depends on SINR primarily measured in symbol-error-rate (SER). A general nonincreasing function is adopted to show the relationship of them, i.e., $\text{SER}_e = f_e(\sqrt{\kappa_e \text{SINR}_e})$. Similarly, the SER for the eavesdropper can be characterized as another nonincreasing function of SINR, which is represented by $\text{SER}_a = f_a(\sqrt{\kappa_a \text{SINR}_a})$. Generally, the form of function $f_e(\cdot)$ and $f_a(\cdot)$ depends on channel characteristics and modulation scheme. In this chapter, we choose the error function as follows

$$f_i(x) = \frac{2}{\sqrt{2\pi}} \int_x^{\infty} e^{-t^2/2} \mathrm{d}t, \ i \in \{e, a\}. \tag{8.7}$$

Next, we consider that the eavesdropper works in active eavesdropping mode. Based on technical implementation in [203], the active jamming mode of the eavesdropper raises the transmission power level of the sensor denoted as $p_1, p_1 > p$ through effecting the reverse training phase such that the channel state information (CSI) is obtained. Denoting $\overline{\text{SINR}}_e$ and $\overline{\text{SINR}}_a$ are denoted as the received SINR at estimator and eavesdropper in active eavesdropping mode. They are given as

$$\overline{\text{SINR}}_e = \frac{g_{s,e} p_1}{g_{a,e} \eta(k) + \sigma_e^2} \tag{8.8}$$

and

$$\overline{\text{SINR}}_a = \frac{g_{s,a} p_1}{g'_{s,a} \xi(k) + \sigma_a^2}, \tag{8.9}$$

where $\eta(k)$ is the jamming power launched by the eavesdropper which has $N-1$ levels, i.e., $\eta(k) \in \boldsymbol{\eta} \triangleq \{\eta_1, \eta_2, \cdots, \eta_{N-1}\}$. When switching to the active mode, the eavesdropper can degrade the packet reception rate by launching jamming noise purposefully such that $\text{SINR}_e \geq \overline{\text{SINR}}_e$.

8.2.3 REMOTE STATE ESTIMATION

Let $\hat{x}_e(k)$ and $\hat{x}_a(k)$ be the estimates of system state $x(k)$ at the estimator and eavesdropper, respectively. The same estimation process for the estimator and eavesdropper runs: Once the estimation information $\hat{x}(k)$ transmitted from the sensor is received by the estimator successfully we have $\theta_e(k) = 1$, otherwise $\theta_e(k) = 0$. When the estimation information $\hat{x}(k)$ transmitted from the sensor is received by the eavesdropper successfully, one has $\theta_a(k) = 1$, otherwise $\theta_a(k) = 0$. The point to point communication link is assumed to be a memoryless packet lossy channel. Thus, $\theta_e(k)$ and $\theta_a(k)$ are two independent Bernoulli random processes such that

$$\Pr\{\theta_e(k) = 1\} = \lambda_e, \ \Pr\{\theta_e(k) = 0\} = 1 - \lambda_e, \tag{8.10}$$
$$\Pr\{\theta_a(k) = 1\} = \lambda_a, \ \Pr\{\theta_a(k) = 0\} = 1 - \lambda_a, \tag{8.11}$$

where $\lambda_e = 1 - f_e(\text{SINR}_e)$ and $\lambda_a = 1 - f_a(\text{SINR}_a)$. Therefore, the reception state and error covariance of a estimator are given by

$$\hat{x}_e(k) = \begin{cases} A\hat{x}_e(k-1), & \text{if } \theta_e(k) = 0 \\ \hat{x}(k), & \text{otherwise}, \end{cases}$$
$$P_e(k) = \begin{cases} h(P_e(k-1)), & \text{if } \theta_e(k) = 0 \\ \bar{P}, & \text{otherwise}. \end{cases} \tag{8.12}$$

The reception state and error covariance of eavesdropper are given by

$$\hat{x}_a(k) = \begin{cases} A\hat{x}_a(k-1), & \text{if } \theta_a(k) = 0 \\ \hat{x}(k), & \text{otherwise,} \end{cases}$$
$$P_a(k) = \begin{cases} h(P_a(k-1)), & \text{if } \theta_a(k) = 0 \\ \bar{P}, & \text{otherwise.} \end{cases} \tag{8.13}$$

For notation simplification, the definition of holding time $\tau_e(k)$ and $\tau_a(k)$ for estimator and eavesdropper to indicate the time duration from the last successful transmission time to time step k is depicted by

$$\tau_e(k) \triangleq k - \max\{l : \theta_e(l) = 1, 0 \leqslant l \leqslant k\},$$
$$\tau_a(k) \triangleq k - \max\{l : \theta_a(l) = 1, 0 \leqslant l \leqslant k\}. \tag{8.14}$$

Before ending this part, some assumptions should be summarized to show a clear expression:

Assumption 2

1) The sensor is installed with two antennas, by which one can transmit the estimation information and the other launches interference noise to affect the eavesdropping process of the attacker.

2) The active eavesdropper operates in a full-duplex mode, that is, it is capable of jamming, pilot contamination, and eavesdropping simultaneously.

Remark 20 *The CSI can not be available for receivers including estimator and active eavesdropper initially. A channel training phase is needed to obtain the CSI. The training phase in practical communication systems creates an exciting opportunity for the eavesdropper to derive a new attack mode called the pilot contamination phenomenon. The pilot contamination attack targets systems in which the transmitter designs its precoder based on the estimates of the legitimate link's CSI. The CSI is obtained with reverse training which means the estimation is done by having the receiver send pilot signals to facilitate the channel estimation at the transmitter. During the reverse training phase, the active eavesdropper sends the pilot signals to fool the transmitter about the correct channel to be estimated. As a result, the transmitter incorrectly designs the precoder which will improve the signal reception at the eavesdropper during data transmission [38, 203]. This leads to* $\overline{SINR_a} > SINR_a$*, and an equivalent effect is given by increasing the transmission power of the transmitter [114].*

The multiple antenna technique for the sensor has been widely used in Wi-Fi, where the injection noise is designed in null space [132] or the antennas work in different frequencies. Thus, the SINR of the sensor is irrespective of the sensor's interference strategy.

8.3 MARKOV GENERAL-SUM GAME FORMULATION

As shown in Fig. 8.1, the capability of the estimator and attacker enables them to obtain the acknowledgement (ACK) feedback information from the estimator transmitted through a reliable link [90, 115, 132], where the ACK feedback information indicates whether the estimation state sent by the sensor has been received by the estimator successfully or not. For example, in transmission control protocol (TCP), the ACK mechanism is adopted to achieve transmission reliability and then provide flow control. With the ACK information, both the sensor and eavesdropper can infer the estimation error covariance at the remote estimator. A similar mechanism is applied for the sensor to infer the estimation error covariance at the eavesdropper. Both sides of sensor and estimator collect their opponent information and make decisions according to the previous time steps. Thus, a dynamic model is more suitable for depicting the interaction between sensor and eavesdropper instead of a static analysis.

A Markov general-sum game is adopted to describe the dynamic process of the attacked CPS, which is mathematically formulated as the sextuplet $< \mathcal{S}, \mathcal{A}_e, \mathcal{A}_a, C_e, C_a, \mathcal{P} >$.

8.3.1 STATE SPACE

The state at time k is defined as the holding times, i.e., $s_k \triangleq (\tau_e(k), \tau_a(k))$, which can take values from the countable state space $\mathcal{S}_\infty \triangleq \{(0,0),(0,1),(1,0),\cdots\} \in \mathbb{N}\times\mathbb{N}$. It is found with $k \to \infty$ an innumberable state space is achieved. But employing a low energy processer and limited random access memory of wireless sensor nodes preclude us adopting innumberable states in a practical application point. A truncated state space $\mathcal{S}_\infty \triangleq \{(0,0),(0,1),(1,0),\cdots,(S,S)\}$ is exploited where the final state (S,S) represents all the states with $\tau_e(k) \geq S, \tau_a(k) \geq S$. It is reasonable by verifying that the estimation error $D(S,S) \triangleq \sum_{k=0}^{\infty} |\text{Tr}[\mathbb{E}\{P_e(k)|\mathcal{S}_\infty\}] - \text{Tr}[\mathbb{E}\{P_a(k)|\mathcal{S}_\infty\}] - \text{Tr}[\mathbb{E}\{P_e(k)|\mathcal{S}\}] + \text{Tr}[\mathbb{E}\{P_a(k)|\mathcal{S}\}]|$ goes to zero with $S \to \infty$ under a nontrivial scenario that the non-truncated Markov chain is bounded.

8.3.2 ACTION SPACE

The action of the sensor is $\xi(k) \in \mathcal{A}_e = \boldsymbol{\xi} \triangleq \{\xi_1, \xi_2, \cdots, \xi_M\}$. For the eavesdropper, denote that $\alpha(k)$ is the operating mode, where $\alpha(k) \in \{0,1\}$ and $\alpha(k) = 0$ represents that it operates in the passive eavesdropping mode and $\alpha(k) = 1$ means that it performs an active jamming mode. When the eavesdropper works in the active mode, $N-1$ power strategies can be chosen to interfere with the transmission link between sensor and estimator, that is, $\eta(k) \in \boldsymbol{\eta} \triangleq \{\eta_1, \eta_2, \cdots, \eta_{N-1}\}$. The eavesdropper's action space is defined as $\mathcal{A}_a \triangleq \{\zeta_1, \zeta_2, \cdots, \zeta_N\}$, where ζ_1 represents that the attacker performs a passive eavesdropping mode, i.e., $\alpha(k) = 0$. Otherwise, $\zeta_l, 2 \leq l \leq N$ represents $\alpha(k) = 1$ and the attacker jams with power η_{l-1}. Therefore, we get that the eavesdropper's strategy at time k satisfies $\zeta(k) \in \mathcal{A}_a$.

The strategy $\pi_e^{(r)}$ denotes the probability of choosing action $\xi_r, r \in \{1, 2, \cdots,$

$M\}$ for sensor. The mixed strategy of the sensor is

$$\vec{\pi}_e = \left[\pi_e^{(1)}, \pi_e^{(2)}, \cdots, \pi_e^{(M)}\right]. \tag{8.15}$$

The probability of choosing strategy $\zeta_t, t \in \{1, 2, \cdots, N\}$ for the eavesdropper is represented by mixed strategy $\pi_a^{(t)}$, and the mixed strategy of the eavesdropper is

$$\vec{\pi}_a = \left[\pi_a^{(1)}, \pi_a^{(2)}, \cdots, \pi_a^{(N)}\right]. \tag{8.16}$$

The strategy sets for two players are

$$\hbar_e = \left\{\vec{\pi}_e \in \mathbb{R}^M, \vec{\pi}_e \geq 0, \sum_{r=1}^{M} \pi_e^{(r)} = 1\right\},$$

$$\hbar_a = \left\{\vec{\pi}_a \in \mathbb{R}^N, \vec{\pi}_a \geq 0, \sum_{t=1}^{N} \pi_a^{(t)} = 1\right\},$$

and we have $\vec{\pi}_e \in \hbar_e$ and $\vec{\pi}_a \in \hbar_a$.

8.3.3 TRANSITION PROBABILITY

The ACKs from the estimator and eavesdropper can be observed by two players. The state of CPS under attack at step k which is denoted as $s(k)$ depends on the last state $s(k-1)$ and policies taken by them. According to equations (8.12) and (8.13), we get the transition probability of system state

$$\Pr\{s(k+1)|s(k), \xi(k), \zeta(k)\} = \begin{cases} (1-\lambda_e)(1-\lambda_a), & \text{if } s(k+1) = (\tau_e(k)+1, \tau_a(k)+1) \\ (1-\lambda_e)\lambda_a, & \text{if } s(k+1) = (\tau_e(k)+1, 0) \\ \lambda_e(1-\lambda_a), & \text{if } s(k+1) = (0, \tau_a(k)+1) \\ \lambda_e\lambda_a, & \text{if } s(k+1) = (0,0) \end{cases} \tag{8.17}$$

From formula (8.17), we find that the transition probabilities are collectively influenced by strategies $\xi(k)$ and $\zeta(k)$, which can not be accessed by players accurately or can not be carried out to be computed precisely. Therefore, to deal with this information limitation and reduce computing overhead, the optimal strategies are obtained by model-free reinforcement learning method in our work.

8.3.4 PAYOFF FUNCTIONS

The expectation of estimation error covariance $\mathbb{E}\{P_i(k)\}, i \in \{e, a\}$ is adopted to quantify the performance of state estimation for players, where

$$\mathbb{E}\{\mathrm{Tr}\{P_e(k)\}\} = \lambda_e \mathrm{Tr}\{\bar{P}\} + (1-\lambda_e)\mathrm{Tr}\{h^{\tau_e(k-1)+1}(\bar{P})\} \tag{8.18}$$

and

$$\mathbb{E}\{\mathrm{Tr}\{P_a(k)\}\} = \lambda_a \mathrm{Tr}\{\bar{P}\} + (1-\lambda_a)\mathrm{Tr}\{h^{\tau_a(k-1)+1}(\bar{P})\}. \tag{8.19}$$

Meanwhile, power consumption should be taken into account for energy-constrained devices. The payoff function of the sensor at time step k is

$$C_e(k) = \xi(k) + \mathbb{E}\{\beta_e \mathrm{Tr}\{P_e(k)\} - (1-\beta_e)\mathrm{Tr}\{P_a(k)\}\}. \tag{8.20}$$

Similarly, the payoff function of the eavesdropper is

$$C_a(k) = \alpha(k)\eta(k) + \mathbb{E}\{\beta_a \mathrm{Tr}\{P_a(k)\} - (1-\beta_a)\mathrm{Tr}\{P_e(k)\}\}. \tag{8.21}$$

In equations (8.20) and (8.21), parameters $\beta_e \in [0,1]$ and $\beta_a \in [0,1]$ are tradeoff factors, where a larger β_e means that the sensor pays more attention to obtaining good estimation performance of the estimator than achieving bad performance of the attacker, and vice versa. The same setting holds for the attacker.

For a long time consideration, the objective of each player is to minimize a discounted sum of payoff function. With a given discount factor $\rho \in [0,1)$, for initial state s_0, the two players take the following values from the game

$$\begin{aligned} J_e(s,\vec{\pi}_e,\vec{\pi}_a) &= \sum_{k=0}^{\infty} \rho^k \mathbb{E}\{C_e(k)|\vec{\pi}_e,\vec{\pi}_a, s=s_0\} \\ J_a(s,\vec{\pi}_e,\vec{\pi}_a) &= \sum_{k=0}^{\infty} \rho^k \mathbb{E}\{C_a(k)|\vec{\pi}_e,\vec{\pi}_a, s=s_0\}. \end{aligned} \tag{8.22}$$

Problem 3 *For the stochastic game of two players, find a Nash equilibrium which is a pair of strategies* $(\vec{\pi}_e^*,\vec{\pi}_a^*)$ *such that*

$$\begin{aligned} J_e(s,\vec{\pi}_e^*,\vec{\pi}_a^*) &\le J_e(s,\vec{\pi}_e,\vec{\pi}_a^*), \vec{\pi}_e \in \hbar_e, \\ J_a(s,\vec{\pi}_e^*,\vec{\pi}_a^*) &\le J_a(s,\vec{\pi}_e^*,\vec{\pi}_a), \vec{\pi}_a \in \hbar_a \end{aligned} \tag{8.23}$$

for all $s \in \mathcal{S}$.

The solution of the Nash equilibrium shows that each player's strategy is the best response to the other's strategy. The following lemma shows for any stochastic game there exists a Nash equilibrium.

Lemma 8.2 *[103] Every general-sum discounted stochastic game has at least one equilibrium point in stationary strategy.*

In general, different information sets can be available for two players through the interactive process if they are endowed with different abilities. The available information history for two players is denoted by $\mathcal{H}^o = \{k, s(0)\}$ if they have an open-loop structure; that is, the actions of players cannot be observed by their opponents. Otherwise, the information set is noted by $\mathcal{H}^c =$

$\{k, s(0), s(1), \cdots, s(k), \xi(0), \zeta(0), \xi(1), \zeta(1), \cdots, \xi(k), \zeta(k)\}$ for two players when the actions taken at each step can be observed by their opponents. Results for the game in equation (8.23) under different history structures are presented in the following parts.

Remark 21 *Note that it is assumed that the ACK information is transmitted by a reliable link in this work. Some future works can also be addressed when the ACK information is transmitted in an unreliable link as can be seen in references [113, 214].*

8.4 SOLUTION TO OPEN-LOOP NONZERO-SUM GAME

As mentioned previously, if the information available for sensor and attacker at time k is $\mathcal{H}^o$, the stochastic game (8.23) for two players is degenerated into an one-stage game as follows.

Problem 4 *Find the Nash equilibrium* (π_e^*, π_u^*) *such that*

$$\begin{aligned} C_e(\pi_e^*, \pi_a^* | s) \leq C_e(\pi_e, \pi_a^* | s), \\ C_a(\pi_e^*, \pi_a^* | s) \leq C_a(\pi_e^*, \pi_a | s) \end{aligned} \tag{8.24}$$

for specific state $s = \{\tau_e, \tau_a\}$.

To exploit the solution of the above nonzero-sum game for sensor and attacker, we suppose that there are two pure strategies for each player. That is, the strategy set of the sensor is $\mathcal{A}_e = \{0, e_1\}$, in which 0 represents no interference noise is launched by the sensor, and otherwise e_1 means interference noise with power e_1 is launched by the sensor to destroy the eavesdropping channel. The strategy set of the attacker is $\mathcal{A}_a = \{0, a_1\}$, where 0 means that the attacker works in a passive eavesdropping mode and otherwise a_1 represents that the attacker interferes with the link between the sensor and estimator with power a_1. The following theorem is given to show the mixed strategies of two players. For notation simplification, we use $\text{SINR}_e(o_2)$ representing the SINR of the sensor with the attacker's strategy o_2 by noticing that the SINR of sensor is irrespective of sensor's interference strategy. Besides, $\text{SINR}_a(o_1, o_2)$ is introduced to depict the SINR of the attacker with the sensor's interference strategy o_1 and the attacker's strategy o_2. Denoting the probability of taking strategy 0 for the sensor is q_e and the probability of taking strategy 0 for the attacker is q_a. The following conclusion is obtained for the one-stage game (8.24).

Theorem 8.1 *If system parameters satisfy* $\lambda_D < 0, 0 \leq q_e^* \leq 1, 0 \leq q_a^* \leq 1$, *the mixed equilibrium strategies for game* (8.24) *are* $([q_e^*, 1 - q_e^*], [q_a^*, 1 - q_a^*])$, *where*

$$q_e^* = \frac{a_1}{\beta_2 \lambda_D Tr(h^{\tau_a+1}(\bar{P}) - \bar{P})} - \frac{\beta_2(\lambda_{a22} - \lambda_{a12}) + (1-\beta_2)(\lambda_{e1} - \lambda_{e2})}{\beta_2 \lambda_D}, \tag{8.25}$$

$$q_a^* = -\frac{e_1}{(1-\beta_1)\lambda_D Tr(h^{\tau_a+1}(\bar{P}) - \bar{P})} + \frac{\lambda_{a22} - \lambda_{a21}}{\lambda_D} \tag{8.26}$$

with

$$\begin{aligned}\lambda_D =&\lambda_{a12}+\lambda_{a21}-\lambda_{a11}-\lambda_{a22},\\ \lambda_{e1} =&f_e(SINR_e(0)),\lambda_{e2}=f_e(\overline{SINR}_e(a_1)),\\ \lambda_{a12} =&f_a(SINR_a(0,0)),\lambda_{a12}=f_a(SINR_a(e_1,0)),\\ \lambda_{a21} =&f_a(\overline{SINR}_a(0,a_1)),\lambda_{a22}=f_a(\overline{SINR}_a(e_1,a_1)).\end{aligned} \tag{8.27}$$

Proof *Let $[q_e,1-q_e]$ and $[q_a,1-q_a]$ be the mixed strategies of the sensor and attacker, respectively. Under state $s=(\tau_e,\tau_a)$, the payoff functions for two players with different strategies are written in the following forms.*

If the sensor takes action 0, the payoff function of the sensor with the attacker's mixed strategy q_a is given by

$$\begin{aligned}&C_e(0,q_a|(\tau_e,\tau_a))\\ =&\beta_1 q_a(\lambda_{e1}\bar{P}+(1-\lambda_{e1})h^{\tau_e+1}(\bar{P}))\\ &+\beta_1(1-q_a)(\lambda_{e2}\bar{P}+(1-\lambda_{e2})h^{\tau_e+1}(\bar{P}))\\ &-(1-\beta_1)q_a(\lambda_{a11}\bar{P}+(1-\lambda_{a11})h^{\tau_a+1}(\bar{P}))\\ &-(1-\beta_1)(1-q_a)(\lambda_{a21}\bar{P}+(1-\lambda_{a21})h^{\tau_a+1}(\bar{P})).\end{aligned} \tag{8.28}$$

On the other hand, if the sensor takes action e_1, the payoff function of the sensor is given in the following with the attacker's mixed strategy q_a

$$\begin{aligned}&C_e(e_1,q_a|(\tau_e,\tau_a))\\ =&e_1+\beta_1 q_a(\lambda_{e1}\bar{P}+(1-\lambda_{e1})h^{\tau_e+1}(\bar{P}))\\ &+\beta_1(1-q_a)(\lambda_{e2}\bar{P}+(1-\lambda_{e2})h^{\tau_e+1}(\bar{P}))\\ &-(1-\beta_1)q_a(\lambda_{a12}\bar{P}+(1-\lambda_{a12})h^{\tau_a+1}(\bar{P}))\\ &-(1-\beta_1)(1-q_a)(\lambda_{a22}\bar{P}+(1-\lambda_{a22})h^{\tau_a+1}(\bar{P})).\end{aligned} \tag{8.29}$$

From the opposite perspective, when the attacker takes action 0, its payoff function is rewritten by

$$\begin{aligned}&C_a(q_e,0|(\tau_e,\tau_a))\\ =&\beta_2 q_e(\lambda_{a11}\bar{P}+(1-\lambda_{a11})h^{\tau_a+1}(\bar{P}))\\ &+\beta_2(1-q_e)(\lambda_{a12}\bar{P}+(1-\lambda_{a12})h^{\tau_a+1}(\bar{P}))\\ &-(1-\beta_2)(\lambda_{e1}\bar{P}+(1-\lambda_{e1})h^{\tau_e+1}(\bar{P})).\end{aligned} \tag{8.30}$$

On the other hand, when the attacker takes action a_1, its payoff function is given by

$$\begin{aligned}&C_a(q_e,a_1|(\tau_e,\tau_a))\\ =&a_1+\beta_2 q_e(\lambda_{a21}\bar{P}+(1-\lambda_{a21})h^{\tau_a+1}(\bar{P}))\\ &+\beta_2(1-q_e)(\lambda_{a22}\bar{P}+(1-\lambda_{a22})h^{\tau_a+1}(\bar{P}))\\ &-(1-\beta_2)(\lambda_{e2}\bar{P}+(1-\lambda_{e2})h^{\tau_e+1}(\bar{P})).\end{aligned} \tag{8.31}$$

With the principle of no difference in mixed Nash equilibrium, letting $C_e(0,q_a|(\tau_e,\tau_a)) = C_e(e_1,q_a|(\tau_e,\tau_a))$*, the optimal value* q_a^* *is obtained as given in equation* (8.26)*. By observing the formula of* q_a^**, if the probability* $0 \le q_a^* \le 1$ *holds, we have* $\lambda_D < 0$*. When* $\lambda_D < 0$ *the optimal response function of the sensor is monotonically increasing with* q_a *and therefore one has*

$$q_e = f_{r1}(q_a) = \begin{cases} 0, & q_a < q_a^*, \\ [0,1], & q_a = q_a^*, \\ 1, & q_a > q_a^*. \end{cases} \tag{8.32}$$

With $C_a(q_e,0|(\tau_e,\tau_a)) = C_a(q_e,a_1|(\tau_e,\tau_a))$*, when* $\lambda_D < 0$*, the optimal response function of the attacker is monotonically decreasing with* q_1 *and it is obtained that*

$$q_a = f_{r2}(q_e) = \begin{cases} 1, & q_e < q_e^*, \\ [0,1], & q_e = q_e^*, \\ 0, & q_e > q_e^*, \end{cases} \tag{8.33}$$

where q_e^* *is given in* (8.25)*. The optimal responses* $q_e = f_{r1}(q_a)$ *and* $q_a = f_{r2}(q_e)$ *are depicted in Fig. 8.2. Thus, the mixed equilibrium is obtained as* $([q_e^*,1-q_e^*],[q_a^*,1-q_a^*])$ *if conditions* $0 \le q_e^* \le 1, 0 \le q_a^* \le 1$ *hold. The proof is completed.*

Remark 22

1) When system parameters make conditions $\lambda_D < 0, 0 \le q_e^* \le 1, 0 \le q_a^* \le 1$ *fail, the pure strategies for two players are obtained with the method of scoring easily.*

2) Note that the given method in Theorem 8.1 is effective when the strategy sets of players are small. Thus, two pure strategies are assumed for each

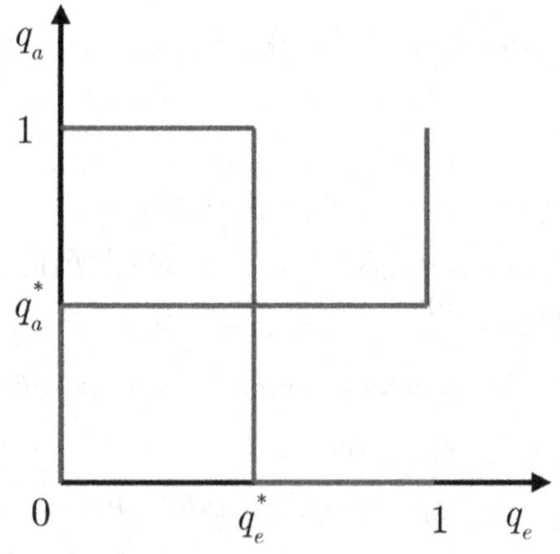

Figure 8.2 The optimal responses for two players.

player to find the closed-form mixed Nash equilibrium in the derivation above. If players' strategy sets are not low dimensional, a general method for finding the mixed Nash equilibrium is presented in the following section.

8.5 SOLUTION TO STOCHASTIC GAME

In this section, the case that information set $\mathcal{H}_c$ is available for two players is studied. And also it is assumed that the game has incomplete but perfect information, meaning that the player does not know the other player's payoff function but it can observe the other player's immediate payoff and previous action. A model-free method is introduced and we extend the Q-learning method for solving a zero-sum stochastic game [115] to a general-sum stochastic game.

Based on the Bellman equation [128], the Q-values for the corresponding sensor and attacker in the Q-learning method are defined as follows

$$Q_i^*(s,\xi,\zeta) = C_i(s,\xi,\zeta) + \rho \sum_{s=1}^{\bar{S}} \Pr\{s^{'}|s,\xi,\zeta\} J_i^*(s,\vec{\pi}_e^*,\vec{\pi}_a^*), \forall i \in \{e,a\}, \tag{8.34}$$

where $\bar{S}$ is the number of total states of the Markov game.

The optimal Q-value of state s and action pair $(\xi(k),\zeta(k))$ is the total discounted reward of a player when players execute actions $(\xi(k),\zeta(k))$ in state s and their Nash equilibrium strategies are $(\vec{\pi}_e^*,\vec{\pi}_a^*)$.

With the Q-learning method, the update rule of Q-values is as follows

$$\begin{aligned} &Q_i(s,\xi,\zeta,k+1) \\ =&(1-\varrho(s,\xi,\zeta,k))Q_i(s,\xi,\zeta,k) \\ &+\varrho(s,\xi,\zeta,k)(C_i(s,\xi,\zeta,k)+\rho \text{Nash}(J_i(s))), \forall i \in \{e,a\} \end{aligned} \tag{8.35}$$

To learn about the Q-values, a player needs to obtain $\bar{S}$ Q-tables for its own Q-values. At the same time, without knowing the other player's Q-values, each player needs to learn about the other player's Q-table for calculating the Nash equilibrium. Assume that player $i, i \in \{e,a\}$ conjectures about the Q-values at the beginning of play $Q_i(s,\xi,\zeta,0) = 0$ for all $i \in \{e,a\}, s \in \mathcal{S}, \xi \in \mathcal{A}_e, \zeta \in \mathcal{A}_a$. The Nash Q-learning procedure is summarized as an algorithm in the following.

Each stage of the stochastic game (8.22) is viewed as a bimatrix game.

Lemma 8.3 *[51] There exists a mixed Nash equilibrium strategy for any finite bimatrix game.*

Different from the solving process in Theorem 8.1, a more general method in which the one-stage nonzero-sum game is turned to solving a nonlinear programming problem is introduced in the stochastic game.

Algorithm 8 Nash Q-learning for each player

1: **Initialize**
2: Letting $k = 0$, get the initial state s_0. For all $s \in \mathcal{S}$, $\xi \in \mathcal{A}_e$ and $\zeta \in \mathcal{A}_a$, $Q_i(s,\xi,\zeta,0) = 0, i \in \{e,a\}$.
3: **Loop**
4: With probability $p_{\exp}$, return action uniformly at random. Otherwise, select $\xi(k), \zeta(k)$ based on $\vec{\pi}_e^*, \vec{\pi}_a^*$ which is the mixed Nash equilibrium solution for two players.
5: Update $Q_i, i \in \{e,a\}$ according to

$$\begin{aligned} &Q_i(s,\xi,\zeta,k+1)\\ =&(1-\varrho(s,\xi,\zeta,k))Q_i(s,\xi,\zeta,k)\\ &+\varrho(s,\xi,\zeta,k)(C_i(s,\xi,\zeta,k)\\ &+\rho\vec{\pi}_e(s(k+1))Q_i(s(k+1),k)\vec{\pi}_a(s(k+1))) \end{aligned} \tag{8.36}$$

where, with an abuse of notation, $Q_i(s(k+1),k) = [Q_i(s,\xi,\zeta,k+1)]_{\xi,\zeta}$.
6: Calculate the Nash equilibrium based on (8.37) and obtain the mixed strategies $\vec{\pi}_e^*, \vec{\pi}_a^*$.
7: Let $k \leftarrow k+1$.

Theorem 8.2 *If and only if there exists a pair* (p_e^*, p_a^*) *such that* $(\vec{\pi}_e^*, \vec{\pi}_a^*, p_e^*, p_a^*)$ *are the solution for nonlinear programming problem*

$$\begin{aligned} &\min_{\vec{\pi}_e,\vec{\pi}_a,p_e,p_a} \quad \vec{\pi}_e^T Q_e \vec{\pi}_a + \vec{\pi}_e^T Q_a \vec{\pi}_a + p_e + p_a\\ &s.t.\ Q_e\vec{\pi}_a \geq -p_e\boldsymbol{1}_M,\ Q_a^T\vec{\pi}_e \geq -p_a\boldsymbol{1}_N,\\ &\vec{\pi}_e \geq 0, \vec{\pi}_a \geq 0, \vec{\pi}_e^T\boldsymbol{1}_M = 1, \vec{\pi}_a^T\boldsymbol{1}_N = 1, \end{aligned} \tag{8.37}$$

the pair $(\vec{\pi}_e^*, \vec{\pi}_e^*)$ *constitutes the mixed Nash equilibrium for two players. In* (8.37), *matrices* Q_e *and* Q_a *represent the Q-tables for a certain state and all actions of two players.*

Proof *Based on constraints in* (8.37), *one has*

$$\vec{\pi}_e^T Q_e \vec{\pi}_a + \vec{\pi}_e^T Q_a \vec{\pi}_a + p_e + p_a \geq 0, \tag{8.38}$$

from which we can see the objective function of (8.37) *is nonnegative. If pair* $(\vec{\pi}_e^*, \vec{\pi}_a^*)$ *is a Nash equilibrium, the following equations*

$$-p_e^* = \vec{\pi}_e^{T*} Q_e \vec{\pi}_a^*, -p_a^* = \vec{\pi}_e^{T*} Q_a \vec{\pi}_a^* \tag{8.39}$$

are feasible. Thus, $(\vec{\pi}_e^*, \vec{\pi}_a^*)$ *is an optimal solution for a nonlinear programming problem in which the objective function equals to zero.*

On the other hand, suppose a solution of a nonlinear programming problem (8.37) *being* $(\vec{\pi}_e^{'}, \vec{\pi}_a^{'}, p_e^{'}, p_a^{'})$. *The feasible solution* $(\vec{\pi}_e^{'}, \vec{\pi}_a^{'}, p_e^{'}, p_a^{'})$ *can meet equations* (8.39). *According to the existence of mixed Nash equilibrium for a bimatrix game, it is concluded that the minimum value of the optimization function in* (8.37) *is nonpositive. Combining with* (8.38), *one has*

$$\vec{\pi}_e'^T Q_e \vec{\pi}_a' + \vec{\pi}_e'^T Q_a \vec{\pi}_a' + p_e' + p_a' = 0. \tag{8.40}$$

For conditions $\vec{\pi}_e^T \boldsymbol{1}_M = 1, \vec{\pi}_a^T \boldsymbol{1}_N = 1$, *we have*

$$\vec{\pi}_e^T Q_e \vec{\pi}_a' \geq -p_e', \vec{\pi}_e'^T Q_a \vec{\pi}_a \geq -p_a', \forall \vec{\pi}_e \geq 0, \forall \vec{\pi}_a \geq 0. \tag{8.41}$$

Thus,

$$\vec{\pi}_e^T Q_e \vec{\pi}_a' + \vec{\pi}_e'^T Q_a \vec{\pi}_a \geq -p_e' - p_a' = \vec{\pi}_e'^T Q_e \vec{\pi}_a' + \vec{\pi}_e'^T Q_a \vec{\pi}_a'. \tag{8.42}$$

Particularly, $\vec{\pi}_e'^T Q_e \vec{\pi}_a' \geq -q_e'$, $\vec{\pi}_e'^T Q_a \vec{\pi}_a' \geq -q_a'$. *With formula* (8.42), $\vec{\pi}_e'^T Q_e \vec{\pi}_a' = -q_e'$, $\vec{\pi}_e'^T Q_a \vec{\pi}_a' = -q_a'$. *And therefore,*

$$\vec{\pi}_e^T Q_e \vec{\pi}_a' \geq \vec{\pi}_e'^T Q_e \vec{\pi}_a', \vec{\pi}_e'^T Q_a \vec{\pi}_a \geq \vec{\pi}_e'^T Q_a \vec{\pi}_a', \tag{8.43}$$

which shows that $(\vec{\pi}_e', \vec{\pi}_a')$ *is the mixed strategy of the bimatrix game* (Q_e, Q_a).

The learning rate in Algorithm 1 satisfies the following assumptions for convergence proof.

Assumption 3

1) $0 \leq \varrho(s,\xi,\zeta,k) < 1$, $\sum_0^\infty \varrho(s,\xi,\zeta,k) = \infty$ *and* $\varrho^2(s,\xi,\zeta,k) < \infty$.

2) Every state and action is visited infinite times. $\varrho(s,\xi,\zeta,k) = 0$, *if* $(s,\xi,\zeta) \neq (s(k),\xi(k),\zeta(k))$.

Assumption 4 *A Nash equilibrium* $(\vec{\pi}_e, \vec{\pi}_a)$ *for bimatrix game* $(Q_e(s), Q_a(s))$ *satisfies one of the following properties*

1) The Nash equilibrium is globally optimal, i.e.,

$$\begin{aligned} &\vec{\pi}_e^*(s) Q_i(s) \vec{\pi}_a^*(s) \leq \vec{\pi}_e(s) Q_i(s) \vec{\pi}_a(s), \\ &\forall i \in \{e,a\}, \forall \vec{\pi}_e \in \hbar_e, \forall \vec{\pi}_a \in \hbar_a. \end{aligned} \tag{8.44}$$

2) If item 1) does not hold, then the player can receive a lower payoff when the other player deviates from the Nash equilibrium, that is,

$$\begin{aligned} &\vec{\pi}_e^*(s) Q_e(s) \vec{\pi}_a^*(s) \geq \vec{\pi}_e^*(s) Q_e(s) \vec{\pi}_a(s), \forall \vec{\pi}_a \in \hbar_a, \\ &\vec{\pi}_e^*(s) Q_a(s) \vec{\pi}_a^*(s) \geq \vec{\pi}_e(s) Q_a(s) \vec{\pi}_a^*(s), \forall \vec{\pi}_e \in \hbar_e. \end{aligned} \tag{8.45}$$

Theorem 8.3 *When Assumptions 3 and 4 hold, the convergence of the Q-learning method for a nonzero-sum stochastic game in Algorithm 8 is guaranteed.*

The proof of Theorem 8.3 is similar to the one in [104]. A large number of iteration and random actions makes item 2) in Assumption 3 set up. By designing a specific learning rate such as in Section Numerical Simulation, item 1) in Assumption 3 is satisfied. Assumption 4 provides sufficient conditions to prove the convergence of the Q-learning algorithm, but these conditions are not necessary in many application experiments [103]. We test Algorithm 1 in the simulation part, which shows that the Q-values converge empirically.

Remark 23 *Note that in formula* (8.22), *the cost function for each player is linear in estimation error covariance and player's power cost. It is known that the mathematical formulation is not needed when finding the solution for a nonzero-sum game in the proposed Q-learning method. Thus, the proposed algorithm is proved to be feasible in finding the Nash equilibrium even when the cost functions are nonconvex, which has wider applicability than the traditional optimization method in which a convex optimization problem must be guaranteed [238].*

8.6 NUMERICAL SIMULATION

In this section, an illustrative example is given to show the effectiveness of the proposed two-player nonzero-sum game for sensor and eavesdropper.

The system parameters of the monitored dynamic process are

$$A = \begin{bmatrix} 1 & 0.5 \\ 0 & 1.05 \end{bmatrix}, C = \begin{bmatrix} 1 & 0 \end{bmatrix},$$
$$Q = \begin{bmatrix} 0.8 & 0 \\ 0 & 0.8 \end{bmatrix}, R = [0.8]. \tag{8.46}$$

When operating the Kalman filtering process, the estimation error covariance converges to

$$\bar{P} = \begin{bmatrix} 0.6083 & 0.4544 \\ 0.4544 & 2.7031 \end{bmatrix} \tag{8.47}$$

with estimation gain $K = [0.7604\ 0.5680]$. The interference power for the sensor is set to be $\xi(k) \in \boldsymbol{\xi} \triangleq \{0,\ 0.1\}$ and the transmission power of the sensor to launch estimation state is $p = 0.2$. The noise power is $\sigma_e^2 = \sigma_a^2 = 0.1$. When the attacker works in an active mode, the transmission power of the sensor increases to $p_1 = 0.5$ and the jamming power is $\eta(k) = 0.1$. Thus, the attack strategy for the eavesdropper is $\zeta = \{0,\ 0.1\}$, where $\zeta_1 = 0$ represents $\alpha(k) = 0$ and $\zeta_2 = 0.1$ denotes $\alpha(k) = 1$ as well as $\eta(k) = 0.1$. The channel gains are $g_{s,e} = 0.9$, $g_{s,a} = 0.8$, $g'_{s,a} = 0.9$, $g_{a,e} = 0.95$. We choose $\beta_e = 0.4$, $\beta_a = 0.5$, and $\rho = 0.3$.

In the one-stage game, based on formulas (8.5)-(8.9), the packet received rates are calculated as $\lambda_{e1} = 0.8347$, $\lambda_{e2} = 0.6694$, $\lambda_{a11} = 0.7981$, $\lambda_{a12} = 0.2054$, $\lambda_{a21} = 0.9789$, $\lambda_{a22} = 0.8110$. The solutions for two players are $q_e^* = 0.7082, q_a^* = 0.8367$.

Consider the truncated system state $S = 2$, that is, there are 9 feasible states in the stochastic game $\mathcal{S} = \{(0,0), (0,1), (1,0),$

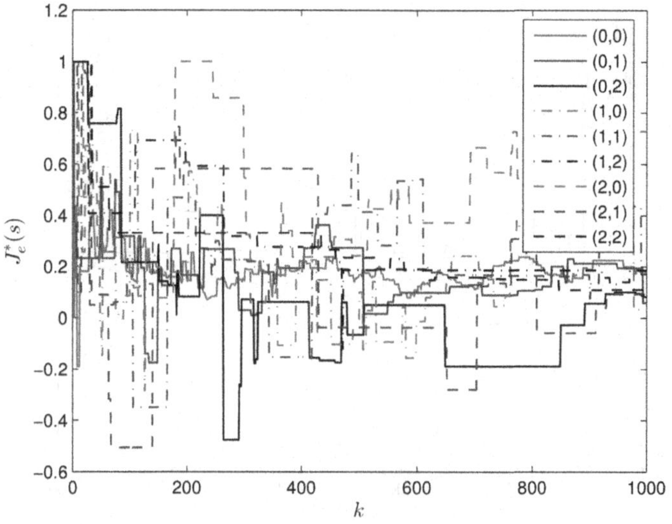

Figure 8.3 Evolution of sensor's payoff value in different states.

$(1,1),(0,2),(1,2),(2,0),(2,1),(2,2)\}$. Choose the learning rate $\varrho(s,\xi,\zeta,k) = 10/(15+\text{count}_k(s,\xi,\zeta))$ that satisfying Assumption 3 and $\text{count}_k(s,\xi,\zeta)$ is the visited times of state s and actions (ξ,ζ) until time step k. The evolution process of the first 1000 steps for all states is given in Figs. 8.3 and 8.4.

The Nash equilibria for different states are listed in the following Table I. The evolutions of mixed strategies in the Q-learning method for sensor and attacker in state $(0,0)$ are presented in Fig. 8.5 and Fig. 8.6, respectively. We can see that the

Table 8.1
The optimal mixed strategies

State	π_e^*	π_a^*
(0,0)	[0.4648 0.5352]	[0.1299 0.8701]
(0,1)	[0 1]	[0 1]
(0,2)	[0 1]	[0 1]
(1,0)	[0 1]	[0 1]
(1,1)	[0.6944 0.3056]	[0.0385 0.9615]
(1,2)	[0 1]	[0 1]
(2,0)	[0.0513 0.9487]	[0.1575 0.8425]
(2,1)	[0 1]	[0 1]
(2,2)	[0.6707 0.3293]	[0.0240 0.9760]

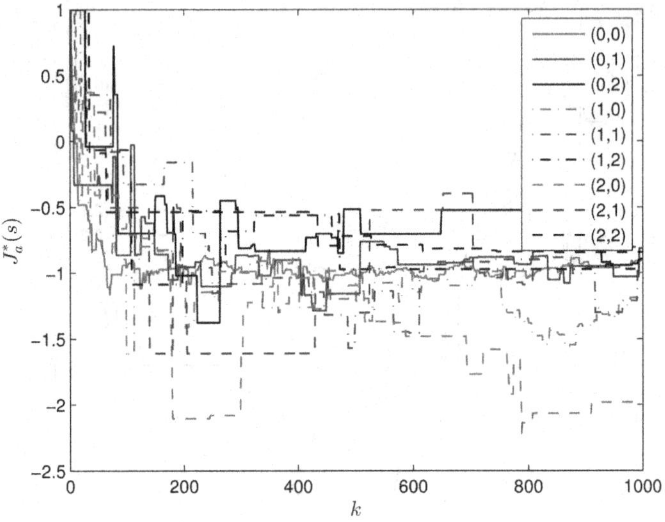

Figure 8.4 Evolution of attacker's payoff value in different states.

sensor will choose a conservative strategy, i.e., not launch any interference noise for energy saving, with probability 0.4648 and launch noise power, i.e., $\xi = 0.1$, with probability 0.5352. In addition, it is known that the attacker works in passive eavesdropping mode with probability 0.1299 and works in active jamming mode with power $\zeta = 0.1$ with probability 0.8701. The convergence of the optimal payoff values for sensor and attacker depicted in Figs. 8.7 and 8.8 shows the effectiveness of the designed Q-learning method in Algorithm 8.1.

We consider the security estimation problem for a geared DC motor system [35]. Setting the sampling time as $0.01s$, we obtain the following discretized system matrix, measurement matrix, and noise covariances

$$A = \begin{bmatrix} 1 & 0.0098 \\ 0 & 0.9653 \end{bmatrix}, C = \begin{bmatrix} 1 & 0 \end{bmatrix},$$
$$Q = \begin{bmatrix} 0.8 & 0 \\ 0 & 0.8 \end{bmatrix}, R = [0.8]. \tag{8.48}$$

The other parameters are the same as above. From the corresponding results given in Table 8.2 and Figs. 8.9-8.12, it is concluded that the proposed method takes effect for state estimation of the geared DC motor system.

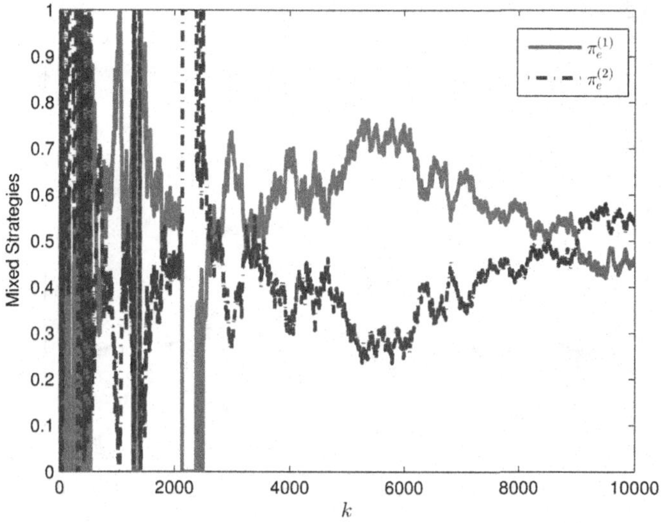

Figure 8.5 Evolution of sensor's strategies in state $(0,0)$.

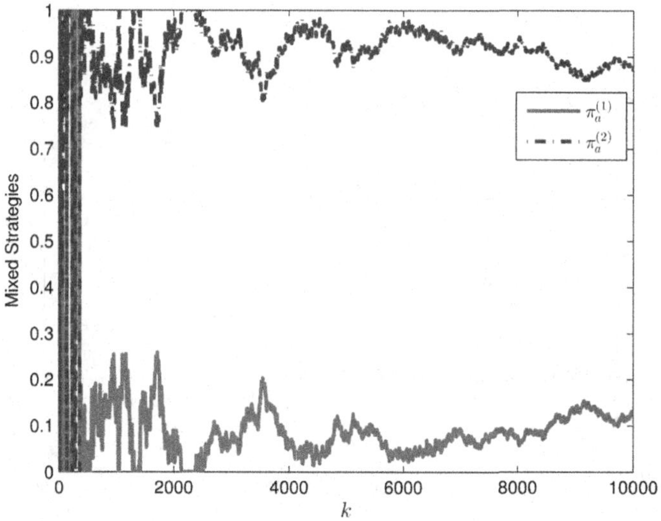

Figure 8.6 Evolution of attacker's strategies in state $(0,0)$.

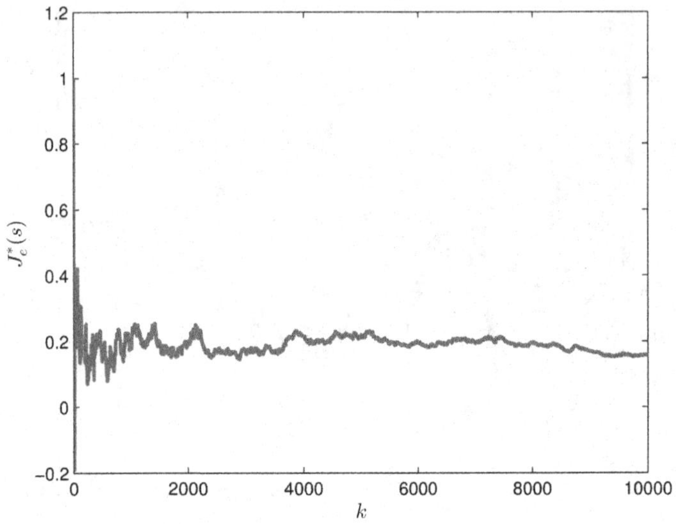

Figure 8.7 Evolution of sensor's optimal payoff value in state $(0,0)$.

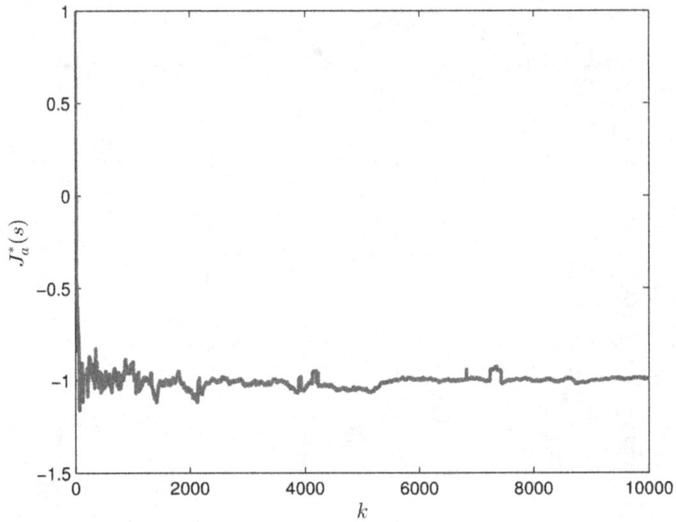

Figure 8.8 Evolution of attacker's optimal payoff value in state $(0,0)$.

Table 8.2
The optimal mixed strategies for a geared DC motor system

State	π_e^*	π_a^*
(0,0)	[0.3162 0.6838]	[0.2691 0.7309]
(0,1)	[0.9654 0.0346]	[0.1449 0.8551]
(0,2)	[0.8243 0.1757]	[0.0968 0.9032]
(1,0)	[0 1]	[1 0]
(1,1)	[0.4952 0.5048]	[0.1305 0.8695]
(1,2)	[0.5367 0.4633]	[0.0487 0.9513]
(2,0)	[0 1]	[1 0]
(2,1)	[0.5553 0.4447]	[0.0677 0.9323]
(2,2)	[0.0002 0.9998]	[0 1]

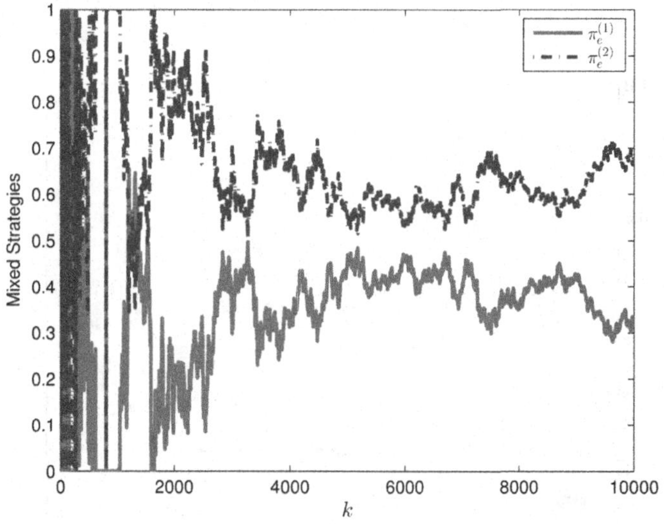

Figure 8.9 Evolution of sensor's strategies in state $(0,0)$ for geared DC motor system.

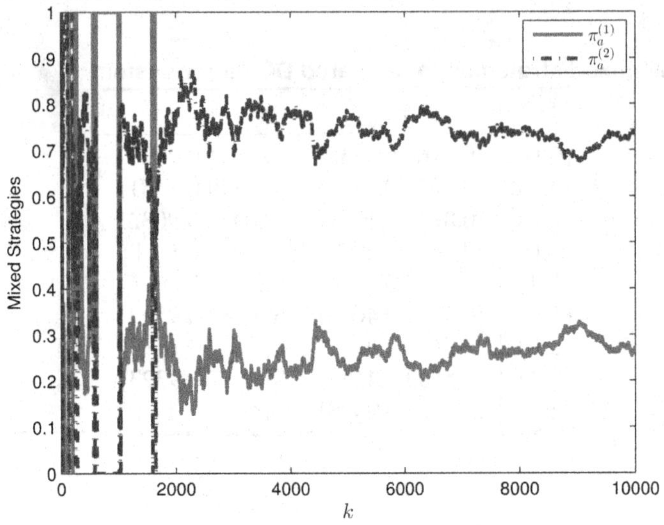

Figure 8.10 Evolution of attacker's strategies in state $(0,0)$ for geared DC motor system.

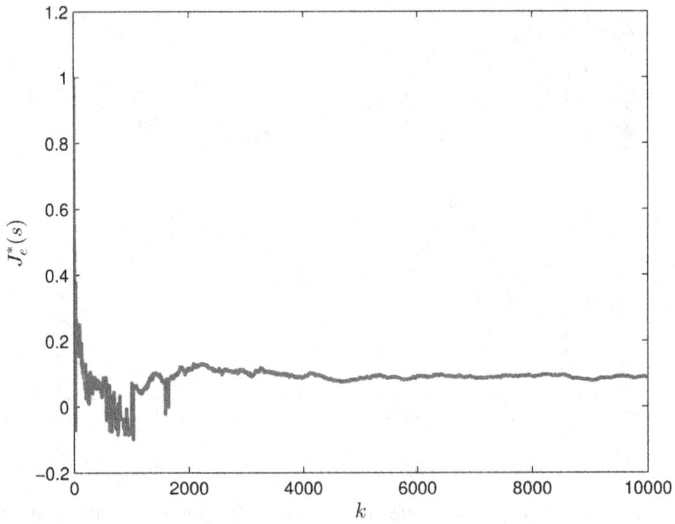

Figure 8.11 Evolution of sensor's optimal payoff value in state $(0,0)$ for geared DC motor system.

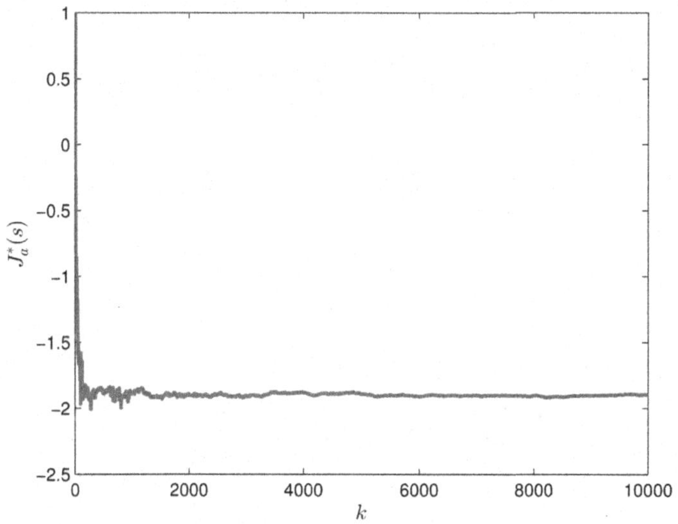

Figure 8.12 Evolution of attacker's optimal payoff value in state $(0, 0)$ for geared DC motor system.

8.7 CONCLUSION

In this chapter, a remote state estimation process under an active eavesdropper for a cyber-physical system has been investigated, including two attacking modes that the eavesdropper can work in which include passive eavesdropping and active jamming. To protect the estimate state from being wiretapped, the sensor launching interference noise to the eavesdropping channel has been designed. With different feedback information sets, a one-stage nonzero-sum game and a long term stochastic game have been constructed for sensor and attacker. Furthermore, corresponding Q-learning and optimization methods have been introduced to solve the problems. Finally, simulations have been provided to verify the feasibility of the proposed methodology.

Section III

Resilient Strategy for CCS Against a Threat

9 Dynamic pricing based resilient strategy design under a jamming attack

9.1 INTRODUCTION

Cloud control system (CCS) is developed to accomplish a coherence control task of a large-scale system relying on advanced cloud computing technology. The CCS facilitates the processing of big data and realization of the control objective benefited from ubiquitous access to shared pools of configuration system resources and high level service. However, CCS faces the challenge of time-delays in data transmission and computing between sensors, controllers, and servers[79, 156, 232].CCS uses wireless network to outsource data processing to a cloud server[85]. However, a wireless network is vulnerable to cyber attacks such as a deception attack and a DoS attack. Therefore, secure transmission of system information in CCS is important.

Game theory is used to study the interaction between system defender and attacker [41, 85, 115, 216]. However, perfect information about other players is not realistic. Some literatures use a Bayesian game or deep reinforcement learning to deal with uncertain information[123, 135]. A time-varying network environment also affects the system performance[21, 91, 252]. The cross-layer design methods have been employed which not only design the estimator/controller to adapt to the attack-induced phenomena, but also develop security strategies to protect the communication network of networked systems[53, 164]. Motivated by the cross-layer method, a co-design to secure the closed-loop control of CCS is addressed in this chapter.

This chapter investigates a dynamic pricing based secure strategy design for closed-loop control of a CCS, considering transmission and computing time-delays. For a communication network, the interaction of transmitter and attacker is modeled as a Stackelberg game, which results in a degradation of SINR and further packet dropout. Under the effect of an attack induced packet dropout, the estimator and predictive control strategies are designed by using a switched system method to deal with time-delays in CCS. A cross-layer mechanism is studied through dynamic pricing to make the system achieve a desired disturbance attention level under constrained information and time-varying networks. The main contributions of this chapter are summarized as follows.

1) An SINR-based Stackelberg game is proposed to model the interaction of transmitter and jammer, and corresponding Stackelberg equilibrium is discussed for two players.
2) Under the effect of attack induced packet dropout, H_∞ performance is analyzed using a switched system method to compensate for time-delays for

CCS. An estimator and predictive controller are designed by solving a series of nonlinear matrix inequalities.

3) A dynamic feedback pricing mechanism is devised such that the disturbance attention level of CCS remains within a desired region under constrained information and time-varying networks.

The remainder of the work is organized as follows: Nomenclature is given in Section 10.2. Problem formulation and objective setup are presented in Section 10.3. The proposed Stackelberg game is analyzed in Section 10.4. In Section 10.5, the H_∞ performance under jamming attack is studied. A dynamic pricing mechanism is given in Section 10.6. Simulation examples are presented in Section 10.7. Conclusions are drawn in Section 10.8.

9.2 NOMENCLATURE

To enhance the readability of this chapter, the adapted notations are summarized in Table 9.1.

9.3 PROBLEM FORMULATION

Fig. 9.1 shows the closed-loop control of a CCS under jamming attack, where the sensor and estimator as well as controller and actuator are linked by wireless networks.

Table 9.1
Notations

Notation	Meaning
η	channel gain
ξ	interference gain
Γ	SINR under jamming attack
L	spreading gain
N_0	background noise
$\bar{\alpha}$	packet delivery rate
$T(J)$	power strategy of transmitter (attacker)
$E(C)$	pricing parameter of transmitter (attacker)
γ	disturbance attention level
h	update period of price strategy
k_e	control gain of dynamic pricing
β_{01}, β_{02}	adjustable parameters in pricing mechanism

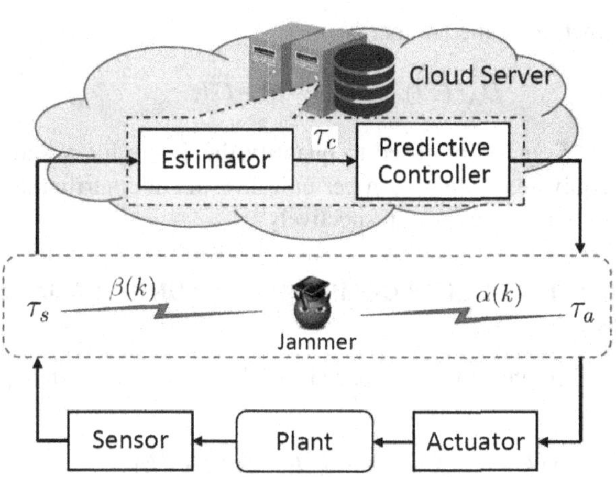

Figure 9.1 CCS under a jamming attack.

9.3.1 COMMUNICATION MODEL UNDER A JAMMING ATTACK

Under the effect of a jamming attack, the received SINR is given by

$$\Gamma = \frac{L\eta T}{\xi J + N_0},$$

where T is the transmission power of transmitter installed in the sensor/controller and J is the power launched by the jammer. Notation η is the channel gain from the plant to the cloud server and ξ is the interference gain between the jammer and receiver. Parameter L is the spread gain of the wireless communication network. N_0 represents the power density of background noise. Based on digital communication theory, the relationship between packet delivery rate and SINR yields

$$\bar{\beta} = 2\mathbf{Q}\left(\sqrt{\kappa\Gamma}\right), \tag{9.1}$$

where

$$\mathbf{Q}(x) \triangleq \frac{1}{\sqrt{2\pi}} \int_0^x \exp(-\tau^2/2)\mathrm{d}\tau$$

and $\kappa > 0$ is a constant.

The transmitter and jammer in the communication network are regarded as two energy constrained players. Different from adopting the SINR as the transmitter's reward function in [41], we choose the logarithmic function of the transmitter's SINR, which can be interpreted as proportional to the Shannon capability. Hence, the utility function of the transmitter yields

$$U_T(T,J) = \ln(1+\Gamma) - ET \tag{9.2}$$

and the utility function of the jammer is

$$U_A(T,J) = -\ln(1+\Gamma) - CJ, \tag{9.3}$$

where parameters E and C are used to quantify the desire for reward by investing power, i.e., the equivalent satisfaction per unit investment contributing to the whole utility, for transmitter and jammer, respectively.

9.3.2 CCS WITH TIME-DELAY COMPENSATION UNDER A JAMMING ATTACK

The following discrete-time state space is used to describe a certain physical plant in CCS

$$\begin{aligned} x(k+1) &= Ax(k) + \alpha(k)Bu(k) + D\omega(k) \\ y(k) &= \beta(k)(Hx(k) + G\omega(k)) \\ z(k) &= Mx(k), \end{aligned} \tag{9.4}$$

where $x(k) \in \mathbb{R}^{n_x}, u(k) \in \mathbb{R}^{n_u}, y(k) \in \mathbb{R}^{n_y}$ are the system state, control input, and measurement output. $\omega(k) \in \mathbb{R}^{n_\omega}$ is the disturbance belonging to $L_2(0,+\infty)$. $z(k) \in \mathbb{R}^{n_z}$ is the output to be regulated. A, B, D, H, G, and M are known matrices with appropriate dimensions. It is assumed that (A, B) is controllable and (A, H) is observable.

Noting that signals are transmitted through networks, communication delay is induced, where the time-delay between sensor and cloud server is denoted as τ_s and τ_a is used to represent the time-delay between cloud server and actuator. Resilient algorithms designed in this chapter are executed in the cloud server and computing time-delay affected by assigned serve resources is denoted as τ_c. To measure the time-delays, time stamps are transmitted together with measurement and control signals. The time-delays in CCS are time-varying and the upper bounds of time-delays in the forward channel, feedback channel, and cloud server are N_a, N_s and N_c, respectively, i.e., $\tau_a \in \{0,1,\cdots,N_a\}$, $\tau_s \in \{0,1,\cdots,N_s\}$ and $\tau_c \in \{0,1,\cdots,N_c\}$.

As shown in Fig. 9.1, it is assumed that the plant and controller in the cloud are linked by wireless networks. Between the plant and cloud server, a jammer tends to interfere with the transmission of measurement and control signals. Binary random processes $\alpha(k)$ and $\beta(k)$ are used to characterize the impact of the jamming attack, where $\alpha(k) = 1$ and $\beta(k) = 1$ represent packets of control input and measurement output that are received error-free, respectively, and otherwise $\alpha(k) = 0$, $\beta(k) = 0$, which yield

$$\begin{aligned} &\Pr\{\alpha(k) = 1\} = \bar{\alpha}, \Pr\{\alpha(k) = 0\} = 1 - \bar{\alpha}, \\ &\Pr\{\beta(k) = 1\} = \bar{\beta}, \Pr\{\beta(k) = 0\} = 1 - \bar{\beta}. \end{aligned}$$

Since not all the system states are available in (9.4), a state estimator is designed in the cloud server first

$$\hat{x}(k+1) = A\hat{x}(k) + \bar{\alpha}Bu(k) + L(y(k) - \bar{\beta}C\hat{x}(k)), \tag{9.5}$$

where $\hat{x}(k)$ is the observed states and L is the estimator gain to be designed. When there is no time-delay, the controller is devised using state feedback control strategy

$$u(k) = K_0\hat{x}(k), \tag{9.6}$$

where K_0 is the controller gain to be determined. Taking the time-varying delays into consideration, the predictive state feedback controller is given as

$$u(k|k-l) = K_l\hat{x}(k-l), l \in \tau, \tag{9.7}$$

where $\tau \triangleq \{0,1,\cdots,N\}$ with $N = N_s + N_c + N_a$. The estimator (9.5) is rewritten as

$$\begin{aligned}\hat{x}(k+1) =&(A-\bar{\beta}LH)\hat{x}(k)+\bar{\alpha}BK_l\hat{x}(k-l)\\&+\beta(k)LHx(k)+\beta(k)LG\omega(k).\end{aligned} \tag{9.8}$$

Thus, the closed-loop system (9.4) is regiven as

$$x(k+1) =Ax(k)+\alpha(k)BK_l\hat{x}(k-l)+D\omega(k), l \in \tau. \tag{9.9}$$

Combining equations (9.8) and (9.9), an augmented switched system is presented as

$$\begin{aligned}\bar{x}(k+1) =&\mathscr{A}_l\bar{x}(k)+\mathscr{D}\omega(k),\\ y(k) =&\beta(k)(\mathscr{H}\bar{x}(k)+G\omega(k)),\\ z(k) =&\mathscr{M}\bar{x}(k),\end{aligned} \tag{9.10}$$

where

$$\begin{aligned}\bar{x}(k) =&[x^T(k),x^T(k-1),\cdots,x^T(k-N),\hat{x}^T(k),\\&\hat{x}^T(k-1),\cdots,\hat{x}^T(k-N)]^T,\\ \mathscr{A}_l =&\begin{bmatrix}\mathscr{A}_l^{1,1} & \mathscr{A}_l^{1,2}\\ \mathscr{A}_l^{2,1} & \mathscr{A}_l^{2,2}\end{bmatrix}, \mathscr{D} = \begin{bmatrix} D \\ 0_{Nn_x\times n_\omega} \\ \beta(k)LG \\ 0_{Nn_x\times n_\omega}\end{bmatrix},\\ \mathscr{H} =&\begin{bmatrix} H & 0_{n_y\times(2N+1)n_x}\end{bmatrix},\\ \mathscr{M} =&\begin{bmatrix} M & 0_{n_z\times(2N+1)n_x}\end{bmatrix}\end{aligned} \tag{9.11}$$

with

$$\begin{aligned}\mathscr{A}_l^{1,1} =&\begin{bmatrix} A & 0_{n_x\times Nn_x}\\ I_{Nn_x} & 0_{Nn_x\times n_x}\end{bmatrix},\\ \mathscr{A}_l^{1,2} =&\begin{bmatrix} 0_{n_x\times ln_x} & \alpha(k)BK_l & 0_{n_x\times(N-l)n_x}\\ & 0_{Nn_x\times(N+1)n_x} & \end{bmatrix},\\ \mathscr{A}_l^{2,1} =&\begin{bmatrix} \beta(k)LH & 0_{n_x\times Nn_x}\\ 0_{Nn_x\times(N+1)n_x} & \end{bmatrix},\\ \mathscr{A}_l^{2,2} =&\begin{bmatrix} A-\bar{\beta}LH & 0_{n_x\times(l-1)n_x} & \bar{\alpha}BK_l & 0_{n_x\times(N-l)n_x}\\ & I_{Nn_x} & & 0_{Nn_x\times n_x}\end{bmatrix}.\end{aligned}$$

The control sequence with time-delay l that arrives at the actuator at time k is denoted by

$$U(k-l) = \begin{bmatrix} u(k-l|k-l) \\ u(k-l+1|k-l) \\ \vdots \\ u(k-l+N|k-l) \end{bmatrix} \tag{9.12}$$

With varying time-delays, all possible available control sequences are

$$U(k-N), U(k-N+1), \cdots, U(k) \tag{9.13}$$

and the control input candidates are

$$u(k|k-N), u(k|k-N+1), \cdots, u(k|k). \tag{9.14}$$

Each of the candidates in (9.14) can compensate for network time-delay, and control input (9.7) is a special case of the improved one (9.14).

Remark 24 *Binary random processes are exploited to depict whether the sensing data and control signals arrive at the cloud server and actuator of the plant under jamming attack, which has been used in works [83, 85, 216] and the references therein. Strategy analysis under a jamming attack should be able to address the problem of packet dropout which is also common in the traditional networked system [125]. However, it is worth mentioning that the packet dropout rate induced by the malicious DoS attacker is much larger compared with the one caused by inherent communication failure [241] and is affected by the defender and attacker's actions. This puts forward a high requirement for resilient strategy design, which should be able to tolerate serious congestions in the communication channel not just occasionally occurring information loss.*

9.3.3 OBJECTIVE SETUP

In this chapter, the jammer, who is smart, can learn the power strategy of the transmitter and then adjust his own interference power. It is assumed that both transmitter and smart jammer have the full knowledge of the channel state information of the communication networks. The smart jammer can observe the existing protection strategy, i.e., transmission strategy T, before choosing his own strategy J which is a worst-case for the transmitter. This can be realized with the attacker being capable of eavesdropping to obtain location knowledge and using physical carrier sensing technology [9, 258]. Even if the attacker does not have the capability of obtaining the transmitter's strategy, the transmitter's strategy designed based on the worst-case is also resilient to the attacker's strategy, which can guarantee the performance of the system [41, 91]. The transmitter can foresee the attacker's strategy and take action defending against the impact. Actually, the transmitter and attacker take actions sequentially. Based on this fact, the power control problem in the presence of a smart jammer is modeled by a Stackelberg game, where the transmitter acts as a leader and the jammer is a follower.

In the game setup, the optimal strategies of transmitter and jammer are taken in the form of Stackelberg equilibrium (SE). Then, the definition of SE for two players is provided in the following.

Definition 9.1 *Denote the Stackelberg game between transmitter and jammer as* $\mathbf{G}_S$. *Then,* T^* *is the SE strategy of the transmitter if*

$$U_T(T^*, \mathcal{S}(T^*)) \geq U_T(T, \mathcal{S}(T)), \forall T \geq 0, \tag{9.15}$$

where $\mathcal{S}(T)$ *is the optimal response of the jammer satisfying*

$$\mathcal{S}(T) = \{J^* \geq 0 | U_A(T, J^*) \geq U_A(T, J), \forall J \geq 0\}. \tag{9.16}$$

The optimal strategy of the jammer is calculated as $J^* = \mathcal{S}(T^*)$. *The set* (T^*, J^*) *is the SE of game* $\mathbf{G}_S$.

In the CCS, the measurement output and control input are transmitted in the form of wireless signals to the destinations, where the received signals are determined by the transmission power of the sensor/controller and jammer. The aggregated impacts of the transmitter and jammer can be quantified by SINR. The objectives integrating the SINR and transmission cost in (9.2) and (9.3) make practical sense for the considered CCS. The objective-oriented decisions of the transmitter and jammer can exert influence on SINR, which further impacts the underlying control performance.

Thus, from the above discussion, the design objective of the security issue in the communication network has been identified. Now, we are in a position to present the design objective of the CCS, that is, design a robust estimator and controller to minimize the following worst-case cost function under the effects of communication delay, computing delay, and jamming attack

$$\Upsilon_\mu^K = \sup \frac{\mathbb{E}\{\sum_{k=0}^K z^T(k)z(k)\}^{\frac{1}{2}}}{\mathbb{E}\{\bar{x}^T(0)S\bar{x}(0) + \sum_{k=0}^K \omega^T(k)\omega(k)\}^{\frac{1}{2}}}, \tag{9.17}$$

where $S > 0$ is a given matrix. For parameterized disturbance attenuation level $\gamma > 0$, problem (9.17) is reformulated as the following design objective for system (9.4)

$$\mathbb{E}\left\{\sum_{k=0}^K z^T(k)z(k)\right\} < \gamma^2 \bar{x}^T(0)S\bar{x}(0) + \gamma^2 \mathbb{E}\left\{\sum_{k=0}^K \omega^T(k)\omega(k)\right\}. \tag{9.18}$$

Remark 25

1) *An attacker endowed with intelligence is considered in this chapter. The defender that takes action first does not know the attacker's strategy beforehand, but the attacker may have partial or full knowledge of the defender's*

strategy. Practically, for the attacker, with more information on the defender's strategy, the probability of launching an attack successfully grows. Thus, the attacker will try his best to collect such information. Accounting for a worst-case that the attacker knows the full knowledge of the defender, a Stackelberg game scheme can be derived such that the defender can design an effective strategy fighting against the attacker.

2) *It should be noted that the addressed attack model has utility functions* (9.2) *and* (9.3) *which are the differences between reward and cost representing the net benefit for two players. Logarithmic functions of SINR are used for the rewards in the objective functions, which are proportional to the Shannon capacity and have been better recognized in the communication community [184].*

9.4 SE STRATEGY FOR TRANSMITTER AND SMART JAMMER

Considering the relationship of two players, we aim at deriving the SE for transmitter and jammer. That is, the transmitter takes action first and the smart jammer learns the transmitter's strategy quickly and takes the corresponding optimal interference strategy. Therefore, in this part, we compute the optimal response of the jammer first for a given strategy of transmitter. Then, the optimal transmission strategy of the transmitter is calculated based on knowing the best response strategy of the jammer.

9.4.1 SMART JAMMER'S OPTIMAL RESPONSE STRATEGY

Let assume that the transmitter's strategy T is given. The smart jammer's optimal response is calculated by solving the following optimization problem.

$$\max_{J\geq 0} U_A(T,J) = -\ln\left(1+\frac{L\eta T}{\xi J+N_0}\right)-CJ$$

Then, the following lemma is obtained.

Lemma 9.1 *Let T be a given strategy of the transmitter. The corresponding optimal strategy of the jammer yields*

$$S(T)=\begin{cases} 0, & \xi/C<N_0,\\ 0, & \xi/C\geq N_0, T<T_1,\\ \frac{1}{2\xi}\left(-2N_0-L\eta T+\sqrt{L^2\eta^2T^2+4\frac{L\eta\xi}{C}T}\right), & \\ & \xi/C\geq N_0, T\geq T_1, \end{cases} \tag{9.19}$$

where $T_1=\frac{1}{L\eta}\frac{N_0^2}{\xi/C-N_0}$.

Proof *The result is obtained by taking the first derivative of $U_A(T,J)$ with respect to J and considering constraints $T\geq 0$ and $J\geq 0$ directly, which is omitted here.*

9.4.2 TRANSMITTER'S OPTIMAL RESPONSE STRATEGY

The transmitter takes actions as a leader, who knows the existence of the smart attacker; that is, the transmitter is aware that the jammer will take the optimal response strategy to maximize its own utility. Thus, the transmitter will take the optimal strategy of the jammer into consideration based on Lemma 9.1. The optimal strategy of the transmitter can be obtained by solving the following optimization problem

$$\max_{T\geq 0} U_T(T,\mathcal{S}(T)) = \ln\left(1+\frac{L\eta T}{\xi\mathcal{S}(T)+N_0}\right)-ET, \tag{9.20}$$

where $\mathcal{S}(T)$ is the optimal response strategy of the jammer given in (9.19).

Substituting (9.19) into equation (9.20), the utility function of the defender can be divided into two cases:

1. When the system parameters satisfy $\xi/C < N_0$ or the two conditions $\xi/C \geq N_0, T < T_1$ hold, i.e., the optimal response of the jammer is $\mathcal{S}(T) = 0$, the optimization problem of the transmitter is reformulated as

$$U_T^{\dagger}(T,\mathcal{S}(T)) = \ln\left(1+\frac{L\eta T}{N_0}\right)-ET \tag{9.21}$$

2. If the conditions $\xi/C \geq N_0$ and $T \geq T_1$ hold, the optimization problem of the transmitter is given by

$$U_T^{\ddagger}(T,\mathcal{S}(T)) = \ln\left(1+\frac{2L\eta T}{-L\eta T+\sqrt{L^2\eta^2T^2+\frac{4L\eta\xi T}{C}}}\right)-ET \tag{9.22}$$

Before giving the optimal strategy of the transmitter by the following lemma, some preliminary notations for cost parameter E are provided as follows

$$E_0 = \sqrt{\frac{L^2\eta^2}{\left(\frac{N_0^2}{\xi/C-N_0}\right)^2+4\frac{\xi}{C}\frac{N_0^2}{\frac{\xi}{C}-N_0}}},$$

$$E_1 = \frac{L\eta}{\frac{N_0^2}{\xi/C-N_0}+N_0},\quad E_2 = \frac{L\eta}{N_0}.$$

Lemma 9.2 *If the game parameters satisfy $\xi/C < N_0$, the optimal strategy of the transmitter is*

$$T^{SE} = \begin{cases} 0, & E > E_2, \\ \frac{1}{E}-\frac{N_0}{L\eta}, & E \leq E_2. \end{cases} \tag{9.23}$$

Otherwise, the optimal response strategy of the transmitter is given by

$$T^{SE} = \begin{cases} 0, & E > E_2, \\ \frac{1}{E} - \frac{N_0}{L\eta}, & E_1 \leq E \leq E_2, \\ \frac{1}{L\eta}\frac{N_0^2}{\xi/C - N_0}, & E_0 < E < E_1, \\ \frac{-2\frac{\xi}{C} + \sqrt{\left(2\frac{\xi}{C}\right)^2 + \frac{L^2\eta^2}{E^2}}}{L\eta}, & E \leq E_0. \end{cases} \tag{9.24}$$

Proof *Utility function $U_T^{\dagger}(T, S(T))$ in forms* (9.21) *and* (9.22) *is strictly concave in T by verifying that its second order derivation is negative. Then, the optimal strategy of the transmitter is calculated as*

$$T_1^{SE} = \frac{1}{E} - \frac{N_0}{L\eta}$$

and

$$T_2^{SE} = \frac{-2\frac{\xi}{C} + \sqrt{\left(2\frac{\xi}{C}\right)^2 + \frac{L^2\eta^2}{E^2}}}{L\eta}$$

for two cases, respectively. Comparing parameters T_1^{SE}, T_2^{SE} with T_1, the relationship between the transmitter's utility function and parameter E is obtained and the optimal strategies for a different range of the parameter E is summarized in equations (9.23) *and* (9.24).

Based on Lemmas 9.1 and 9.2, the game equilibrium of two players is given in the following theorem.

Theorem 9.1 *For Stackelberg game $\mathbf{G}_s$, solution (T^{SE}, J^{SE}) is*

Case 1: $\xi/C < N_0$

$$(T^{SE}, J^{SE}) = \begin{cases} (0,0), & E > E_2, \\ (\frac{1}{E} - \frac{N_0}{L\eta}, 0), & E_1 \leq E \leq E_2. \end{cases}$$

Case 2: $\xi/C \geq N_0$

$$(T^{SE}, J^{SE}) = \begin{cases} (0,0), & E > E_2, \\ \left(\frac{1}{E} - \frac{N_0}{L\eta}, 0\right), & E_1 \leq E \leq E_2, \\ \left(\frac{1}{L\eta}\frac{N_0^2}{\xi/C - N_0}, 0\right), & E_0 < E < E_1, \\ \left(\frac{-2\frac{\xi}{C} + \sqrt{\left(2\frac{\xi}{C}\right)^2 + \frac{L^2\eta^2}{E^2}}}{L\eta}, J_0\right), & E \leq E_0, \end{cases}$$

$$\Sigma_{1l} = \begin{bmatrix} \bar{\mathscr{A}}_l^T P_j \bar{\mathscr{A}}_l - P_l + \Psi_1 + \mathscr{M}^T \mathscr{M} & * \\ \bar{\mathscr{D}}^T P_j \bar{\mathscr{A}}_l + (\bar{\beta} - \bar{\beta}^2) \mathscr{D}_0^T P_j \bar{I}_1 L \bar{H}_1 & \bar{\mathscr{D}}^T P_j \bar{\mathscr{D}} + (\bar{\beta} - \bar{\beta}^2) \mathscr{D}_0^T P_j \mathscr{D}_0 - \gamma^2 I_{n_\omega} \end{bmatrix} < 0 \quad (9.25)$$

where

$$J_0 = \frac{1}{2\xi}\left(-2N_0 + 2\frac{\xi}{C} - \sqrt{4\frac{\xi^2}{C^2} + \frac{L^2\eta^2}{E^2} + \frac{L\eta}{E}}\right).$$

Proof *The results are obtained by plugging* (9.23) *and* (9.24) *into equation* (9.19).

Up to now, the SE of the transmitter and jammer have been derived. When both sides of the two players adopt rational strategies, the packet delivery rate at the estimator is given by

$$\bar{\beta} = 2\mathbf{Q}\left(\sqrt{\kappa \frac{L\eta T^{SE}}{\xi J^{SE} + N_0}}\right).$$

9.5 H_∞ PERFORMANCE ANALYSIS FOR CCS UNDER A JAMMING ATTACK

In this section, the H_∞ performance is analyzed for the designed estimation and control strategies in the cloud server where the jamming attack is taken into account. Then, the estimator and controller are designed by finding the optimal solution for a series of nonlinear matrix inequalities.

9.5.1 STABILITY AND H_∞ PERFORMANCE ANALYSIS FOR CCS

The analysis of H_∞ performance for augmented system (9.9) is given in this part.

Theorem 9.2 *For a given constant* $\gamma > 0$*, if there exist matrices* $P_l, l \in \tau$ *such that inequalities* (9.25),

$$P_l < \gamma^2 S \quad (9.26)$$

hold for all $l, j \in \tau$*, system* (9.9) *is asymptotically stable in the mean square sense with the disturbance attention level* γ*, where inequality* (9.25) *is given in the top of* *the next page, in which*

$$\bar{\mathscr{A}}_l = \begin{bmatrix} \bar{\mathscr{A}}_l^{1,1} & \bar{\mathscr{A}}_l^{1,2} \\ \bar{\mathscr{A}}_l^{2,1} & \bar{\mathscr{A}}_l^{2,2} \end{bmatrix}, \bar{\mathscr{D}} = \begin{bmatrix} D \\ 0_{Nn_x \times n_\omega} \\ \bar{\beta}LG \\ 0_{Nn_x \times n_\omega} \end{bmatrix},$$

$$\begin{aligned} \Psi_1 =& (\bar{\beta}-\bar{\beta}^2)(\bar{I}_1 L\bar{H}_1)^T P_j \bar{I}_1 L\bar{H}_1 \\ &+ (\bar{\alpha}-\bar{\alpha}^2)(\bar{B}_1 K_l \bar{I}_1^T)^T P_j \bar{B}_1 K_l \bar{I}_1^T, \\ \bar{I}_1 =& \begin{bmatrix} 0_{n_x \times (N+1)n_x} & I_{n_x} & 0_{n_x \times Nn_x} \end{bmatrix}^T, \\ \bar{H}_1 =& \begin{bmatrix} H & 0_{n_y \times (2N+1)n_x} \end{bmatrix}, \\ \mathscr{D}_0 =& \begin{bmatrix} 0_{n_\omega \times (N+1)n_x} & (LG)^T & 0_{n_\omega \times Nn_x} \end{bmatrix}^T \end{aligned}$$

with

$$\begin{aligned} \bar{\mathscr{A}}_l^{1,2} &= \begin{bmatrix} 0_{n_x \times ln_x} & \bar{\alpha}BK_l & 0_{n_x \times (N-l)n_x} \\ & 0_{Nn_x \times (N+1)n_x} & \end{bmatrix}, \\ \bar{\mathscr{A}}_l^{2,1} &= \begin{bmatrix} \bar{\beta}LH & 0_{n_x \times Nn_x} \\ 0_{Nn_x \times (N+1)n_x} & \end{bmatrix}, \\ \bar{B}_1 &= \begin{bmatrix} B^T & 0_{n_u \times (2N+1)n_x} \end{bmatrix}^T. \end{aligned}$$

Proof *Choose the following switched Lyapunov function*

$$V(k,\bar{x}(k)) = \bar{x}^T(k) P_l \bar{x}(k),$$

where $P_l > 0, l \in \tau$ satisfies matrix inequalities (9.25). By denoting that

$$\zeta(k) = \begin{bmatrix} \bar{x}(k) \\ \omega(k) \end{bmatrix}, \tilde{\mathscr{D}} = \begin{bmatrix} 0_{(N+1)n_x \times n_\omega} \\ (\beta(k)-\bar{\beta})LG \\ 0_{Nn_x \times n_\omega} \end{bmatrix},$$

$$\tilde{\mathscr{A}}_l = \begin{bmatrix} 0_{n_x \times (N+l+1)n_x} & (\alpha(k)-\bar{\alpha})BK_l & 0_{n_x \times (N-l)n_x} \\ 0_{Nn_x \times (2N+2)n_x} & & \\ (\beta(k)-\bar{\beta})LH & 0_{n_x \times (2N+1)n_x} & \\ 0_{Nn_x \times (2N+2)n_x} & & \end{bmatrix},$$

the difference of $V(k,\bar{x}(k))$ along with (9.9) is calculated as

$$\begin{aligned} &\mathbb{E}\{\Delta V(k)\} \\ =&\mathbb{E}\{\bar{x}^T(k+1) P_j \bar{x}(k+1) - \bar{x}^T(k) P_l \bar{x}(k)\} \\ =&\bar{x}^T(k) \bar{\mathscr{A}}_l^T P_j \bar{\mathscr{A}}_l \bar{x}(k) + 2\bar{x}^T(k) \bar{\mathscr{A}}_l^T P_j \bar{\mathscr{D}} \omega(k) \\ &+ \omega^T(k) \bar{\mathscr{D}}^T P_j \bar{\mathscr{D}} \omega(k) \\ &+ \bar{x}^T(k) \mathbb{E}\{\tilde{\mathscr{A}}_l^T P_j \tilde{\mathscr{A}}_l\} \bar{x}(k) + 2\bar{x}^T(k) \mathbb{E}\{\tilde{\mathscr{A}}_l^T P_j \tilde{\mathscr{D}}\} \omega(k) \\ &+ \omega^T(k) \mathbb{E}\{\tilde{\mathscr{D}}^T P_j \tilde{\mathscr{D}}\} \omega(k) - \bar{x}^T(k) P_l \bar{x}(k), \end{aligned}$$

which should be satisfied with arbitrary switching laws. Then, we have

$$\mathbb{E}\{\Delta V(k)\} + \mathbb{E}\{z^T(k)z(k)\} - \gamma^2\omega^T(k)\omega(k) = \zeta^T(k)\Sigma_{1l}\zeta(k). \tag{9.27}$$

When $\omega(k) = 0$, according to inequality (9.25), it is obtained that $\mathbb{E}\{\Delta V(k)\} < 0$, which implies that the closed-loop system (9.9) is asymptotically stable in the mean square sense under switching.

Summing up both sides of equation (9.27), it yields inequality (9.18), which means that the H_∞ attenuation level is less than the given value γ for system (9.9). This completes the proof.

Notice that Theorem 9.2 provides sufficient conditions of H_∞ control for CCS with considering time-delay and a jamming attack. In the next part, we will solve a series of optimization problems to obtain the gains for CCS.

9.5.2 DESIGN OF ESTIMATOR AND CONTROLLER

In this subsection, Theorem 9.2 is extended to devise the estimator gain L and controller gains $K_l, l \in \tau$ for system (9.9).

Theorem 9.3 *If there exist matrices $P_l, l \in \tau$ such that matrix inequality (9.28) holds for any $l, j \in \tau$, where inequality (9.28) is given at the top of the next page, then system (9.9) is asymptotically stable in the mean square sense with an H_∞ performance γ.*

Proof *By using Shur complement Lemma [81], $\Sigma_{1l} < 0$ is equivalent to $\Sigma_{2l} < 0$.*

Note that inequality (9.28) is not a linear matrix inequality, and a cone complementary linearization approach is applied. By using a related iterative algorithm, the suboptimal minimum disturbance attenuation level γ can be obtained. By replacing P_j^{-1} with W_j in Σ_{2l}, we get inequality (9.29).

$$\Sigma_{2l} = \begin{bmatrix} -P_l + \mathscr{M}^T\mathscr{M} & * & * & * & * \\ 0 & -\gamma^2 I_{n_\omega} & * & * & * \\ \bar{\mathscr{A}}_l & \bar{\mathscr{D}} & -P_j^{-1} & * & * \\ \sqrt{\bar{\beta}-\bar{\beta}^2}\bar{I}_1 L\bar{H}_1 & \sqrt{\bar{\beta}-\bar{\beta}^2}\bar{\mathscr{D}}_0 & 0 & -P_j^{-1} & * \\ \sqrt{\bar{\alpha}-\bar{\alpha}^2}\bar{B}_1 K_l \bar{I}_1^T & 0 & 0 & 0 & -P_j^{-1} \end{bmatrix} < 0 \tag{9.28}$$

$$\Sigma_{3l} = \begin{bmatrix} -P_l + \mathscr{M}^T\mathscr{M} & * & * & * & * \\ 0 & -\gamma^2 I_{n_\omega} & * & * & * \\ \bar{\mathscr{A}}_l & \bar{\mathscr{D}} & -W_j & * & * \\ \sqrt{\bar{\beta}-\bar{\beta}^2}\bar{I}_1 L\bar{H}_1 & \sqrt{\bar{\beta}-\bar{\beta}^2}\bar{\mathscr{D}}_0 & 0 & -W_j & * \\ \sqrt{\bar{\alpha}-\bar{\alpha}^2}\bar{B}_1 K_l \bar{I}_1^T & 0 & 0 & 0 & -W_j \end{bmatrix} < 0 \tag{9.29}$$

Solving the nonlinear matrix inequality $\Sigma_{2l} < 0$ is converted to solving the optimization problem

$$\begin{aligned} &\min \operatorname{tr}(P_j W_j) \\ &s.t. \text{ inequality (9.29)}, \\ &\begin{bmatrix} P_j & I \\ I & W_j \end{bmatrix} \geq 0,\ j \in \tau. \end{aligned} \tag{9.30}$$

Algorithm 1 is used to solve the minimum optimization problem in (9.17). Note that, $\Sigma_{2l} < 0$ is used as a stopping criterion, and suboptimal disturbance attenuation level γ is obtained within a specific iterations.

Algorithm 9 Find the optimal disturbance attenuation level for specific $\bar{\alpha}$

1: Obtain system matrices A, B, D, H, G and M. Assume that $\bar{\alpha} = \bar{\beta}$. For specific packet delivery rate $\bar{\alpha}$, take a large enough disturbance attenuation level γ. Choose a small enough scalar $\Delta\gamma$.
2: **while** $\gamma > 0$ **do**
3:    Find feasible solution $[P(j), W(j), K(l), L], l, j \in \tau$ for LMIs (9.26) and (9.29). Set $k = 0, P^0(l) = P(l), W^0(l) = W(l), \forall l \in \tau$.
4:    Solve the following LMI optimization problem:

$$\begin{aligned} &\min \sum_{j=0}^{N} P_j^k W_j + P_j W_j^k \\ &s.t.\ \Sigma_{3l} < 0, \\ &\begin{bmatrix} P_j & I \\ I & W_j \end{bmatrix} \geq 0. \end{aligned} \tag{9.31}$$

5:    **if** conditions (9.26) and (9.28) hold **then**
6:       $\gamma \leftarrow \gamma - \Delta\gamma$.
7:    **else if** $k < K$ **then**
8:       $k \leftarrow k + 1$.
9:       $P_j^{k+1} = P_j$, $W_j^{k+1} = W_j$, and go to step 4.
10:    **else**
11:       Break and output $\hat{\gamma}$.
12:    **end if**
13: **end while**

9.6 RESILIENT PRICING MECHANISM FOR CROSS-LAYER DESIGN

9.6.1 CROSS-LAYER DESIGN

The derivation in Section 9.4 is to obtain a static solution for two players based on the assumption that the transmitter knows the attacker's parameters. However, the transmitter has difficulty to attain parameters of the jammer, for instance, C and ξ. How does the transmitter design a resilient strategy to derive the system performance from an equilibrium to a desired region under constrained information and time-varying networks? A dynamic pricing mechanism is devised in this part to solve this problem. Without loss of generality, sensor and controller acting as transmitter have the same transmission strategy and the packet delivery rate of forward and feedback links is denoted by $\bar{\alpha}$.

The price parameter of the transmitter, which can also stand for the desire of QoS for a transmitter, can be decided based on the observed gradient of the cost function at each time slot. The iterative formulation for SINR by adopting a gradient based algorithm is given by

$$\begin{aligned}\Gamma(n+1) =&\Gamma(n)+h\left(\frac{\partial U_T(\Gamma(n))}{\partial T(\Gamma(n))}*\frac{\partial T(\Gamma(n))}{\partial \Gamma(n)}\right)\\ =&\Gamma(n)+h\left(\mathcal{F}(\Gamma(n))-E(n)\varpi(n)\right),\end{aligned} \tag{9.32}$$

where h is the iteration period. $\varpi(n)=\frac{\xi J+N_0}{L\eta}$ and

$$\mathcal{F}(\Gamma(n)) = \begin{cases} \frac{1}{\Gamma(n)+\frac{N_0}{\xi J+N_0}}, \xi/C < N_0 \text{ or } \xi/C \geq N_0, \Gamma(n) < \Gamma_1, \\ \frac{1}{\Gamma(n)\sqrt{1+\frac{4\xi}{C\Gamma(n)(\xi J+N_0)}}}, \xi/C \geq N_0, \Gamma(n) \geq \Gamma_1 \end{cases}$$

with $\Gamma_1=\frac{N_0^2}{(\xi/C-N_0)(\xi J+N_0)}$.

Theorem 9.4 *Considering dynamics* (9.32), *if the following pricing mechanism,*

$$E(n)=-\mathcal{U}(n)=-(k_e s(n)-\hat{\mathcal{Z}}(n)/b), \tag{9.33}$$

is applied, where

$$\begin{aligned}\hat{\Gamma}(n+1) =&\hat{\Gamma}(n)+h\hat{\mathcal{Z}}(n)-\beta_{01}(\hat{\Gamma}(n)-\Gamma(n))+hb\mathcal{U}(n),\\ \hat{\mathcal{Z}}(n+1) =&\hat{\mathcal{Z}}(n)-\beta_{02}(\hat{\Gamma}(n)-\Gamma(n))\end{aligned} \tag{9.34}$$

and $s(n)=\Gamma^*-\hat{\Gamma}(n)$ *with* k_e, β_{01}, *and* β_{02} *being adjustable parameters, then we obtain that the SINR* $\Gamma(n)$ *achieves its objective value* Γ^* *with a bounded error* ϵ, *where*

$$\begin{aligned}\epsilon =& \sqrt{\tau(\|e(0)\|,n)+\varphi(\|\varepsilon(n)\|_\infty)}\\ &+\sqrt{\varsigma(s(0),n)+\psi\left(\sup_{0\leq l\leq n}\sqrt{\tau(\|e(0)\|,l)+\varphi(\|\varepsilon(l)\|_\infty)}\right)}.\end{aligned}$$

Proof *The iterative process of* (9.32) *can be rewritten as*

$$\Gamma(n+1)=\Gamma(n)+h\mathcal{Z}(n)+hb\mathcal{U}(n), \tag{9.35}$$

where

$$\mathcal{Z}(n) = \mathcal{F}(\Gamma(n)) + \mathcal{U}(n)\varpi(n) - b\mathcal{U}(n).$$

Denoting $e_1(n) = \hat{\Gamma}(n) - \Gamma(n)$ *and* $e_2(n) = \hat{\mathcal{Z}}(n) - \mathcal{Z}(n)$, *according to* (9.34) *and* (9.35), *we have*

$$e(n+1) = \begin{bmatrix} e_1(n) \\ e_2(n) \end{bmatrix} = \mathcal{A}e(n) + \varepsilon(n), \tag{9.36}$$

where

$$\mathcal{A} = \begin{bmatrix} 1-\beta_{01} & h \\ -\beta_{02} & 1 \end{bmatrix}, \varepsilon(n) = \begin{bmatrix} 0 \\ \mathcal{Z}(n) - \mathcal{Z}(n+1) \end{bmatrix}.$$

Choose a Lyapunov function

$$\mathcal{V}_e(n) = e^T(n)\mathcal{P}_e e(n);$$

one has that

$$\lambda_{\min}\{\mathcal{P}_e\}\|e(n)\|^2 \leq \mathcal{V}_e(n) \leq \lambda_{\max}\{\mathcal{P}_e\}\|e(n)\|^2 \tag{9.37}$$

with $\mathcal{P}_e > 0$. *The difference of the Lyapunov function is*

$$\begin{aligned}\Delta\mathcal{V}_e(n) =& e^T(n+1)\mathcal{P}_e e(n+1) - e^T(n)\mathcal{P}_e e(n) \\ =& e^T(n)(\mathcal{A}^T\mathcal{P}_e\mathcal{A} - \mathcal{P}_e)e(n) + 2\varepsilon^T(n)\mathcal{P}_e\mathcal{A}e(n) \\ &+ \varepsilon^T(n)\mathcal{P}_e\varepsilon(n).\end{aligned}$$

If there exists a matrix $Q > 0$ *satisfying*

$$\mathcal{A}^T\mathcal{P}_e\mathcal{A} - \mathcal{P}_e = -Q, \tag{9.38}$$

by applying the inequality

$$2\varepsilon^T(n)\mathcal{P}_e\mathcal{A}e(n) \leq ae^T(n)Qe(n) + \frac{1}{a}\varepsilon^T(n)\mathcal{P}_e\mathcal{A}Q^{-1}\mathcal{A}^T\mathcal{P}_e\varepsilon(n),$$

where $a > 0$, *we have*

$$\Delta\mathcal{V}_e(n) \leq (a\lambda_{\max}\{Q\} - \lambda_{\min}\{Q\})\|e(n)\|^2 + \lambda_{\max}\left\{\mathcal{P}_e + \frac{1}{a}\mathcal{P}_e\mathcal{A}Q^{-1}\mathcal{A}^T\mathcal{P}_e\right\}\|\varepsilon(n)\|^2.$$

Applying (9.37), *one has that*

$$\begin{aligned}&\lambda_{\min}\{\mathcal{P}_e\}\|e(n)\|^2 - \lambda_{\max}\{\mathcal{P}_e\}\|e(n-1)\|^2 \\ \leq& (a\lambda_{\max}\{Q\} - \lambda_{\min}\{Q\})\|e(n-1)\|^2 + \lambda_{\max}\left\{\mathcal{P}_e + \frac{1}{a}\mathcal{P}_e\mathcal{A}Q^{-1}\mathcal{A}^T\mathcal{P}_e\right\}\|\varepsilon(n-1)\|^2.\end{aligned}$$

If there exists

$$\max\left\{0, \frac{\lambda_{\min}\{Q\}-\lambda_{\max}\{\mathcal{P}_e\}}{\lambda_{\max}\{Q\}}\right\} \le a \le \frac{\lambda_{\min}\{\mathcal{P}_e\}+\lambda_{\min}\{Q\}-\lambda_{\max}\{\mathcal{P}_e\}}{\lambda_{\max}\{Q\}}, \tag{9.39}$$

we have

$$\|e(n)\|^2 \le \tau(\|e(0)\|, n) + \varphi(\|\varepsilon(n)\|_\infty)$$

with

$$\tau(\|e(0)\|, n) = \left(\frac{\lambda_{\max}\{\mathcal{P}_e\}+a\lambda_{\max}\{Q\}-\lambda_{\min}\{Q\}}{\lambda_{\min}\{\mathcal{P}_e\}}\right)^n \|e(0)\|^2,$$

$$\varphi(\|\varepsilon(n)\|) = \frac{\lambda_{\max}\{\mathcal{P}_e+\frac{1}{a}\mathcal{P}_e\mathcal{A}Q^{-1}\mathcal{A}^T\mathcal{P}_e\}}{\lambda_{\min}\{\mathcal{P}_e\}+\lambda_{\min}\{Q\}-a\lambda_{\max}\{Q\}-\lambda_{\max}\{\mathcal{P}_e\}}\|\varepsilon(n)\|_\infty^2$$

and $\tau(\cdot,\cdot)$, $\varphi(\cdot)$ being $\mathcal{KL}$-function and $\mathcal{K}_\infty$-function, respectively. The error system (9.36) is input-to-state stable (ISS) [153].

With

$$s(n) = \Gamma^* - \hat{\Gamma}(n), \tag{9.40}$$

we have

$$s(n+1) = (1-hk_eb)s(n) + \beta_{01}e_1(n).$$

Similar to the deduction above, let us construct a Lyapunov function

$$\mathcal{V}_s(n) = s^2(n),$$

and one has that

$$\Delta\mathcal{V}_s(n) \le -(1-c)qs^2(n) + \beta_{01}^2\left(1+\frac{(1-hk_eb)^2}{cq}\right)e_1^2(n)$$

with $q > 0$,

$$k_e^2h^2b^2 - 2k_ehb = -q \tag{9.41}$$

and

$$\max\{0, (q-1)/q\} < c < 1. \tag{9.42}$$

It can be derived that

$$s^2(n) \le \varsigma(s(0), n) + \psi(\|e(n)\|_\infty),$$

where

$$\varsigma(s(0), n) = (1-q+cq)^n s^2(0),$$

$$\psi(\|e(n)\|_\infty) = \beta_{01}^2\frac{cq+(1-hk_eb)^2}{cq^2(1-c)}\|e(n)\|_\infty^2.$$

We can also conclude that system (9.40) is ISS. The revolution of SINR tends to its objective value Γ^* with a bounded error, which satisfies

$$|\Gamma^* - \Gamma(n)| \leq |s(n)| + \|e(n)\| \leq \epsilon.$$

This completes the proof.

Remark 26 *We can see that the accurate knowledge of term $\mathcal{F}(\Gamma(n))$ is not prerequisite in Theorem 4. It is worth mentioning that even if the system parameters have fluctuations/variations, they can be estimated in an online manner by the designed estimator* (9.34) *and then compensated by the proposed pricing mechanism. Thus, the transmitter in the security game requires less prior knowledge about the jammer and can achieve the desired SINR just by the observed gradient while interacting repeatedly. Notice that the addressed scheme of this chapter is motivated by the extended state observer (ESO) method researched in disturbance rejection control as in many works [102, 136, 242]. An ESO-based pricing mechanism is designed for the transmitter to achieve desirable performance and the convergence performance is proved by using ISS theory.*

The explicit process of the resilient strategy for CCS executed in the cloud server is summarized in Algorithm 2.

Algorithm 10 Dynamic pricing algorithm of CCS

1: Initialize communication parameters $L, \eta, \xi, N_0, \kappa$ and price parameters E, C.
2: Choose parameters $k_e, \beta_{01}, \beta_{02}, h$. Verifying if there exist $Q > 0, \mathcal{P}_e > 0, q > 0$ and scalars a, c satisfying formulas (9.38), (9.39), (9.41) and (9.42); if not, re-select, otherwise go to the next *Step*.
3: Set the desired estimation performance γ_d. Inquire about the desired packet delivery rate $\bar{\alpha}^*$ using Algorithm 1.
4: Calculate the required SINR Γ^* with inequality (9.43).
5: Obtain the estimation of $\Gamma(n)$ with (9.34).
6: Compute the price strategy by using (9.33).
7: The cloud server sends the strategy to the power transmitter in sensors. The transmitter changes his desire for QoS according to the received price strategy.

The required SINR Γ^* is calculated according to inequality

$$\bar{\alpha}^* \leq 2\mathbf{Q}(\kappa(\Gamma^* - \epsilon)). \tag{9.43}$$

Remark 27 *The dynamic pricing system* (9.32) *is proved to be ISS, which means SINR $\Gamma(n)$ can be controlled to be Γ^* with a small error. So if the predetermined disturbance attenuation performance is guaranteed, the required SINR is calculated with inequality* (9.43)*, which leads to the results being conservative. The upper bound of error ϵ can be reduced by adjusting parameters a, c, k_e, β_{01} and β_{02} such that the conservativeness of the dynamic pricing method is reduced.*

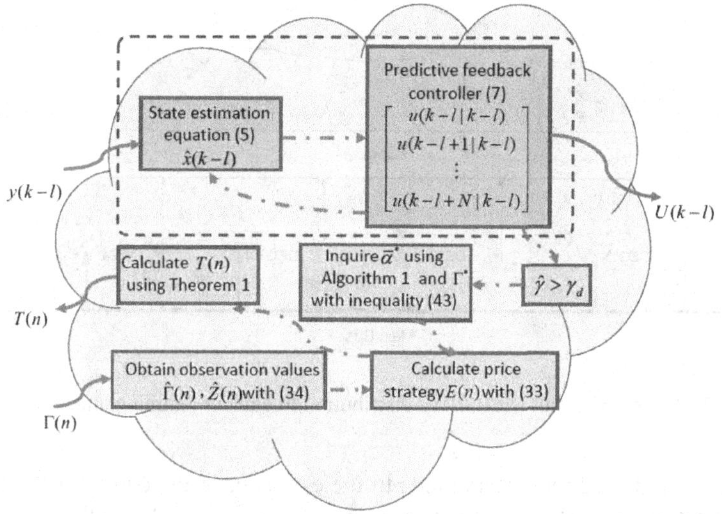

Figure 9.2 Resilient algorithm executed in cloud server.

Remark 28 *The cloud platform provides storage, computing, and control services which are shared for all end users. The requests from a user are mapped as a set of workflows. The workflows can be dealt with in parallel and the whole computing time is reduced by using scheduling algorithms. For example, when Algorithm 1 is used to find specific $\bar{\alpha}^*$ corresponding to γ_d, with different initial values of $\bar{\alpha}$ being set, Algorithm 1 can be executed simultaneously in different serve units, i.e., containers, and computing time can be reduced significantly [54]. Notice that this chapter focuses on resilient strategy design for one physical plant in CCS. Practically, there are a number of control systems that are independent or interrelated access to the cloud server. Thus, the computing time and system performance are affected by serve resource allocated to the service requests of a specific plant. The resilient scheme executed in the cloud server is shown in Fig. 9.2, where based on measurement $y(k-l)$, the estimation state $\hat{x}(k-l)$ and control sequence $U(k-l)$ are calculated with equations* (9.5) *and* (9.7). *The procedure of the dynamic pricing mechanism is also illustrated in Fig. 9.2, which operates in a larger time-scale than the control process.*

9.7 NUMERICAL SIMULATION

We use an IEEE 4-bus distribution line power grid system as shown in Fig. 9.3 to verify the effectiveness of the proposed methodology in this chapter [15, 144]. In Fig. 9.3, the power grid system outsources data storage, handling, and strategy calculation to the cloud server through transmitting data with communication networks subject to jamming attack. Voltage sensors installed in the main bus of the power grid monitor

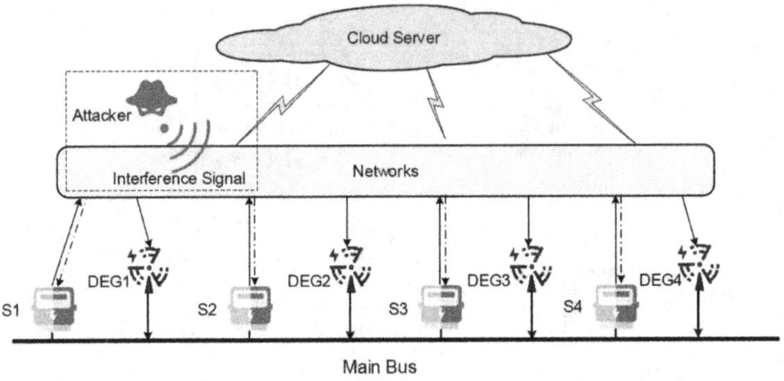

Figure 9.3 Power grid with IEEE 4-bus distribution line under jamming attack.

the voltages and send the observations to the estimator in the cloud server through communication networks. The raw measurements are dealt with and the controller is designed in the cloud server, and then control indexes are sent to distributed energy generators (DEGs) to stabilize the voltages at points of common couplings (PCCs) to reference values, where the PCCs are the points where buses connect to the main bus shown in Fig. 9.3.

The measured voltages of sensors are denoted by $\{\bar{y}_i(t)\}_{i=\{1,\cdots,4\}}$. The DEGs are modeled as a voltage resource whose voltages are denoted by $\{v_{pi}(t)\}_{i=\{1,\cdots,4\}}$ and the voltages at PCCs are $\{v_i(t)\}_{i=\{1,\cdots,4\}}$. Defining $\bar{y}(t) = [\bar{y}_1(t), \bar{y}_2(t), \bar{y}_3(t), \bar{y}_4(t)]^T$, $v_p(t) = [v_{p1}(t), v_{p2}(t), v_{p3}(t), v_{p4}(t)]^T$, and $v(t) = [v_1(t), v_2(t), v_3(t), v_4(t)]^T$, the dynamics of the power system are written in the following form

$$\begin{aligned} \dot{x}(t) &= A_c x(t) + B_c u(t) + D_c \omega(t), \\ \bar{y}(t) &= H_c x(t) + G_c \omega(t), \end{aligned} \tag{9.44}$$

where system state $x(t) = v(t) - v_{ref}$ is the PCC state voltage deviation, v_{ref} is the PCC reference voltage, control input $u(t) = v_p(t) - v_{pref}$ is the DEG control input deviation, v_{pref} is the reference control effort. $\bar{y}(t)$ is the bus voltage measured by sensors. The system matrices A_c, B_c and D_c are given by

$$A_c = \begin{bmatrix} 175.9 & 176.8 & 511 & 1036 \\ -350 & 0 & 0 & 0 \\ -544.2 & -474.8 & -408.8 & -828.8 \\ -119.7 & -554.6 & -968.8 & -1077.5 \end{bmatrix},$$

$$B_c = \begin{bmatrix} 0.8 & 334.2 & 525.17 & -103.6 \\ -350 & 0 & 0 & 0 \\ -69.3 & -66.1 & -420.1 & -828.8 \\ -434.9 & -414.2 & -108.7 & -1077.5 \end{bmatrix},$$

$$D_c = \begin{bmatrix} 1 & 0 & 1 & 0 \end{bmatrix}^T.$$

The measurement matrices are given by

$$H_c = \begin{bmatrix} 1 & 1 & 0 & 0 \\ 0 & 0 & 1 & 0 \\ 0 & 1 & 0 & 1 \\ 0 & 0 & 0 & 1 \end{bmatrix}, G_c = \begin{bmatrix} 1 & 0 & 0 & 0 \end{bmatrix}^T.$$

To guarantee the power grid system operates stably under a jamming attack, the measured information is sent to the estimator in the cloud server, estimator and controller gains are calculated in the cloud server according to Algorithm 1, and control signals are transmitted to the power system. The sampling period is $T_s = 0.003s$ and the time-delay is $0.006s$, i.e., $N = 2$. Assume that under the effect of jamming attack, the packet delivery rate $\bar{\alpha} = 0.9$. The disturbance attenuation level is set to be $\gamma = 0.1$. Estimation and control gains are given by

$$L = \begin{bmatrix} 0.6443 & 0.1983 & -0.4944 & 0.3886 \\ 0.1983 & -0.2471 & 0.5217 & -0.3681 \\ -0.4944 & 0.5217 & 0.1034 & -0.6559 \\ 0.3886 & -0.3681 & -0.6559 & 0.8300 \end{bmatrix},$$

$$K_1 = \begin{bmatrix} -0.0071 & 0.5179 & -0.3625 & 0.0822 \\ 0.5179 & -0.5711 & 0.3489 & -0.1159 \\ -0.3625 & 0.3489 & 0.0040 & 0.1405 \\ 0.0822 & -0.1159 & 0.1405 & -0.1460 \end{bmatrix},$$

$$K_2 = \begin{bmatrix} -0.2968 & 0.3854 & -0.4062 & -0.0174 \\ 0.3854 & -0.6629 & 0.2878 & -0.1291 \\ -0.4062 & 0.2878 & -0.3059 & 0.1668 \\ -0.0174 & -0.1291 & 0.1668 & -0.0977 \end{bmatrix},$$

$$K_3 = \begin{bmatrix} -0.2709 & 0.1944 & -0.1925 & -0.0346 \\ 0.1944 & -0.2651 & 0.0868 & -0.0446 \\ -0.1925 & 0.0868 & -0.2161 & 0.0517 \\ -0.0346 & -0.0446 & 0.0517 & 0.0030 \end{bmatrix}.$$

$\omega(k)$ is a bounded noise given by $\sin(k)/k$. The evolution of system states is depicted in Fig. 9.4.

The parameters in the attack model of equations (9.2) and (9.3) are set as $L = 6$, $\eta = 0.85$, $\xi = 0.25$, $N_0 = 0.1$. The pricing parameters of two players are $E = 2$ and $C = 0.5$. According to Theorem 1, the SE is calculated as $(T^*, J^*) = (0.3410, 1.2219)$ and the SINR is $\Gamma^* = 4.2891$. With scalar $\kappa = 0.1$ and Algorithm 1, the disturbance attenuation level $\hat{\gamma}$ is calculated as 0.0914. Assume that the objective disturbance attenuation level is $\gamma_d = 0.09$. Based on equation (9.43), the packet dropout rate and SINR are calculated as 0.3460 and 4.44. Choosing parameters $h = 0.01$, $k_e = 1.5$, $\beta_{01} = 0.15$, $\beta_{02} = 7$, by using the dynamic pricing mechanism (9.33) depicted by Fig. 9.5(a), the SINR is adjusted as Fig. 9.5(b) and the system disturbance attention level can achieve its objective value as shown in Fig. 9.5(c).

We give an illustration for the running process of the proposed resilient scheme in a power grid system in practical terms. The cloud server obtains system information and

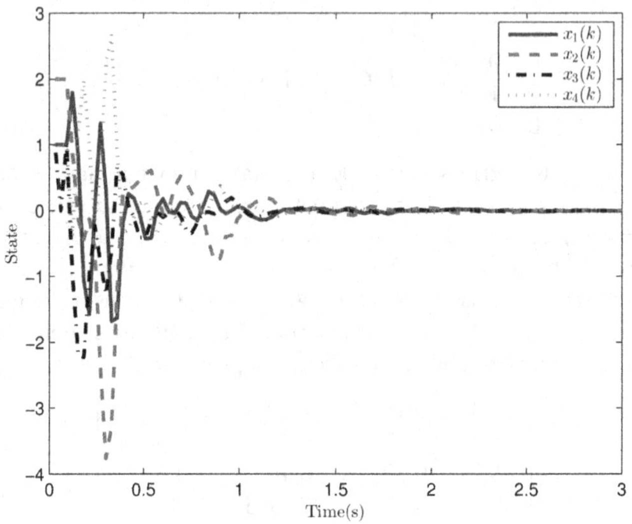

Figure 9.4 Evolution of system states.

communication parameters by gathering large amounts of data from the power grid and operating system recognition or reinforcement learning approaches. Estimator and controller gains are obtained by solving optimization problem (9.30) iteratively in the cloud server. As shown in Figs. 9.2 and 9.3, based on voltage values measured and sent by sensors in the main bus, a predictive control sequence is computed and sent to the DEGs who can choose an appropriate control command according to time stamps and adjust their input voltages to stabilize the voltages of PCCs to reference values. Besides, based on the system information, Algorithm 1 is executed in the cloud server. When the disturbance attenuation level cannot meet the demand under the impact of a jamming attack, the cloud server will find out the required SINR Γ^* for desired performance γ_d according to Algorithm 1. Then, price strategy (9.33) in Theorem 4 is calculated based on real-time SINR $\Gamma(n)$ and objective SINR Γ^*. With price strategy $E(n)$, the transmitter's strategy is calculated based on equation (9.25) and acknowledgements are sent to sensor/controller to increase or decrease the transmission power. The adjustment time depends on the operation of the physical plant, parameters in pricing mechanism, i.e., k_e, β_{01} and β_{02}. From Figs. 9.4 and 9.5(a), it is seen that the dynamic adjustment process is realized in about 20 minutes, i.e., $2s * 600$ iterations.

Assume that the channel gain η yields exponential distribution and the attacker is irrational and changes his strategy randomly, for instance, $J(n)$ takes values 2.5, 1.5 and 2 at steps 400, 800, and 1200, respectively. From Fig. 9.6(a), we can see that

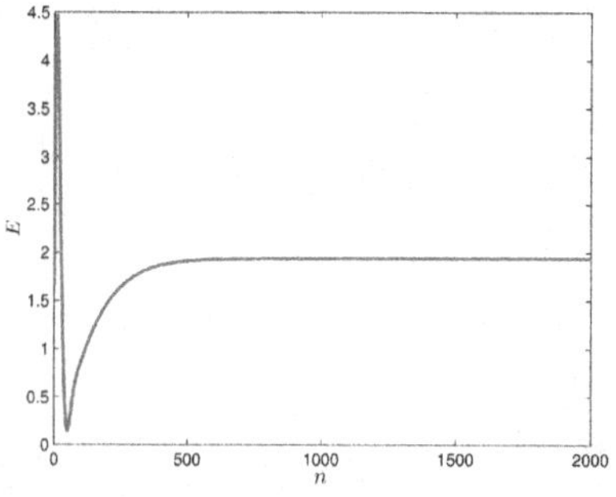

(a)Pricing parameter.

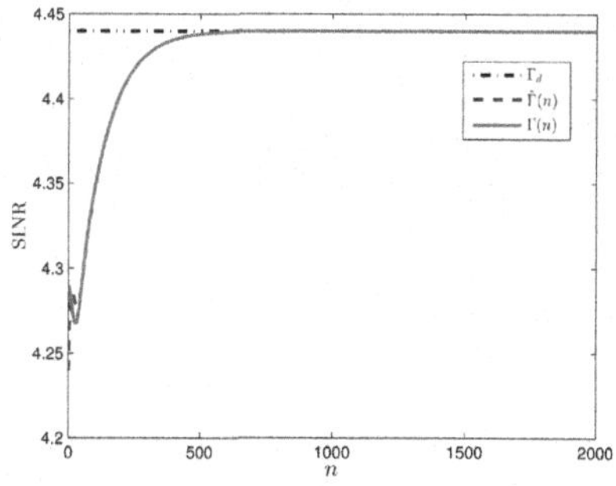

(b) SINR.

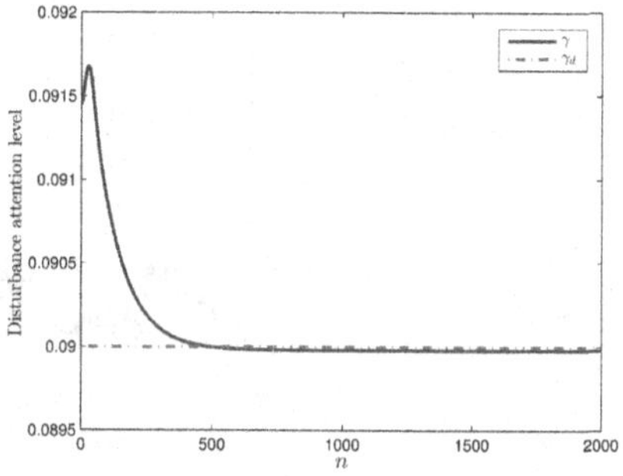

(c) Estimation performance.

Figure 9.5 Evolution results by using dynamic pricing mechanism.

the SINR can achieve its optimal value 4.44 accurately with time-varying networks and the attacker's irrational strategy. Moreover, the system performance is derived into the desired region as shown in Fig. 9.6(b). The evolution of pricing parameter E and observation value $\hat{\mathcal{Z}}(n)$ are depicted by Figs. 9.6(c) and (d), respectively. It can be seen that the parameters E and $\hat{\mathcal{Z}}(n)$ are affected by time-varying gains and attacker's strategy.

Fig. 9.6 depicts the results when networks change randomly and the attacker takes irrational strategies. Results in Fig. 9.6 illustrate that with the proposed dynamic pricing mechanism, the networks change and the attacker's strategy can be observed effectively; the designed price strategy makes the system achieve a desired performance. Above all, the dynamic pricing mechanism can guarantee a given secure performance for the power system in spite of jamming attacks and environment uncertainties, which makes the power grid system more resilient.

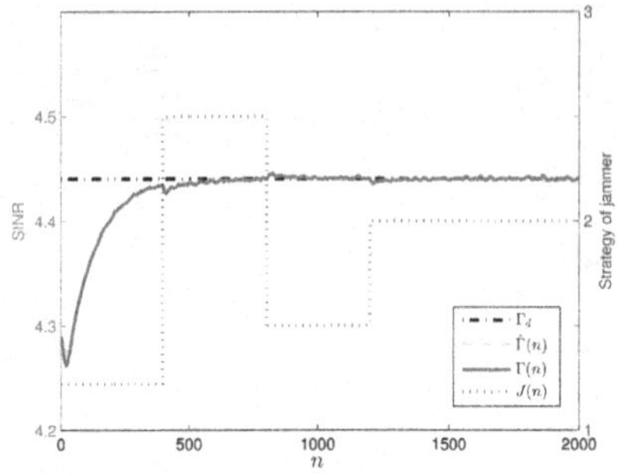

(a) SINR.

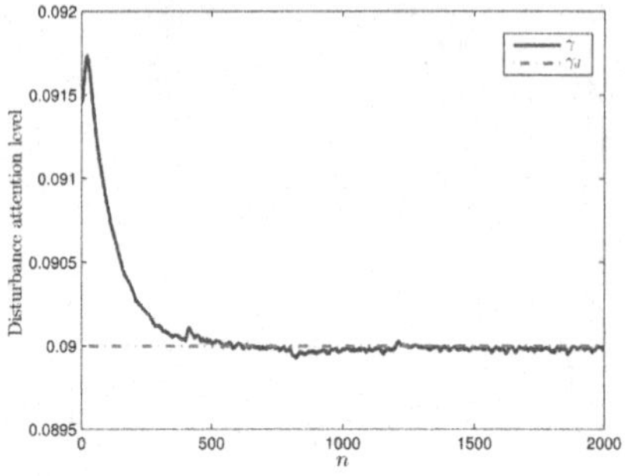

(b) Estimation performance.

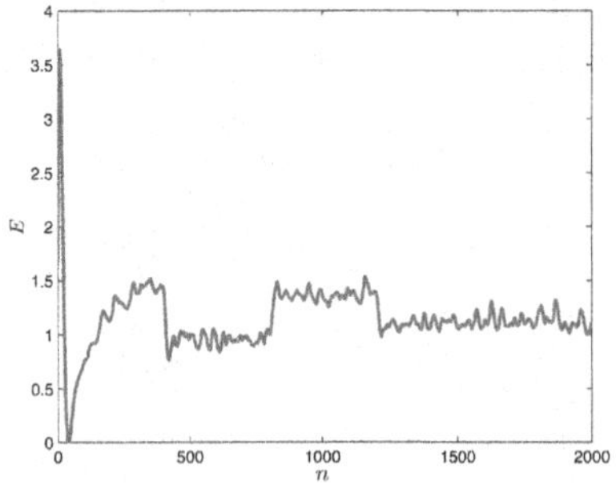

(c) Pricing parameter.

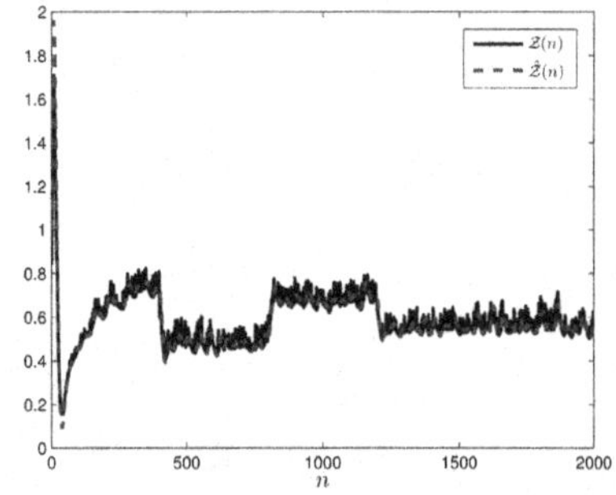

(d) $\mathcal{Z}(n)$ and $\hat{\mathcal{Z}}(n)$.

Figure 9.6 Evolution results with time-varying networks and attacker's irrational strategies.

9.8 CONCLUSION

This chapter has investigated a resilient defense problem for a CCS with time-delays suffering from a jamming attack. The degradation of system performance affected by the jamming attack has been presented. A Stackelberg game has been studied to describe the interaction of transmitter and jammer. On account of the game equilibria of two players, the disturbance attenuation level of CCS with time-delay has been obtained. A novel cross-layer dynamic pricing mechanism has been devised to drive the system performance of CCS to a desired region under constrained information and time-varying networks. Simulation results have been provided to verify the proposed methodology.

10 Stackelberg-game-based defense analysis against advanced persistent threats

10.1 INTRODUCTION

A cloud control system (CCS) is a remote control system that uses networked control system (NCS) and cloud computing technology to connect many distributed devices and outsource data and controller tasks to the cloud [227]. The cloud enables bidirectional information transmission between sensors, actuators, and controllers. However, CCS faces reliability and security issues due to the openness of communication networks and the outsourced manner [227, 229]. The main sources of insecurity are communication links and cloud service [257].

The attacks on communication links between physical plants and the cloud of CCS are classified as two types: integrity attack [218] and availability attack [111, 216]. Besides the communication links, the security of cloud service also plays a key role for reliable operation of CCS. The security challenges of the cloud service mainly include threats in identifying and accessing management, virtualization, data storage, data and computational integrity, and so on [253]. A new attack called advanced persistent threats (APTs) tries to steal information from a target cyber system like CCS without being noticed [27]. APTs are hard to detect and defend against because they are complex, hidden, continuous, and targeted [152, 253]. Game theory can help study the interaction of defender and APT attacker. A stealthy takeover game has been used to model this interaction [146]. A contract-based Flipcloud game has been used to evaluate the security risk and cloud QoS under APTs [97], where a pricing mechanism for security as a service has been designed for the physical plant control.

Multiple serve units in the CCS that combines advantages of NCS and cloud computing technology provide on-demand control as a service [229] for multiple physical plants. The service provider will allocate the service resources to fulfill plants' control tasks and meanwhile allocate the defense resources to secure the cloud service. The contributions are summarized as follows:

(1) Compared with works [97, 257], which focus on designing secure mechanism for a single physical plant, this chapter studies strategic defense by optimally allocating resources on account of the large-scale and distribution nature of CCS.
(2) With considering a decision sequence, the interaction of defender and attacker is modeled by a Stackelberg game with both sides subject to resource constraints.

(3) The optimal solutions for both sides under different types of budget constraints are analyzed and given by solving a mixed-integer nonlinear programming (MINLP) problem.

The remainder of the chapter is organized as follows: The preliminaries of system framework and the game model are set up in Section 11.2. The proposed Stackelberg game is analyzed in Section 11.3. In Section 11.4, we extend to investigating the cases with limited defense resource and limited number of protected servers. Section 11.5 extends to cases with limited defense resource and a number of protected servers. Simulation examples are presented to verify our main results in Section 11.6. Conclusions are drawn in Section 11.6.

10.2 PROBLEM FORMULATION

We consider a CCS suffering from APTs in the cloud as depicted in Fig. 10.1. Optimal controllers are designed for physical plants in the CCS. Based on the optimal control results, a defense and attack model is constructed by using a game theoretic approach.

10.2.1 CCS UNDER MALICIOUS ATTACKS

A CCS is studied in this chapter as shown in Fig. 10.1, which allows heterogeneous components to provide services in an integrated system. In the CCS, cloud service devices and multiple physical systems are jointed together by communication networks. The measured data of sensors are sent to controllers in the cloud through up-links and the calculated control commands are sent back to the actuators via down-links. Specifically, the large amount of collected sensor data can be stored and aggregated in the cloud while the controller can retrieve the data and compute the control command

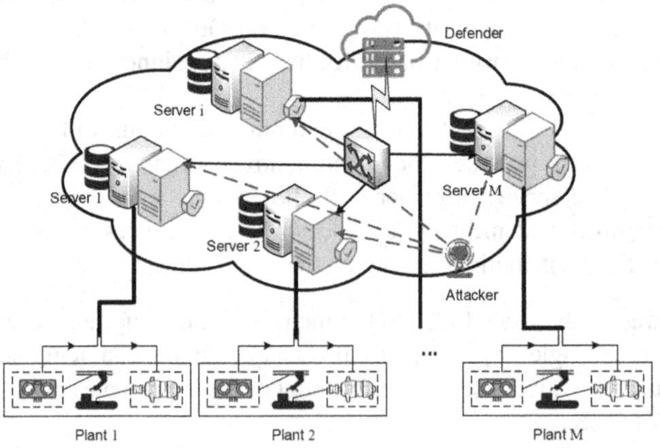

Figure 10.1 CCS under APTs.

on the cloud. Hence, this cloud-enabled framework, i.e., CCS, provides an efficient approach for remote control of physical plants. A cloud service provider allocates the service resources comprising data aggregation, storage, and processing to physical plants such that the service of automation satisfies the performance requirement of each physical system.

However, the cloud layer can be insecure, since it faces cyber threats known as APTs [27] which can lead to complete compromise of the cloud without being detected. This type of attack endowed with stealthiness and a persistent nature renders the current defense mechanisms such as a cryptography approach and intrusion detection inapplicable.

Confronted with APTs, the cloud service provider must make a defense investment for different serve units when he allocates service resources to different physical systems. Meanwhile, the attacker of APTs may also allocate his limited attack resources to different servers. Therefore, to create a mechanism for secure control as a service for the CCS, we aim at investigating the defense investment of a cloud service provider when taking the countermeasure of attacker into consideration to create a worst-case for improving the QoS of physical plants.

10.2.2 OPTIMAL CONTROL OF PHYSICAL PLANT

The devices in the CCS perform various tasks. To assess the performance of CCS, we need to consider the dynamics of physical plants. Specially, it is considered that there are M independent systems employing the cloud service simultaneously in the CCS. The discrete-time dynamics of device i under unreliable cloud service and transmission latency is captured as

$$x_i(k+1) = A_i x_i(k) + v_i(k) B_i u_i(k-d_i), \tag{10.1}$$

where $x_i(k) \in \mathbb{R}^{n_{x_i}}$ is the state, $u_i(k-d_i) \in \mathbb{R}^{n_{u_i}}$ is the control input with time delay $d_i \geq 0$. A_i and B_i are time-invariant system matrices with appropriate dimensions. The initial values $x_i(0), u_i(l), l = -d_i, \cdots, -1$, for all $i \in \mathcal{M} \triangleq \{1, 2, \cdots, M\}$ are known. The stochastic process $\{v_i(k)\}$ is used to model the vulnerability of the cloud, which captures whether the information is stored, handled, and transmitted successfully in the cloud.

Remark 29 *Notice that this chapter focuses on the security of CCS under APTs and resource allocations of defender and attacker. We only consider the input delay for the CCS, if the state delay in the feedback channel is present, the optimal controller is known to take the same form, and a prediction method can be used to compensate the state delay [88]. On the other hand, a constant time delay d_i is included in this chapter, where d_i is the maximum step of the time delay of plant i in the CCS. A buffer is assumed to be installed in the actuator of each physical plant, with which the optimal controller* (10.4) *can guarantee the stability of CCS with random time delay in networks.*

The CCS has the capacity of dealing with complex computation and storing big data. The devices in the CCS maintain constant communication with the cloud to collect and store the sensor data, then process information and calculate the control input for each physical plant. The physical plants whose performances are dependent on the QoS of the cloud will make sure the trustworthiness of the cloud. Thus, the stochastic variable $\{v_i(k)\}$ can model the impact of the cloud service's unreliability under APTs.

It is assumed that the communications between the cloud and the physical devices are secure in the CCS and the time delay induced by networks is considered. The degradation of the system performance results from the loss of sensing and control information caused by APTs in the cloud. Without loss of generality, let $v_i(k)$ be a Bernoulli random variable which yields

$$v_i(k) = \begin{cases} 1, \text{ with probability } \rho_i, \\ 0, \text{ with probability } 1-\rho_i, \end{cases} \tag{10.2}$$

where $v_i(k) = 0$ means that the data collection, storage and computing service of the cloud is disrupted and makes control inputs unavailable for the actuators. Otherwise, if the data collection and storage can meet the demand and computing service operates normally, $v_i(k) = 1$. ρ_i is the delivery rate of data packets of control input for subsystem i, and it can also represent the QoS of the cloud in the CCS.

The optimal control scheme is considered for physical plants in an infinite time horizon. With given cloud QoS parameter ρ_i, the physical plant i wants to minimize the quadratic cost function as

$$J_i(x_i(0), u_i(k)) = \sum_{k=0}^{\infty} \mathbb{E}\{x_i^T(k)Qx_i(k) + v_i(k)u_i^T(k-d_i)Ru_i(k-d_i)\}, \tag{10.3}$$

where $Q \geq 0$ and $R > 0$ are two weighting matrices capturing the cost of the state derivation and control effort. To simplify the exposition, we focus on the case that Q, R are identity matrices with appropriate dimensions, and the following lemma is introduced to give the optimal control strategy and minimum system performance.

Lemma 10.1 *If the system (A_i, B_i) is stabilizable, there exists a unique solution $P_i > 0$ satisfying the following delay-dependent algebraic Riccati equation*

$$P_i = A_i^T P_i A_i + I - \Pi_i^T \Psi_i^{-1} \Pi_i$$

with

$$\Psi_i = \rho_i^2 B_i^T P_i B_i + (\rho_i - \rho_i^2) B_i^T (A_i^T)^{d_i} P_i A_i^{d_i} B_i + (\rho_i - \rho_i^2) \sum_{l=0}^{d_i-1} B_i^T (A_i^T)^l A_i^l B_i + \rho_i I,$$

$$\Pi_i = \rho_i B_i^T P_i A_i.$$

The optimal control input satisfying

$$u_i^*(k-d_i) = -\Psi_i^{-1} \Pi_i \hat{x}_i(k|k-d_i), k \geq d_i \tag{10.4}$$

can stabilize system (A_i, B_i) *and minimize the cost function* (10.3)*, where*

$$\hat{x}_i(k|k-d_i) = A^{d_i}x_i(k-d_i) + \sum_{l=1}^{d_i} A_i^{l-1}B_iu_i(k-d_i-l).$$

The optimal cost is given by

$$J_i^* = x_i^T(0)P_ix_i(0) - \sum_{k=0}^{d_i-1} u_i^T(k-d_i)u_i(k-d_i) + \sum_{k=0}^{d_i-1} \mathbb{E}\{\Delta_i^T\Psi_i\Delta_i\} \tag{10.5}$$

with

$$\Delta_i = u_i(k-d_i) + \Psi_i^{-1}\Pi_i\hat{x}_i(k|k-d_i).$$

Proof *According to Theorem 3 in [88], the result can be derived directly by substituting parameters* $A, \bar{A}, B, \bar{B}, \omega(k)$ *with corresponding* $A_i, 0, \rho_iB_i, B_i, v_i(k)-\rho_i$ *in this chapter for all* $i \in \mathcal{M}$.

10.3 DEFENSE AND ATTACK GAME SETUP

10.3.1 DEFENSE AND ATTACK MODEL

To defend against APTs, an effective countermeasure is to invest in each serve unit to control the cloud resources with high frequency [97]. When the cloud service provider, denoted as a defender in the secure problem, invests to control the cloud, the information can be collected, handled and sent correctly with high probability. In [97], for the cloud service of a single physical plant, the defense and attack frequencies defined as the defender and attacker's strategies are assumed to be optimizable without budget constraints. In this chapter, we research a CCS which contains multiple servers assigned to different control systems. The resource budgets of defender and attacker must be considered in CCS because the resources cannot always satisfy the requirement or are expensive for a large-scale system. Since the defense budget is limited, the defender needs to balance the investment on each server. The defense strategy allocated to server i is denoted as ξ_i with $0 \le \xi_i \le \xi_i^{\max}, i \in \mathcal{M}$; then the defense strategy of CCS is written as a vector

$$\boldsymbol{\xi} \triangleq [\xi_1, \xi_2, \cdots, \xi_M]^T.$$

The total cost for such a defense plan is denoted as

$$C_d = \mathbf{1}^T \cdot \boldsymbol{\xi}.$$

It is assumed that a fixed attack investment g for each server can be exploited by the attacker, but with constrained equipment, the attacker can only disrupt R, $R < M$, serve units at the same time. The strategy of the attacker is expressed as

$$\boldsymbol{\gamma} \triangleq [\gamma_1, \gamma_2, \cdots, \gamma_M]^T,$$

where $\gamma_i \in \{0,1\}, i \in \mathcal{M}$ represents whether the attacker launches an attack to server i.

Intuitively, under the defense investment ξ_i and attack strategy $\gamma_i = 1$, the probability ρ_i that the data packet can be transmitted successfully to the actuator of plant i is monotonically increasing with respect to ξ_i, which is denoted as function $f_i(\cdot) : \mathbb{R}^+ \cup \{0\} \to \mathbb{R}^+ \cup \{0\}$ [97], i.e.,

$$\rho_i = f_i(\xi_i), f_i(0) = 0, \tag{10.6}$$

where the function $f_i(\cdot), i \in \mathcal{M}$ depending on the server's configuration and the physical plant's characteristic is defined as the reward of the defender. On the other hand, if the attacker does not launch an attack to server i, i.e., $\gamma_i = 0$, the packet delivery rate of plant i in the CCS is denoted as $\rho_i = c_i$, which is a constant that does not vary with the investment ξ_i and satisfies

$$c_i > f_i(\xi_i), \forall\, 0 \le \xi_i \le \xi_i^{\max}, \forall i \in \mathcal{M}. \tag{10.7}$$

Remark 30 *Instead of analyzing the performance cost J_i^* in secure strategy design which will make the problem intractable, we define the QoS of the cloud, that is, the packet delivery rate ρ_i, as the reward of the defender. Since it is known that the cost value of the physical plant is decreasing with the delivery probability by Monte-Carlo simulation [169], this setup is reasonable.*

10.3.2 GAME SETUP

In this work, we focus on optimizing the performance of CCS under interaction of both defender and attacker. Since defender and attacker are two sides that have many strategies, the problem of the CCS under ATPs is investigated from a game-theoretic point of view.

The defender who aims at securing the CCS wants to maximize the packet delivery rate of all physical systems while taking the total cost of the defense plan into account. Then, the payoff function of the defender is expressed as

$$\mathcal{U}_d(\xi, \gamma) = \mathcal{R}_d - \beta C_d, \tag{10.8}$$

where

$$\mathcal{R}_d = (\mathbf{1} - \gamma)^T \boldsymbol{c} + \gamma^T \boldsymbol{f}(\xi)$$

is the reward function including the packet delivery rate under or not under attack. Notation β is a weighting parameter which can reflect the preference of the defender. The action of the defender is taken from set $\mathbf{A}_d \triangleq [\mathbf{0}, \xi^{\max}]$. Notation $\boldsymbol{c} \triangleq [c_1, c_2, \cdots, c_M]^T$ is the packet delivery rate if there is no attack on the physical plants.

For the attacker, an opponent objective is endowed which aims to minimize the packet delivery rate. Thus, we define the payoff for the attacker as

$$\mathcal{U}_a(\xi, \gamma) = -\mathcal{R}_d, \tag{10.9}$$

which is subject to the constraint $\mathbf{1}^T \gamma \le R$.

Proposition 2 *The payoff function $\mathcal{U}_a(\xi,\gamma)$ is monotonically increasing with respect to attack strategy γ.*

Proof *It is known that attacker's utility function yields*

$$\mathcal{U}_a(\xi,\gamma) = -(\mathbf{1}-\gamma)^T c - \gamma^T f(\xi) = -\mathbf{1}^T c + \gamma^T (c - f(\xi)).$$

According to inequality (10.7), *one has that* $\mathbf{c} - \boldsymbol{f}(\xi) \geq \mathbf{0}$. *It is concluded that* $\mathcal{U}_a(\xi,\gamma)$ *is monotonically increasing in* γ.

Based on Proposition 1, it is not difficult to show that the optimal payoff of the attacker is achieved when $\mathbf{1}^T\gamma = R$ and the number of all the strategies of the attacker is $\mathbb{C}_M^R$. The set of attack action is defined as

$$\mathbf{A}_a \triangleq \left\{ \gamma_i, \forall i \in \mathcal{M} \middle| \sum_{i=1}^{M} \gamma_i = R \right\} = \{\gamma_1, \gamma_2, \cdots, \gamma_L\},$$

where $L = \mathbb{C}_M^R$. Then, the attacker's strategy is represented as $\gamma_l \in \mathbf{A}_a$, $l \in \mathcal{L} \triangleq \{1, 2, \cdots, L\}$.

Compared with most of the presented literature on system security [134, 234] that players take actions simultaneously, that is, the analysis is provided based on the concept of 'Nash equilibrium', we consider a more actual case that the attacker is intelligent and the players take actions sequentially in this chapter. It is reasonable to assume that the defender that takes action first does not know the attacker's strategy beforehand, but the attacker may have partial or full knowledge of the defender's strategy. Practically, the attacker will try his best to acquire such information and with more information being collected, the probability of launching a successful attack always grows. Therefore, we consider a worst-case that the attacker has full knowledge of the defender, which derives a Stackelberg game scheme, in which the defender is a leader and the attacker acts as a follower [41]. Different from [41] considering a SINR-based model of the physical layer, a problem on defense resource allocation and attack strategy choice is investigated in this chapter.

Problem 5 *Denote the game between defender and attacker as $\mathbf{G}_S$. Find the defender's strategy $\xi^* \in \mathbf{A}_d$ such that*

$$\mathcal{U}_d(\xi^*, \Gamma(\xi^*)) \geq \mathcal{U}_d(\xi, \Gamma(\xi)), \forall \xi \in \mathbf{A}_d,$$

where $\Gamma(\xi)$ is the optimal response of the attacker satisfying

$$\Gamma(\xi) = \{\psi \in \mathbf{A}_a | \mathcal{U}_a(\xi,\psi) \geq \mathcal{U}_a(\xi,\gamma), \forall \gamma \in \mathbf{A}_a\}.$$

Find the optimal strategy of the attacker $\gamma^* = \Gamma(\xi^*)$. Then, obtain the set (ξ^*, γ^*) which is a Stackelberg equilibrium of the game between defender and attacker in the CCS.

10.4 STACKELBERG GAME ANALYSIS

The Stackelberg game of CCS denoted by $\mathbf{G}_S$ is executed as follows: The optimal response strategy of the attacker is computed for a given strategy of the defender. Then, we calculate the optimal strategy of the defender based on the knowledge of the optimal response strategy of attacker. Above all, the solution for the Stackelberg game of defender and attacker described in *Problem 1* is summarized in the following theorem.

Theorem 10.1 *The Stackelberg security game for CCS is equivalent to solve the maximin problem*

$$\max_{\xi \in \mathbf{A}_d} \min_{\gamma \in \mathbf{A}_a} \mathcal{U}_d(\xi, \gamma). \tag{10.10}$$

The solution to security game $\mathbf{G}_S$ satisfies the following properties:

1) *The optimal strategy of defender $\boldsymbol{\xi}^*$ satisfies the solution of*

$$\begin{aligned} &\max_{\xi \in \mathbf{A}_d} \varepsilon \\ &s.t. \ (\mathbf{1} - \gamma_l)^T \mathbf{c} + \gamma_l^T f(\xi) - \beta \mathbf{1}^T \xi \geq \varepsilon, \forall l \in \mathcal{L}. \end{aligned} \tag{10.11}$$

2) *The optimal strategy of attacker is expressed as*

$$\gamma^* = \arg\min_{l \in \mathcal{L}} \{(\mathbf{1} - \gamma_l)^T \mathbf{c} + \gamma_l^T f(\xi^*)\}. \tag{10.12}$$

Proof *As in previous discussions, the decisions are made sequentially in the Stakelberg game. The defender in CCS first gives a defense investment plan; then the attacker observes the existing protection action and makes a choice to launch an attack to those serve units such that the greatest damage to the CCS is produced. With a given defense strategy $\boldsymbol{\xi}$, the attacker's optimal strategy is calculated as*

$$\boldsymbol{\Gamma}(\xi) = \arg\max_{\gamma \in \mathbf{A}_a} \mathcal{U}_a(\xi, \gamma).$$

Then, the defender chooses $\boldsymbol{\xi}^*$ to maximize his payoff under given $\boldsymbol{\Gamma}(\xi)$, which is written as

$$\xi^* = \arg\max_{\xi \in \mathbf{A}_d} \mathcal{U}_d(\xi, \boldsymbol{\Gamma}(\xi)).$$

By observing the functions (10.8) *and* (10.9)*, obviously, we have the following conclusion*

$$\boldsymbol{\Gamma}(\xi) = \arg\max_{\gamma \in \mathbf{A}_a} \mathcal{U}_a(\xi, \gamma) = \arg\min_{\gamma \in \mathbf{A}_a} \mathcal{U}_d(\xi, \gamma).$$

Therefore, the Stackelberg game of CCS is converted into solving

$$\max_{\xi \in \mathbf{A}_d} \min_{\gamma \in \mathbf{A}_a} \mathcal{U}_d(\xi, \gamma). \tag{10.13}$$

Then, making use of the Wald's maximin model, problem (10.13) *has an equivalent formula*

$$\begin{aligned}
&\max_{\xi\in\mathbf{A}_d}\min_{\gamma\in\mathbf{A}_a} \mathcal{U}_d(\xi,\gamma)\\
&= \max_{\xi\in\mathbf{A}_d}\min_{l\in\mathcal{L}}\{\mathcal{U}_d(\xi,\gamma_1),\mathcal{U}_d(\xi,\gamma_2),\cdots,\mathcal{U}_d(\xi,\gamma_L)\}\\
&= \max_{\xi\in\mathbf{A}_d,\varepsilon\in\mathbb{R}}\{\varepsilon|\varepsilon\le\mathcal{U}_d(\xi,\gamma_l),\forall l\in\mathcal{L}\},
\end{aligned} \tag{10.14}$$

which is equivalent to solve the problem given by

$$\begin{aligned}
&\max_{\xi\in\mathbf{A}_d,\varepsilon\in\mathbb{R}} \quad \varepsilon\\
&s.t.\ (\mathbf{1}-\gamma_l)^T\mathbf{c}+\gamma_l^T f(\xi)-\beta\mathbf{1}^T\xi\ge\varepsilon,\forall l\in\mathcal{L}.
\end{aligned}$$

This completes the proof of Item 1).

After obtaining ξ^*, the attacker's optimal attack vector is calculated as

$$\gamma^* = \arg\min_{l\in\mathcal{L}}\{(\mathbf{1}-\gamma_l)^T\mathbf{c}+\gamma_l^T f(\xi^*)\}.$$

Item 2) is obtained. This ends the proof.

Problem (10.11) can be rewritten as a compact form and yields

$$\begin{aligned}
&\max_{\xi\in\mathbf{A}_d,\varepsilon\in\mathbb{R}} \quad \varepsilon\\
&s.t.\ \mathcal{F}(\xi)+\mathcal{B}\ge\varepsilon\mathbf{1},
\end{aligned} \tag{10.15}$$

where $\mathcal{F}(\xi) = [\mathcal{F}_1(\xi),\mathcal{F}_2(\xi),\cdots,\mathcal{F}_L(\xi)]^T$ with $\mathcal{F}_l(\xi) = \sum_{i=1}^M(\gamma_{l,i}f_i(\xi_i)-\beta\xi_i),\forall l\in\mathcal{L}$, $\mathcal{B} = [\mathcal{B}_1,\mathcal{B}_2,\cdots,\mathcal{B}_L]^T$ with $\mathcal{B}_l = (\mathbf{1}-\gamma_l)^T\mathbf{c},\forall l\in\mathcal{L}$.

Let us choose function $f_i(\cdot)$ with the form satisfying the conditions in formula (10.6) and (10.7) as follows

$$f_i(\xi_i) = c_i(1-e^{-b_i\xi_i}),\forall i\in\mathcal{M}, \tag{10.16}$$

where $c_i > 0, b_i > 0$ depend on the characteristics of device i. Variables in the defender's optimization problem (10.15) are reformulated as $\mathcal{F}_l(\xi) = \sum_{i=1}^M(\gamma_{l,i}c_i(1-e^{-b_i\xi_i})-\beta\xi_i),\forall l\in\mathcal{L}$ and $\mathcal{B}_l = (\mathbf{1}-\gamma_l)^T\mathbf{c},\forall l\in\mathcal{L}$. Note that the function $f_i(\cdot)$ in (10.16) is chosen based on the concept of marginal utility in economic theory, in which the growth rate of function $f_i(\cdot)$ decreases with respect to ξ_i, $\forall i\in\mathcal{M}$.

10.5 EXTENDING TO CASES WITH LIMITED DEFENSE RESOURCE AND NUMBER OF PROTECTED SERVERS

The problem considered in the previous section is with an explicit constraint of resource only for the attacker, while for the defender a soft constraint, that is, a penalty term $-\beta\mathbf{1}^T\xi$, is imposed in the objective function $\mathcal{U}_d$. However, in certain cases, the total defense budget is limited and the total number of the servers that can be protected at the same time is limited because of physical restriction. We will extend our work to these more practical aspects in this part.

10.5.1 CASE OF LIMITED DEFENSE RESOURCE CONSTRAINT

We first investigate that the defender has a total budget limitation denoted as Ω. It is reasonable that the punishment term of investment cost will not be considered in the utility of defender, i.e., $\beta = 0$. Therefore, the problem (10.15) can be reformulated based on the previous discussions.

Corollary 4 *The optimal defense resource allocation* $\boldsymbol{\xi}$ *for limited defense budget* Ω *is obtained by solving*

$$\begin{aligned} &\max_{\xi \in \mathbf{A}_d, \varrho \in \mathbb{R}} \varrho \\ &s.t.\ \tilde{\mathcal{F}}(\boldsymbol{\xi}) + \mathcal{B} \geq \varrho \mathbf{1},\ \mathbf{1}^T \boldsymbol{\xi} \leq \Omega, \end{aligned} \tag{10.17}$$

where $\tilde{\mathcal{F}}(\boldsymbol{\xi}) = [\tilde{\mathcal{F}}_1(\boldsymbol{\xi}), \tilde{\mathcal{F}}_2(\boldsymbol{\xi}), \cdots, \tilde{\mathcal{F}}_L(\boldsymbol{\xi})]^T$ with $\tilde{\mathcal{F}}_l(\boldsymbol{\xi}) = \sum_{i=1}^{M} \gamma_{l,i} f_i(\xi_i)$.

The above problem (10.17) to maximize auxiliary variable ϱ with fixed defense constraint Ω is equivalent to its dual problem that minimizes the variable Ω under a constraint with fixed value ϱ, that is,

$$\begin{aligned} &\min_{\xi \in \mathbf{A}_d, \Omega \in \mathbb{R}^*} \Omega \\ &s.t.\ \tilde{\mathcal{F}}(\boldsymbol{\xi}) + \mathcal{B} \geq \varrho \mathbf{1},\ \mathbf{1}^T \boldsymbol{\xi} \leq \Omega. \end{aligned} \tag{10.18}$$

Eliminating the auxiliary variable Ω, problem (10.18) is equivalent to the one given as

$$\begin{aligned} &\min_{\xi \in \mathbf{A}_d} \mathbf{1}^T \boldsymbol{\xi} \\ &s.t.\ \tilde{\mathcal{F}}(\boldsymbol{\xi}) + \mathcal{B} \geq \varrho \mathbf{1}. \end{aligned} \tag{10.19}$$

In problem (10.19), the parameter ϱ can be interpreted as a minimum requirement of QoS needed by the CCS. Now we talk about the corresponding estimation of parameter ϱ with a fixed defense budget Ω. Following the constraint in problem (10.19), one has that

$$\begin{aligned} \varrho &\leq \tilde{\mathcal{F}}_l(\boldsymbol{\xi}) + \mathcal{B}_l, \forall l \in \mathcal{L} \\ &\leq \max_{l \in \mathcal{L}} \left(\max_{i \in \mathcal{M}} \gamma_{l,i} \tilde{f}_i \cdot \sum_{i=1}^{M} \xi_i + \sum_{i=1}^{M} (1 - \gamma_{l,i}) c_i \right) \\ &\leq \hat{b}_\gamma \Omega + \hat{c}_\gamma, \end{aligned} \tag{10.20}$$

where $\hat{b}_\gamma \triangleq \max_{l \in \mathcal{L}} \max_{i \in \mathcal{M}} \gamma_{l,i} \tilde{f}_i$ with $\tilde{f}_i = \left.\frac{\partial f_i(\xi_i)}{\partial \xi_i}\right|_{\xi_i = 0}$ and $\hat{c}_\gamma \triangleq \max_{l \in \mathcal{L}} \sum_{i=1}^{M} (1 - \gamma_{l,i}) c_i$. The value ϱ can be chosen based on inequality (10.20) and with several trials. On the other hand, for a given performance requirement ϱ if the minimized defense cost $\mathbf{1}^T \boldsymbol{\xi}^*$ is larger than the available budget Ω, it means that the ideal performance is not able to be achieved.

Table 10.1
Reward values of defender

	Defense $\theta_i = 1$	No defense $\theta_i = 0$
Attack $\gamma_i = 1$	$f_i(\xi_i)$	0
No attack $\gamma_i = 0$	c_i	c_i

10.5.2 EXTENDING TO CASE OF LIMITED NUMBER OF PROTECTED SERVERS

In this part, we consider an extended problem in which the number of protected serve units is limited. Intuitively, the more serve units are protected, the easier the system performance of CCS can be achieved. In other words, if more numbers of serve units are protected, the defense investment can be reduced for predetermined system performance. The high cost of defense infrastructure is the hindrance for large-scale deployment. Therefore, it is essential to find the best selection of a limited number of protected serve units, which is also of great importance in real applications.

Let a binary variable $\theta_i \in \{0,1\}$ represent whether the serve unit i is protected. The reward functions of the defender at serve unit i for different cases are listed in Table 10.1. The other main problem considered in this chapter is addressed as follows:

Problem 6 *On account of problem* (10.19), *find the optimal strategy* $(\boldsymbol{\xi}^*, \boldsymbol{\theta}^*)$ *for the defender by solving*

$$\begin{aligned} &\min_{\boldsymbol{\xi}\in\mathbf{A}_d,\boldsymbol{\theta}\in\mathbf{A}_\theta} \boldsymbol{1}^T\boldsymbol{\xi} \\ &s.t.\ \bar{\mathcal{F}}(\boldsymbol{\xi},\boldsymbol{\theta})+\mathcal{B} \geq \varrho\boldsymbol{1},\ \boldsymbol{1}^T\boldsymbol{\theta} \leq \Theta, \end{aligned} \tag{10.21}$$

where $\bar{\mathcal{F}}(\boldsymbol{\xi},\boldsymbol{\theta}) = [\bar{\mathcal{F}}_1(\boldsymbol{\xi},\boldsymbol{\theta}),\cdots,\bar{\mathcal{F}}_L(\boldsymbol{\xi},\boldsymbol{\theta})]^T$ *with* $\bar{\mathcal{F}}_l(\boldsymbol{\xi},\boldsymbol{\theta}) = \sum_{i=1}^M \gamma_{l,i}\theta_i f_i(\xi_i)$, $\boldsymbol{\theta} = [\theta_1,\theta_2,\cdots,\theta_M]^T$ *and* $\mathbf{A}_\theta \triangleq \{0,1\}^M$. *Find the optimal attack strategy* $\boldsymbol{\gamma}^*$ *such that*

$$\mathcal{U}_a(\boldsymbol{\xi}^*,\boldsymbol{\theta}^*,\boldsymbol{\gamma}^*) \geq \mathcal{U}_a(\boldsymbol{\xi}^*,\boldsymbol{\theta}^*,\boldsymbol{\gamma}), \forall\boldsymbol{\gamma}\in\mathbf{A}_a,$$

where $\mathcal{U}_a(\boldsymbol{\xi},\boldsymbol{\theta},\boldsymbol{\gamma}) = -\bar{\mathcal{F}}(\boldsymbol{\xi},\boldsymbol{\theta}) - \mathcal{B}$.

The following proposition is introduced to verify the convexity of problem (10.21) [86].

Proposition 3 *Problem* (10.21) *is proved to be a convex mixed-integer problem with the following statements holding.*

1) $\mathbf{A}_d$ *is a nonempty convex and compact set in* $\mathbb{R}^M$. $\mathbf{A}_\theta$ *is a finite integer set.*
2) *Relax* θ_i *to be a real variable in the range of [0,1] for all* $i \in \mathcal{M}$. *Obviously,* $f^{obj}(\boldsymbol{\xi}) \triangleq \boldsymbol{1}^T\boldsymbol{\xi}$ *is convex in* $\boldsymbol{\xi}$ *and* $g_2^{con}(\boldsymbol{\theta}) \triangleq \boldsymbol{1}^T\boldsymbol{\theta} - \Theta$ *is convex with respect to* $\boldsymbol{\theta}$. *The first constraint is divided into L constraints which are denoted as*

$$g_{1,l}^{con}(\boldsymbol{\xi},\boldsymbol{\theta}) \triangleq \varrho - \sum_{i=1}^{M}\left(\gamma_{l,i}\theta_i f_i(\xi_i) + (1-\gamma_{l,i})c_i\right), l \in \mathcal{L}.$$

The Hessian matrix of $g_{1,l}^{con}(\boldsymbol{\xi},\boldsymbol{\theta})$ calculated by $H_l = diag\{[c_1 b_1^2 e^{-b_1\xi_1},\cdots, c_M b_M^2 e^{-b_M\xi_M}, 0,\cdots,0]\}$ is positive semi-definite, which concludes that $g_{1,l}^{con}(\boldsymbol{\xi},\boldsymbol{\theta})$ is convex in $\boldsymbol{\xi}$ and $\boldsymbol{\theta}$ for all $l \in \mathcal{L}$.

Problem 2 is an MINLP problem and the Generalized Benders Decomposition (GBD) method is an effective approach to solve this problem with guaranteed optimality [39]. Based on the GBD method, optimization problem (10.21) is converted into solving the following master problem

$$\begin{aligned}&\min_{\boldsymbol{\theta}\in\{0,1\}^M,\underline{B}\in\mathbb{R}} \underline{B}\\ &s.t.\ L(\boldsymbol{\xi},\boldsymbol{\lambda}) \le \underline{B},\ \boldsymbol{u}^T(\mathbf{1}^T\boldsymbol{\theta}-\Theta)\le 0,\end{aligned} \tag{10.22}$$

the subproblem

$$\begin{aligned}&\min_{\boldsymbol{\xi}\in\mathbf{A}_d} \mathbf{1}^T\boldsymbol{\xi}\\ &s.t.\ \bar{\mathcal{F}}(\boldsymbol{\xi})+\mathcal{B}\ge \varrho\mathbf{1},\end{aligned} \tag{10.23}$$

and feasibility check problem

$$\begin{aligned}&\min_{\boldsymbol{\xi}\in\mathbf{A}_d,\vartheta\in\mathbb{R}^+} \vartheta\\ &s.t.\ \vartheta\mathbf{1}\ge \varrho\mathbf{1}-\bar{\mathcal{F}}(\boldsymbol{\xi})-\mathcal{B},\end{aligned} \tag{10.24}$$

where

$$L(\boldsymbol{\xi},\boldsymbol{\theta},\boldsymbol{\lambda}) = \mathbf{1}^T\boldsymbol{\xi}+\boldsymbol{\lambda}^T(\varrho\mathbf{1}-\bar{\mathcal{F}}(\boldsymbol{\xi})-\mathcal{B}) \tag{10.25}$$

is the Lagrangian function of problem (10.21). $\boldsymbol{u}$ is the multiplier when solving the Lagrangian dual problem of (10.24).

With given values of integer variables, the MINLP problem is reduced to subproblem (10.23) to obtain the values of continuous variables. The master problem (10.22) is an integer programming problem, where the integers are regarded as the variables and only the integer constraints are considered. The feasibility check problem (10.24) is constructed to update the constraint in (10.22) when subproblem (10.23) is infeasible. The iterative process of the GBD method is depicted by a flow diagram shown in Fig. 10.2, in which $\aleph$ is a large enough constant and ϵ is chosen as a small enough constant that represents the iteration precision. $\mathbb{I}^{(k)}$ and $\mathbb{J}^{(k)}$ are two sets with elements of iteration steps.

Theorem 10.2 *The proposed secure resource allocation scheme shown in Fig. 10.2 converges to the optimal solution $(\boldsymbol{\xi}^*,\boldsymbol{\theta}^*)$ with a finite number of iterations.*

Proof *Let ℓ^* denote the optimal value of $\mathbf{1}^T\boldsymbol{\xi}$ in problem* (10.21). *Based on the flow diagram of Fig. 10.2, it is obvious that $\underline{B}^{(k-1)} \le \underline{B}^{(k)} \le \ell^* \le \overline{B}^{(k)} \le \overline{B}^{(k-1)}$ for each $k \ge 1$. If the algorithm stops at the kth iteration, then it is obtained that $\overline{B}^{(k)} = \ell^* = \underline{B}^{(k)}$ with a small enough error derivation ϵ and the optimal solution for problem* (10.21) *is $(\boldsymbol{\xi}^*,\boldsymbol{\theta}^*)$.*

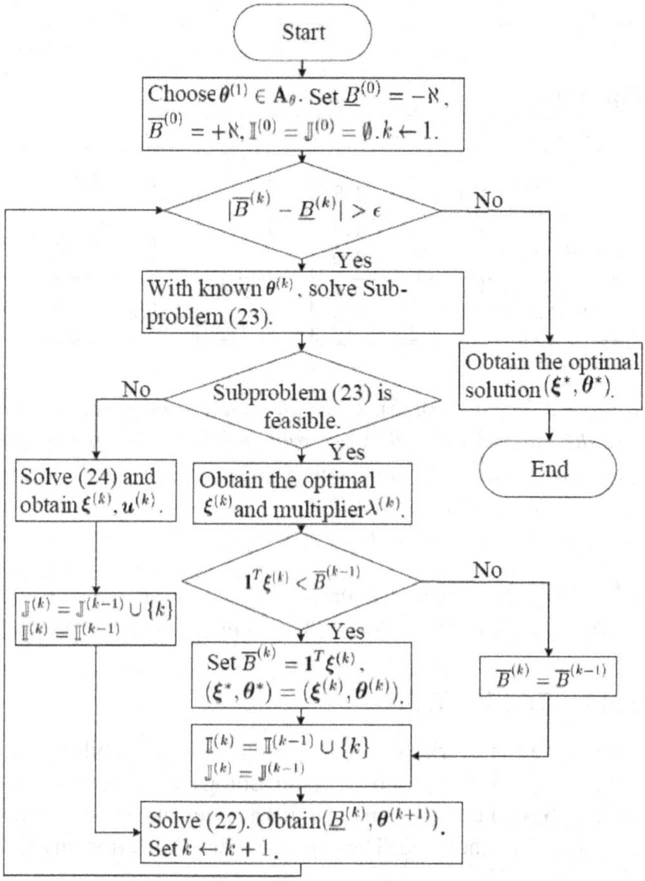

Figure 10.2 Flow diagram for solving the proposed secure scheme.

The convergence will be proved by verifying that if the algorithm does not stop at iteration k, the solution $\boldsymbol{\theta}^{(k+1)}$ will not repeat any previous solutions $\boldsymbol{\theta}^{(1)}, \cdots, \boldsymbol{\theta}^{(k)}$. A proof by contradiction is exploited for the following two cases: 1) *For* $1 \leq l \leq k$, *if Subproblem* (10.23) *is feasible, then* $l \in \mathbb{I}^k$. *Since* $(\boldsymbol{\xi}^{(l)}, \boldsymbol{\lambda}^{(l)})$ *is an optimal primal-dual pair of Subproblem* (10.23) *with known* $\boldsymbol{\theta}^{(l)}$, *the Karush-Kuhn-Tucker conditions show that* $\boldsymbol{\lambda}^{(l)})^T(\varrho \boldsymbol{1} - \bar{\mathcal{F}}(\boldsymbol{\xi}) - \mathcal{B}) = 0$. *Thus,*

$$L(\boldsymbol{\xi}^{(l)}, \boldsymbol{\theta}^{(l)}, \boldsymbol{\lambda}^{(l)}) = \boldsymbol{1}^T \boldsymbol{\xi}^{(l)} \geq \overline{B}^{(l)} \geq \overline{B}^{(k)} > \underline{B}^{(k)}. \tag{10.26}$$

If the optimal solution $\boldsymbol{\theta}^{(k+1)} = \boldsymbol{\theta}^{(l)}$, *the first constraint in master problem* (10.22) *becomes*

$$\underline{B}^{(k)} \geq L(\boldsymbol{\xi}^{(l)}, \boldsymbol{\theta}^{(l)}, \boldsymbol{\lambda}^{(l)})$$

Table 10.2
System parameters

Parameter	A_i	B_i	b_i	c_i
Plant 1	$\begin{bmatrix} 1.7 & -1.3 \\ 1.6 & -1.8 \end{bmatrix}$	$\begin{bmatrix} 1.0 \\ 2.0 \end{bmatrix}$	1.8	0.98
Plant 2	$\begin{bmatrix} 1.8 & -1.4 \\ 1.8 & -1.9 \end{bmatrix}$	$\begin{bmatrix} 1.7 \\ 3.4 \end{bmatrix}$	1.9	0.93
Plant 3	$\begin{bmatrix} 1.4 & -1.1 \\ 1.3 & -1.5 \end{bmatrix}$	$\begin{bmatrix} 0.8 \\ 1.6 \end{bmatrix}$	1.6	1

which is in contradiction with (10.26). 2) *Besides, if Subproblem* (10.23) *is infeasible,* $l \in \mathbb{J}^k$. *Because the optimal value* $\vartheta^{(l)}$ *of problem* (10.24) *is positive, it follows the dual problem that* $\vartheta^{(l)} = \boldsymbol{u}^{(l)^T}(\boldsymbol{1}^T\boldsymbol{\theta}^{(l)} - \Theta^{(l)})$, *which violates the second constraint in problem* (10.22), *i.e.,*

$$\boldsymbol{u}^{(l)^T}(\boldsymbol{1}^T\boldsymbol{\theta}^{(l)} - \Theta^{(l)}) \leq 0.$$

Therefore, $\boldsymbol{\theta}^{(k+1)}$ *will not repeat the previous solutions* $\boldsymbol{\theta}^{(1)}, \cdots, \boldsymbol{\theta}^{(k)}$. *Then, the algorithm will converge in a finite iteration with a finite integer strategy set* $\mathbf{A}_\theta$.

10.6 RESULT VERIFICATION

In this section, we aim to verify the effectiveness and applicability of the proposed method. For this purpose, the proposed methodology is applied to the numerical simulations of a CCS with three agents. Comparison results between schemes in this chapter and [97], [157] are included. The experimental verification on a CCS platform is also provided.

10.6.1 STRATEGY STUDY

A CCS consisting of three accessed agents with parameters in Table 10.2 [156] is considered as an example to verify the performance of the defense strategy against APTs.

Three agents access the same cloud and are assigned to different serve units to collect sensing measurements, process data, and generate control instructions for each agent. To illustrate the basic idea and procedure of our chapter, let us assume that the attacker can attack $R = 2$ serve units simultaneously. Consequently, based on Proposition 1, we have $\mathbf{A}_a = \{[1,1,0]^T, [0,1,1]^T, [1,0,1]^T\}$. Assume that the reward of agent i is $f_i(\xi_i) = c_i(1 - e^{-b_i\xi_i}), \forall i \in \{1,2,3\}$. The coefficients in $f_i(\cdot), i \in \{1,2,3\}$ are given in Table 10.2. Set $\xi_1^{\max} = \xi_2^{\max} = \xi_3^{\max} = 3$.

Fig. 10.3 depicts the total investment of the defender versus parameters β and b, where we assume $b = b_1 = b_2 = b_3$. The results in Fig. 10.3 show the total investment is near zero with a large β and a small b, which reveals the defender is not willing to

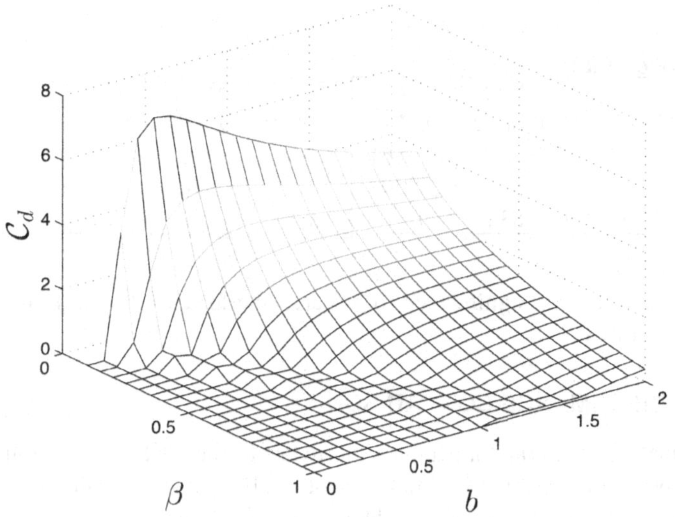

Figure 10.3 Defender's investment versus β and b.

invest when cost is high and reward is low. On the contrary, when β is small and b is large, there's no need to invest much to achieve a high utility so the cost decreases.

Then, to investigate the influence of limitation of protected serve units, we enlarge the CCS and assume that there are 5 agents accessing the CCS. The attacker can launch attacks to 4 serve units and there are $\mathbb{C}_5^4$ strategies of the attacker, i.e.,

$$\mathbf{A}_a = \{[1,1,1,1,0]^T,\ [1,1,1,0,1]^T,\ [1,1,0,1,1]^T,\\ [1,0,1,1,1]^T,\ [0,1,1,1,1]^T\}.$$

Coefficients in the reward function $f_i, \forall i \in \{1,2,3,4,5\}$ are given as $b_1 = 1.8$, $b_2 = 1.9$, $b_3 = 1.6$, $b_4 = 1.5$, $b_5 = 1.6$ and $c_1 = 0.95$, $c_2 = 0.9$, $c_3 = 0.98$, $c_4 = 0.93$, $c_5 = 1$.

Table 10.3 presents the corresponding defense investment of optimal defense strategies under different numbers of limited protected units Θ and expected performances ϱ. Table 10.3 shows that when the number of protected units increases, the expected performance can be achieved with lower investment. In other words, the expected performance can be realized easier with a larger protected units.

10.6.2 SCENARIO COMPARISON

In this part, three scenarios, including SE strategy in this chapter, NE strategy in [157] and random strategy, are considered for comparison. The comparative results in Fig. 10.4 show that SE strategy leads to higher utilities for both players than NE and random strategies. We conclude that attacker endowed with intelligence can achieve

Table 10.3
Defense investment

	$\Theta=5$	$\Theta=4$	$\Theta=3$	$\Theta=2$	$\Theta=1$
$\varrho=1$	0.0619	0.0619	0.0619	0.0621	0.0659
$\varrho=2$	0.9677	1.0561	1.3414	n/a	n/a
$\varrho=3$	2.3168	2.8997	n/a	n/a	n/a
$\varrho=4$	4.8348	n/a	n/a	n/a	n/a

high utility and it is of significance to research the leader-follower framework for secure design of CCS.

10.6.3 PERFORMANCE COMPARISON

Under the effect of random input time delay in the CCS, state evolutions are compared between using the optimal controller (10.4) and controller (21) in [97]. Assume that the upper bound of time delay $d_i = 3$ for all $i \in \mathcal{M}$. Fig. 10.5 shows the evolutions of states for agent 1 in the CCS, which illustrates that the controller given in this chapter performs better and the states of the agent in the CCS may diverge if the controller is designed without considering time delay in transmission networks.

10.6.4 EXPERIMENT VERIFICATION

To further illustrate the validity and applicability, the proposed scheme is applied to a platform of CCS, which consists of E-puck wheeled mobile robots, a Nokov motion capture system (NMCS), a local controller, and a cloud server shown in Fig. 10.6. The NMCS is equipped with eight cameras to provide real time localization of E-pucks. The cloud server provides service for time delay tolerant system performance that needs to deal with a large amount of data. The local controller receives commands

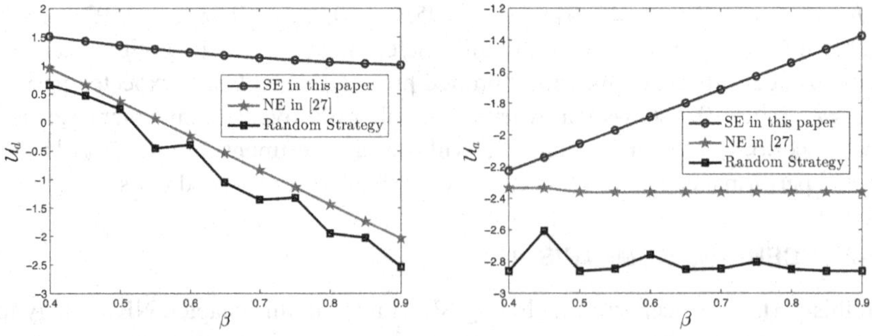

(a) Utility of defender versus β. (b) Utility of attacker versus β.

Figure 10.4 Utility comparisons among different scenarios.

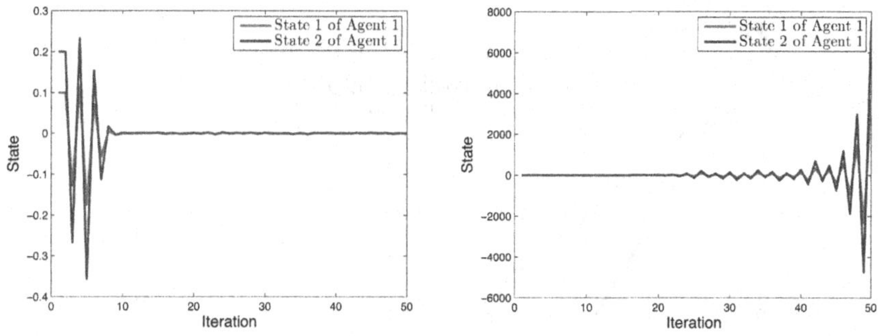

(a) State evolution using controller in this chapter.

(b) State evolution using controller in [97].

Figure 10.5 Performance comparison with random transmission time delay.

from the cloud server and sends them to E-pucks. Meanwhile, the local controller can also provide real-time control service.

In this chapter, to verify the effectiveness of the proposed secure scheme, we aim to control one E-puck from (1m, 0m) to (0m, 0m). As in Fig. 10.6, the local controller receives position information from the E-puck and then sends it to the cloud server. The cloud server chooses a corresponding algorithm to satisfy system performance and sends the commands to the local controller. Subsequently, the control commands are transmitted to the E-puck. The sampling period is 0.02s and its obtained packet dropout rate is approximate 1% by testing. The following three control scenarios are explored:

1) Controller (10.4) designed in this chapter is applied without attack.
2) An artifical attack by a possessing cloud server with probability $\rho = 0.5$ is performed, which is realized by interrupting the cloud service in a high frequency [97]. Controller (10.4) designed in this chapter is applied.
3) Controller (21) in [97] is used for the CCS when no attack exists.

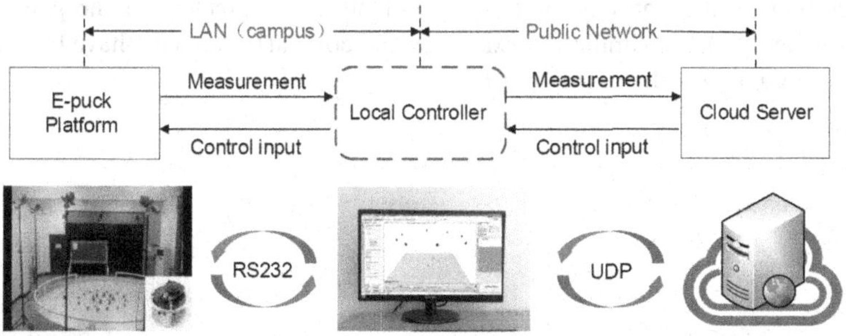

Figure 10.6 CCS platform.

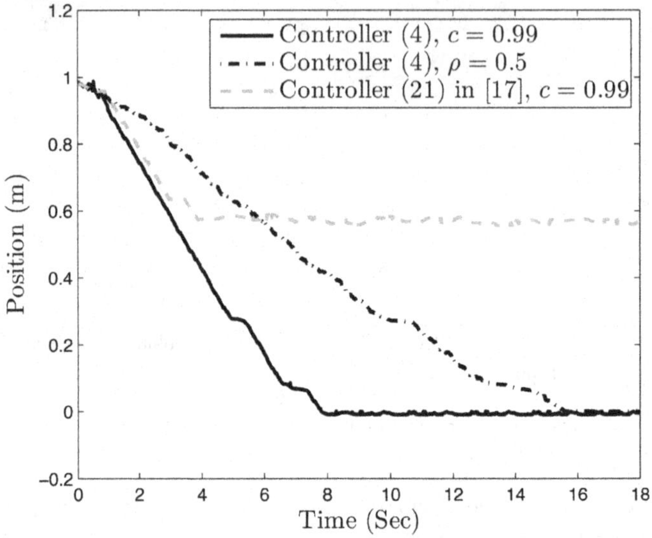

Figure 10.7 Experiment results of different control scenarios.

The positions of E-puck in different scenarios are depicted in Fig. 10.7, from which we can see the E-puck moves slower with attack than without attack; that is, the system performance becomes worse if there exists an attack. Moveover, when using controller (21) in [97], the E-puck cannot move to the target location, and it turns around at about (0.57m, 0m), which illustrates it is essential to take time delay into account when designing a controller for CCS.

10.7 CONCLUSION

A novel resource allocation problem for CCS has been studied in this chapter. Considering a hierarchical scheme, the defender and attacker have been modeled by using a Stackelberg game for resource limited players. For different types of resource budget, the optimal solutions of defender and attacker for the game have been provided. Finally, simulation examples and comparison results have been given to verify the main results of this work.

Bibliography

1. Al-Tamimi A, Lewis F L, and Abu-Khalaf M. Model-free q-learning designs for linear discrete-time zero-sum games with application to H_∞ control. *Automatica*, 43(3):473–481, 2007.
2. Ameli A, Hooshyar A, El-Saadany E F, and Youssef A M. Attack detection and identification for automatic generation control systems. *IEEE Transactions on Power Systems*, 33(5):4760–4774, 2018.
3. Biron Z A, Dey S, and Pisu P. Real-time detection and estimation of denial of service attack in connected vehicle systems. *IEEE Transactions on Intelligent Transportation Systems*, 19(12):3893–3902, 2018.
4. Cetinkaya A, Ishii H, and Hayakawa T. Networked control under random and malicious packet losses. *IEEE Transactions on Automatic Control*, 62(5):2434–2449, 2016.
5. Diro A A and Chilamkurti N. Distributed attack detection scheme using deep learning approach for internet of things. *Future Generation Computer Systems*, 82:761–768, 2018.
6. Goldsmith A. *Wireless Communications*. Cambridge University Press, 2005.
7. Gupta A, Langbort C, and Basar T. Optimal control in the presence of an intelligent jammer with limited actions. In *49th IEEE Conference on Decision and Control (CDC)*, pages 1096–1101. IEEE, 2010.
8. Khazraei A, Kebriaei H, and F R Salmasi. Replay attack detection in a multi agent system using stability analysis and loss effective watermarking. In *2017 American Control Conference (ACC)*, pages 4778–4783. IEEE, 2017.
9. Mukherjee A and Swindlehurst A L. Jamming games in the mimo wiretap channel with an active eavesdropper. *IEEE Transactions on Signal Processing*, 61(1):82–91, 2012.
10. Mustafa A, Modares H, and Moghadam R. Resilient synchronization of distributed multi-agent systems under attacks. *Automatica*, 115:108869, 2020.
11. Regalia P A, Khisti A, Liang Y, and Tomasin S. Secure communications via physical-layer and information-theoretic techniques. *Proc. IEEE*, 103(10):1698–1701, 2015.
12. Teixeira A, Pérez D, Sandberg H, and Johansson K H. Attack models and scenarios for networked control systems. In *Proceedings of the 1st International Conference on High Confidence Networked Systems*, pages 55–64, 2012.
13. Tewari A. *Automatic Control of Atmospheric and Space Flight Vehicles*. Springer, 2011.
14. Bequette B. *Process Dynamics: Modeling, Analysis, and Simulation*. Prentice Hall PTR, Upper Saddle River, NJ, 1998.
15. Chen B, Ho D W C, Zhang W A, and Yu L. Distributed dimensionality reduction fusion estimation for cyber-physical systems under dos attacks. *IEEE Transactions on Systems, Man, and Cybernetics: Systems*, 49(2):455–468, 2017.

16. Fang B, Du A, Zhang X, and Wang Z. Research on the international strategy for national cyberspace security. *Strategic Study of Chinese Academy of Engineering*, 18(6):13–16, 2016.
17. Kailkhura B, Han Y S, Brahma S, and Varshney P K. Distributed bayesian detection in the presence of byzantine data. *IEEE Transactions on Signal Processing*, 63(19):5250–5263, 2015.
18. Qin B, Yan H, Zhang H, Wang Y, and Yang S X. Enhanced reduced-order extended state observer for motion control of differential driven mobile robot. *IEEE Transactions on Cybernetics*, 2021.
19. Radhakisan B and Helen G. Cyber-physical systems. *The Impact of Control Technology*, 12(1):161–166, 2011.
20. Shen B, Wang Z, Shu H, and Wei G. Robust H_∞ finite-horizon filtering with randomly occurred nonlinearities and quantization effects. *Automatica*, 46(11):1743–1751, 2010.
21. Wang B, Wu Y, Liu K J R, and Clancy T C. An anti-jamming stochastic game for cognitive radio networks. *IEEE Journal on Selected Areas in Communications*, 29(4):877–889, 2011.
22. De Persis C and Tesi P. Input-to-state stabilizing control under denial-of-service. *IEEE Transactions on Automatic Control*, 60(11):2930–2944, 2015.
23. De Persis C and Tesi P. Networked control of nonlinear systems under denial-of-service. *Systems & Control Letters*, 96:124–131, 2016.
24. Fang C, Qi Y, Cheng P, and Zheng W X. Optimal periodic watermarking schedule for replay attack detection in cyber–physical systems. *Automatica*, 112:108698, 2020.
25. Lee C, Shim H, and Eun Y. On redundant observability: From security index to attack detection and resilient state estimation. *IEEE Transactions on Automatic Control*, 64(2):775–782, 2018.
26. Li C, Chen Y, and Shang Y. A review of industrial big data for decision making in intelligent manufacturing. *Engineering Science and Technology, an International Journal*, 29:101021, 2022.
27. Tankard C. Advanced persistent threats and how to monitor and deter them. *Network Security*, 2011(8):16–19, 2011.
28. Wang C, Zuo Z, Qi Z, and Ding Z. Predictor-based extended-state-observer design for consensus of mass with delays and disturbances. *IEEE Transactions on Cybernetics*, 49(4):1259–1269, 2018.
29. Wen C, Wang Z, Liu Q, and Alsaadi F E. Recursive distributed filtering for a class of state-saturated systems with fading measurements and quantization effects. *IEEE Transactions on Systems, Man, and Cybernetics: Systems*, 48(6):930–941, 2016.
30. Yang J C and Fang B X. Security model and key technologies for the internet of things. *The Journal of China Universities of Posts and Telecommunications*, 18:109–112, 2011.
31. Ding D, Han Q L, Xiang Y, Ge X, and Zhang X M. A survey on security control and attack detection for industrial cyber-physical systems. *Neurocomputing*, 275:1674–1683, 2018.

32. Ding D, Han Q L, Wang Z, and Ge X. Recursive filtering of distributed cyber-physical systems with attack detection. *IEEE Transactions on Systems, Man, and Cybernetics: Systems*, 51(10):6466–6476, 2020.
33. Ding D, Wang Z, Shen B, and Dong H. Envelope-constrained H_∞ filtering with fading measurements and randomly occurring nonlinearities: The finite horizon case. *Automatica*, 55:37–45, 2015.
34. Ding D, Wang Z, Ho D W C, and Wei G. Distributed recursive filtering for stochastic systems under uniform quantizations and deception attacks through sensor networks. *Automatica*, 78:231–240, 2017.
35. Ding D, Wang Z, Wei G, and Alsaadi F E. Event-based security control for discrete-time stochastic systems. *IET Control Theory & Applications*, 10(15):1808–1815, 2016.
36. Ding D, Wang Z, Han Q L, and Wei G. Security control for discrete-time stochastic nonlinear systems subject to deception attacks. *IEEE Transactions on Systems, Man, and Cybernetics: Systems*, 48(5):779–789, 2016.
37. Kim K D and Kumar P. Cyber–physical systems: A perspective at the centennial. *Proceedings of the IEEE*, 100(Special Centennial Issue):1287–1308, 2012.
38. Kudathanthirige D and Baduge G A A. Effects of pilot contamination attacks in multi-cell multi-user massive mimo relay networks. *IEEE Transactions on Communications*, 67(6):3905–3922, 2019.
39. Li D, Sun X, et al. *Nonlinear Integer Programming*, volume 84. Springer, 2006.
40. Wang D, Wang Z, Shen B, and Alsaadi F E. Security-guaranteed filtering for discrete-time stochastic delayed systems with randomly occurring sensor saturations and deception attacks. *International Journal of Robust and Nonlinear Control*, 27(7):1194–1208, 2017.
41. Yang D, Xue G, Zhang J, Richa A, and Fang X. Coping with a smart jammer in wireless networks: A stackelberg game approach. *IEEE Transactions on Wireless Communications*, 12(8):4038–4047, 2013.
42. Yang D, Ren W, Liu X, and Chen W. Decentralized event-triggered consensus for linear multi-agent systems under general directed graphs. *Automatica*, 69:242–249, 2016.
43. Ye D and Luo S. A co-design methodology for cyber-physical systems under actuator fault and cyber attack. *Journal of the Franklin Institute*, 356(4):1856–1879, 2019.
44. Ye D and Zhang T Y. Summation detector for false data-injection attack in cyber-physical systems. *IEEE Transactions on Cybernetics*, 50(6):2338–2345, 2019.
45. Ye D, Zhang T Y, and Guo G. Stochastic coding detection scheme in cyber-physical systems against replay attack. *Information Sciences*, 481:432–444, 2019.
46. Zhang D and Feng G. A new switched system approach to leader–follower consensus of heterogeneous linear multiagent systems with dos attack. *IEEE Transactions on Systems, Man, and Cybernetics: Systems*, 51(2):1258–1266, 2019.

47. Zhang D, Song H, and Yu L. Robust fuzzy-model-based filtering for nonlinear cyber-physical systems with multiple stochastic incomplete measurements. *IEEE Transactions on Systems, Man, and Cybernetics: Systems*, 47(8):1826–1838, 2016.
48. Zhang D, Liu L, and Feng G. Consensus of heterogeneous linear multiagent systems subject to aperiodic sampled-data and dos attack. *IEEE Transactions on Cybernetics*, 49(4):1501–1511, 2018.
49. Zhang D, Shi P, Wang Q G, and Yu L. Analysis and synthesis of networked control systems: A survey of recent advances and challenges. *ISA Transactions*, 66:376–392, 2017.
50. Altman E, Avrachenkov K, and Garnaev A. Jamming in wireless networks under uncertainty. *Mobile Networks and Applications*, 16:246–254, 2011.
51. Nash J F. Non-cooperative games. *Annals of Mathematics*, 54(2):286–295, 1951.
52. Pasqualetti F, Dörfler F, and Bullo F. Attack detection and identification in cyber-physical systems. *IEEE Transactions on Automatic Control*, 58(11):2715–2729, 2013.
53. Pasqualetti F, Dorfler F, and Bullo F. Control-theoretic methods for cyber-physical security: Geometric principles for optimal cross-layer resilient control systems. *IEEE Control Systems Magazine*, 35(1):110–127, 2015.
54. Chen Z G, Zhan Z H, Lin Y, Gong Y J, Gu T L, Zhao F, Yuan H Q, Chen X, Li Q, and Zhang J. Multiobjective cloud workflow scheduling: A multiple populations ant colony system approach. *IEEE Transactions on Cybernetics*, 49(8):2912–2926, 2018.
55. Guo X G, Wang J L, Liao F, and Wang D. Quantized H_∞ consensus of multiagent systems with quantization mismatch under switching weighted topologies. *IEEE Transactions on Control of Network Systems*, 4(2):202–212, 2015.
56. Guo X G, Zhang D Y, Wang J L, Park J H, and Guo L. Event-triggered observer-based H_∞ consensus control and fault detection of multiagent systems under stochastic false data injection attacks. *IEEE Transactions on Network Science and Engineering*, 9(2):481–494, 2021.
57. Hasslinger G and Hohlfeld O. The gilbert-elliott model for packet loss in real time services on the internet. In *14th GI/ITG Conference-Measurement, Modelling and Evalutation of Computer and Communication Systems*, pages 1–15. VDE, 2008.
58. Li Y G and Yang G H. Optimal stealthy innovation-based attacks with historical data in cyber-physical systems. *IEEE Transactions on Systems, Man, and Cybernetics: Systems*, 51(6):3401–3411, 2019.
59. Li Y G and Yang G H. Worst-case ϵ-stealthy false data injection attacks in cyber-physical systems. *Information Sciences*, 515:352–364, 2020.
60. Nan G and Chao J. Interpretation of "cyber-physical systems whitepaper (2017)"(part one). *Inf. Technol. Standard.*, 4:36–40, 2017.
61. Wang G. *Research on privacy protection and accuracy of localization in the Internet of Things*. PhD thesis, Nanjing University of Posts and Telecommunications, 2019.

62. Wu G, Sun J, and Chen J. A survey on the security of cyber-physical systems. *Control Theory and Technology*, 14(1):2–10, 2016.
63. Wu G, Sun J, and Chen J. Optimal data injection attacks in cyber-physical systems. *IEEE Transactions on Cybernetics*, 48(12):3302–3312, 2018.
64. Dong H, Wang Z, Shen B, and Ding D. Variance-constrained H_∞ control for a class of nonlinear stochastic discrete time-varying systems: The event-triggered design. *Automatica*, 72:28–36, 2016.
65. Fawzi H, Tabuada P, and Diggavi S. Secure estimation and control for cyber-physical systems under adversarial attacks. *IEEE Transactions on Automatic Control*, 59(6):1454–1467, 2014.
66. Gao H, Chen T, and Wang L. Robust fault detection with missing measurements. *International Journal of Control*, 81(5):804–819, 2008.
67. Liu H. Sinr-based multi-channel power schedule under dos attacks: A stackelberg game approach with incomplete information. *Automatica*, 100:274–280, 2019.
68. Modares H, Moghadam R, Lewis F L, and Davoudi A. Static output-feedback synchronisation of multi-agent systems: A secure and unified approach. *IET Control Theory & Applications*, 12(8):1095–1106, 2018.
69. Movric K H and Lewis F L. Cooperative optimal control for multi-agent systems on directed graph topologies. *IEEE Transactions on Automatic Control*, 59(3):769–774, 2013.
70. Niu H, Sahoo A, Bhowmick C, and Jagannathan S. Attack detection in linear networked control systems by using learning methodology. In *2019 IEEE Conference on Control Technology and Applications (CCTA)*, pages 148–153. IEEE, 2019.
71. Niu H, Bhowmick C, and Jagannathan S. Attack detection and approximation in nonlinear networked control systems using neural networks. *IEEE Transactions on Neural Networks and Learning Systems*, 31(1):235–245, 2019.
72. Niu H and Jagannathan S. Flow-based attack detection and accommodation for networked control systems. *International Journal of Control*, 94(3):834–847, 2021.
73. Pang Z H, Liu G P, Zhou D, Hou F, and Sun D. Two-channel against output tracking control of networked systems. *IEEE Transactions on Industrial Electronics*, 63(5):3242–3251, 2016.
74. Song H, Shi P, Zhang W A, Lim C C, and Yu L. Distributed H_∞ estimation in sensor networks with two-channel stochastic attacks. *IEEE Transactions on Cybernetics*, 50(2):465–475, 2018.
75. Song H, Shi P, Lim C C, Zhang W A, and Yu L. Set-membership estimation for complex networks subject to linear and nonlinear bounded attacks. *IEEE Transactions on Neural Networks and Learning Systems*, 31(1):163–173, 2019.
76. Song H, Shi P, Lim C C, Zhang W A, and L Yu. Attack and estimator design for multi-sensor systems with undetectable adversary. *Automatica*, 109:108545, 2019.
77. Sun H. *Security control of networked systems under denial of service attacks.* PhD thesis, Shanghai University, 2019.

78. Watkins C J C H and Dayan P. Q-learning. *Machine Learning*, 8:279–292, 1992.
79. Yang H, Ju S, Xia Y, and Zhang J. Predictive cloud control for networked multiagent systems with quantized signals under dos attacks. *IEEE Transactions on Systems, Man, and Cybernetics: Systems*, 51(2):1345–1353, 2019.
80. Yang H, Xia Y, and Shi P. Stabilization of networked control systems with nonuniform random sampling periods. *International Journal of Robust and Nonlinear Control*, 21(5):501–526, 2011.
81. Yang H, Xia Y, Shi P, and Zhao L. *Analysis and Synthesis of Delta Operator Systems*, volume 430. Springer, 2012.
82. Yang H, Xu Y, and Zhang J. Event-driven control for networked control systems with quantization and markov packet losses. *IEEE Transactions on Cybernetics*, 47(8):2235–2243, 2016.
83. Yuan H and Xia Y. Resilient strategy design for cyber-physical system under dos attack over a multi-channel framework. *Information Sciences*, 454:312–327, 2018.
84. Yuan H, Xia Y, and Yang H. Resilient state estimation of cyber-physical system with multichannel transmission under dos attack. *IEEE Transactions on Systems, Man, and Cybernetics: Systems*, 51(11):6926–6937, 2020.
85. Yuan H, Xia Y, Yang H, and Yuan Y. Resilient control for wireless networked control systems under dos attack via a hierarchical game. *International Journal of Robust and Nonlinear Control*, 28(15):4604–4623, 2018.
86. Zhang H, Jiang C, Mao X, and Chen H H. Interference-limited resource optimization in cognitive femtocells with fairness and imperfect spectrum sensing. *IEEE Transactions on Vehicular Technology*, 65(3):1761–1771, 2015.
87. Zhang H and Lewis F L. Adaptive cooperative tracking control of higher-order nonlinear systems with unknown dynamics. *Automatica*, 48(7):1432–1439, 2012.
88. Zhang H, Li L, Xu J, and Fu M. Linear quadratic regulation and stabilization of discrete-time systems with delay and multiplicative noise. *IEEE Transactions on Automatic Control*, 60(10):2599–2613, 2015.
89. Zhang H, Cheng P, Shi L, and Chen J. Optimal denial-of-service attack scheduling with energy constraint. *IEEE Transactions on Automatic Control*, 60(11):3023–3028, 2015.
90. Zhang H, Cheng P, Shi L, and Chen J. Optimal dos attack scheduling in wireless networked control system. *IEEE Transactions on Control Systems Technology*, 24(3):843–852, 2015.
91. Zhang H and Zheng W X. Denial-of-service power dispatch against linear quadratic control via a fading channel. *IEEE Transactions on Automatic Control*, 63(9):3032–3039, 2018.
92. Zhang H, Qi Y, Zhou H, Zhang J, and Sun J. Testing and defending methods against dos attack in state estimation. *Asian Journal of Control*, 19(4):1295–1305, 2017.
93. Zhang H, Qi Y, Wu J, Fu L, and He L. Dos attack energy management against remote state estimation. *IEEE Transactions on Control of Network Systems*, 5(1):383–394, 2016.

94. Zhou H, Chen J, Zheng H, and Wu J. Energy efficiency and contact opportunities tradeoff in opportunistic mobile networks. *IEEE Transactions on Vehicular Technology*, 65(5):3723–3734, 2015.
95. Ghafir I, Hammoudeh M, Prenosil V, Han L, Hegarty R, Rabie K, and Aparicio-Navarro F J. Detection of advanced persistent threat using machine-learning correlation analysis. *Future Generation Computer Systems*, 89:349–359, 2018.
96. Chen J, Touati C, and Zhu Q. A dynamic game approach to strategic design of secure and resilient infrastructure network. *IEEE Transactions on Information Forensics and Security*, 15:462–474, 2019.
97. Chen J and Zhu Q. Security as a service for cloud-enabled internet of controlled things under advanced persistent threats: A contract design approach. *IEEE Transactions on Information Forensics and Security*, 12(11):2736–2750, 2017.
98. Duan J, Zeng W, and Chow M. Resilient distributed dc optimal power flow against data integrity attack. *IEEE Transactions on Smart Grid*, 9(4):3543–3552, 2016.
99. Giraldo J, Cárdenas A, and Quijano N. Integrity attacks on real-time pricing in smart grids: Impact and countermeasures. *IEEE Transactions on Smart Grid*, 8(5):2249–2257, 2016.
100. Giraldo J, Urbina D, Cardenas A, Valente J, Faisal M, Ruths J, Tippenhauer N O, Sandberg H, and Candell R. A survey of physics-based attack detection in cyber-physical systems. *ACM Computing Surveys (CSUR)*, 51(4):1–36, 2018.
101. Giraldo J, Sarkar E, Cardenas A A, Maniatakos M, and Kantarcioglu M. Security and privacy in cyber-physical systems: A survey of surveys. *IEEE Design & Test*, 34(4):7–17, 2017.
102. Han J. From pid to active disturbance rejection control. *IEEE Transactions on Industrial Electronics*, 56(3):900–906, 2009.
103. Hu J and Wellman M P. Nash q-learning for general-sum stochastic games. *Journal of Machine Learning Research*, 4(Nov):1039–1069, 2003.
104. Hu J, Wellman M P, et al. Multiagent reinforcement learning: Theoretical framework and an algorithm. In *ICML*, volume 98, pages 242–250, 1998.
105. Hu J, Wang Z, Liu S, and Gao H. A variance-constrained approach to recursive state estimation for time-varying complex networks with missing measurements. *Automatica*, 64:155–162, 2016.
106. Li J, Xing R, Su Z, Zhang N, Hui Y, Luan T H, and Shan H. Trust based secure content delivery in vehicular networks: A bargaining game theoretical approach. *IEEE Transactions on Vehicular Technology*, 69(3):3267–3279, 2020.
107. Luo J, Andrian J H, and Zhou C. Bit error rate analysis of jamming for ofdm systems. In *2007 Wireless Telecommunications Symposium*, pages 1–8. IEEE, 2007.
108. Moon J and Basar T. Minimax control over unreliable communication channels. *Automatica*, 59:182–193, 2015.
109. Pawlick J, Chen J, and Zhu Q. istrict: An interdependent strategic trust mechanism for the cloud-enabled internet of controlled things. *IEEE Transactions on Information Forensics and Security*, 14(6):1654–1669, 2018.

110. Proakis J and Salehi M. *Digital Communications*. 5th ed. McGrawHill, 2007.
111. Qin J, Li M, Shi L, and Yu X. Optimal denial-of-service attack scheduling with energy constraint over packet-dropping networks. *IEEE Transactions on Automatic Control*, 63(6):1648–1663, 2017.
112. Befekadu G K, Gupta V, and Antsaklis P J. Risk-sensitive control under markov modulated denial-of-service (dos) attack strategies. *IEEE Transactions on Automatic Control*, 60(12):3299–3304, 2015.
113. Ding K, Ren X, Quevedo D E, Dey S, and Shi L. Defensive deception against reactive jamming attacks in remote state estimation. *Automatica*, 113:108680, 2020.
114. Ding K, Ren X, Leong A S, Quevedo D E, and Shi L. Remote state estimation in the presence of an active eavesdropper. *IEEE Transactions on Automatic Control*, 66(1):229–244, 2020.
115. Ding K, Li Y, Quevedo D E, Dey S, and Shi L. A multi-channel transmission schedule for remote state estimation under dos attacks. *Automatica*, 78:194–201, 2017.
116. Hamedani K, Liu L, Atat R, Wu J, and Yi Y. Reservoir computing meets smart grids: Attack detection using delayed feedback networks. *IEEE Transactions on Industrial Informatics*, 14(2):734–743, 2017.
117. Tugnait J K. Detection of active eavesdropping attack by spoofing relay in multiple antenna systems. *IEEE Wireless Communications Letters*, 5(5):460–463, 2016.
118. Wang K, Yuan L, Miyazaki T, Chen Y, and Zhang Y. Jamming and eavesdropping defense in green cyber–physical transportation systems using a stackelberg game. *IEEE Transactions on Industrial Informatics*, 14(9):4232–4242, 2018.
119. An L and Yang G H. Secure state estimation against sparse sensor attacks with adaptive switching mechanism. *IEEE Transactions on Automatic Control*, 63(8):2596–2603, 2017.
120. An L and Yang G H. Decentralized adaptive fuzzy secure control for nonlinear uncertain interconnected systems against intermittent dos attacks. *IEEE Transactions on Cybernetics*, 49(3):827–838, 2018.
121. An L and Yang G H. Distributed secure state estimation for cyber–physical systems under sensor attacks. *Automatica*, 107:526–538, 2019.
122. Ding L, Han Q L, Ning B, and Yue D. Distributed resilient finite-time secondary control for heterogeneous battery energy storage systems under denial-of-service attacks. *IEEE Transactions on Industrial Informatics*, 16(7):4909–4919, 2019.
123. Jia L, Yao F, Sun Y, Niu Y, and Zhu Y. Bayesian stackelberg game for antijamming transmission with incomplete information. *IEEE Communications Letters*, 20(10):1991–1994, 2016.
124. Lei L, Yang W, Yang C, and Shi H B. False data injection attack on consensus-based distributed estimation. *International Journal of Robust and Nonlinear Control*, 27(9):1419–1432, 2017.

125. Li L, Yu D, Xia Y, and Yang H. Stochastic stability of a modified unscented kalman filter with stochastic nonlinearities and multiple fading measurements. *Journal of the Franklin Institute*, 354(2):650–667, 2017.
126. Li L, Yu D, Xia Y, and Yang H. Remote nonlinear state estimation with stochastic event-triggered sensor schedule. *IEEE Transactions on Cybernetics*, 49(3):734–745, 2018.
127. Li L, Yang H, Xia Y, and Yang H. Event-based distributed state estimation for linear systems under unknown input and false data injection attack. *Signal Processing*, 170:107423, 2020.
128. Littman M L. Markov games as a framework for multi-agent reinforcement learning. In *Machine Learning Proceedings 1994*, pages 157–163. Elsevier, 1994.
129. Ma L, Wang Z, and Lam H K. Mean-square H_∞ consensus control for a class of nonlinear time-varying stochastic multiagent systems: The finite-horizon case. *IEEE Transactions on Systems, Man, and Cybernetics: Systems*, 47(7):1050–1060, 2016.
130. Ma L, Wang Z, Han Q L, and Lam H K. Variance-constrained distributed filtering for time-varying systems with multiplicative noises and deception attacks over sensor networks. *IEEE Sensors Journal*, 17(7):2279–2288, 2017.
131. Sadeghikhorami L, Zamani M, Chen Z, and Safavi A A. A secure control mechanism for network environments. *Journal of the Franklin Institute*, 357(17):12264–12280, 2020.
132. Wang L, Cao X, Sun B, Zhang H, and Sun C. Optimal schedule of secure transmissions for remote state estimation against eavesdropping. *IEEE Transactions on Industrial Informatics*, 17(3):1987–1997, 2020.
133. Wang L, Wang Z, Han Q L, and Wei G. Event-based variance-constrained H_∞ filtering for stochastic parameter systems over sensor networks with successive missing measurements. *IEEE Transactions on Cybernetics*, 48(3):1007–1017, 2017.
134. Xiao L, Xu D, Xie C, Mandayam N B, and Poor H V. Cloud storage defense against advanced persistent threats: A prospect theoretic study. *IEEE Journal on Selected Areas in Communications*, 35(3):534–544, 2017.
135. Xiao L, Li Y, Han G, Dai H, and Poor H V. A secure mobile crowdsensing game with deep reinforcement learning. *IEEE Transactions on Information Forensics and Security*, 13(1):35–47, 2017.
136. Zhao L, Yang Y, Xia Y, and Liu Z. Active disturbance rejection position control for a magnetic rodless pneumatic cylinder. *IEEE Transactions on Industrial Electronics*, 62(9):5838–5846, 2015.
137. Zhao Y L, Zhang J J, and Song Y X. Research on the problem of search games on a lattice under the constraint of multiple factors. *Mathematics in Practice and Theory*, 47(11):135–141, 2017.
138. Zhu L, Tang X, Shen M, Du X, and Guizani M. Privacy-preserving ddos attack detection using cross-domain traffic in software defined networks. *IEEE Journal on Selected Areas in Communications*, 36(3):628–643, 2018.

139. Dimitris M and Ekaterini V. A cloud-based cyber-physical system for adaptive shop-floor scheduling and condition-based maintenance. *Journal of Manufacturing Systems*, 47:179–198, 2018.
140. Li X M, Zhou Q, Li P, Li H, and Lu R. Event-triggered consensus control for multi-agent systems against false data-injection attacks. *IEEE Transactions on Cybernetics*, 50(5):1856–1866, 2019.
141. Long M, Wu C H, and Hung J Y. Denial of service attacks on network-based control systems: Impact and mitigation. *IEEE Transactions on Industrial Informatics*, 1(2):85–96, 2005.
142. Min M, Xiao L, Xie C, Hajimirsadeghi M, and Mandayam N B. Defense against advanced persistent threats in dynamic cloud storage: A colonel blotto game approach. *IEEE Internet of Things Journal*, 5(6):4250–4261, 2018.
143. Pirani M, Taylor J A, and Sinopoli B. Attack resilient interconnected second order systems: A game-theoretic approach. In *2019 IEEE 58th Conference on Decision and Control (CDC)*, pages 4391–4396. IEEE, 2019.
144. Rana M, Li L, and Su S W. Distributed state estimation over unreliable communication networks with an application to smart grids. *IEEE Transactions on Green Communications and Networking*, 1(1):89–96, 2017.
145. Ruan M, Ahmad M, and Wang Y. Secure and privacy-preserving average consensus. In *Proceedings of the 2017 Workshop on Cyber-physical Systems Security and Privacy*, pages 123–129, 2017.
146. Van Dijk M, Juels A, Oprea A, and Rivest R L. Flipit: The game of "stealthy takeover". *Journal of Cryptology*, 26:655–713, 2013.
147. Zhu M and Martinez S. On the performance analysis of resilient networked control systems under replay attacks. *IEEE Transactions on Automatic Control*, 59(3):804–808, 2013.
148. Gilbert E N. Capacity of a burst-noise channel. *Bell System Technical Journal*, 39(5):1253–1265, 1960.
149. Kosut O, Jia L, Thomas R J, and Tong L. Limiting false data attacks on power system state estimation. In *2010 44th Annual Conference on Information Sciences and Systems (CISS)*, pages 1–6. IEEE, 2010.
150. Da Costa K A P, Papa J P, Lisboa C O, Munoz R, and De Albuquerque V H C. Internet of things: A survey on machine learning-based intrusion detection approaches. *Computer Networks*, 151:147–157, 2019.
151. Hovareshti P, Gupta V, and Baras J S. Sensor scheduling using smart sensors. In *2007 46th IEEE Conference on Decision and Control*, pages 494–499. IEEE, 2007.
152. Hu P, Li H, Fu H, Cansever D, and Mohapatra P. Dynamic defense strategy against advanced persistent threat with insiders. In *2015 IEEE Conference on Computer Communications (INFOCOM)*, pages 747–755. IEEE, 2015.
153. Jiang Z P and Wang Y. Input-to-state stability for discrete-time nonlinear systems. *Automatica*, 37(6):857–869, 2001.
154. Kaur P, Kaur D, and Mahajan R. Wormhole attack detection technique in mobile ad hoc networks. *Wireless Personal Communications*, 97:2939–2950, 2017.

155. Li P, Yang X, Xiong Q, Wen J, and Tang Y. Defending against the advanced persistent threat: An optimal control approach. *Security and Communication Networks*, 2018:1–14, 2018.
156. Liu G P. Predictive control of networked multiagent systems via cloud computing. *IEEE Transactions on Cybernetics*, 47(8):1852–1859, 2017.
157. Shukla P, Chakrabortty A, and Duel-Hallen A. A cyber-security investment game for networked control systems. In *2019 American Control Conference (ACC)*, pages 2297–2302. IEEE, 2019.
158. Suchomski P. A j-lossless coprime factorisation approach to H_∞ control in delta domain. *Automatica*, 38(10):1807–1814, 2002.
159. Zhang P, Zhou M, and Fortino G. Security and trust issues in fog computing: A survey. *Future Generation Computer Systems*, 88:16–27, 2018.
160. Han Q, Yang B, Wang X, Ma K, Chen C, and Guan X. Hierarchical-game-based uplink power control in femtocell networks. *IEEE Transactions on Vehicular Technology*, 63(6):2819–2835, 2014.
161. James J Q, Hou Y, and Li V O K. Online false data injection attack detection with wavelet transform and deep neural networks. *IEEE Transactions on Industrial Informatics*, 14(7):3271–3280, 2018.
162. Li Q, Xia L, and Song R. Novel resilient structure of output formation tracking of heterogeneous systems with unknown leader under contested environments. *IEEE Transactions on Systems, Man, and Cybernetics: Systems*, 51(11):6819–6829, 2020.
163. Wang Q, Tai W, Tang Y, Ni M, and You S. A two-layer game theoretical attack-defense model for a false data injection attack against power systems. *International Journal of Electrical Power & Energy Systems*, 104:169–177, 2019.
164. Zhu Q and Basar T. Game-theoretic methods for robustness, security, and resilience of cyberphysical control systems: Games-in-games principle for optimal cross-layer resilient control systems. *IEEE Control Systems Magazine*, 35(1):46–65, 2015.
165. Deng R, Xiao G, and Lu R. Defending against false data injection attacks on power system state estimation. *IEEE Transactions on Industrial Informatics*, 13(1):198–207, 2015.
166. Ma R, Shi P, Wang Z, and Wu L. Resilient filtering for cyber-physical systems under denial-of-service attacks. *International Journal of Robust and Nonlinear Control*, 30(5):1754–1769, 2020.
167. Zhang R and Venkitasubramaniam P. Stealthy control signal attacks in linear quadratic gaussian control systems: Detectability reward tradeoff. *IEEE Transactions on Information Forensics and Security*, 12(7):1555–1570, 2017.
168. Zhang R and Zhu Q. A game-theoretic approach to design secure and resilient distributed support vector machines. *IEEE Ttransactions on Neural Networks and Learning Systems*, 29(11):5512–5527, 2018.
169. Amin S, Schwartz G A, and Sastry S S. Security of interdependent and identical networked control systems. *Automatica*, 49(1):186–192, 2013.

187. Dong T and Gong Y. Leader-following secure consensus for second-order multi-agent systems with nonlinear dynamics and event-triggered control strategy under dos attack. *Neurocomputing*, 416:95–102, 2020.
188. Kailath T, Sayed A H, and Hassibi B. *Linear Estimation.* Prentice Hall, 2000.
189. Ma C Y T, Yau D K Y, Lou X, and Rao N S V. Markov game analysis for attack-defense of power networks under possible misinformation. *IEEE Transactions on Power Systems*, 28(2):1676–1686, 2012.
190. Senthilkumar T and Balasubramaniam P. Delay-dependent robust stabilization and H_∞ control for nonlinear stochastic systems with markovian jump parameters and interval time-varying delays. *Journal of Optimization Theory and Applications*, 151:100–120, 2011.
191. Senthilkumar T and Balasubramaniam P. Non-fragile robust stabilization and H_∞ control for uncertain stochastic time delay systems with markovian jump parameters and nonlinear disturbances. *International Journal of Adaptive Control and Signal Processing*, 28(3-5):464–478, 2014.
192. Sun H T, Peng C, Zhou P, and Wang Z W. A brief overview on secure control of networked systems. *Advances in Manufacturing*, 5:243–250, 2017.
193. Dolk V, Tesi P, De Persis C, and Heemels W P M H. Event-triggered control systems under denial-of-service attacks. *IEEE Transactions on Control of Network Systems*, 4(1):93–105, 2016.
194. Al-Dabbagh A W, Li Y, and Chen T. An intrusion detection system for cyber attacks in wireless networked control systems. *IEEE Transactions on Circuits and Systems II: Express Briefs*, 65(8):1049–1053, 2017.
195. He W, Gao X, Zhong W, and Qian F. Secure impulsive synchronization control of multi-agent systems under deception attacks. *Information Sciences*, 459:354–368, 2018.
196. Jiang W, Ma Z, and Deng X. An attack-defense game based reliability analysis approach for wireless sensor networks. *International Journal of Distributed Sensor Networks*, 15(4):1550147719841293, 2019.
197. Yang W, Zhang Y, Chen G, Yang C, and Shi L. Distributed filtering under false data injection attacks. *Automatica*, 102:34–44, 2019.
198. Yang W, Zheng Z, Chen G, Tang Y, and Wang X. Security analysis of a distributed networked system under eavesdropping attacks. *IEEE Transactions on Circuits and Systems II: Express Briefs*, 67(7):1254–1258, 2019.
199. Yu W and Liu K J R. Secure cooperation in autonomous mobile ad-hoc networks under noise and imperfect monitoring: A game-theoretic approach. *IEEE Transactions on Information Forensics and Security*, 3(2):317–330, 2008.
200. Ge X and Han Q L. Distributed event-triggered H_∞ filtering over sensor networks with communication delays. *Information Sciences*, 291:128–142, 2015.
201. Ge X, Han Q L, Zhong M, and Zhang X M. Distributed krein space-based attack detection over sensor networks under deception attacks. *Automatica*, 109:108557, 2019.

202. Ren X and Mo Y. Secure detection: Performance metric and sensor deployment strategy. *IEEE Transactions on Signal Processing*, 66(17):4450–4460, 2018.
203. Zhou X, Maham B, and Hjorungnes A. Pilot contamination for active eavesdropping. *IEEE Transactions on Wireless Communications*, 11(3):903–907, 2012.
204. Ali Y, Xia Y, Ma L, and Hammad A. Secure design for cloud control system against distributed denial of service attack. *Control Theory and Technology*, 16(1):14–24, 2018.
205. Chen Y, Huang S, Liu F, Wang Z, and Sun X. Evaluation of reinforcement learning-based false data injection attack to automatic voltage control. *IEEE Transactions on Smart Grid*, 10(2):2158–2169, 2018.
206. Chen Y, Kar S, and Moura J M F. Dynamic attack detection in cyber-physical systems with side initial state information. *IEEE Transactions on Automatic Control*, 62(9):4618–4624, 2016.
207. Chen Y, Kar S, and Moura J M F. Cyber-physical attacks with control objectives. *IEEE Transactions on Automatic Control*, 63(5):1418–1425, 2017.
208. Chen Y, Kar S, and Moura J M F. Optimal attack strategies subject to detection constraints against cyber-physical systems. *IEEE Transactions on Control of Network Systems*, 5(3):1157–1168, 2017.
209. Hu Y, Sanjab A, and Saad W. Dynamic psychological game theory for secure internet of battlefield things (iobt) systems. *IEEE Internet of Things Journal*, 6(2):3712–3726, 2019.
210. Huang Y, Chen J, Huang L, and Zhu Q. Dynamic games for secure and resilient control system design. *National Science Review*, 7(7):1125–1141, 2020.
211. Keller J Y and Sauter D. Monitoring of stealthy attack in networked control systems. In *2013 Conference on Control and Fault-Tolerant Systems (SysTol)*, pages 462–467. IEEE, 2013.
212. Li Y, Shi D, and Chen T. False data injection attacks on networked control systems: A stackelberg game analysis. *IEEE Transactions on Automatic Control*, 63(10):3503–3509, 2018.
213. Li Y, Shi D, and Chen T. Secure analysis of dynamic networks under pinning attacks against synchronization. *Automatica*, 111:108576, 2020.
214. Li Y, Quevedo D E, Dey S, and Shi L. Fake-acknowledgment attack on ack-based sensor power schedule for remote state estimation. In *2015 54th IEEE Conference on Decision and Control (CDC)*, pages 5795–5800. IEEE, 2015.
215. Li Y, Quevedo D E, Dey S, and Shi L. A game-theoretic approach to fake-acknowledgment attack on cyber-physical systems. *IEEE Transactions on Signal and Information Processing over Networks*, 3(1):1–11, 2016.
216. Li Y, Quevedo D E, Dey S, and Shi L. Sinr-based dos attack on remote state estimation: A game-theoretic approach. *IEEE Transactions on Control of Network Systems*, 4(3):632–642, 2016.
217. Li Y, Shi L, Cheng P, Chen J, and Quevedo D E. Jamming attacks on remote state estimation in cyber-physical systems: A game-theoretic approach. *IEEE Transactions on Automatic Control*, 60(10):2831–2836, 2015.

218. Li Y, Shi L, and Chen T. Detection against linear deception attacks on multi-sensor remote state estimation. *IEEE Transactions on Control of Network Systems*, 5(3):846–856, 2017.
219. Lu A Y and Yang G H. Secure luenberger-like observers for cyber–physical systems under sparse actuator and sensor attacks. *Automatica*, 98:124–129, 2018.
220. Lu A Y and Yang G H. Secure switched observers for cyber-physical systems under sparse sensor attacks: A set cover approach. *IEEE Transactions on Automatic Control*, 64(9):3949–3955, 2019.
221. Lv Y, Zhou J, Wen G, Yu X, and Huang T. Fully distributed adaptive nn-based consensus protocol for nonlinear mass: An attack-free approach. *IEEE Transactions on Neural Networks and Learning Systems*, 33(4):1561–1570, 2020.
222. Mi Y, Fu Y, Wang C, and Wang P. Decentralized sliding mode load frequency control for multi-area power systems. *IEEE Transactions on Power Systems*, 28(4):4301–4309, 2013.
223. Mo Y, Garone E, and Sinopoli B. Lqg control with markovian packet loss. In *2013 European Control Conference (ECC)*, pages 2380–2385. IEEE, 2013.
224. Mo Y, Chabukswar R, and Sinopoli B. Detecting integrity attacks on scada systems. *IEEE Transactions on Control Systems Technology*, 22(4):1396–1407, 2013.
225. Shoukry Y and Tabuada P. Event-triggered state observers for sparse sensor noise/attacks. *IEEE Transactions on Automatic Control*, 61(8):2079–2091, 2015.
226. Wang Y, Li J, Meng K, Lin C, and Cheng X. Modeling and security analysis of enterprise network using attack–defense stochastic game petri nets. *Security and Communication Networks*, 6(1):89–99, 2013.
227. Xia Y. From networked control systems to cloud control systems. In *Proceedings of the 31st Chinese Control Conference*, pages 5878–5883. IEEE, 2012.
228. Xia Y. Cloud control systems. *IEEE/CAA Journal of Automatica Sinica*, 2(2):134–142, 2015.
229. Xia Y. Cloud control systems and their challenges. *Acta Automatica Sinica*, 42(1):1–12, 2016.
230. Xia Y, Yan C, Wang X, and Song X. Intelligent transportation cyber-physical cloud control systems. *Acta Automatica Sinica*, 45(1):132–142, 2019.
231. Xia Y, Li H, Zhang J, et al. The interaction between control and computing theories: Cloud control systems. *Journal of Command and Control*, 3(2):99–118, 2017.
232. Xia Y, Qin Y, Zhai D, and Chai S. Further results on cloud control systems. *Science China Information Sciences*, 59:1–5, 2016.
233. Yang Y, Xu H, and Yue D. Observer-based distributed secure consensus control of a class of linear multi-agent systems subject to random attacks. *IEEE Transactions on Circuits and Systems I: Regular Papers*, 66(8):3089–3099, 2019.

234. Yuan Y and Sun F. Data fusion-based resilient control system under dos attacks: A game theoretic approach. *International Journal of Control, Automation and Systems*, 13:513–520, 2015.
235. Yuan Y, Sun F, and Zhu Q. Resilient control in the presence of dos attack: Switched system approach. *International Journal of Control, Automation and Systems*, 13:1423–1435, 2015.
236. Yuan Y, Yuan H, Ho D W C, and Guo L. Resilient control of wireless networked control system under denial-of-service attacks: A cross-layer design approach. *IEEE Transactions on Cybernetics*, 50(1):48–60, 2018.
237. Yuan Y, Yuan H, Guo L, and Yang H. Multi-tasking optimal control of networked control systems: A delta operator approach. *International Journal of Robust and Nonlinear Control*, 27(16):2842–2860, 2017.
238. Yuan Y, Yuan H, Guo L, Yang H, and Sun S. Resilient control of networked control system under dos attacks: A unified game approach. *IEEE Transactions on Industrial Informatics*, 12(5):1786–1794, 2016.
239. Yuan Y, Yuan H, Wang Z, Guo L, and Yang H. Optimal control for networked control systems with disturbances: A delta operator approach. *IET Control Theory & Applications*, 11(9):1325–1332, 2017.
240. Yuan Y, Guo L, and Wang Z. Composite control of linear quadratic games in delta domain with disturbance observers. *Journal of the Franklin Institute*, 354(4):1673–1695, 2017.
241. Yuan Y, Zhang P, Guo L, and Yang H. Towards quantifying the impact of randomly occurred attacks on a class of networked control systems. *Journal of the Franklin Institute*, 354(12):4966–4988, 2017.
242. Yuan Y, Zhang P, Wang Z, Guo L, and Yang H. Active disturbance rejection control for the ranger neutral buoyancy vehicle: A delta operator approach. *IEEE Transactions on Industrial Electronics*, 64(12):9410–9420, 2017.
243. Yuan Y, Wang Z, and Guo L. Event-triggered strategy design for discrete-time nonlinear quadratic games with disturbance compensations: The noncooperative case. *IEEE Transactions on Systems, Man, and Cybernetics: Systems*, 48(11):1885–1896, 2017.
244. Bai C Z, Pasqualetti F, and Gupta V. Data-injection attacks in stochastic control systems: Detectability and performance tradeoffs. *Automatica*, 82:251–260, 2017.
245. Bawany N Z, Shamsi J A, and Salah K. Ddos attack detection and mitigation using sdn: methods, practices, and solutions. *Arabian Journal for Science and Engineering*, 42:425–441, 2017.
246. Feng Z and Hu G. Secure cooperative event-triggered control of linear multiagent systems under dos attacks. *IEEE Transactions on Control Systems Technology*, 28(3):741–752, 2019.
247. Feng Z, Wen G, and Hu G. Distributed secure coordinated control for multiagent systems under strategic attacks. *IEEE Transactions on Cybernetics*, 47(5):1273–1284, 2016.

248. Guo Z, Shi D, Johansson K H, and Shi L. Optimal linear cyber-attack on remote state estimation. *IEEE Transactions on Control of Network Systems*, 4(1):4–13, 2016.
249. Guo Z, Shi D, Johansson K H, and Shi L. Worst-case innovation-based integrity attacks with side information on remote state estimation. *IEEE Transactions on Control of Network Systems*, 6(1):48–59, 2018.
250. Guo Z, Shi D, Johansson K H, and Shi L. Worst-case stealthy innovation-based linear attack on remote state estimation. *Automatica*, 89:117–124, 2018.
251. Guo B Z and Zhao Z L. *Active Disturbance Rejection Control for Nonlinear Systems: An Introduction*. John Wiley & Sons, 2017.
252. Liu Z, Wang J, Xia Y, Fan R, Jiang H, and Yang H. Power allocation robust to time-varying wireless channels in femtocell networks. *IEEE Transactions on Vehicular Technology*, 65(4):2806–2815, 2015.
253. Su Z, Xu Q, Luo J, Pu H, Peng Y, and Lu R. A secure content caching scheme for disaster backup in fog computing enabled mobile social networks. *IEEE Transactions on Industrial Informatics*, 14(10):4579–4589, 2018.
254. Tang Z, Kuijper M, Chong M S, Mareels I, and Leckie C. Linear system security—detection and correction of adversarial sensor attacks in the noise-free case. *Automatica*, 101:53–59, 2019.
255. Wang Z, Wang D, Shen B, and Alsaadi F E. Centralized security-guaranteed filtering in multirate-sensor fusion under deception attacks. *Journal of the Franklin Institute*, 355(1):406–420, 2018.
256. Wang Z, Yang F, Ho D W C, and Liu X. Robust H_∞ filtering for stochastic time-delay systems with missing measurements. *IEEE Transactions on Signal Processing*, 54(7):2579–2587, 2006.
257. Xu Z and Zhu Q. Secure and resilient control design for cloud enabled networked control systems. In *Proceedings of the First ACM Workshop on Cyber-Physical Systems-Security and/or Privacy*, pages 31–42, 2015.
258. Zheng Z, Haas Z J, and Kieburg M. Secrecy rate of cooperative mimo in the presence of a location constrained eavesdropper. *IEEE Transactions on Communications*, 67(2):1356–1370, 2018.

Index

Printed in the United States
by Baker & Taylor Publisher Services

Printed in the United States
by Baker & Taylor Publisher Services

170. Geirhofer S, Tong L, and Sadler B M. Cognitive medium access: Constraining interference based on experimental models. *IEEE Journal on Selected Areas in Communications*, 26(1):95–105, 2008.
171. Guan S and Wang L. Uncertainty analysis of cloud control system with its controller design. *Acta Automatica Sinica*, 10, 2019.
172. Hasan S, Dubey A, Karsai G, and Koutsoukos X. A game-theoretic approach for power systems defense against dynamic cyber-attacks. *International Journal of Electrical Power & Energy Systems*, 115:105432, 2020.
173. Hu S, Yue D, Chen X, Cheng Z, and Xie X. Resilient H_∞ filtering for event-triggered networked systems under nonperiodic dos jamming attacks. *IEEE Transactions on Systems, Man, and Cybernetics: Systems*, 51(3):1392–1403, 2019.
174. Hu S, Yue D, Xie X, Chen X, and Yin X. Resilient event-triggered controller synthesis of networked control systems under periodic dos jamming attacks. *IEEE Transactions on Cybernetics*, 49(12):4271–4281, 2018.
175. Hu S, Yuan P, Yue D, Dou C, Cheng Z, and Zhang Y. Attack-resilient event-triggered controller design of dc microgrids under dos attacks. *IEEE Transactions on Circuits and Systems I: Regular Papers*, 67(2):699–710, 2019.
176. Hu S, Cheng Z, Yue D, Dou C, and Xue Y. Bandwidth allocation-based switched dynamic triggering control against dos attacks. *IEEE Transactions on Systems, Man, and Cybernetics: Systems*, 51(10):6050–6061, 2019.
177. Leong A S, Quevedo D E, Dolz D, and Dey S. Transmission scheduling for remote state estimation over packet dropping links in the presence of an eavesdropper. *IEEE Transactions on Automatic Control*, 64(9):3732–3739, 2018.
178. Liu S, Wei G, Song Y, and Liu Y. Extended kalman filtering for stochastic nonlinear systems with randomly occurring cyber attacks. *Neurocomputing*, 207:708–716, 2016.
179. Mahmoud M S and Xia Y. *Networked Control Systems: Cloud Control and Secure Control*. Butterworth-Heinemann, 2019.
180. Raghavan T E S and Filar J A. Algorithms for stochastic games—a survey. *Zeitschrift für Operations Research*, 35(6):437–472, 1991.
181. Shapley L S. Stochastic games. *Proceedings of the Nnational Academy of Sciences*, 39(10):1095–1100, 1953.
182. Xiao S, Ge X, Han Q, and Zhang Y. Distributed resilient estimator design for positive systems under topological attacks. *IEEE Transactions on Cybernetics*, 51(7):3676–3686, 2020.
183. Xu S, Yan Z, Zhang L, and Tang C. Cyber physical system: features, architecture, and research challenges. *Journal of Computer Applications*, 33(S2):1–5, 2013.
184. Alpcan T, Basar T, Srikant R, and Altman E. Cdma uplink power control as a noncooperative game. *Wireless Networks*, 8:659–670, 2002.
185. Basar T and Olsder G J. *Dynamic Noncooperative Game Theory*. SIAM, 1998.
186. Basar T and Bernhard P. *H_∞ Optimal Control and Related Minimax Design Problems: A Dynamic Game Approach*. Springer Science & Business Media, 2008.